CW00735483

This is book number ___917___ of a limited edition of 1000 copies.
Signed by author Gary James.

Manchester City
Women

**An Oral
History**
by Gary James

J A M E S
W A R D

First published in 2019 by James Ward, PO Box 901, Halifax HX1 9UX
Info@manchesterfootball.org

Design by Trevor Hartley

The publisher makes no representation, express or implied, with regard to the
accuracy of the information contained in this book and cannot accept any legal
responsibility for any errors or omissions that may be made.

A CIP catalogue record for this book is available from the British Library.
ISBN: 9780955812798

Printed in the UK by Mixam

AUTOGRAPHS

HISTORICAL/FACTUAL

From Maine Men To Banana Citizens (1989), Temple Press

The Pride of Manchester (with Steve Cawley, 1991), ACL & Polar

Manchester: The Greatest City (1997 & 2002), Polar Publishing

Farewell To Maine Road (2003), Polar Publishing

Manchester City Hall Of Fame (2005), Hamlyn

Manchester City The Complete Record (2006), Breedon Books

Manchester City: 125 Years Of Football (2006 & 2007), At Heart Publications

Manchester: A Football History (2008 & 2010), James Ward

The Big Book Of City (2009), James Ward

The Big Book of United (2011), James Ward

Manchester: The City Years (2012), James Ward

Manchester City Folklore (2018), Conker Editions

The Emergence of Footballing Cultures: Manchester 1840-1919 (2019), Manchester University Press

FICTION

Atkinson For England (with Mark Brown, 2001), Empire

BIOGRAPHY

Football With A Smile: The Authorised Biography of Joe Mercer, OBE (1993 & 1994), ACL & Polar

Joe Mercer, OBE: Football With A Smile (2010), James Ward

TELEVISION

The History Of Football (2007), Channel M

Manchester City
Women
An Oral History

Gary James

Contents

Foreword

The original aim of this project was to capture the memories of women and men who had played or been involved with the creation and development of Manchester City Women since its formation in 1988. However, what developed over the months extended far beyond this. The project became a way of telling unknown histories, it became a way of compiling statistics that had never been formally recorded before and it became

Steph Alder, Manchester City's archivist.

a way of connecting people. What this has meant for the Manchester City archive is immeasurable. In a place where once no records sat now resides a rich and varied collection, a collection that will be preserved forever as a testament to the last 31 years of Manchester City Women.

Gary has been researching and writing about Manchester football since the mid-1980s. He has written several significant publications and a variety of articles on the region's games, clubs, players and personalities as well as being a regular contributor to the Manchester City match programme for 25 years. This new book addresses an area of Manchester City Football Club's history that has never before been explored in print. It is written and researched by a man whose passion for Manchester City has never faltered and who was cheering on from the side lines at the first Manchester City Ladies game back in November 1988. He has spent the last two years tirelessly interviewing and championing the voices of Manchester City Ladies and the journey through to Manchester City Women as we know it today. I am grateful for Gary's dedication and determination in what has been a fantastic revelation of the stories of women throughout this previously untold history.

As the women's game progresses so too will our archive. The oral history project may have come to an end, but it is just the beginning of collecting more stories and the archives that come with them. The Manchester City Football Club is a richer place for it!

Stephanie Alder
Manchester City Archivist

The Oral History Project

For the last few years I have been interviewing former players, coaches, administrators, fans and others connected with Manchester City's women's team. This has been part of a project established by myself with the full support of Steph Alder, City's archivist, to capture the history of the team from its formation in 1988 through to the modern day. Steph has been a great supporter of the project and, from the moment I first suggested it, she has been keen to ensure City has supported it.

There were two main reasons to begin the project: The first was to ensure the full history of the team was recognised and the second was to develop an archive of material connected with the women's team at Manchester City. The idea was to interview a number of women, initially set at fifteen, who would be able to explain their involvement. The aim was to ensure every period of the club's existence was covered. Using interviews, i.e. an oral history approach, seemed an appropriate way to capture the stories as I wanted to ensure there was an authenticity about the material captured. Interviewing those who participated allowed me to capture the stories and feelings of those involved.

The authenticity of sources has been important throughout my work. Alongside this I have been determined to ensure my own independence and objectivity as a historian, even though I was at some of the events captured within this book. It is vital objectivity is maintained and, as Holt comments, 'history is an almost inexhaustible source' of facts and from which 'any number of conclusions can be drawn according to the inclination of the

Gary James at a City Women supporters meeting.

Gary James chatting with members of the supporters club at the Dick, Kerr Ladies Football Cup 2019.

historian'. [1] The need to read widely, critically and contextually is essential and this book, like all of my publications. draws extensively on primary and secondary sources. My research for this project has included secondary sources, such as modern day articles on the early years of the club, and a variety of primary sources. This includes newspapers as well as other contemporary publications, films, illustrations, periodicals, maps, meeting minutes, reports and accounts, personal correspondence, diaries and football related ephemera such as tickets, programmes and photographs. [2] The triangulation of sources has also been important to me. [3]

Although archival research, triangulation of sources and the establishment of a historical truth has been my main method of historical research, it is important to stress that the significant focus for this project has been that of performing research by gathering oral testimony. I interviewed a variety of people with the aim of capturing every angle of the club, though it is clear that no publication could ever hope to capture every moment, story or voice. I planned interviews around a series of key questions but also allowed a degree of flexibility and established an environment that allowed each interviewee to feel confident and free to speak.

Articles on oral history began to appear in the 1960s, and by the 1970s debates were taking place on the appropriateness of the technique and its significance. [4] In 1978 Thompson argued that oral history enabled hidden histories of individuals to be uncovered and that it enabled democratic history-making whereby the stories of any individual could be recorded via an accessible technique. [5] Mitchell described the approach as a 'distinctly valuable source' and recognised its ability to direct researchers to other primary sources. [6] I think it is fairly obvious to anyone reading this book that gender inequality still exists with the history of female activities and the voices of women often excluded from traditional sources. This shaped my thought processes while establishing the project and it became obvious to me that focusing only on the written record would not unearth the history of this club. The voices of those who participated had to be heard if we ever hope to fill in the gaps of both our knowledge and of the history of football. Women have been playing football longer in the Manchester region than either Manchester City or Manchester United have existed in their present form. There are reports of games in the region as far back as the 1880s and yet there is little if any published material properly recording Mancunian football as experienced by women. Until their experiences are properly captured and reported we cannot hope to have a true history of football in the region or at our club. Oral history and this book are a start but they are not the end of the journey (I will be contributing further by publishing a detailed analysis of women and football at a later date).

While performing oral research it is important to recognise that the interviewee may be taking a position which may exclude or silence voices, for example by focusing on a particular line of questioning or by ignoring some voices, and that memory itself is selective. [7] Despite the pitfalls, an oral history approach was still the right one to take. It fitted the subject perfectly and allowed those involved to speak freely about their experiences. During my interviews I became aware that some individuals chose what to recall and may not always discuss their real memory of the event and, even if they do discuss and recall every detail, it is possible that their memories have become distorted over time. [8] To limit this triangulation with contemporary sources and gathering oral testimony from other interviewees with similar

[1] Holt, *Sport in History* 34, no.1 (2013), 3.

[2] Examples of archives utilised include the family collections of City players, coaches, supporters and managers, and those of Manchester City, National Football Museum, British Library and public libraries/collections across Britain.

[3] The triangulation of sources is also necessary and important and can be explained briefly by the research into City's first FA Cup season. An error in the original report for a regional cup tie v Crewe from the 1989-90 season meant that had become fixed in the minds of many as a FA Cup quarter-final. Triangulation with FA records and other newspapers eventually led to the right conclusion which was that the game in question was the regional league's equivalent of a FA Cup, competed by all teams affiliated to that league but it was not the national FA Cup. Accepting the views of several interviewees and of a report produced would have seemed sensible but it is the historian's duty to dig deep and to review every detail to ensure accuracy.

[4] E.D. Swain, 'Oral History in the Archives: Its Documentary Role in the Twenty-First Century', *The American Archivist* 66, no.1 (2003), 142.

[5] A. Thomson, 'Oral History and Community History in Britain: Personal and Critical Reflections on Twenty-Five Years of Continuity and Change', *Oral History* 36, no. 1 (2008), 96.

[6] D.J. Mitchell, 'Living Documents: Oral and Biography', *Biography* 3, no.4 (1980), 284.

[7] Thomson, *Oral History*, 98-99.

experience, allows comparisons of 'truth' to be made to establish a historical truth in the same manner as with other sources. I have utilised oral testimony in most of my works post 1991, especially in *Farewell To Maine Road* and in my biographical publications, and this method enables the 'turning-point moments' of a life to be documented, while establishing the character and personality of the individual through anecdotes, interesting stories and life facts. [9]

It is obvious to anyone who has attended one of my talks, book events or seen interviews with me that I am a man. Some academics suggested when I first explained about the project that I was unsuitable for the role as I was a man and I would find interviewing women about their sporting experiences difficult. The suggestion being that women will only talk with women about their experiences. This is of course ridiculous and shows a level of academic prejudice that undermines research. None of the people interviewed had an issue with my gender, just as none of the male footballers have ever had an issue with the fact that I can't kick a ball; or that I may be a different ethnicity; or that I have never scored the goal in a major football final. However, it is true that anyone embarking on a project like this must

The trophies at the International Football History Conference 2019

[8] K.C. Guan, 'Oral Histories in the Making of Our Memories and Heritage', *Asian Journal of Social Science* 36, no.3-4 (2008), 612-628.
[9] N.K. Denzin, *Interpretive Biography* (London: Sage, 1989), 7; Sidney Lee, *Principles of Biography* (Cambridge: Cambridge University Press, 1911), 8-9.
[10] G. Letherby, 'Gender-Sensitive Methodologies', in V. Robinson & D. Richardson (eds) *Introducing Gender & Women's Studies* (London: Palgrave, 2015), 89-90.

do their research and must ensure they fully understand the interviewee's background.

As I attended games between 1988 and 1992 I was aware of some of the situations discussed during the interviews but I always attempted to remain interviewer rather than commentator, even when some interviewees asked for my own memories. Interviewees often have their own idea of what an interviewer may want to hear too and the experiences of both can influence the story recorded. [10] It was important I was given each interviewee's story as they remembered it, without my influence. No person's story could ever be described as a true factual account of any particular moment and this is certainly true for footballing moments – how many of us have heard an account of a game we've been to and thought 'that's not how I saw it'? – but I have striven to ensure this is as accurate a record of the club's history as possible, told by the people who were there.

The oral testimony gathered for this book over a three year period was utilised to provide context and to establish the life of Manchester City's women's team via the stories of those who connected with it, and their vivid, emotional and entertaining stories provide a central thread, allowing the evolution of the club between 1988 and 2019 to be reported and considered. This book adds to debates about women's football and demonstrates how the club became established as a key feature of modern Manchester's sporting landscape. It is inevitably impossible to include every moment and trend witnessed, but it is hoped that enough spread has been included to engage the reader and provide an overview of the development of Manchester City's women's team.

I would like to end this introduction by making a couple of points. First, there are still many stories, voices and memories to be rediscovered. There have been hundreds of players over the years and there is so much more to uncover. If you played for Manchester City Ladies or Women at any point during its existence and have stories to tell or objects, images, programmes etc. then please contact Steph Alder at Manchester City. She is determined to create a strong archive. Second, this book contains match details for every season in the club's history. Gathering this information was never my intention, nor was it something I expected to include in the book. However, as time wore on I decided it would add reference points to the overall story. These statistics though are far from complete and I need your help. If you have line-ups and details for any of the missing games then please get in touch either via Steph at Manchester City or via my facebook.com/garyjames4 or twitter: @garyjameswriter

Finally, thanks for buying this book and supporting this project.

Dr Gary James

The 30th anniversary was marked in several ways, including through the match programme itself. The City-Arsenal WSL match programme, December 2018, was designed to look similar to the first programme ever issued by City Ladies.

MANCHESTER CITY Ladies F. C.

MANCHESTER CITY V AUSTRALIA U18'S PRICE 50p

MANCHESTER CITY

v ARSENAL WOMEN • 02.12.2018
OFFICIAL MATCHDAY PROGRAMME £1.50

Women's Super League

ETIHAD AIRWAYS   SAP NISSAN QNET

In The Beginning

Although recent years have seen football played by women reach new heights across Europe with the establishment of national leagues and various competitions, it would be wrong for any publication on one of today's prominent clubs to begin without recognising the history of the game. Women have been playing football for centuries but their history has often been excluded, ignored or down-played by those chronicling the male version of the game. Newspaper articles of children playing in the nineteenth century are typically discussed in academic and other publications as if these were communities of boys playing but was that actually the case? There are plenty of examples from the nineteenth century of boys specifically being mentioned as playing but at other times reports talk of children – does this indicate a gender mix? It is impossible to state of course, but to assume reports discussing children only mean boys appears incorrect, particularly in working class, industrial areas of our cities where boys and girls did at times share activities. Girls and boys worked in the mills in industrial Manchester with little, if any, differentiation in physical activity. If they worked together then surely they would also play together? We will never know unless we find specific examples of female activity.

We do know that some women were playing football in Manchester during the 1880s and that exhibition games were staged that attracted crowds greater than – or at least comparable with – the earliest incarnations of both City and United. This publication cannot possibly do justice to

left displayed in the second half last week,

Lady Footballers.

A match has been arranged to take place on the City ground on Wednesday afternoon next between Dick Kerr's Ladies' team, of Preston, and Messrs. J. Lyons and Co., Ltd., Ladies' team, of London, for the championship of England. Hitherto Dick Kerr's team has remained unbeaten, but this record is to be seriously challenged by the Metropolitan team of Lyons' ladies. The entire proceeds of this match will be handed over to the Lord-Mayor of Manchester's Fund for the destroyed French town of Mezieres.   J. R. C,

BRANSBY WILLIAMS AND THE RIVALS CAPTAINS.

The Manchester Football News, 19 November 1921 showing details of a game at Hyde Road between Dick Kerr's Ladies and Lyons... and a photo from the game itself.

those women who participated in football prior to the 1980s, that will come in a future book, but it must be recognised and recorded that within both the city and region of Manchester women were active participants and attendees at football games from football's beginning as a professional sport through to the modern era. In the 1880s there were games in Manchester, while female support for men's teams was commented on often, particularly in connection with the 1885 Manchester Cup Final and the first successes of United and City.

Both Hyde Road, City's original home, and Old Trafford staged games between women, while City also had discounted season tickets for women from the beginning of the club. Those tickets continued into the period post-World War Two, suggesting there was demand, and photos exist of women at male football matches throughout the sport's history in Manchester.

In terms of playing, occasional exhibition games were staged but it was the advent of World War One that led to a significant increase in women playing the sport as munitions, factory and other teams were established, often with a charitable aspect. Games were staged across the Manchester region and competitions were established. Few questioned the role of women playing during this time but once the war was over the situation changed. Women's football continued to develop with significant crowds for one-off games being reported. The most famous team of the era

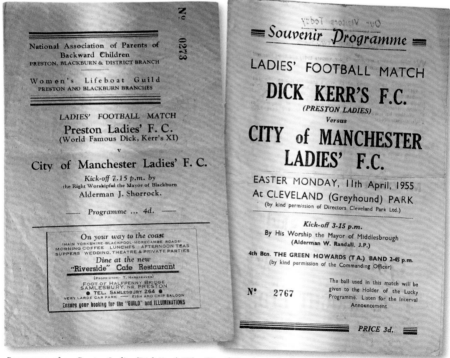

Programmes from Preston Ladies (Dick Kerr's XI) v City of Manchester Ladies in the 1950s...

was Dick Kerr's Ladies, from Preston, and they did play at City's Hyde Road ground. However, despite of – or probably because of – its popularity the Football Association took steps to stop women from playing the sport. They ultimately banned women's games from any club ground affiliated to the FA which in effect meant the game itself was banned. The two main reasons given were that the game was medically unsuitable for women and that some people, mainly men, were profiteering from the games with gate receipts not always finding their way to the charities that games were staged for. Medical evidence was provided – though it could easily be challenged by those in support of women playing the game – and steps could have been taken to limit profiteering

if the FA had taken a stronger interest in promoting the sport themselves. The end result was that football for women was pushed to the margins with games taking place on park pitches or venues with no FA connection. This ban remained in force from 1921 until 1971 with clubs and individuals being punished at various times during the ban.

Women did not stop playing of course, though it meant that only the most committed teams and individuals continued. Dick Kerr's continued to play and promote the sport whenever they could. They survived into the 1970s but from a local perspective it was a Manchester team that became the force post 1945. Manchester Corinthians became established in 1949 by Peter Ashley who wanted to help his daughter play football. The name was selected to establish that this was a team with Corinthian values with women from a variety of backgrounds working together. A sister club called Nomads was established and the two teams played each other, and others, in exhibition games and charity matches. City goalkeeper Bert Trautmann acted as an ambassador for the team on a tour of Germany and the club prospered for many years. In fact it was still going strong into the 1980s and some of the women who went on to play for Manchester City Ladies later that decade did appear for Corinthians during the 1970s and 1980s including Bev Weir, Lesley Wright, Rhoda Taylor, Janice Smith, Lesley Peters, Nicky Hunt and Rita Howard. This connection provides an unbroken link for Mancunian women's football from the 1940s through to the present day and this is important when considering how society views social activities. Some of those guiding principles of the Corinthians remained crucial in City Ladies development into

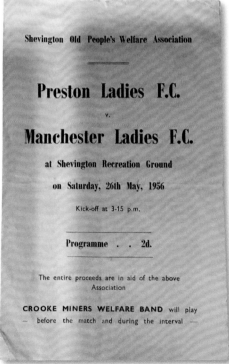

Shevington Old People's Welfare Association

Preston Ladies F.C.

v.

Manchester Ladies F.C.

at Shevington Recreation Ground

on Saturday, 26th May, 1956

Kick-off at 3-15 p.m.

Programme . . 2d.

The entire proceeds are in aid of the above Association

CROOKE MINERS WELFARE BAND will play — before the match and during the interval —

... and Preston Ladies v Manchester Ladies in 1956.

recent times. Rita Howard, for example, was a captain of the Corinthians and she went on to captain City and manage the club, providing an authoritative voice into the 2000s. Rita: "Corinthians was a fabulous community developing the talents of young girls."

By the 1980s women's football was in a different place than when Corinthians was established over thirty years earlier. The ban had been lifted, a women's FA had been established and a related FA Cup was being staged annually, but the game remained an amateur activity played, predominantly, on park and recreational ground pitches. There were regional leagues and some games were staged at football grounds by this time, but professional men's Football League clubs rarely became involved in promoting or working with women's football. There

Wednesday.

Bert Trautmann, Manchester City's German goalkeeper, kicked off in an international women's football match in which England and West Germany drew 1-1 at Stuttgart yesterday.

Bert Trautmann at a game in Stuttgart between England (actually Corinthians) and Germany in 1957.

The Manchester Corinthians 1982 in their green and black shirts with seven players who went on to play for Manchester City: (Names with a C in brackets after played for City) Bev Weir (C), Rhoda Taylor (C), Lesley Wright (C), Janice Smith (C), Val Hall, Lesley Peters (C), Mary Delruy. Front row form the left: Estelle Scruton, Angie Fletcher, Wendy Crossland, Elizabeth Dean, Rita Doherty (later Rita Howard) (C), ?, Nicky Hunt (C).

ATHERTON FESTIVAL OF SPORT

A LADIES FOOTBALL MATCH

on ATHERTON COLLIERIES F. C. GROUND

SUNDAY, AUGUST 9TH, 1970,
kick-off 2-45 p.m.

CORINTHIANS
NOMADS

These are two of the finest teams in the Country.
You will be amazed at their ability.

Admission by Programme 1/-

Hunt & Mansley, Printers, Atherton. Tel. 3141.

LADIE'S FOOTBALL MATCH
IN AID OF

THE MULTIPLE SCLEROSIS SOCIETY
(SALFORD & DISTRICT BRANCH)

CORINTHIAN LADIES
v
NOMADS

at the SPORTS GROUND, PEEL PARK
SALFORD 5

on SUNDAY, MARCH 21st 1971
KICK-OFF 3·0 P.M.

ADMISSION BY PROGRAMME
10 p. (2s 0d)

CORINTHIAN LADIES (Manchester)
(Colours : Black & White)

1	HAZEL BANCROFT	7	MARGARET WHITWORTH
2	EILEEN GAY	8	MARGARET WILDE
3	BARBARA HOPWOOD	9	MARGARET TEMPLE
4	CAROL AIKIN	10	YVONNE CRAVEN
5	ALICE INGHAM	11	JEAN WILSON
6	CATHLEEN HARVEY		

CORINTHIAN LADIES (Manchester) are the oldest existing Ladies' Football Club in the country. They have toured Germany, Holland, Venezuela, British Guiana, South America, Italy, France, Morocco and Tunisia and have raised over a quarter of a million pounds for charities.
During its lifetime the Club have won 56 Trophies, the most recent being the Reims International Tournament, 1970; Northern Tournament 1970; Macclesfield Tournament, 1971; Three Counties League Runners up, 1972; Leicester Tournament, 1972.

FODENS LADIES
(Colours : Amber)

1	ANGELA WATSON	7	SUE FISH
2	SUE TAYLOR	8	SYLVIA GORE
3	ELAINE BROWN	9	SUE CARTER
4	KATHLEEN STEENSON	10	JEANNIE ALLOTT
5	SHEILA PARKER	11	LESLEY CAULDWELL
6	LYNE ARSTALL	12	S. HAMNER or P. McDEVITT

FODENS LADIES are old friends of the Corinthian Ladies and have played matches against each other for many years, since Foden Ladies was was formed 15 years ago. Fodens victories are numerous, as they were the winners of the Three Counties League Trophy, 1972; Macclesfield Tournament, 1972; and Runners-up in the Deal Tournament, 1972.
The following players:- Sheila Parker, Sylvia Gore and Jenny Allott. (Fodens) and Jean Wilson, (Corinthians) were all picked recently for the first ever England Ladies' Soccer squad, for which they are to be congratulated.

Referee : Mr. A. PHILLIPS (Buxton)
Linesmen : Mr. K. DUNN and Mr. F. JOHNSON

---

were fan clubs who established teams using the male clubs' names but these were not official parts of the male club. This changed by the end of the 1980s. It was a time when attitudes were changing within professional male football but even then it was the efforts of individuals that started the process.

Roger Reade worked for the Professional Footballers' Association (PFA) at this time: "I think it was June 1986 when I started with the Football in the Community Scheme and City were one of the pilot six clubs along with United, Bolton, Bury, Oldham and Preston. The remit, or the target, really was to embrace the idea that we would encourage more people to come to football, show an interest in football, play in activities, not necessarily exclusively football, but to generate that interest that would then encourage attendances. 1985-86 season I think was one of the worst for football league attendances. It reached an all-time low and, whilst I wouldn't want the PFA's Football in the Community to claim the credit as there were lots of factors, attendances from 1986-87 started going back up again. It was partly because of the increased interest in the game, alongside the security. The game started becoming popular again and particularly amongst that new young generation.

"It was a poor time for football and one of the things I've learnt over the years is that I think a lot of Board of Directors of football clubs in the 60s and 70s were very reactionary. They didn't really embrace the idea of change until 1969, when a wonderful report was written by Sir Norman Chester, as he became, which was the first time that anyone had the vision to say, look, we're not getting 50% of the population at football games; we need to do more to encourage women to have an interest in the game; to come to games and hopefully even to play the game as well and even in 1969 people in football didn't really react to that.

"I don't think they really related the idea that actually it could be good for the game because more and more women coming to the game brings increasing amounts of money in to the game which, in turn, means you can improve your facilities, improve women's facilities, which were almost non-existent in the 1960s. It was not until the early 1980s really when the idea of Football in the Community was born and the idea of extending an arm to the whole wider community - men, women, boys, girls, senior citizens, people with disabilities, the whole of society… the concept of embracing everybody in the community was first born.

"The PFA took the lead because they recognised an opportunity to work with Government, where the Government would fund the fledgling Football in the Community scheme to get it off the ground. What the FA and the Football League recognised at a very early stage was that if

they didn't go along with the PFA, they may get left behind. The PFA were the visionaries in the early days - they had the vision for embracing that wider community and, of course, girls and women were a big target area from day one in 1986."

The PFA's Football in the Community was piloted in the North West and City was one of that first batch of clubs. Roger Reade knew that City would be supportive and a welcoming club: "City were absolutely brilliant. I can remember discussions with secretary Bernard Halford and he said this is exactly what we want to do, to add to what we've already got, because City's footprint in 1986 was still miles ahead of any other club. At the time they had Maine Road, which was being used for community activities and they had Platt Lane, the training complex. They had the social club with events for the local community. They had a mix of ages."

The first significant attempts at formalising City's community activities came in the 1960s. The club founded its Social Club in the mid 1960s and then established the Junior Blues at the start of the 1970s. While these may be looked upon today as focusing on support and match attending fans the truth was that in 60s and 70s Manchester the Social Club became an important facility in Moss Side, staging activities for locals as well as fans. In Arthur Hopcraft's *The Football Man* the author dedicated significant space to the Social Club, highlighting its significance bridging the gap between the club and the community. [1] It was viewed as a great example of how to create facilities for the community. In 1979, under the direction of director Bill Adams, and with significant support from Manchester City Council, the Blues invested in their Platt Lane facilities with the specific aim of opening up the then first team training centre to the community. "The Manchester City Way" as it became

The Manchester City Social Club in 1987.

known became a model for other clubs with City heralded as pioneers. By 1986 there were 1200 users per week with four full-time and twenty part-time staff. The focus was on sport with men & women participating in a variety of activities including football, netball, rounders, cricket and hockey. Women did play football as part of these initiatives with Rita Howard, future captain and manager of Manchester City Ladies, training there with other women. Former City player and 1956 FA Cup winner Dave Ewing trained female footballers at Platt Lane.

Women's football was certainly being played at City's Platt Lane from the 1970s with the 1979 launch of the Manchester City Way strengthening activities, but it wasn't until the formation of the Football in the Community programme that steps were taken to establish a specific Manchester City women's team. Ian Lees was one of the programme's staff in 1988: "It was around September 1988. Roger Reade gave me the

opportunity to work with Man City on various projects, including senior citizens, boys, girls, and then the pilot project with ladies came along."

According to Roger and Ian the PFA provided the initial funding for staff. Roger: "It was effectively the PFA in the founder days because the funding came through a Government Scheme called the Community Programme, hence the name Community Programme in Professional Football. Effectively the initial employees for the first four or five years were employed by the PFA." The PFA also supported the Women's Football Association (WFA), which was ran at the time by Linda Whitehead, the organisation's secretary. Roger remembers that the PFA, then based in Manchester's Corn Exchange, helped Linda obtain offices in the same building for the WFA: "She moved to the Corn Exchange and of course the rent was so low then at the old Corn Exchange building, that she was able to get a bit closer to balancing the books. She was brilliant and she did everything she could to encourage us. At the PFA we had this belief, even in the mid '80s, that every club would have a women's team and that every club would have feeder teams at different age groups leading up to the women's team. It was a bold statement which actually never came to full fruition. Linda worked tirelessly for the women's football. She was such a hard worker. Such a fantastic dedicated person to the growth of the women's game."

According to the WFA's chair Richard Faulkner writing in 1989: "The decision to move the WFA office to Manchester was taken before I became your chairman, but I can assure members that the arrangements are working well. It was not appropriate for the WFA to be administered from a room little larger than a cupboard over a garage (despite the prestige of a Hyde Park address), and the Manchester premises are more in keeping with what is needed." [2] At the WFA council meeting in June 1989 it was revealed that membership of the WFA increased by 26 clubs since the move to Manchester with 249 clubs affiliated by that time. [3] The view was that Linda Whitehead had performed a superb job with the office move: "The secretary was congratulated on obtaining excellent premises at such a low cost." [4]

In 1990 Linda explained the reasons for moving the WFA to Manchester: "The move… was a conscious one for a number of reasons, one of which was to develop a working relationship with the Professional Footballers Association and their 'Football in the Community Programme'. The

Association is very much aware of the need to increase awareness and participation in our sport and assistance is essential by various organisations if we are to really stand a chance of gaining national recognition. The PFA Community programme has given us the opportunity of promoting our sport within the footballing communities of the North West and we are now moving further afield in the hope that we can establish more women's teams throughout the Football League." [5]

The PFA's Football in the Community and the club's Platt Lane facility staff were not the only people connected with City that seemed to be promoting women playing football, the Supporters' Club also encouraged competition. As with male members of the organisation, each year the various branches of the organisation could enter women's teams into a Supporters Club tournament. Usually these were 6-a-side competitions and it is known they were being played during the 1970s and 1980s and possibly in earlier decades. [6]

By the summer of 1988 Kevin Glendon, a former City and Burnley midfielder, was running City's version of Football in the Community and with the desire of the PFA and WFA to encourage male clubs to promote women's football a perfect storm occurred in which Manchester City was to play a leading role. Neil Mather was one of City's community officers at this time: "I was a member of City staff and we were always looking for new ideas. We were not at the level we are today, but we were ahead of all

[1] A. Hopcraft, *The Football Man: People and Passions in Soccer* (London: Collins, 1968)

[2] WFA Chairman's report by Richard Faulkner, August 19, 1989, held at the British Library

[3] WFA Ltd Council meeting, June 3, 1989, held at the British Library

[4] WFA minutes of an officers meeting 19/11/88 held at MUFC, November 19, 1988, 2. Material stored at the British library.

[5] Manchester City Ladies v Australia U18s match programme, January 28, 1990.

[6] For example, The Manchester City FC Supporters Club handbook on 1983-84 carries information on the 1982-83 competition, which was won by Piccadilly branch who beat Leicester & Rugby branch 3-0 on penalties.

[7] *Fives Fun*, South Manchester Reporter, September 16, 1988, 23.

[8] *It's a Man's Game?*, King of the Kippax, issue 5 (1989).

top flight teams in terms of our community work. We staged community football tournaments and I ended up suggesting we do one for women. Local businesses entered and some of the women who went on to play for City Ladies, as we were initially called, competed. They talked to me and said that it'd be a great move if City set a team up. Various discussions took place and then I approached the club."

The first tournament held was won by a team often reported as being called Szererlmey Restoration, but this was actually the renowned local club FC Redstar, several members of which would later join City either as players, or in the case of Jane Morley as a coach and manager. Redstar's sponsors were Szererlmey Restoration, hence the confusion. They beat the Midland Bank following an exciting penalty shoot-out in the final.

As with the formation of most sports clubs there are differing views of the specific incidents that led to the creation of Manchester City Ladies amongst those working for Football in the Community and Manchester City but evidence shows that Kevin Glendon, as the leader of the community programme at City, first publicly mentioned the creation of the club in an article on 16 September 1988. [7] This had followed the tournament that Neil Mather mentioned and general consensus suggests the article had followed meetings which had been attended by the City Football in the Community staff. In 1989 Neil explained: "Being someone who enjoys a challenge (either that or I am a sucker) I decided to take on the all new Manchester City Ladies team." [8]

In 2018 Neil added: "I didn't want to just set up a women's team, the whole idea was to be Manchester City and I was very aware that, although there were a number of teams… off the top of my head: Oldham…

Millwall… but they were all, without being disrespectful, lower division sort of teams and there was no big team, although City at the time weren't exactly ripping up trees, they were still a major club. So I wanted us to become the first big club, if you like, to have a women's team. So, the first thing was to go to Bernard Halford, the Club Secretary, and get his permission. I had to get his permission and I've got to be honest with you, he was great. He just said 'fantastic. What do you need?' and I said not really an awful lot. We'll use Platt Lane and if we could get a kit? Immediately he said 'Well that's fine, off you go. We're fine with you to do it.'

"I then went to see Glyn Pardoe, who bizarrely was a youth team coach but was also in charge of the kit as well. I can still picture it today because all the kit was put in store cupboards that ran down the tunnel…. big white cupboards right down the tunnel at Maine Road. Glyn went in to this cupboard and got a whole kit out. It was huge but it was the smallest they had. It was like a youth team kit; sort of like an under 16. He basically said 'that's all we've got' and I thought that it was brilliant. I didn't expect the support - and so we had a kit."

Ian Lees remembers Kevin Glendon asking him to get involved too: "Kevin told us we were going to create this Ladies team. There were five of us, of which I had to be included, because I was the only one that had a driving licence to drive the bus! So I got to drive the bus and then we got a schedule of where we would train on a certain night."

Neil: "We had been given the go ahead so the next thing was to see if we could get players, so I organised trial nights at Platt Lane. We put it in the club programme; put it in the *Manchester Evening News*… I don't know what I expected, maybe 20 kids, 20 girls to rock up and there was over 70

prestigious ...
with 19 wins out of 22 games.

ton's."

FIVES FUN!

By MARK FREEMAN

ite trailing 1-0 after 0 minutes.

New boy Jim Cameron scored his ifth goal of the season midway through he second half to ull Road back.

Newcastle insisted n playing the offside rap but time after ime Road broke hrough and should ave won by two or hree.

Maine Road have layed six games, von four and drawn wo.

The second team ost 2-1 to Chadderon in the Reserve eague tournament.

Boss call

LETCHER Moss angers are desperate-y looking for two mangers to help with their ve junior teams.

The club are also ooking for sponsors for heir successful under 1's and under 15s.

If you can help, ring igel Hanson on 442 373.

OKALL ON ANGLING

MANCHESTER CITY'S Football and the Community scheme gave the ladies a chance to show off their soccer skills last week.

Teams from all over Manchester took part in the tournament including a team from this newspaper (pictured above, left-right: Joanne Allison, Rachel Ashbrook, Joanne Tulip, Clare Hare, Jennifer Allison and Sue Pritchard).

The Reporter team faced some stiff opposition in their group, playing sides from Manchester City, Brother and GM Police.

For the record, our girls lost 3-0 to GM Police, drew 1-1 with Brother and lost 3-0 to Manchester City.

The tournament was eventually won by Szererlmey Restoration who beat Midland Bank following an exciting penalty shoot-out.

The competition was a huge success and attracted hundreds of spectators.

Manchester City Football and the Community are starting a Ladies 11-a-side team. Anybody interested should ring Kevin Glendon on 226 1782.

Five-goal Celts

The South Manchester Reporter feature (16 September 1988) on the 5-a-side tournament. This is the article that inspired Kate Themen to call City from a call box.

at one. It was chaos to be honest with you. Luckily I had a lot of the lads, the qualified coaches, and split them into groups. I said to the other coaches 'just try and whittle it down a wee bit' because there were some girls that turned up that were City fans that just wanted to be there really... but couldn't play. There were others that were clearly exceptionally good footballers and were already playing at other clubs as well. We had to hastily do another session where we did like an X Factor type training. We finished up with about 30 odd and then we whittled that down to a squad of probably about 20 or something like that but I was also aware at the time that a lot of players, like Lesley Wright, Rhoda Taylor and Rita Howard were all playing for clubs. They'd already started their season because this would have been about October."

Those playing for other clubs had a dilemma, do they jump ship and join the new City club or do they wait and see how it progresses. As City were only able to play friendly matches in their first season players from other clubs did join for occasional games with Heidi Ward, from Redstar, playing in the inaugural game against Oldham Athletic in November 1988 while Lesley Wright, Rhoda Taylor, Nicky Hunt and Rita Howard, all from Woodley Ladies (the renamed Manchester Corinthians), made their debuts in the third game, away to Burnley in January 1989. Others joined at stages over the course of the following year as the team entered competitions and joined a league.

Throughout 1988 and 1989 those involved with the new team felt extremely motivated by the whole affair. Though little was openly discussed at the time Manchester City Ladies was a forward looking team, bringing together women from a variety of social backgrounds. Ian Lees remembers this as a real strength: "We talk a lot about diversity today but back then we didn't. It wasn't something we ever considered because, if you actually go back and think about it, that first team was diverse. We had married players, we had players who would describe themselves as gay/lesbian, we had different ethnicities and religions… but we never discussed any of that because we were a team. This was normal. No one judged anyone else on anything but their ability to play football – or to contribute to the team. It was how it should be but so often isn't. It was great."

Women came from all over the Manchester conurbation to play for the club. Kate Themen was one of the players who joined Manchester City at the start of the women's club. She had been living in Whaley Bridge, south of the city and also in south Manchester prior to joining the club. In September 1988 she spotted the article in the *South Manchester Reporter*: "There was a little piece and there were the contact details if you were interested in joining the new team. I rang the number and I remember being at the phone box: 'oh you've got this thing about the women's team…' and I guess it was Kevin Glendon I was talking to. I remember ringing and asking what was happening and things like this. They were just possibly gathering names and what have you, but I rang that number from a call box. I don't know how they got back in touch but they did to tell me when and where the training session was."

Living in Whaley Bridge there had been little scope to play football, so the newspaper article was enough to inspire Kate to make that connection: "There weren't any teams where I was from. I was in Whaley Bridge… it's like the back end of nowhere. I'd maybe had a little kick about with friends but nothing. So, to get the chance of playing football… Why not? Playing football - that's not something that was really an opportunity. I'd heard of Corinthians and Doncaster Belles. Leasowe Pacific…. I kind of knew these things and there were other bits I was aware of…. My Mum playing football, possibly once or twice. There might have been some charity game she played in. I'm sure it was just loads of men laughing at them as well. I've kind of got these memories of that. There weren't opportunities. So, to play football and wear a Manchester City shirt. That's a kid's dream!"

Kate Themen

CHILDREN IN NEED APPEAL

City officials were delighted to become involved with this year's Children in Need Appeal, following a request to Maine Road by G.M.R. (formerly B.B.C. Radio Manchester) for a fund raising event next week.

The Great Maine Road Run will take place around the track surrounding the playing area when various companies and organisations will be entering teams and hoping to raise sponsorship cash.

Former Radio Two D.J. and television presenter Ray Moore, the original "bog-eyed jogger", who took to the streets to raise money for the annual B.B.C. organised appeal, hopes to be at Maine Road next Friday, despite being stricken with cancer and he will defy doctor's orders to link up with G.M.R.'s Allan Beswick in the live broadcast from the ground. Sadly, Ray will not be able to run himself but he feels very strongly about the Children in Need Appeal and will no doubt offer suitable encouragement to the runners.

Teams representing our own Junior Blues, the Football in the Community project and Brother, City's major sponsors, will be taking part and Jimmy Frizzell will don a tracksuit to raise cash for the appeal, with bids or pledges being made to the radio station.

The Great Maine Road Run will be between 6 a.m. and 9 a.m. next Friday and teams wishing to participate should contact Janet Boulding or Joanne Cartwright at G.M.R. on 228 3434.

FOOTBALL AND THE COMMUNITY

The winners of the first North West teacher/pupil Superstars Competition held at Maine Road recently were Bob Christie and Patrick Bruce of Brineleas School in Crewe while the runners-up were Alec O'Neil and Leighton Shaw from Old Moat School in Manchester.

Because of the success of this competition, you will be pleased to know that a similar venture is being organised for the New Year.

Congratulations are also due to another winner from a recent Superstars Competition, Ian Brassel, who outplayed the 40 other boys taking part to land the first prize.

Another community programme success took place at half-term in the shape of the Soccer School. We must apologise to disappointed parents whose children were unable to take part due to the limited number of places and as with the 'Birthday Treat', please book well in advance.

This coming Wednesday at 8.00 p.m. we will be holding a Video Trivia Quiz night in the City Social Club. Team tickets can be obtained from Neil Mather. For those not taking part, entry is by payment of 50p on the night. For further details contact us on 226 1782.

The turnout for the first ladies coaching lessons was unbelievable! 33 ladies turned out on the night and we are now in the process of organising the team to represent Manchester City. Anyone still interested in joining should come to the next training session this Monday, 8.00 p.m.-10.00 p.m. at the Platt Lane Complex.

John Hudson, Activity Organiser.

/ HYDE GROUP

The first training session is mentioned in the men's match programme.

Kate somehow received notification of the date and time of the first training session at Platt Lane and she attended: "I remember turning up. They must have put us in to groups and stuff because obviously they've got these girls who have gone down and I'm guessing most of us had definitely not had any sort of coaching. They gave us small matches, like training things, to assess us. I always remember just being so enthusiastic. I had absolutely no football skill whatsoever but had that whole enthusiasm for it. I was not particularly adept at playing football, but I was putting a lot of physical effort in to it."

Kate was one of 33 women and girls at the first session on 31 October 1988 with 70 turning up for the second. Two others who had seen the newspaper features were Debbie Darbyshire and Rowena Foxwell. At the time they had never met but through the establishment of the women's team they became great friends. Rowena: "Myself and my best friend used to go Maine Road and it was a mid-week game I think. I'd left school in the July, so I'd just started work and obviously I was looking for some sports and things having come out of that type of thing. I saw it in the match programme. My friend isn't sporty at all, so I thought well I'm going to have to go on my own, but I want to go, so that's where I saw it. It must have been in the programme because I used to read it from start to finish back in the day. It must have been quite a decent size for us to notice it as well."

When she arrived at training Rowena looked for a friendly face and she saw Debbie Darbyshire: "You're there and you're

SPORTS EXTRA

By MARK FREEMAN

SHARPSHOOTING girls are queuing up for a chance to pull on the famous sky blue strip and represent Manchester City.

The club has just launched a Ladies team which they hope will see off opposition from other North West clubs.

Neil Mather who works for the club's Football and the Community scheme is putting the girls through their paces.

Neil is pictured above with (from left to right) Paula Hinchcliffe, 16, from Burnge, Michelle Mather, 15, from Fallowfield, Donna Harris, 25, also from Fallowfield and Lisa Hayes, 15, from Withington.

On Sunday the girls play their first game against Oldham at Boundary Park, and the week after December 5 they play a return game at Platt Lane.

Other fixtures have been lined up against Burnley and Bury.

Cpompetitipon for places in the team is very fierce with more than 30 girls turning up for training every week.

---

thinking, do I know anybody? Do I know what's going on? But I think from the first minute we sort of noticed that we probably stood on our own. I can't remember anybody else from that session on that first night that we know now, but that's not to say they weren't there." Debbie: "We clicked straight away. So out of 33 me and Rowena picked each other out. " Sadly, Rowena passed away in 2019, shortly after the 30th anniversary reunion but was one of the first, and most enthusiastic, former players to engage with this book. Her friendship with

Debbie, and many other members of the team, lasted, demonstrating the bonds that can be created through sport and shared visions.

At school Rowena had been quite sporty: "I used to do every single sport that was going, I absolutely loved my sport, whether it was netball, hockey, swimming, athletics, whatever it was. I didn't ever play football for school because there wasn't a girls football team, but obviously just a kick-about whenever you got the chance. I suppose coming to football specifically was

Rowena Foxwell and Debbie Darbyshire pictured in the early 1990s.

more about the love for City and the thought of playing in a City shirt than it was the fact it was women's football."

As Kate mentioned, the first training sessions had been arranged to gauge interest and to identify who had the right skills or enthusiasm. Debbie, having never played before, remembers some of the issues some women faced: "To start off we were dreadful. We were falling over. Some were running for the same ball, despite some of us watching football and knowing how football was played. We were so giddy we just all wanted to get involved." Rowena: "I think there was three camps probably. You had people who had no idea. No clue about the game and they'd never played before. You had girls that were absolutely amazing. I can think of one or two with a brilliant left foot, brilliant right foot, whatever it was. They might have grown up in a family of brothers but they had the ability and then you had probably the likes of us we knew what we needed to do but perhaps our ability wasn't to the

standard of those that had that natural flair I think."

The club, delighted with the interest generated at these sessions, organised its inaugural game to take place at Boundary Park against Oldham Athletic Ladies on 27 November 1988. The historic first goal scorer was Donna Haynes, who also scored City's third in a 4-1 victory, while former Redstar midfielder Heidi Ward also netted twice. Neil: "Teams wanted to play us because of our name I guess. We often had games organised through our Football in the Community contacts. I got in touch with a lot of community officers around the country really and I said if you've got a women's team can we play you and even better I'd try and arrange games to coincide with a men's game, so we could play the women's game in the morning and then the men's game in the afternoon. That happened at numerous clubs. We did a bit of a nationwide tour playing friendlies that first season."

While Neil and the other community coaches were all qualified coaches none of them had managed or coached a women's team before: "I was a fully qualified FA Coach. I'd done my badges… We'd all done our badges so we were all fully qualified… all knew what we were doing. I'd never ran a team before as such, but I'd done numerous coaching jobs but it was the admin of it that was hard for me because the coaching side was easy, I know football, I know what I'm doing with football, know how to coach players and stuff like that. It was the admin that I found the tricky bit, this is why Linda Whitehead at the WFA was invaluable to me. It wasn't just like right well we coach the team and manage the team, it was get the fixtures…join a league… enter the WFA Cup… all new experiences."

As Neil commented getting support from the WFA was vital and, with the PFA's connections to the WFA and a shared view of how the game could develop, Linda Whitehead was keen to help Manchester City however she could. Neil: "The 'men's' FA had nothing to do with women's football whatsoever, in any way. They were not interested. The women's FA was ran out of the Corn Exchange, at the very top of the Corn Exchange. I'll never forget it… the old lifts where you had to pull the gates closed and stuff like that and it was a tiny office. It was just one woman, Linda Whitehead, in this office and she ran the whole of the women's game from this office, which was remarkable really. So I went to her and said, 'Can we join?' and

to be fair Linda was delighted because you know for the prestige of the women's game to have teams like Manchester City keen on joining, promoting and developing the game was a big deal really.

"So they were chuffed to bits. They were desperate to get us in. So she basically said 'definitely… crack on!' I went to Linda on numerous occasions for help… 'how do I do this' and 'what do I do here' and so on. I can't speak highly enough of Linda because she helped enormously. And from then on in it was just a case of finding out off Linda. who had got the teams, organising some friendlies, so we could keep busy for that first season, because the season had already started."

The first mention of Manchester City in WFA minutes occurs at the start of 1989 when it was recorded: "The number of clubs affiliated at present is 233 of which 35 are 5-a-side clubs and 9 are school teams. Six new clubs have affiliated since November, another being a professional Football League club. It is anticipated that more Professional Clubs will affiliate a Ladies team within the next few months. New clubs since December: Columbo St Non-league (London); Sussex University (non-League); Manchester

Neil Mather in November 1989 wearing the yellow kit worn by City's men's team in an embarrassing 4-0 defeat by Arsenal, 14 October 1989. City vowed they would never wear yellow again and some of the shirts were given to City's community staff to use.

City (Non-League); Mayflower Ladies (Non-League); Kings College (Non-League); Redbridge (Southwark & District League)." [9] This was followed in March with further comments from the WFA's development officer: "Football League Clubs: Miss Bilton reported that more Football League clubs were now starting ladies teams, latest to do so are Hull City and Manchester City. The development report was accepted by the members." [10] To join the WFA in 1988-89 clubs had to pay a membership fee of £17.25 for new teams and then £34.50 in subsequent years. [11]

After that initial game at Oldham there were a series of friendly games organised with the second match being the return game with Oldham, staged at City's Platt Lane training ground. At the time this was the main training facility for the entire Football League club, not simply the community initiatives, and it was located a short walk from the Maine Road Stadium on a historic site that had been utilised for rugby and football from as early as the 1880s, possibly earlier.

Traveling to games was often an issue, as it was for all women's teams at this time. Players would often have to drive, or be driven by family members, in a convoy of vehicles to games but City did also provide the club's minibus whenever they could. Neil: "If you had a fleet of cars there were always problems… Somebody gets lost and there's no satnav then and all that lot and you've got to get across to Merseyside or you've got to get across to here, there and everywhere and you know and three cars turn up and

A City minibus, c.1980.

four have gone in the opposite direction and stuff like that. So to have the mini bus was amazing. It added to the impression of the club… added to our stature I guess.

"We looked quality, because we had good kit, we had tracksuits, so all the girls came out in the tracksuit and I'm big on that as well, I think if you look good and you feel good you play better. The more professional you are, even at amateur level, the more likely you are to be successful. We had certain fixtures at Platt Lane – where the men's reserves would play. The club made sure that we were sorted, you know, the club were fabulous."

The progress of the team was reported regularly in the men's first team match programme during the 1988-89 season, with Neil Mather, his coaching team and the players themselves, working tirelessly to promote the club and women's football in general. Neil continued to meet with the WFA and they helped the club join the North West League Second Division in 1989. They also perceived City as a pioneering club.

Linda Whitehead publicly praised the club in 1990: "Manchester City, one of the first professional Football League clubs to form a women's team and affiliate to the WFA, have worked hard over the last 18 months to promote the club and women's football and we are extremely grateful for their support." [12]

It is worth noting that by January 1990 14 Football League clubs had set up women's teams affiliated to the WFA, and back in 1988 some reports claimed City were the fourth team, after

Millwall, Bradford and Hull, to set up a female team. This point is often forgotten today when some in the game talk of the history and heritage of clubs who dominated the game during the 2000s. [13]

Under the original title of Manchester City Ladies Football Club the women's side ended their first competitive campaign in the North West League Second Division fourth, narrowly missing out on promotion but they had already attracted national attention with various TV features including a popular appearance on the children's show *WAC90*. That feature included interviews with first team players and was used to encourage girls and young women to take up the game.

The club participated in tournaments, including one at another relatively new club, Arsenal Ladies, and Neil Mather organised friendly games, often tied in with the male first team fixtures such as against Brentford prior to a City FA Cup tie there and against Bradford City on the morning of the men's promotion game in 1989. That year the increased activities of City's Football in the Community, which of course included the development of the women's team, brought recognition of City's investment in community initiatives at the first Football Trust's Community Club of the Year awards with City winning the Second Division prize and £20,000 to put into community activities. Around this time articles often

Roger Reade

talked of City as being the first club to take community activities seriously and Roger Reade, who spent many years at the PFA working on the Football in the Community Scheme, claimed City to be the perfect model.

Roger is rightly proud of the PFA's achievements too and has diaries and records of meetings with the WFA where the PFA and Linda Whitehead would discuss how to get male Football League clubs involved with the women's game. This is often overlooked and the PFA are often perceived as an organisation focusing solely on protecting the rights of professional male footballers, but in the 1980s they worked hard to persuade clubs to connect to their communities and to encourage others to take up football. Roger: "Of course, there was a drive to improve the popularity of football in general. If we could do that then we might boost attendances at Football League games, so that's when the focus came on to getting more girls and women involved. We'd limited resources and so much of the work was about going in to schools and schools would welcome you with open arms because any new resource helped the teachers, because they were so stretched, even in those days. Of course what used to happen was we'd go in to schools and they'd say 'you can take the boys for football, but the girls will be playing netball', or they'll be playing hockey or whatever, and

[9] WFA Secretaries report (undated but early 1989), believed to be January, stored at the British Library
[10] WFA Council minutes, March 4, 1989, 8. Stored at the British Library.
[11] WFA AGM 1989, September 10, 1988, held at the British Library.
[12] Manchester City Ladies v Australia U18s match programme, January 28, 1990.
[13] Manchester City Ladies v Australia U18s match programme, January 28, 1990.

The City team at Platt Lane in 1989.

we said 'hang on a minute, no, what if the girls want to play football?' They said 'no, they won't'. We challenged that and a few schools started letting the girls play with the boys and that became the forerunner for the FA changing their rules to embrace the idea of boys and girls at primary school age playing mixed football."

It is often overlooked now but the efforts of Linda Whitehead and the PFA to work together was perceived as a major strength back in 1989. In the WFA's submission to the Sports Council it was documented that: "Since the WFA's move of headquarters from central London to central Manchester where the PFA headquarters are based, a closer working relationship has materialised. The PFA organise a community programme which we are gradually becoming more and more involved in. The PFA organise community schemes in conjunction with Football League clubs and we hope to encourage all these clubs that take part in the scheme to include girls and women's football in their programme, and eventually affiliate

their team with the WFA. We envisage strengthening our ties with the PFA and the Community programme scheme over the next few years." [14]

Neil Mather remembers the importance of the community programme at City during the late 1980s: "Even though the first team was struggling the club understood how important the community scheme was. They got that working with the community, whether that was with the women's team, local schools or disadvantaged groups, was important. The club took a lot of stick for what was happening on the pitch, but as far as community was concerned City was better than probably all top flight teams. They definitely knew how to work with the community more than United for example."

In January 1990 City's former male first team goalkeeper Alex Williams re-joined the club to manage its community activities after a spell playing in Scotland and at Port Vale. His playing career had seen him leave City in 1986 and ended through injury in 1988, after which he worked as Port Vale's Football in

Girls put Colin top of list

MANCHESTER City's thriving women's soccer team have "signed" Colin Hendry as their first president.

The team, quarter-finalists in the WFA Cup and Stretford Fives winners, who are on a six-game unbeaten run, invited Colin to accept the honour after he topped a poll.

He will be an active president and help them with coaching.

Women's team captain Rita Howard with Colin Hendry and Fives trophy.

the Community officer. After 1990 the club's community activities grew significantly and the name was eventually changed to City in the Community and Alex has provided a consistent and welcoming face throughout the 30 years since he returned. He has worked tirelessly for CITC, deservedly being awarded an MBE for his work over the years and he remains an important ambassadorial figure. When he arrived in 1990 City Ladies were already viewed positively by the main club at the time and first team star and Scottish international Colin Hendry became the women's club's president in March 1990. He had watched the team defeat the leading side in the region, St. Helens, 3-1 in a cup competition. At the time, Hendry commented: "I hope that by becoming president it will encourage more publicity for women's football." [15]

Involving Hendry was a significant move by Neil Mather and part of his long term plan: "I wanted us to play at the highest level possible. At that time, United had a team, run by fans with no affiliation to the club, but I don't think any of the current names in the top level of the women's game had a team at the time we were formed. I may be wrong, but I remember that Arsenal was formed about the same time as us. Arsenal took a major step by putting players on YTS contracts which, basically, meant that for the first time women could go and earn money – not much – from football. That's how they became a force. At City we had no chance of doing that. You know it annoys me a little that City has been perceived as a new team by many, and yet we were the first major League club in the north to establish a team."

Articles appeared in the programme and in newspapers, and the team was used to demonstrate how football clubs were moving away from their 1970s/80s image of a male dominated environment, leading

[14] *Professional Footballers Association – Community Programme*, Sports Council Submission 1989-1993, (Manchester: WFA Ltd, 1989), 6.
[15] Manchester Evening News, March 1990 (specific date unknown).

Neil Mather and Godfrey Williams.

to an appearance on the Granada TV documentary series *World In Action*. Neil: "I will always be immensely proud of what we – the coaches, players and supporters – had achieved at the start and of what City were doing for the sport. I love how City have embraced women's football again in recent years and I've attended a few games. It really is excellent. The support the team gets is great and it will continue to grow. I do remember that back in our first years we had a crowd of about 150 for the derby match, but, generally, we were supported by family members, partners and friends. We had some good coaches like Godfrey Williams and John Fox, and they were enthusiastic for what we were doing, and of course the players who made it a success at that time."

As Neil suggested, like most women's clubs of that era, the team was supported at each match by a dedicated group of supporters that included parents, husbands, partners, children and friends. Leading striker Donna Haynes commented in 1990: "My boyfriend never misses a game. I want to get to the top and he supports me. Women can be just as good as men, and we can't wait to prove it." That year two of the club's players, Joni Davies and Rachel O'Shaughnessy, were selected for trials for the Welsh squad.

The first steps had been taken and Manchester City Ladies as it was called at the time was perceived as a positive force in women's football.

CITY GIRLS HEADING FOR GLORY

WITH Manchester City heading right back to the first division the club's ladies team is planning for glory days too.

The team (pictured left), formed last November have an impressive record — played four, won three and drawn one.

Next month they are hoping for more wins against Burnley, Crewe and Manchester University.

Recently the team became only the fourth side from a professional club to become affiliated to the Women's FA.

And next season the girls hope to join a North West League against sides from other professional clubs in the region.

The First Game

After Neil Mather had instigated a number of training sessions for the newly formed team he persuaded near neighbours Oldham Athletic to provide the opponents for the club's first ever game. This was a first for Oldham too as their team had been recently established and it soon became clear City's team were the better of the two.

Oldham kindly offered their Boundary Park stadium for the historic first match, meaning that the first Manchester City Ladies game of all time was played in a then Second Division Football League stadium, with a capacity of 21,962. No one paid to watch and the game wasn't publicised but the significance of playing on a professional men's pitch and in a major stadium that would host top flight male games in 1991 should not be overlooked. For Neil Mather this in itself was an achievement: "That was awesome. I mean to say to go there and its proper changing rooms and it's a stadium... a proper stadium. That was amazing. The whole experience of that first game was amazing and to win it as well was fantastic, because Oldham weren't a bad side by the way as well, you know, they weren't a bad side. The opportunity to do that... we were very lucky in a way. They had the plastic pitch and all of that too."

Ian Lees, another member of City's Community team, refereed many of the club's opening games. He also drove the minibus. He remembers another City staff member getting involved: "Louisa Felton. I worked with her in the Commercial Department. She was keen to play. She supported City. Once she'd heard I think she ran across to Kevin Glendon and said 'put my name down, 1 want to be part of this."

Donna Haynes (left) and Heidi Ward (right) scored in the first game in December 1988.

Left to right:
Ian Lees.
The captain for the
first game, Louisa
Felton.
Kate Themen and
Michelle Mather.
Debbie Darbyshire
(back) and Rowena
Foxwell.

Someone who played in that game was Rowena Foxwell. In 2018 she remembered how quick the journey was from the first training session to the first game: "It was so rapid. I can't remember how we got to the game in the sense of how we got from that first session to how it came about to a team. I don't think I ever analysed it because I was too young to know any different. At that age you just do it but we were playing on a proper pitch; using a proper dressing room! We were excited, definitely. Now you'd look back and think about it more. My youngest son is in awe: 'You played football? You played for City? How much did they pay you?' We know it wasn't like that."

Debbie Darbyshire, another member of that initial team, agrees that it was difficult to understand the significance at the time: "I don't think it was a case of 'oh my God, I'm playing for City', I think it's more 'hey, we've got a City shirt. We're having a laugh. We've got a game.' I don't think it clicked that we were actually part of something."

Kate Themen played in that game and was not particularly impressed with the plastic pitch: "The pitch was bloody awful!

Surfaces then were pretty dreadful. Totally unsuitable for playing football and it doesn't matter how new some of us were at playing football, that was unsuitable for playing at any sort of level." Rowena Foxwell: 'We couldn't cope with the balance, because we played our first game on the plastic pitch, we were sort of getting used to the ball, next minute, bouncing so high, it was like wooh, a bit strange."

It was a new experience for Kate who hadn't played for a team before: "I remember being afraid to go in for tackles, because of the burns. Also you get your foot stuck and the danger of like jarring yourself and all these sort of things… I remember having kind of quite a lot of anxieties around that, around the surface." Kate remembers that she did manage to charge down the wing at one point during the match and put in a cross: "A really, really good cross but no one jumped for it. That was it and you know what I was dead chuffed with myself. I managed to curl my foot around it and probably put the only decent cross in I ever did."

There were mistakes in the game with

Oldham Ladies v. Man. City Ladies
At Boundary Park

OLDHAM ... 1   v.   MAN. CITY ... 4
City scorers: Donna Hayes 2; Heidi Ward 2.

An outstanding performance from City in this their first match of the season.

City took control straight from the start and demonstrated an accurate passing game, Oldham finding it hard to live with the Blues. Despite all the early pressure, it was the home side who nearly ntook an unexpected lead, only to be denied by a magnificent save from Flynn.

That near shock over, City pushed forward and the deadlock was broken when Haynes cut in from the left and finished with a far post shot, from then on it was all City, Haynes hit the post, Ward had a goal-bound effort cleared off the line before stabbing home City's second from a Burnett cross.

The second half started in similar vein and Mornson was desparately unlucky, to see her 20 yard drive cannon off the bar. It was only a matter of time before it was 3-0 and Haynes was the scorer again, latching onto a fine defence-splitting through ball from skipper Felton. Ward then grabbed her second, evading two challenges before scoring.

City had a lapse in concentration and left Flynn stranded and Oldham got a consolation goal. Notable performances for City, Haynes and Ward for all round work, Felton — who emerged as mid-field playmaker, Burnett — good old fashioned wing play and Mather, cool and calm at the back.

City team: M. Flynn, R. Foxwell, T. Slack, M. Cox, M. Mather, L. Burnett, K. Thomson, L. Felton (Capt.), A. Ward, D. Haynes, A. Hewnelt; Subs: C. Morrison, M. Braddock, D. Davies, A. Marland, D. Darbyshire, D. Crystal, B. Emerson.

LADIES FOOTBALL IN REDDISH

ARE THERE any ladies who are in, or run a Ladies Football Team who would be interested in playing against Manchester City Ladies.

They play in the evenings, under floodlights on the all-weather pitch at Platt Lane, Fallowfield. To arrange dates and times, please contact Louisa Felton on 061-226 1191 office hours.

Also, I would be interested in taking team photos and match reports for inclusion in the paper and I can be contacted on 061-432 5379.

Len Duckett

the mix of novices, experienced players, and dedicated fans learning how each other played. Heidi Ward, who scored twice in this match, had been playing for FC Redstar for a few years prior to joining City: "It was the final year of my A Levels when City started and I was playing for Redstar in the North West League. My Mum, who worked at City then said they're starting a team, 'do you want to go to training?' So, I went along to see what it was going to be like, and I ended up playing in the friendlies that season. Getting to training was a bit of a faff, but I got to as many as I could, but I was still officially signed for Redstar, so at the end of that season, I had to go to Redstar to ask permission to go to play with City instead. If I'm being honest I just wanted to play football, but then the opportunity to play football in a City shirt was just like a massive draw I couldn't turn down."

Heidi played in most of the friendlies during the 1988-89 season while continuing to play for FC Redstar in League games: " I only remember that first game at Oldham now because of a couple of photographs and I know that my Dad was there as well. He videoed some of it but I can't find the video.

41

I remember that we had a few girls that had never really played football before and then a couple of us had played football before, so it was a big sort of mis-match of players. I remember that we had a hand-me-down kit from the youth team so it didn't fit properly. It was as if we were wearing hot pants and big shirts!"

In difficult light and wearing the men's team's hand-me-downs City's women took to the field for their first fixture. The Blues took control from the start but struggled to make their dominance tell initially. In fact it was Oldham who came closest to scoring in the opening minutes forcing City 'keeper Michelle Flynn to make a magnificent save.

Despite this scare City remained in overall control of the play and the deadlock was finally broken when Donna Haynes cut in from the left and finished with a far post shot to become the club's historic first goalscorer. Moments later she hit the post again. This was followed by an attempt from Heidi Ward who saw her goal-bound effort

cleared off the line. Ward did make it 2-0 soon after though when she stabbed home from Lisa Burnett's cross.

In the second half the Blues had a 20 yard shot cannon off the bar before Haynes managed to make it 3-0. She latched on to a fine defence-splitting through ball from captain Louisa Felton. Heidi Ward netted her second of the game soon after when she evaded two challenges before scoring. Neil: "Do you know I can't remember the first goal by Donna Haynes if I'm honest, but I can remember Heidi's from the edge of the box… I can still picture Heidi's strike from the edge of the box flying in to the far corner, I can't remember the second of Donna's but the one goal I remember from that game was one of Heidi's."

Heidi is more doubtful of the quality of the goal: "I can't remember that much about the day never mind the goal. Neil describes how I scored and describes the goal as if it's one of the best he's ever seen. I doubt that. I can't remember. If we ever find my dad's

Goalkeeper Michelle Flynn

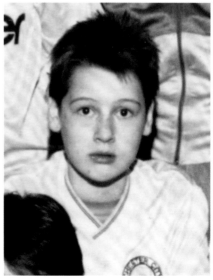

Donna Davies

video tape of the game then we'll probably see that it just rolls in! For me Donna Haynes was the star of that team. She was great. They called her Mara-Donna because she was quite short and she'd dribble with the ball... she'd get around people and had a good shot. She was a really good player."

Neil agrees: "I remember Donna coming and thinking this girl is amazing. She'd played a bit and then she'd had a baby and she'd packed it in. She had so much ability, I mean as good a footballer... I don't give a monkeys whether we're talking about men or women... Donna Haynes could play quality football. She had everything, all the tricks, all the finishes. She could finish, chip, strike through the ball, head it, anything... she was a wonderful footballer. That day at Oldham with Donna and Heidi... those two girls up front and we won that game 4-1 and I thought look at them... I'll never forget that game."

Despite a late consolation goal for Oldham the Blues were thoroughly deserving of their 4-1 victory. A report of the game highlighted: "notable performances for City: Haynes and Ward for all round work; Felton – who emerged as midfield playmaker; Burnett – good old fashioned wing play; and Mather – cool and calm at the back." [1]

For Rowena Foxwell the game improved confidence and spirit amongst the team: "Winning the game boosted us even more back then. It's 'oh we've won, we can do this, we've won a game.' Then it was 'who's the next one?' We're ready to play again."

Kate Themen was equally positive: "I enjoyed it and there was the whole social things as well. I didn't think 'yes, I'm making a statement.' I play drums as well and I'd been playing drums at the time. I remember the day I wanted to play drums. I was five years old and someone had made a model drum kit for a competition or something and one of the teachers played it and I thought, yes, I'm going to do that. It was the same with the football, it was never unusual.

Alison Hewlett

Michelle Cox

It's just I really like this, I really love football. I was a City fan and I got to wear a City shirt and play football and that's big."

Neil Mather's sister Michelle was a member of City's first team: "I was dragged to Platt Lane by Neil following the advert going in the 'papers as I could play and had knowledge of the game. He didn't think many would turn up so I was there to make up the numbers." She was selected to play against Oldham: "That first game at Boundary Park... Being so proud to wear the same shirt as my heroes and to step on to the same field as the players who I'd watched from the terraces from being seven years old. My memory of the game was being frozen because Neil made us go out in shorts and short sleeved shirts and refused to let us wear base layers as 'you'll move more to stay warm', racing into the changing room at half time and fighting with the girls over the small blow heater on the wall."

Ian Lees: "Playing that first game was a success and ensuring the club continued beyond that moment and game was important. That it continued and prospered is down to a lot of different people. And actually ultimately it's down to also having access to facilities; what resources were available to support it, because without those hours of those activity community organisers you wouldn't have had those games and those training sessions. It took a lot of people to develop the women's team and without City's community scheme it may never have happened."

Neil Mather: "It's a nice thing to look at and say we played in a real stadium... the first game... we won the game and everything was perfect really, everything went well." City's exciting mix of experienced players, City fans and newcomers to playing the sport had made their mark. Some would remain involved for several years and friendships were developed that have lasted.

■ Sunday 27 November 1988
Oldham Athletic 1 Manchester City 4
City Scorers: Donna Haynes 2, Heidi Ward 2
Venue: Boundary Park
Team: Michelle Flynn, Rowena Foxwell, Tonia Slack, Michelle Cox, Michelle Mather, Lisa Burnett, Kate Themen, Louisa Felton (captain), Heidi Ward, Donna Haynes, Alison Hewlett. Subs: C Morrison, M Braddock, Donna Davies, A Marland, Debbie Darbyshire, D Crystal & B Emerson.

---

[1] A report of the game exists from an unknown newspaper. Part of it was republished in G. James & K. Mellor, *From Maine Men to Banana Citizens*, (Nottingham: Temple Press, 1989), 134. The names of some of the players were incorrectly recorded in that report while some first names remain unclear. All contemporary newspapers covering the Oldham region have been consulted.

The Family Tree

While Manchester City Ladies was established in 1988 the roots of the organisation go back much further. Several clubs contributed players in the early years with Woodley Ladies and FC Redstar two of the most prominent. This diagram depicts how those clubs fed into the earlier years of Manchester City's women's team.

MANCHESTER CORINTHIANS

Established 1949

Renamed Woodley Ladies

MANCHESTER UNITED

Established 1977 as Manchester United Supporters Club Ladies, becoming Manchester United Ladies for the 1989-90 season.

FC REDSTAR

Formed as a breakaway from Manchester United in 1985.

MANCHESTER CITY LADIES

Established 1988

Prominent players who moved to Manchester City in 1988-90 include:
Rhoda Taylor
Lesley Wright
Rita Howard
Lesley Wright
Nicky Hunt
Bev Weir

Prominent players who moved to Manchester City in 1988-90 include:
Heidi Ward
Joni Davies
Bev Harrop

Jane Morley, who went on to manager City Ladies, would subsequently make the move, contributing to the club's development at various levels.

Corinthians players Rhoda Taylor, Lesley Wright and Rita Doherty (who became City's captain Rita Howard) in 1982.

Manchester Corinthians was established in 1949 by Peter Ashley, who wanted to increase opportunities for his daughter to play football. In the mid-1950s City goalkeeper Bert Trautmann acted as their ambassador on a tour of Germany. Gladys and George Aiken took over the running of the club as time moved on and, following their divorce, George remained involved until his death. Due to ground issues the club was renamed Woodley Ladies during the mid-1980s.

FC Redstar was established in 1985 when Jane Morley, Bev Harrop and several other prominent members of the Manchester United Ladies team felt dissatisfied with the club's ambition. They wanted to compete in the North West regional league but the committee at the time wanted to focus on success in Manchester based leagues. Redstar joined the North West Women's Football League at the start of 1985 and, after a difficult first season, became established as a prominent club in the Manchester area by the time of City's formation in 1988. In 1988 Redstar's official home ground was the Kendal Sports Club in Stretford, though their initial home had been only a mile or so north of the present day Etihad Stadium.

TODAYS VISITORS

May I now take this opportunity to welcome todays visitors F.C. Redstar, who play all their home games at Kendal Sports Club in Stretford.

F.C. Redstar was formed during the summer 1985 and was made up from a collection of players from The Greater Manchester Womens Football League.

They joined The North West Womens Football League at the start of the 1985/86 season and found a big difference between the two Leagues, their first season was difficult and at the end of a very grueling season they finished around mid table and were left to pick up the pieces, and try again.

Their second season was much more rewarding and after getting their act together, they finished as runners up in the second division which earned them their promotion into the first division.

Their stay in the first division was short, but sweet and they feel they learned a lot from it. Now they are hoping that with their past experiences, new management and new players, that this season will be very rewarding for everyone concerned with Redstar.

May I now wish them every success with their aims.

Former Redstar player Joni Davies.

FC Redstar 1988 with Heidi Ward (back row, far left).

REDSTAR

(SKY BLUE SHIRTS, NAVY SHORTS)

TEAM TO BE PICKED FROM

T. JORDAN (Capt)
J. KENNEDY
J. MORLEY
P. ROBERTS
B. HARROP
J. DAVIES
Ni JORDAN
D. COOK
J. GOLLAND
H. WARD
Vi SUNGAY
J. TURNER
T. BURROWS
H. ROBERTS

Finding Their Feet

After the first game at Oldham Neil Mather organised a return with the Latics and then a trip to Burnley in January 1989. The teams changed at Burnley's Turf Moor and then travelled uphill to an open pitch with no facilities. The ground had goalposts but no nets. Despite the rather poor quality of the venue and facilities this was another step forward for the fledgling club. Several new players, most notably players from Woodley (the renamed Manchester Corinthians) had joined and made their debuts at Burnley.

Neil Mather had ambition for the team by this time: "I thought it would have a life, yes, I could see us joining the League the next year. I knew that we had a nucleus of good players. What used to always bug me was the fact that people used to laugh it off. They don't laugh it off any more because they see it on TV, but nobody ever saw that on TV. If you saw Heidi Ward play, if you saw Donna Haynes play, you'd go these girls could play football. These weren't mugs. I knew there was a nucleus of players waiting in the wings to come in that was going to make us even better, so I could see us going forward and joining the League and the club growing and growing. Could I see what has happened now? No. But nobody could, but I could see us being an established women's team and I wanted it to carry on and carry on and carry on and it did."

Action from City's visit to Burnley and the Shirt worn by Rhoda Taylor in that game.

Left to right: Neil Mather, assistant manager John Fox and coach Mike Day.

One of the new influx of players was Lesley Wright: "While at Woodley Ladies, the renamed Corinthians, I heard that City were thinking of starting a team. So a few of us left Woodley and that caused a bit of a fallout. It still happens now that groups will move from one team to another, putting the other in jeopardy. When I joined City there were some who perhaps couldn't kick a ball as well as we'd have liked but they were keen. Some just wanted to play for City and that gave them a desire that perhaps wasn't there for all. Starting City was important and it meant everything to some to wear that shirt. I felt bad leaving Woodley but I had to go with my heart. We must remember that the City Supporters Club used to organise five-a-side tournaments. I used to play in that. This was before the City Ladies team was established."

Heidi Ward (2nd back left) and Joni Davies (bottom middle) at a MCFC Supporters Club competition at Platt Lane with first team men's 'keeper Eric Nixon.

FOOTBALL AND THE COMMUNITY

St. Edward's Primary School, who represented Manchester City in the G-Mex Schools Soccer Six, lost to Leeds United 2-1 in the final, and so ended as the runners-up. It was a tremendous effort by the youngsters and City striker Paul Moulden went along to the school on Friday to present the players with their trophy. Congratulations to all who took part from the staff on the Community Programme.

Over the next few weeks, we will be visiting hospitals and schools with some first team players, chatting to as many people as possible and hopefully cheering up a few patients! The Community Programme has also organised a Christmas party for OAP's and we will be the guests at a Christmas party at a school for the mentally handicapped.

On Monday, our ladies football team took on Oldham Athletic and this time drew 1-1.

Finally, we wish everyone involved with the Club and all the supporters a happy Christmas and a prosperous New Year.

Above: From the City men's match programme 17 December 1988.

FC Redstar's Joni Davies had also participated in those 5-a-sides for a supporters branch, alongside Heidi Ward. She became a member of the new City team too, as did Gail Rothwell, now Redston: "I'd played before, like even for men's teams and everything else, but when we started getting players, we got players from Redstar like Joni Davies and Vanessa Bungay too. We started getting these players and I thought, yes, this is what we want, you know, so I was more enthusiastic at the fact that we're getting these players in now and you know even the training was different, it was more serious."

Team selection became more difficult as Neil and the coaches had to juggle the needs of finding a squad of quality alongside the needs of both the new players and the large number who had been keen at the initial training sessions. When it came to specific games though there was also a more practical element. Rita Howard: "When it came to team selection that was down to Neil but often it was 'who've we got?' There'd be work commitments, social life commitments and so on. It took some time to take off."

City attracted players from all over Greater Manchester and beyond, and getting to training for some could be difficult. Heidi Ward: "Because of where I lived and I couldn't drive getting to training was a bit of a faff, but I got to as many as I could. I was still officially signed for Redstar when I played in those friendlies during 1988-89

Rhoda Taylor

Carol Woodall

Michelle Mather

49

In the distance Joni Davies and Lesley Wright leave the field against Bradford in May 1989.

for City so at the end of that season I had to go to Redstar to ask permission to play with City. But because it was my A Level year, I was planning to go off to university, so I didn't actually take part in much of what was going on at the start of the 1989-90 season and then I didn't go to university in the end, so I came back to play for City.

"Redstar was a team of girls that had played football before and knew about positioning and they were quite experienced. I was sort of learning from Redstar, because I'd never played in a proper team before them. They were all experienced players and I started playing for them when I was about 14. At City we had Neil who was more of a proper coach, and then we got this influx of girls that had been playing football for quite a long time, so it sort of changed the dynamics of the team."

Heidi enjoyed her experience at City and that first season of friendly matches had some memorable moments: "I suppose

I had confidence that I'd played in a league before so I sort of knew what to expect in the game. Some of the girls had never played like a 90 minute game of football before, so it obviously must have helped, yes. We played a lot of friendlies. We went down to Brentford when the men's team had a cup game against Brentford and we went down in the mini bus. We played against a team that I don't think had played before and I remember in the dressing rooms one of the Brentford girls saying 'don't you all sound like you come from Coronation Street!' And then Donna Haynes said 'oh you all sound like you come from Eastenders!' And there was just a little bit of banter and I think we beat them but I can't really remember the game."

Most of the teams City faced in their inaugural season were the community teams of men's clubs. Some were already established, others were playing their first game. Opponents included Crewe Alexandra, Chester City and Bradford. Lady

Blues defender Helen Hempenstall made her debut against Chester (3/5/89): "I remember my first game. We won 12-0 I got player of the match and I scored the twelfth goal. City was more organised than I'd experienced at Lady Blues."

After a 3-0 victory over Crewe at Platt Lane three days later the Blues faced Bradford City. Heidi Ward: "I remember the Bradford game because it was the day of the promotion game for the men so we went along as City fans to watch the City-Bradford game in Bradford. We played the Bradford girls before the match and I remember that one because I was warming up and got injured in the warm-up! I didn't actually play. I hadn't warmed up properly and I was kicking a football around. I should have done a few stretches, I think that's what it was. I still got to watch both the matches

afterwards – the women and the men. I didn't want to miss City."

Kate Themen did make it on to the pitch though and remembers the game because it brought a significant moment in her City career: "I scored like an 18 yarder. I was on the edge of the box and I curled it in. And I ran to the middle of the pitch and celebrated. I think we'd gone up on the mini bus in the morning." Neil Mather: "I remember that really well and I really remember beating Bradford, because it was a big deal. They were a good team." Bradford were an established team and that game was included in a feature on Bradford City Ladies that appeared in Football Monthly.

Although she can't remember which game this was Kate Themen is aware of one of her other actions that season: "I came on as sub for a match, and I was a bit late

Below: The Bradford v City game was featured in Football Monthly magazine.

IT'S A MAN'S GAME? ....

The following week February 12th (are you still following me?) it was back to the plastic at Oldham hoping Oldham's keeper modelled herself on Mr. Rhodes.

Now we've got some publicity we'll get you supporting the other City team, bring your bananas!! Come and admire Michelle 'Dibble' Flynn, Michelle 'Reddo' Mather (exceptional football talent runs in the family) or 'Mara' Donna Haynes all finds from nowhere.

I've enjoyed the experience even though we have to be at the ground an hour before kick-off to give them some time to get changed, why does it take you so long girls??

So come on all you City fans get supporting the girls, and watch a consistent team for a change!!

NEIL MATHER APRIL '89

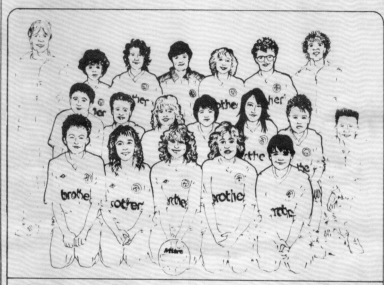

Back row

L-R Mike Day (coach) Donna Haynes, Michelle Cox, Michelle Flynn, Pat Barnes, Rita Howard (team captain) Neil Mather (manger)

Middle row

L-R Carol Woodall, Rhoda Taylor, Nicky Hunt, Michelle Mather, Rowena Foxwell, Donna Davies, John Fox (Assistant manager)

Front row

L-R Lesley Wright, Louis Felton (club captain) Debbie Darbyshire, Joanne Hardy, Alison Hewnett.

⑨

From the fanzine King of the Kippax.

coming in on a tackle. I got a load of abuse from the people watching at the time – 'don't know what you've brought her on for, dirty git.' The other player had a kind of a rip down their leg and showing the ref - 'have you checked the studs' and all this sort of stuff. These were quite traditional games. There could be quite a bit of blood and thunder and what have you."

Michelle Mather played in a lot of the 1988-89 friendlies too: "My strongest memories are of the camaraderie we had and how dedicated we all were. For a group of girls thrown together, who came from all backgrounds we quickly became a family who worked so hard for each other which made each game special. As I was in the original team it was mostly about establishing the team and getting set-up."

I'm honoured that I was there from the start and helped develop a team that now leads the way in women's football."

She believes, as do most of the others who played during the club's formative years, that even with their first game City had found one of their greatest ever players: "Donna Haynes is still one of the best players I have watched at any level and a pleasure to play with." Inevitably, Michelle is keen also to remember the role her brother played in establishing the team: "Neil was the driving force behind it all and was so dedicated to promoting the women's game and to having a successful team at City."

The last game of the 1988-89 season is a long-forgotten first derby match with United. This has become one of the most difficult games to track down. A list of

City towards the end of the 1988-89 season at Platt Lane.

Pat Barnes *Nicky Hunt* *Rita Howard* *Joanne Hardy*

results was published in a feature Neil Mather did for the fanzine *King of the Kippax* and that included a 4-2 defeat at home to Manchester United. None of the players seem to remember this defeat although Heidi Ward has a recollection of a meeting with United during that first season: "I'm sure we played it at United's training ground because there was quite a few people that came to watch as well and I just remember, because I played on the wing, I remember running up the wing, but I can't remember the score or anything." If this is correct then that game would have been played at The Cliff, a venue Manchester United Ladies had used often, but whether this is the 4-2 defeat mentioned in *King of the Kippax* is uncertain.

The first season of friendlies ended after the Manchester United defeat, which in itself occurred some time after the men's season had ended. Excluding the Brentford game (as this was played indoors and was more of a tournament/5 a-side style series of games) the record was Played 12 Won 9 Drew 1 Lost 1 with 56 goals for and 15 against. Neil was proud of that season and the role City's community team had played: "Manchester City's community scheme has always been one of the best, even going back when I started there, we were winning awards. There's a picture of the community lads on the Maine Road pitch after we'd won an award somewhere. It was always one of the best and that's the reason it started. Let's get it right… because the community scheme were constantly on the lookout to do everything for the community… Without Kevin Glendon, who was the Community Officer at the time, it wouldn't have happened. He pushed us as staff to sort of do everything and make sure everything was covered. The community was very important."

Manchester City Women Firsts

T he City Ladies team has a long and distinguished history, and was established as a part of the main club via an initiative in 1988. Here are a few of the club's early firsts:

First Training Session:
■ 31 October 1988 at MCFC's Platt Lane Training Complex. This was the home of Manchester City's first team and reserves training centre. 33 women and girls attended the first session.

First Games:
■ Sunday 27 November 1988
Oldham Athletic 1
Manchester City 4
City Scorers: Donna Haynes 2, Heidi Ward 2.
Venue: Boundary Park
Team: M Flynn, R Foxwell, T Slack, M Cox, M Mather, L Burnett, K Themen, L Felton (captain), H Ward, D Haynes, A Hewlett. Subs: C Morrison, M Braddock, D Davies, A Marland, D Darbyshire, D Crystal & B Emerson.

■ Monday 12 December 1988 (6pm kick off) **Manchester City 1 Oldham Athletic 1**
City Scorer: Heidi Ward
Venue: Platt Lane
Team: M Flynn, D Davies, K Themen, M Hewlett, M Braddock, P Hinchcliffe, T Slack, M Mather, L Felton, D Haynes, A Marsland,

MANCHESTER CITY LADIES

Manchester City Ladies . . . 1   v   Oldham Ladies . . . 1
Platt Lane, Monday December 12, 1988

THIS return game started where the first game ended with city putting pressure on Oldham's goal. D. Haynes cut in on the right and her shot was headed over, from the corner Oldham cleared easily. Oldham now settled to a good rhythm, in their first attack L. Morgan had a good shot well saved by City 'keeper M. Flynn.

N. Prenty played a good ball into City's penalty area but a good tackle from D. Davies saved City. Oldham had a series of corners, but could not capitalise on them. H. Ward had a good run down the left wing, only to see her low shot turned away for a corner, from the corner D. Haynes nearly opened the scoring but her shot was just wide.

Both teams were playing some good football, Midfielder S. Leach for Oldham fired in a low shot which was well saved by Flynn, from the kick out Haynes ran through the Oldham defence only to be denied by Oldham 'keeper D. Vance who stood her ground and saved well.

Oldham pressed forward and were awarded a corner on the right, the ball came into the crowded area, and fell to D. Jones who scored with a good left foot drive. As half time approached Oldham pressed to increase their lead.

The second half started with City bringing on three substitutes, and began pressing for a goal which came from H. Ward, a good drive into the bottom left hand corner of the Oldham net.

Oldham's forwards were pressing City's defence and pegged them back in their own half of the field for long periods, the only City player to relieve the pressure was D. Haynes who broke out but Oldham's 'keeper was up to form and saved well.

Then again D. Haynes started a move down the left, laid the ball into L. Felton, her hard shot was kicked away by keeper Vance, and was called upon again as H. Ward fired in another hard shot. The game was now end to end and City wasted some good moves.

Oldham's L. Morgan was taken off with an injury to her ankle, which weakened Oldham's side as she was one of their better players. Haynes for City was getting in good positions but her crosses were too hard and chances were being wasted. At the final whistle a 1 - 1 draw was a fair result.

Teams were: City — M. Flynn, D. Davies, K. Themen, M. Hewlent, M. Braddock, P. Hinchcliffe, T. Slack, M. Mather, L. Felton, D. Haynes, A. Marsland, D. Darbyshire, R. Foxwell, L. Burnett, H. Ward, C. Morgson, H. Clark, J. Walsh.

Oldham — D. Vance, S. Leach, L. Morgan, N. Prenty, L. Stansfield, M Pearson, L. Jones, H. Grime, J. Herd, S. Ryer, D. Jones, J Hartley.

Team photos next week.

Len Duckett.

Left: A report of the first home game ever played by Manchester City Ladies

D Darbyshire, R Foxwell, L Burnett, H Ward, C Morgson, H Clark & J Walsh. Record of who started/subs bench not kept.

■ Sunday 22 January 1989
Burnley 3 Manchester City 5
City Scorers: Donna Haynes (2), Rhoda Taylor (2) and Nicky Hunt
Venue: Burnley
Specific details still being researched. Video footage of this game, filmed by Crosland Ward (father of Heidi Ward) exists.

First Goal:
■ **Donna Haynes**, v Oldham Athletic, 27 November 1988
"City pushed forward and the deadlock was broken when Haynes cut in from the left and finished with a far post shot. From then on it was all City."

Donna Haynes was the club's top scorer in 1988-89 with 22 goals and was voted the Players' Player of the Year. Other awards went to Donna Davies (Young Player of the Year), Nicky Hunt (Manager's Player of the Year) and Patricia Barnes (Sportswoman of the Year).

First Women's FA Cup Tie:
■ 17 September 1989
Wigan 7 Manchester City 2
City Scorers: Lesley Peters (28 mins) & Donna Haynes (32)
Wigan Scorers: L Arstall (14 & 60), K Harding (19), V McLeod (33), J Wood (41), S Entwistle (87) & C Leach (89).

First Women's FA Cup Goal:
■ **Lesley Peters**, v Wigan Athletic, 17 September 1989

First Promotion:
■ At the end of the 1990-91 season the Blues were promoted from Bass North West Regional League Division Two to Bass North West Regional League Division One – at the time the highest level of football available (there was no national league)

First Divisional Title:
■ 1997-98 North West Women's Regional League Division Two. P20 W18 D2 L0 F102 A26 Pts 56 GD 76. This was an incredible season with City promoted after an unbeaten season back to the top tier of regional football.

First League Title:
■ 1999-2000 North West Women's Regional League Premier Division. P18 W15 D2 L1 F71 A20 Pts 47 GD 51. After finishing second in 1999 the Blues won the League the following season. Football had been restructured in 1998 which meant that City now joined the Northern Combination for the 2000-01 season.

Donna Haynes.

First Major National Trophy:
▧ 2014 FA WSL Continental Cup – **Arsenal 0 City 1** (Christiansen 73), attendance 3,697 (Adams Park, High Wycombe)

First WSL Title:
▧ 2016 – P16, W13, D3, L0, GF 36, GA 4, Pts 42, GD 32.

First WSL Goal:
▧ **Toni Duggan** v Arsenal, 18 May 2014

First FA Cup Success:
▧ 2016-17 – **Birmingham City 1** (Wellings 73) **City 4** (Bronze 18, Christiansen 25, Lloyd 32 & Scott 80), attendance 35,271 (Wembley)

Above right: 2014 Continental Cup success - Blandie from the Supporters Club with players Emma Lipman, Chelsea Nightingale and Danielle Lea.

Right: The first manager Neil Mather with Toni Duggan, who scored the first City goal in the WSL.

Below: 2017 FA Cup success.

57

The 1989-90 squad at Maine Road.

Joining a League

During the 1988-89 season as City participated in a series of friendlies manager Neil Mather decided to take the club into league competition. At that time there was no national league or even a pyramid structure, and so the highest level of competition open to the club was the North West Women's Regional Football League which was itself being restructured as part of a directive from the WFA. The belief was that each region should have one major league, comprising of several divisions to allow progression within the sport for any progressive team. These were the first steps towards a national period, though that was still some way off. The new league structure was to commence from 1989 with the North West Women's Regional Football League comprising of four divisions which were to be established out of existing leagues including the Greater Manchester & Merseyside League and the North West Women's Football League. [1]

The North West Women's Regional Football League could trace its history through many prominent competitions across the region, one of which was the North West Lancashire Ladies League, established in 1970. The Greater Manchester & District Women's Football League had been established in 1982 with the Manchester United Supporters club being founder members.

The restructure was going on without much involvement from City, and those running the game in the north west were perhaps not entirely as obvious to Neil Mather as they ought to be. Understandably, with the confused nature of the region's leagues in 1988 Neil sought the advice of WFA secretary Linda Whitehead. Neil: "I remember being sat in her room trying to fathom what steps we needed to take. She was helpful and saw City's involvement as a step forward. She talked me through everything and helped enormously. I was also invited to the Women's FA Cup final and it felt as if, within the women's game, there was a lot of support for each other. Linda was pushing for the game to spread and the arrival of clubs like City was seen as significant. I'm certain that we were the first major side to set up a women's team and she really encouraged us."

Debbie Darbyshire remembers that Neil soon announced his grand plan: "I can remember Neil setting out his vision. It was quite soon after we started with the games that Neil was talking about joining the League. That's when we started attracting the players, like the ones from the old Corinthians." Rowena Foxwell saw this as being the start of a change in direction and attitude: "I think once that decision to go in the League was made it changed the feel of it. This wasn't just a kickabout… you know like the lads from the pub having a kickabout and maybe the odd game or two. It was sort of three or four wins in 'we'll join the League next year' and lots of people started joining."

---

[1] Details of the north west leagues and the restructure can be traced through the programmes of various clubs, including *Manchester United Ladies FC v Manchester City Ladies FC*, November 27, 1994, 5-6 and *Ladyblues FC v FC Redstar*, September 8, 1988, 7-8.

Neil: "We played friendlies and then joined the North-West League Second Division. There was no national league back then, but the regional league was supportive. It did surprise me how far we had to travel for games though. During the first year or so we played all over the north-west, Yorkshire, London and anywhere really we could get a game or enter a tournament. That was a bit of a shock."

It is significant that City were parachuted straight into the Second Division of the League for the first full season of both the competition and the club. Some of City's opponents may not have realised that this was a new club due to the nature of the league restructure, but the club's status, achieved through the male Football League side, had established City as a name that had to be beat. As Neil mentioned, the League included teams from a variety of places.

In its four divisions were clubs from north Wales, Merseyside, Greater Manchester, Lancashire, Cheshire and Staffordshire with a variety of experience and varying number of players. Each division was supposed to contain ten clubs but some withdrew during the season on occasion as travel, costs and the ability to field a full team meant they were unable to complete fixtures. City had no such problem in 1989. In fact a reserve team had been established within weeks of the first game at Oldham in November 1988.

Neil: "We had lots of young girls with potential, so it was dead important to get a reserve team established and get them games quickly. This was another headache, if you like, but again, we had such a big squad and such a lot of people that wanted to play. That was brilliant. So I wanted to make sure everybody got games and nobody

Training at Platt Lane, 1989.

was discarded and nobody felt that they were being pushed out. But I was equally aware that when we joined the North West League, with the squad we had then, if I'd have gone out on that first day of that League season with the team I had at Oldham we'd have got annihilated. In fact, early doors, we struggled a wee bit to sort of get going. It was dead important to have some established players as well, which we did. But, you know, the reserves were dead important as well to me and to everybody else."

Of the players Neil brought in there was one he had hoped to persuade to join City since the club was established: "Lesley Peters was one of the top players in the north west. She was a red (Manchester United fan) as well. She took a bit of persuading, being honest, but Lesley was an excellent player. I mean they were all good players but I was always after Lesley.

"People saw that we were doing it right. That we had the kit... the mini bus... people saw that we were doing that and we were well run and we did proper training sessions. We had proper coaches and to be fair, it is true to say that, a lot of teams just had Dads running them or whatever. We had proper coaches and proper training sessions and the training sessions were right. It wasn't just 'let's get a ball and kick a ball about'. We trained and we worked on things and we talked. It was quality. It was always good quality. You know we even had a goalie coach, John Fox. I mean nobody else had that. Short of offering money, which obviously you couldn't do, it was as professional as it possibly could be and I think players realised that. We had a lot of issues, early doors, with other teams. We were very unpopular with other teams because a lot of players wanted to come and play for us."

Gail Redston, then Rothwell, joined the team during its first season of 1988-89 and remembers the mix of results when they joined the league well: "Well I mean we were some days getting battered. But we were still

Training at Platt Lane, 1989.

finding our feet. We had a mix of abilities and the way I look at it if you haven't got that nucleus of players, even whether they can or they can't play, you won't get anywhere. If they show an interest and it's pushing us along that's great. We started getting these players and I thought, 'yes, this is what we want'. So I was more enthusiastic at the fact that we're getting these players in now and you know even the training was different. It was more serious. Neil was really good at organising the training facilities and I think the nucleus of girls we had were a good set of girls. I think it helps when you can go training and you enjoy it and you've got at least 30 odd players there. Whereas if you go in to other clubs and you're thinking 'I've only got 12!' You can't train with 12... you can't progress."

City's opening game in the Second Division of the regional league was an 11-0 defeat at Chorley, prompting several discussions on what was needed to compete at this level. The following week's game at home to Broadoak was postponed but City did manage to play a friendly with Burnley instead which they won 4-1. Sadly, the next competitive fixture was the Women's FA Cup tie at Wigan Athletic. It was another disappointing day with City suffering a 7-2 defeat against a team established in 1984.

Another heavy defeat followed in a league game at Rossendale. Lesley Wright: "I remember we had to play at Rossendale. We were used to traveling but this seemed like the end of the world. It was September, cold and up in the hills miles from Manchester and another 7-2 defeat! A lot of teams were out to beat us because they saw us as a major scalp. We weren't the best by a long way because we were still trying to mould our team whereas other clubs, who may have had less talented players overall, had been established some time and worked as a team. That first year we were trying to get there

but you realise that you're not as good as you thought you were as a team."

The club's historic first competitive victory came on 1 October 1989. City defeated FC Redstar 7-2 with goals from Nicky Hunt, Rhoda Taylor, Lesley Peters (3), Rachel O'Shaughnessy & Donna Haynes. The win lifted the club off the bottom for the first time but postponements over the following weeks prevented the club from establishing momentum. There were also some disciplinary issues with manager Neil Mather involved occasionally: "I tell you what I wasn't brilliant at, at the beginning... because I was a player myself, strangely enough, I never got sent off ever as a player, so on the pitch I was quite controlled and I think it was because I could personally do something about it on the pitch. I could change the game by playing. I found it very difficult being a manager and not having any power and I used to lose my rag consistently. The one thing about the women's game at the beginning the refereeing level was poor, very poor. It was often the referees that couldn't get a game, you know, in the men's level, and the other thing that was bizarre about it, when I think about it now, you had to find your own ref, which sounds ridiculous, but you had to find your own ref. So you had to go around and scrape for the ref, which was often hard.

"If you got a ref, you used that ref every week. So I remember the lad's name now that we used - Ian Neve his name was. We had him most weeks so he knew us quite well. Ian was unscrupulously fair and often actually went the other way around and gave us nowt because I think he wanted to make sure it was fair. At other clubs you'd literally not get a decision off them because these referees are refereeing every week.

"I'll never forget Clitheroe away. Clitheroe were run by the Chairman of the North West League as well and they weren't

Training at the Maine Road first team gym, 1989.

that keen on us because they thought we were big time Charlies and so on and so forth. A lot of teams early on wanted to slap us, and again quite rightly so. And we went there and the referee was terrible. He'd sent Lesley (Wright) off and then he sent Carol (Woodall) off. He sent Carol off bizarrely because a girl stood on her back and Carol jumped up and lifted the shirt up to show the stud marks on her back. She said what are you going to do about this and he sent her off for lifting her shirt up! So he sent her off, so I invariably give him some stick. I'll never forget Heidi (Ward) trying to pull me back actually and stop me from doing it, but she failed miserably. So they sent me off. It's on a park pitch away at Clitheroe, so I'm like 'where do I go?' You can't go up in to a stand on a park pitch, so I kind of stood there and then he said 'right, I'm not starting the game until you go.' And I went 'go where?' and he went 'I don't care, you've just got to go.' So I walked off and the pitch was at the side of a road so I went on to the road. The pitch was sort of covered by trees and bushes to obviously stop the ball going on the road and so I hid behind the bushes. The players still talk about it to this day, they couldn't see me but they could still hear me, barking instructions at them. Then the referee stopped the game again because he could hear me but he didn't know where I was. He came looking for me. And then he sort of peered through these trees and he said 'I've sent you off.' I said 'well I'm off aren't I? Where am I supposed to go? Leave Clitheroe? What do you want me to do?' He replied: 'I don't know.' So he walks back on to the pitch and carries on. I spent the rest of the game sort of yelling at them through a gap in a bush that I'd found."

The day got worse for City. Neil: "He then sent another player off… he finished up sending three players off and me… Oh and my mother, who was 4'10". She was a tiny little woman and she gave him the biggest rollicking of his life after the game. She collared him outside the changing room… gave him a right rollicking… full throttle

The fanzine Electric Blue's first edition included a feature on the women's team in 1989.

and when we got the FA report through talking about all the sending of and that the club's in trouble… But the main thing was – and I can see this to this day – that he said 'a spectator called me a Little Hitler' and that was my Mum! We got more in trouble for my Mum calling him a Little Hitler than the girls and me getting sent off!"

Despite the disciplinary matters and the unsettled nature of the opening months, that first league season did see some great victories, such as a comfortable 9-0 win over Petros, but also some heavy defeats, including an end-to-end 10-5 defeat to Lady Blues from Ashton-under-Lyne. Amazingly City won the return 4-1 on the last day of the league season. That win ensured the team finished their first campaign in fourth place after an unbeaten league run of eight games. It was some achievement after the disappointing start. Unfortunately, such was the nature of the competition that both Petros and FC Redstar were forced to withdraw from the league during the season as they were unable to field teams. The loss of Redstar was upsetting to several Blues who had played for the club previously and as one of the closest clubs to City, geographically, it was almost inevitable that the pulling power of City would attract talented local players.

Jane Morley was a key figure behind FC Redstar at the time: "Neil did what he had to do to develop City but it affected other clubs. He knew how good Redstar was and he openly told me that he needed to get City Ladies up and running. He asked me to bring Redstar down to Platt Lane to do some training, maybe have a training match where Redstar could show some of the less experienced how they played and so on. We went down there and before I knew it some of our players were on their way to City. FC Redstar could not compete with the lure of Manchester City. The training facilities at Platt Lane were like a gold mine to the rest of us. We wanted that as it was streets ahead of anything we had. Neil sold the club well. Sadly whenever a new club is formed another is put at risk. Players move on to the new ones and take their friends and that still happens."

Lesley Wright: "Redstar were a better team than City at that time. A much better team but City had the name and, although we now know what happened to City in the years that followed, back then they were the ambitious, forward looking team that was going places. It still happens now. Salford City's women's team received the backing from the United Class of 92 and suddenly they're attracting players from all over. Ellen Thornton, who used to be at City, is their

City Ladies get a sponsor! Reported in the men's programme of 23 September 1989.

captain. They've wiped the floor with others. When we left Corinthians, or Woodley as it had become by then, they struggled and finished too."

Neil Mather understood the situation and did feel sorry for clubs that could no longer compete for players: "I can understand why they were upset because it was hard to compete against Manchester City. I mean you know it was difficult. I was given a really bad name for a while. I don't know who did this but somebody did a cartoon of me that actually Linda Whitehead had pinned up in her office as a laugh, of me with a City kit on and a coat. I had sweets in my coat and puppies at my feet...enticing players to come and play for City. So I got an awful name but the truth was I didn't go around poaching players because I didn't have to. People wanted to come and play for Man City. When they saw what we were doing people wanted to be involved in it, so although I was desperately unpopular at first, the truth was that it wasn't me. It was the Club that attracted them."

Neil did have a lot of players show interest in joining: "We were knocking players back to be honest with you. It sounds sort of harsh almost but I didn't want to discard the original team that had come in and a number of them had never played football competitively, like my sister, a great example, I mean Michelle had never played football competitively, but she could play. She played in school playgrounds and she'd done things like that, but she'd never played for a team. It was difficult that period."

Rita Howard, a former Manchester Corinthians/Woodley captain had played in some of the friendlies in 1989 and became one of City's leaders both on the pitch and off it: "I'd been captain at Corinthians for

a very long time. I was captain when I was 16 and the leadership role felt well. When I joined City I think Lesley Wright, as another established player and obviously talented, was made captain initially. I think that was the right thing too because Neil probably knew Lesley more and she was a Blue. She was a good leader. Then I became the captain of City at some point during that first year. It was frustrating at times that first year or so because we were trying to establish a team. We had such a mix. In my younger days I was quite hot headed and wasn't particularly tolerant. I know I wasn't. I'm sure many people would agree and I'm sure some disliked me because of that. I can only be honest and I found it difficult at times when there were people who couldn't play at the standard I'd been used to. I found it difficult."

Maine Road, 1989.

1990s Season Summary

The first league campaign ended in 1990 with City fourth in the North West Women's Regional League Second Division. That season had included a memorable Divisional Cup quarter-final tie with Crewe, although such was the lack of knowledge in the wider community that this has often been listed as a WFA Cup quarter-final tie in local media and in some Manchester City material. That game was played in March 1990 and saw City losing 4-3 with only seven minutes remaining. Manager Neil Mather made a couple of substitutions to try and get at least an equaliser but Crewe netted a fifth in injury time. England international Kerry Davies played for Crewe and City boss Neil Mather felt she was the difference between the teams: "She was an England player and she'd been over to the States. We battered them actually. We were the better team, but she was on another planet. I mean obviously international players are on a different level too but she was incredible. It was like sticking Messi in the middle of an average men's team. We just couldn't stop her. We just couldn't. We were the better side. If you took her out of the side we would have beaten them comfortably because we were way better than they were but she was just that magic. Quarter finals in our first season- we were that close!"

Despite this cup run Neil Mather was somewhat dissatisfied with how City's

Lesley Wright

competitive life had begun: "We started awful in the first year. I think by Christmas we'd only got a handful of points and it was always going to be a case of it's going to take a bit of effort and time, because we were a new team and a lot of the players hadn't played together and so on and so forth. Bit by bit we got better and then in the second year we got promoted because we were very strong in the second year. Very, very, very strong. We had a good FA Cup run as well. We got better and better and better, and we were quite a good side. By the end of that second year we were a very strong side."

By this time the squad had strengthened with older, experienced players often helping younger team members. Helen Hempenstall, a former Lady Blues player, was keen to learn: "I think Lesley Wright kept the team together. She kept it all tight at the back. I played at the back with her and I learnt a lot from her. Because I was next to her I knew how important she was. If I missed something she always got it. She always encouraged me and kept shouting 'different class, different class'. You learn from the people around you and I listened to her. Before every game she came to speak to me. She'd put her arm around me and reassure me. She'd tell me not to worry about anything. Most of the time travelling to away games I'd go with Lesley in the car. We used to have a laugh. I remember one day we were travelling to an away game some distance away and we stopped for petrol and all got out. I lit up a fag and everyone else jumped back in the car screaming! I didn't even think! When we got to the ground they all told Neil Mather and I think he worried that he could've lost half his team. At another game I was sat in the middle and as we got out the person before me slammed the door back. It hit my head and I had a big lump for the game."

Helen enjoyed the 1990-91 season and there was one game in particular that the entire team looked forward to – the first competitive Manchester City-United derby game: "I remember when we played United (30/9/90) and Neil (Helen's boyfriend, now husband) and all his mates came to watch us. There were a lot of people there that day. United had a decent team then. It was always a difficult game against United. They had a right-winger… We never got on. Every time we played each other we were at each other all the way through the game. Me and Carol Woodall were having a go at her. The referee told Lesley Wright 'Tell both your full backs to shut their mouths otherwise they'll both be off!' We just didn't get along and before every game I thought I'll get in their first. 'I'm having her.' Neil Mather still talks about it."

City won that first competitive derby 4-3 with goals from Rhoda Taylor (8 min), Rachel O'Shaughnessy (43 mins), Jenny Newton (50 mins) and Lesley Peters. Neil Mather: "United were the top side, you know, and beating them was so good for morale. The men's team were a good side in the early 90s when City Ladies carried on developing, you know. This was the Howard Kendall era, and City had top five finishes. City were one of the top five or six teams in the country at the time, so it was fabulous for women's football to have Man City, you know."

Neil worked incredibly hard to ensure the parent club supported the venture and there were several notable achievements: "I managed to get us a club president from the men's first team, Colin Hendry. He tried to get involved as well. I mean he didn't do an awful lot, but he showed interest in it. He came to watch a game or two and stuff like that."

Gail Redston remembers that it was important to have men's first team players involved: "Yes. There's a photograph somewhere of me, Michelle Mather, Donna Haynes and Nicola Jones with Colin Hendry at Maine Road. It was important to have that connection to us and to the club. Colin wished us all the best and then encouraged us just to 'keep at it.' I never forget, once, because we used to borrow the mini bus off Alex Williams, who in 1990 was in charge of the Community team. They'd had the Junior Blues on a Sunday morning at the City Social Club and Colin was a guest and he had parked his car right behind the mini bus. We were playing away and I was supposed to be driving the minibus but I couldn't get out. We had to go and say 'Colin, you need to move your car' but instead he gave us the keys. So I gets in this men's first team player's car to move it. Colin's not a small bloke and the seat is like right at the back. So I'm pushing the seat forward… pulling it forward. I move the car and then try to put his seat back… what's up with this? It won't go back! I had to leave it. We're then driving away from Maine Road and heading up to Preston. Suddenly, we're at this roundabout near the Mancunian Way and Colin is in the lane next to us. He's got the window down. He's screaming 'what have you done to my seat?' He's screaming at me and I'm calling back 'nothing!' I look at him and he's all hunched up! His steering wheel under his chin."

Despite the car seat issues Colin

Colin Hendry, Gail Duncan, Michelle Mather, Nicola Jones and Donna Haynes at Maine Road, March 1990.

remained involved and attended some City Ladies games. He wasn't the only first team member to do so. Neil: "Paul Lake came, Wayne Biggins... I think Andy Dibble came as well. We used to get the players. They didn't have to...it was just me mithering them in the changing room going 'can you come and do this.' They – I mean the club, the players... everybody, was supportive. Getting Colin as president was important it brought publicity. The players met him and I mean imagine that one of the first team players – a Scottish international - rocking up at training the buzz was huge and so Colin was a big name."

In terms of the Ladies' own squad, Neil was proud of the opportunities it gave young women: 'Tracey Blanchard was a kid. She was about 15 when she first come and she was such a talented player. I was dead proud, because you could see these were girls that

obviously loved football, could play football, but never got opportunities. I remember an interview with one of the players and she said that they wanted to play football but they didn't have anywhere to go. They couldn't play anywhere until we set up the team. We were giving them that chance to play football and, like Tracey, for all their lives you know? Look at Gail [Redston]... still playing in her early sixties! So that's a fabulous thing isn't it?"

City became recognised quickly as a prominent women's club. So much so that Linda Whitehead at the Women's FA promoted them often. She also encouraged media companies to speak with them. Neil: "Linda was superb. Partly thanks to her we got two Swedish girls that had played in the Swedish League. They had come over as au pairs I think but they wanted to continue to play football. They were excellent because the Swedish League was way better than the English, you know, and they came over and played and you could see there was definitely something significant happening in their football culture that we didn't have. I think they were put in contact with us via Linda at the WFA. The WFA was always promoting us. In January 1990 we played the Australian Under 18s. Linda said that they were coming over and they've asked 'who can we play?' Her response was 'well, Manchester City are the biggest team' and we got them."

Neil's comments about Linda Whitehead's support are accurate. A review of the WFA minutes, held at the British Library, for the 1989-90 season show that some WFA committee members were disappointed that the Australian team was not playing established women's teams in southern England. Linda had to defend their decision to play in Manchester and highlighted the publicity opportunities. She also pointed out that the Australians were keen to play against a prominent name in football with Manchester City ultimately being chosen.

Neil Mather: "What an honour! This was their international under 18s team. I mean they beat us. Not by many though. It was only 3-1 but you could see their development. You could see what they had and that was a great honour. Such a good crowd that day and they'd brought a whole squad and they'd come in the full Australian tracksuits and the kit. It was just magnificent. They were fantastic and they were so complimentary to us because they could see what we were trying to do as well. We played at the University Grounds and it was good quality. I remember that one because City had said you could play at Platt Lane and when they came the weather was typical Manchester weather. It was shocking for about two weeks and the pitch was really heavy and in the end they went 'no, you can't do it.' City's men's first team used to train on it and play on it and there was only one pitch."

Rita Howard remembers the game for one specific reason: "I remember playing in that game against Australia. I was pregnant at the time and I knew I was pregnant but only I knew. It would've been unfair if I'd told anyone."

The Australia game ended in a 3-1

MANCHESTER CITY v AUSTRALIA U18'S PRICE 50p

City girls aim for title shot

By Sian Webley

MANCHESTER City Ladies start the new season with an away match at Rossendale, on Sunday, with sights firmly fixed on the North West Women's League second division title and promotion to the top flight.

Manager, Neil Mather says: "If we don't win it we'll certainly be in the running. Last season we finished fourth after a bad start. This time provided we start strongly we'll be there".

But the City girls have a tough opening programme, after Rossendale they have successive away fixtures at Daresbury and Chorley, and their first home match is THE big one - deadly rivals Manchester United, who also have title ambitions.

Anyone who imagines ladies football is sissy would change their mind after a look at City's injury list.

Donna Haynes broke an ankle in a pre-season friendly and will be out of action until October, but Karen Bretherton who fractured her skull last season is happily "back with a vengance", says Neil.

Quality

He feels that this time round he will have more quality players available, at least 18 compared to the bare essential squad of just 12, last season.

Top scorer, Lesley Peters has shown good form in pre-season matches, while Rachael O'Shaugh-nessy is aiming to gain a

defeat with Welsh trialist Joni Davies scoring City's consolation on 28 January 1990. That season had ended with City finishing fourth in the second tier of the four-tier North-West Women's Regional Football League – a creditable position for any club in their first competitive season. The following season, 1990-91, brought some high profile games

1990-91 Back (L to R): Neil Mather, Malin Karlsson, Heidi Ward, Rita Howard, Michelle Flynn, Sally Rustige, Jane Marcus, Tracey Blanchard, Godfrey Williams. Front: Rhoda Taylor, Michelle Brady, Lesley Wright, Helen Hempenstall, Gail Duncan, Donna Haynes, Joni Davies.

and some great publicity City's way but most importantly it had seen the team grow and compete, earning promotion to the highest level possible. One of the team's Swedish players, Malin Karlsson, netted twice in the last league game of the season – a 5-1 victory over Daresbury at the University Grounds. Rhoda Taylor (2) and Michelle Brady netted the other City goals that day. The connection with City's men's team was strong and many members of the men's squad attended the annual awards event for the women on 16 May 1991. Helen Hempenstall remembers it well: "At the end of that season I got the young player of the year award at the club. I didn't know this and I wasn't going to go to the awards do but people kept saying I should go. I think they knew. Anyway, I went and I got the young player of the year award presented by Colin Hendry."

From a coaching perspective Godfrey Williams had officially joined Neil as his assistant at the start of the 1990-91 season but this was to be the last for Neil himself. An opportunity for him to manage the Stockport County Football in the Community Scheme had appeared and the more significant role meant he left Manchester City, the club that became his legacy: "Gaining promotion in 1991 was a real achievement. Our first success, but for me it was the end of an era. I was working for City but I was just one of the Community team and the job came up as top man at Stockport County's community team. It was the Manager – the equivalent role that Kevin Glendon had had at City and now Alex Williams had. I knew that I was never going to get Alex's job, with the best will in the

Blues are up!

MANCHESTER City women guaranteed promotion to Division One on Tuesday when they ended the season with a crushing 5-1 victory over Daresbury at Platt Lane.

Two days earlier second place Rivacre had beaten City 4-2, with Donna Haynes and Rhoda Taylor City's scorers, but the team were determined to finish with a bang and they gave Daresbury a real thrashing.

Rhoda Taylor and Michelle Brady struck to put City in a commanding position.

world, so the Stockport job came up and I'd been with City since '86, so I thought I'd go for it."

Neil was no longer the driving force behind the team at City. In his place as City manager came experienced captain Rita Howard. Rita was not an employee of Manchester City but the club remained an official part of City's community scheme and the manager of the Community Scheme, Alex Williams, continued to support the club's efforts, though financial support was often difficult in the years that followed, especially when the men's team began its fall down the divisions.

Rita managed a good group of players with strong support from Godfrey Williams and had been a prominent player and captain in the Manchester region since the 1970s. Former Manchester United and

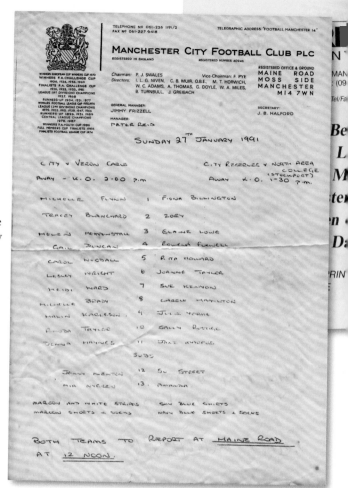

FC Redstar player Bev Harrop joined City shortly before the managerial change: "Rita was great. She gave me my first game and she played me at left full back. The next time she put me in at right full back and we had a decent year. That first season Rita gave me manager's player of the year." Rita and Bev went on to play or work together with City for the following decade. In fact in 2019 they appeared in a Manchester City team together that reached the final of the Dick, Kerr Ladies Walking Football Cup. The rest of that team was made up of City players

from the 1980s and 1990s: Lesley Wright, Anita Clarke, Rhoda Taylor, Heidi Ward (now James) and Gail Redston. Another player who had hoped to participate in that tournament was a key member of the early 1990s squad Nicky Hunt. Rita: "Nicky Hunt had the best left leg of any player I have ever seen. She was a great footballer."

Under Rita and in the top flight of regional football for the first time the season took some time to get going. This season saw the establishment of a national league and a second regionalised tier. Meaning that

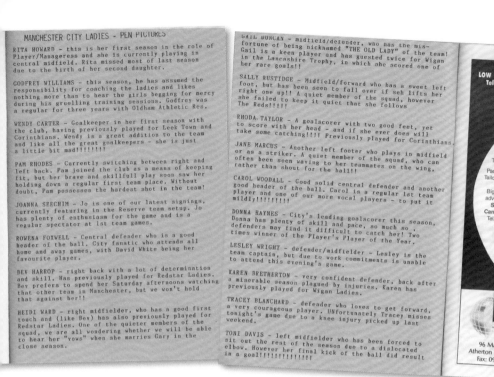

RITA HOWARD - this is her first season in the role of Player/Manageress and she is currently playing in central midfield. Rita missed most of last season due to the birth of her second daughter.

GODFREY WILLIAMS - this season, he has assumed the responsibility for coaching the ladies and likes nothing more than to hear the girls begging for mercy during his gruelling training sessions. Godfrey was a regular for three years with Oldham Athletic Res.

WENDY CARTER - Goalkeeper in her first season with the club, having previously played for Leek Town and Corinthians. Wendy is a great addition to the team and like all the great goalkeepers - she is just a little bit mad!!!!!!!!

PAM RHODES - Currently switching between right and left back. Pam joined the club as a means of keeping fit, but her brave and skillfull play soon saw her holding down a regular first team place. Without doubt, Pam possesses the hardest shot in the team!

JOANNA SEECHIM - Jo is one of our latest signings, currently featuring in the Reserve team setup. Jo has plenty of enthusiasm for the game and is a regular feature at 1st team games.

ROWENA FOXWELL - Central defender who is a good header of the ball. City fanatic who attends all home and away games, with David White being her favourite player.

BEV HARROP - right back with a lot of determination and skill. Has previously played for Redstar Ladies. Bev prefers to spend her Saturday afternoons watching that other team in Manchester, but we won't hold that against her!!

HEIDI WARD - right midfielder, who has a good first touch and (like Bev) has also previously played for Redstar Ladies. One of the quieter members of the squad, we are all wondering whether we will be able to hear her "vows" when she marries Gary in the close season.

GAIL DUNCAN - midfield/defender, who has the misfortune of being nicknamed "THE OLD LADY" of the team! Gail is a keen player and has guested twice for Wigan in the Lancashire Trophy, in which she scored one of her rare goals!!

SALLY RUSTIDGE - Midfield/forward who has a sweet left foot, but has been seen to fall over if seh lifts her right one up!! A quiet member of the squad, however she failed to keep it quiet that she follows The Reds!!!!!

RHODA TAYLOR - A goalscorer with two good feet, yet to score with her head - and if she ever does will take some catching!!!! Previously played for Corinthians.

JANE MARCUS - Another left footer who plays in midfield or as a striker. A quiet member of the squad, who can often been seen waving to her teammates on the wing, rather than shout for the ball!!

CAROL WOODALL - Good solid central defender and another good header of the ball. Carol is a regular 1st team player and one of our more vocal players - to put it mildly!!!!!!!!

DONNA HAYNES - City's leading goalscorer this season, Donna has plenty of skill and pace, so much so, defenders may find it difficult to catch her! Two times winner of the Player's Player of the Year.

LESLEY WRIGHT - defender/midfielder - Lesley is the team captain, but due to work commitments is unable to attend this evening's game.

KAREN BRETHERTON - very confident defender, back after a miserable season plagued by injuries. Karen has previously played for Wigan Ladies.

TRACEY BLANCHARD - defender who loves to get forward, a very courageous player. UNfortunately Tracey misses tonight's game due to a knee injury picked up last weekend.

TONI DAVIS - left midfielder who has been forced to sit out the rest of the season due to a dislocated elbow. However her final kick of the ball did result in a goal!!!!!!!!!!!!

Pen Pictures of City's 1991-92 squad in the programme for the Atherton charity game.

City were now playing in the equivalent of a third tier – it is somewhat ironic that City's promotion saw them rise from the second highest tier available in 1990-91 to the third tier in 1991-92!

A 4-1 defeat at leading side Leasowe Pacific (Rita had scored for City) on the opening day was followed by another 4-1 defeat at home to Huddersfield in the FA Cup and a 2-2 draw in the league with Vauxhall. There had been a couple of postponements – including what was scheduled to be the first competitive top flight Manchester derby on 8 September 1991 – and then came on 13 October 1991 a trip to a familiar local side Wigan. Helen Hempenstall: "We seemed to play at Wigan a lot. Next to the baked beans factory. I remember feeling sick on a Sunday morning and all you could smell were baked beans."

A number of friendships had developed over the years between City and Wigan with some City players guesting for Wigan in tournaments. City also supported the charitable efforts of the Prescott Family, committee members and programme producers for Wigan, including City playing in a fundraising game against Atherton organised by the Prescotts in February 1992.

The game with Wigan was an important step in this first North West top flight season and the Blues achieved a 3-2 victory, lifting them to fifth in a division of ten clubs. Mixed results followed and then on 19 January the Blues achieved their first double of the season beating Wigan 4-1. Form dipped again as the season proved to be a taxing one and on 22 March 1992 Bev Harrop netted the only goal of the game with Wythenshawe. City were sixth after this match but the final three league games ended in defeat and they finished 8th – just

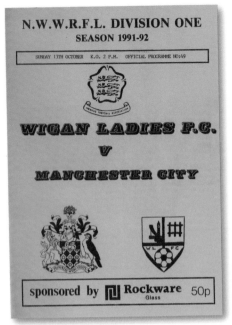

off the pitch and went to the side of the pitch. I shouted 'what are you doing?' She said "I'm sitting on the side. It's where I'm always put when the game's on.' It was funny at the time but I remember thinking that that was real commitment. To keep coming back when you're not being selected. You need people like that but it is an issue if you can't give everyone a game. You always need to try and balance up winning a match with giving chances."

City were still part of the parent club via City's community programme but, following Neil's departure the previous year, obtaining kit was now not as straightforward as before. Assistant manager Godfrey Williams, who had been a footballer with Oldham Athletic, worked for the kit manufacturer Umbro and would raise money for the team by selling football name cards and perform other fundraising duties. For the 1992-93 season, City's second in the North West Women's Regional Football League top division, he had raised enough to buy an entire kit from Umbro. Godfrey: "We all needed to do our bit. When you're involved with a football team it's never just about playing or coaching on a Sunday. It's about raising money to ensure the club has a future." Godfrey is one of many unsung heroes at

above the relegation zone. For Rita this had been an acceptable first season in her new role as manager, but she wanted more. She also felt she was still learning: "I remember there was this one player at training. We'd been training and then we said 'right, get in to your normal positions. We're having a training game.' This particular player walked

The City Squad, c.1992

City who worked tirelessly to support the club both on and off the pitch. The kit he purchased for the club in 1992 was not a recognisable Manchester City shirt, it was a generic Umbro yellow kit. Rita Howard: "Even when we wore a yellow and blue kit – it was anything we could get at one point – we were still Manchester City. We were always Manchester City. Always. We were perceived as that and we saw ourselves as that. The men's match programme carried articles on us occasionally – I don't know who sent those in. It wasn't me, but they were there."

Research for this book has shown that some of the match and league details the team played in are recorded incorrectly in the men's match programmes, however the visibility that was given to the team was important. Occasionally, it brought a few supporters to games, especially games with United which were perceived by the wider public as derbies, and often it would encourage girls or young women to seek out the club. Many of the women playing for City in the 1980s have mentioned how they found out via newspapers, match programmes and magazines that there were women's teams and this method of discovering teams carried on into the 2000s.

Nationally there still remained little coverage of women and football. Rita Howard: "Despite the closeness with City I don't think I ever thought back then that women's football was progressing into what we have now. More girls began to play which was encouraging and down to the efforts of a lot of people. I wish I had seen what was coming… I wish I'd been born later so that I could have played now. There was a professional league in Italy in the early nineties and one of the girls I used to play with in the Three Counties League, Kerry Davis, went off to play in Italy. She played at Crewe and was a really good player.

"One of the frustrations for me is that when I was at my peak is that I didn't play for England – there I've said it! I've put it out there! Because I honestly think given the coaching now I'd have definitely made it but back then a few of us felt there seemed to be a clique around the England team. I remember playing in a representative game - the North West versus the North East. Gillian Coulthard, who played for Doncaster Belles was playing in that game. Kerry was playing too. We won 1-0 and I crossed to Kerry who scored a great header. It was a great game and I played really well. Everything was perfect and I'd marked Gillian out of the game. The next week the England squad was announced and Kerry and Gillian were in it but I'm nowhere to be seen. I have no idea why and a few people who had seen me told me I should be there, but I stood no chance for some reason. Opportunity is everything and I suppose, without a national league then, the fact that every week I was playing in Woodley, Manchester or Crewe and not in London, or where the selectors were based, meant that I stood little chance of being spotted. Once City Ladies began and started developing as a team we were really good and I think quite a few of us could've made it at the highest club level we have today. There just wasn't that opportunity then. Without a national league it was impossible to tell."

1992-93 was another mixed season in the top division of the North West league. The Blues were knocked out of the FA Cup in their first competitive game of the season by local rivals Broadoak but managed to win three of the following four league games, including a historic 3-1 victory over Manchester Belle Vue (this was Belle Vue's first game at this level) with goals from Lesley Wright, Tracey Blanchard and Bev Weir. That win placed City top of the league but the following six league games all ended in high scoring defeats, including the derby match with United. City had raced to a 2-0 lead in the first thirty minutes but United fought back and won 5-2. A 2-1 win in the return derby (a double from Sue Donbavond) and a 5-3 win at Broadoak helped the Blues finish fourth but the fragility of the league structure and of some teams competing meant that one club folded and Crewe withdrew from the league during the season. Newcomers Manchester Belle Vue ended the season runners-up to Wigan. There was some positive news at the annual league awards when Rhoda Taylor won the league's player of the year award in June 1993.

City were now an established team playing in the North West Women's Regional Football League's top division, but making the next step was proving difficult. Bev Harrop: "Those years were tough at times but the friendships got us through. Every single one of us got on and we were very much a team and it was that that got us through. We had Rita coaching us. We played some tough games you know and it was the fact that we were fitter than a lot of other teams that had got us through. Rita always said to us 'last 20 minutes, last 20 minutes' and a lot of games we did. We could score two, three, four goals in the last 20 minutes, of games, to get us through something that might have been 0-0 for an hour." Rita Howard agrees: "It's difficult to recall individual successes as a player at City. We achieved promotion early on but we didn't win leagues and cups back then like we did when I was at Corinthians. But I loved it still."

In 1993-94 the Blues finished ninth and the following season were seventh. Another seventh place finish came in 1995-96 before the club suffered in the 1996-97. Managerial changes, players moving on, injuries and periods of maternity leave all impacted

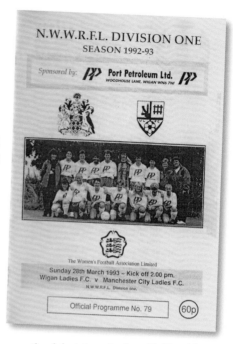

on the club at times in the mid-90s with several longstanding players taking time out to focus on family matters. Rita Howard had handed over the managerial reigns to Godfrey Williams at times and in 1994-95 he was officially listed as the manager. Jane Morley, one of the former FC Redstar founders along with Bev Harrop, also took on the role. Jane: "I managed Manchester City Ladies twice. The first time was when Gail (Redston) and Bev (Harrop) were playing and we were at Wythenshawe Town. It was before we had a junior set up and I did it for a year. They were still very much a one-man band then. It was before Gary Moores and Derek Heath arrived. City didn't have a manager at the time and I was asked if I'd do it. I did and brought a few girls who I knew like Paula Roberts – my best friend. I think I came in half way through a season and between us we all managed to get enough players in to see out the season. Then it came to the end of the season and there were some tensions and I left as manager. I continued to come with Lesley Wright and then suddenly there were all these young people and I started to get involved in training them, then managing them. Next thing we're entering tournaments and we were attracting good, young players. It was a great period."

Before the transformation that Jane mentioned the club had to rely on a band of women to keep it operating. These were dark days in terms of finances and results but not in terms of the feeling that this was a group of women working together to play football and to keep a club afloat. Once the men's team began to struggle in 1996 support for the women's team seemed to vanish according to some. Bev Harrop: "We struggled. It was very difficult. There was no more support from the club. We had no financial help and we had to pay for everything ourselves. Things didn't come cheap."

Despite having less direct support Lesley Wright remained convinced that this was still Manchester City: "It always felt as if we were part of Manchester City to me. We had struggles and support from the club varied but we were always part of it. That never changed." As with Manchester United and other teams of this period the male club was supportive but not directly involved in setting the agenda or direction of the club. Alex Williams and the community team at City still provided kit from time to time and in 1995 chairman Francis Lee appeared on a team photograph with City Ladies, but as the men's team struggled the women's team had little support when their own crises occurred. The 1996-97 saw the most significant crisis according to some.

The men's team were enduring their own problems when City Ladies were relegated in 1996-97. That season the club struggled for players as well as positive results on the

December 1996, City's new kit.

pitch. Reno Dionisiou, who worked with Bev Harrop on the buses, was the manager and worked hard to promote the club and encourage close co-operation with the men's club. According to Gail Redston, who was performing coaching duties herself around this time: "He was quite good, Reno, as doing the admin side, which is a massive help. When you're a player and you're like player/manager, and you've got to organise and make the phone calls and there's a game on… 'is this on? Make sure all the team sheets are right' and so on, it's quite difficult."

In December 1996 Reno managed to persuade the club to donate an away kit for the team and there were the usual features in the men's match programme but these days were bleak on the pitch. The season started with a 5-1 defeat at home to Radcliffe Borough on 1 September and a 14-1 defeat at Manchester Belle Vue. A 1-1 draw followed at Newsham but the club just could not get any momentum going because of a large number of postponements. Playing on Sunday afternoons often meant that pitches were in a poor state in wet weather as men's teams typically used those same facilities on Saturdays and Sunday mornings. It is known that in 1996-97 at least eleven games were postponed, including a run of four successive league matches. For the first time since formation the club's existence seemed in jeopardy.

Rita Howard: "I remember that period because I had finished playing but I was still involved. There were a lot of discussions about 'where do we go? How do we keep going?' I don't really recall much about the specifics because I had three children by then and I wasn't playing so life had different priorities for me."

In the middle of a gloomy period there was a training session which proved to be the most important the club had experienced since the original sessions

staged in October 1988. The specific date has not been identified and people's accounts do vary but it seems this occurred early in the season. According to a number of players approximately eight people turned up for training one evening. It was a pivotal moment when the future of the club was debated at length. Lesley Wright: "I remember sitting in the changing room and people discussing it. Some wanted us to go and join with Stockport but I think I was one of the ones who was saying 'no, let's knock it on the head. I'm not going to Stockport.' We decided to stay and carry on."

Louise Wakefield was a young player at this time and remembers the state of the place when she arrived: "We didn't have anybody. There was Lesley Wright, Gail, Bev Harrop, Jane Morley… They did everything and we had nothing. We had to go beg, steal and borrow a kit. They were doing it all between them… organising the games, everything. It was 96-97, and you didn't have a mobile and there were no emails, so they had to do a lot of leg work, you know. They had to literally go to places. They couldn't send an e-mail or send a text they had to go literally and do all the leg work for everything, even to go and get players. Sometimes they'd knock on doors to get messages passed on."

Louise is convinced that without those people the club would have folded in 1997: "It wouldn't have existed. No, it definitely wouldn't and Bev was a massive United fan. So was Jane. So for them to go and push all out for Man City Ladies… you'd think that they'd go and help United, but no. This was their club and I would say that they definitely saved that club. Without them… especially Gail and Bev – they did a lot for me. They got me there and looked after me throughout the years. I wouldn't have been able to get there if it wasn't for Bev originally. She used to come and pick me up and stuff because I was only 17. I was only in college and didn't have a car or owt. I'm from Salford, so to get to Platt Lane on a Friday night at 8 o'clock was too difficult for me then. Bev would talk me through everything on the way home after a game 'you need to start doing this Louise… you need to start doing that, you're panicking too much.' Bev was very cool and calm on the ball. I was always looking for the Hollywood pass and she'd say 'you've got to stop looking for that.' So Bev would talk you through everything after the game; you'd have Lesley Wright talking you through during the game; and then if Gail ever came up to me, after the game and said I did dead well, then I was made up because Gail wasn't the type. She'd always encourage me… well played and all that but she wasn't the type to sit down and go 'you played really well then.' She said that to everybody because she kept everybody together, but if she personally said it to you 'it meant more.'"

Despite the lack of numbers at this time Louise felt she had joined the right club: "To be fair going to City was the best thing because they really, really looked after me. It wasn't about it being City because I'm a

■ THE BLUES SISTERS: Manchester City Ladies team with, right, defender Gail Rothwell and striker Louise Wakefield

Girls on the ball

PLAYING football was a way of life for Gail Rothwell from around the age of five. She was more or less forced into it. "I had four brothers all older than me. Mum was chuffed when she had a little girl, but every time she put me in a little dress, they changed me and put me in shorts and boots and had me kicking a ball about with them."

Gail even played for her primary school, which made her a pioneer in those days around 30 years ago. "We had to always ask permission from the other teams, for a girl to play. When I was 14 or 15, I signed for the Corinthians, who were like the first ladies team in Manchester."

Now, at the age of 36, Gail plays in defence for Manchester City Ladies FC (founded 1989) at the time of a world boom in women's football. Last summer saw its first full medal appearance in the Olympic Games, with the USA beating China in the final in Atlanta.

In Britain, woman-to-woman marking is a tactical fact of football life. Before this season's Charity Shield match at Wembley between the Premiership men of Manchester United and Newcastle, the respective ladies' clubs played a keenly-contested 20-minute curtain-raiser.

The number of women players officially registered has tripled in the last seven years to 21,500, with 1,350 teams, says FA spokeswoman Katherine Knight.

Louise Wakefield is a 17-year-old star striker for City Ladies on a Sunday. When it comes to men's football, she is actually a United supporter, ogling David Beckham at Old Trafford, where she works in the kitchens on match days and manages to glimpse a bit of the game.

"I played for the United women's team for two years and I was getting fed up. So I contacted Gail and I signed for City."

The second row in the derby against United this season, in pull City level when they were trailing 3-1. I asked her about men who say women know nothing about football.

"I say come and watch me, and I'll show you. A lot of women are better than men. Some of them are built like men as well."

NO fewer than 35 clubs now compete in four divisions of the North West Women's Regional Football League alone. Next her up are the youth and south premier leagues, then the national league. Manchester, it was summoned this week, will soon have its first girls' football league, following a successful five-a-side trial tournament. So great is the growth in popularity of football with the fair sex that the FA is undertaking a complete reorganisation of it next year.

For Gail that cannot come too soon. Britain is lagging behind, she says. "In Italy women's football is professional. In America they get scholarships in the colleges. In Holland all the amateur grounds are like the Vauxhall Conference, only better. It's just amazing."

"The majority of girls in this country play in the park, raising money from

Like their professional male counterparts, Manchester City ladies football team are not doing very well. They wrote to the Evening News Postbag recently hoping to interest some new players. But women's football is booming nationwide and this week it was announced that Manchester will soon have its first girls' football league, following a successful five-a-side trial tournament

BY KEITH WARD

football cards and subs from the players," says Sharon Wilson, 28-year-old secretary of the North West Women's League, says: "We had five or six new teams starting last year and the numbers are increasing."

Living in Blackpool, she plays midfield for Fushion le Fylde, the team managed by her husband Graham, who, like her, is a Manchester United fan.

"I have to take notice of what he says, otherwise I'd be on the subs' bench," she laughs. "We have players aged from 14 to 40. We are just as physical as the men. It's not bandbags at 10 paces stuff."

Do they ever come along too watch? "A few." Presumably some more interested in watching the women than the football? "That's a typical male outlook," scolds Sharon.

Mark Reagan, a 35-year-old Bury fan, is fixtures secretary of the North West Women's League, as well as managing Haslingden Ladies. "About seven years ago I was working with a girl who played for the team and she said they needed a manager. I had done some FA coaching courses so I volunteered."

What sort of reaction does he get from his mates? Says Mark: "Negative reactions are disappearing. Probably more than half the teams in our league are managed by men. Genuine football fans react quite positively. Some are surprised we play a full 90 minutes."

Mark is married, with two daughters aged seven and five. Neither Katrina nor Roxey yet shows an interest in playing, he says. Wife Gillian hates football, but doesn't mind him managing a women's team.

"She may joke about it in her friends. But it's like any other hobby. If I was stamp collecting, I'd go off for a couple of hours doing that. What's the difference?"

What about the practical problems - he is surely ruled offside if he tries to enter the ladies' dressing room to give them a pep talk?

"Yes. While they are getting changed before the game, or in the showers afterwards, I am outside in the cold," laughs Mark. "You hold your team talk on the pitch, or I go in pre-match before they get changed."

Manchester City Ladies FC are also managed by a man, 32-year-old bus driver Rino Dimauro. His team suffers uncomfortable parallels with their male counterparts at Maine Road. The Ladies are currently bottom of their regional First Division (although Rino's job is thought to be safe). How did he get involved in the first place?

"Last season I was running a team Sunday team but I was getting quite that Sunday team and I was getting all those coming for Sunday morning games straight from a Saturday night out. I knew one of the ladies' team, Beverley Harron, from work. She said they were looking for a manager, did I fancy the job?

"My first reaction was to say 'no'. But I agreed to go down and have a look, and to be quite honest, I was really surprised. The standard is really high."

RINO wrote to the Evening News Postbag recently asking for new players. "We had about 12 phone calls, of which about half came down, which about half came down. Some of them were a bit young, only about 12 or 13. In this league, I want them to be able to look after themselves."

Rino is unmarried and lives with his

United fan, you know. It was that they really looked after me. They came and got me every week and even supported me outside of football. They were just really good with the girls. You'd go and they'd just look after you. They were a lot older than me - I was only young, so they just kind of mothered you."

Louise remembers her debut game during this period: "We couldn't get in the changing rooms because there was no key. So at one point we were like 'oh, we're just going to have to get changed outside.' We didn't as we eventually got in somehow but we obviously had to put our own nets up. You were all on each other's shoulders putting the nets up and then we didn't even have time to warm up because of the time it took and we were already late because of the dressing room problem. The ref's ready and he's not happy. I think we just scraped 11 players that day for my first game. At times we'd draft players in who couldn't kick a ball just to make up the numbers.

"At my first game we had no manager on the side, because Gail and Lesley were running the club and they were playing, so we actually had nobody on the sideline. I can't remember who was captain, but it would've been one of them probably. So we had just scraped to get changed…we just scraped to get the game together and

Unusual Hobbies

Based in the Finance Department at Cheadle Heath, Sally Rustige is a football fanatic. She plays 5-a-side twice a week with her colleagues (her and nine lads, lonely in the changing rooms), then when the weekend arrives she puts on her boots to represent Manchester City Ladies even though she is a keen Manchester United Fan!

City Ladies, unlike the first team, are riding high at the moment with a table-topping eight wins and one draw from nine fixtures. The high point of Sally's season so far was a game against Crewe Ladies at Maine Road during the half-time

interval in front of 27,000 spectators. Sally's team ran-out 1-0 winners and City's first team went on to do the same. Ladies first!

Coverage of City occurred in a variety of places. This 1996-97 piece appeared in the works magazine for Sally Rustige's employer.

I remember turning around and there was nobody on the sideline because the manager, the secretary, everybody, they were players."

The idea that at this point the club consisted of everybody in the 11 that played that day and no one in support may have put off some young players but Louise had a different view: "I loved that. Do you know what I mean? We were all there. It was 'us' and then I loved it as well because I thought 'well I'm not getting subbed.' I'd been with Manchester United before City and at that time they had a structure, a manager… everything. It was from one extreme to the other, but I loved City more for it. My first season we used to get battered and I'm talking double figures sometimes. We got a few youngsters coming in. Jane Clark started the same day as me. She brought a couple of friends with her."

City was relegated at the end of the 1996-97 season. This was the first relegation the team had ever endured and meant the 1997-98 season would be played in the second level of the North West Women's Regional Football League for the first time since their promotion in 1991. While the relegation was obviously a disappointment it actually came at a time when the club had started to restructure. According to Louise Wakefield Reno Dionisiou, City's coach who had been brought in by Bev Harrop helped: "Reno got Derek Heath involved and that's when Derek got us a reserve team; started the youth section and he built on all that. He brought a lot from Stockport like Lindsay Savage and others. He brought a lot over. In the space of about six months it was like a whole different structure and you could see it all starting to pan out. Suddenly we had some kids playing over there… we've got an under 10s now… we've got a reserves now. To me Reno had got that club up and running and yet again it was Bev Harrop that brought him in. I was young and I was

City Ladies on the Maine Road pitch, 1997.

hyper. I turned up and played football. I didn't get involved with the politics, but after those rough, rough times… those heavy defeats… no goal keeper… mud up to there… he had changed the whole structure of it." Louise is full of praise for the efforts of Reno to bring Derek in while others focus mostly on Derek's achievements after arriving. Lesley Wright: "Derek Heath came along from Stockport with an idea. Stockport had a group of girls but at that time Stockport didn't want to, or couldn't, develop a structure. He suggested that he could bring the girls and build a proper structure from the bottom all the way. So Stockport's under 14 team became City's and players like Lindsay Savage arrived, as did Derek Heath and (future chairman) Gary Moores. There were also under-10s and under-12s which myself and Jane Morley decided to take on."

Louise Wakefield: "We gradually improved. We got a few results. We wasn't getting battered every week and then we started signing the right players for the right positions at the right time. They all came in and they all gelled with the team and it worked and we all got on. I poached goalkeeper Vicki Bloor… she's my best friend now and I've been bridesmaid for her twice. I poached her from Stockport. Every position that we were weak on was the right fit. It all just kind of fell in to place. I ended up with a serious injury at 18. I snapped my shin in half at Platt Lane, so I was out, so it was around about that time, because then when I came back, we'd won the league in 1998. I played towards the end and towards the beginning of the 1997-98 season, but in the middle I was out."

The arrival of Derek Heath from Stockport was significant. It helped bring new players and brought people keen to contribute to the administrative duties of the club. One of these was Gary Moores: "I fulfilled a few roles over the years but from 1999-2000 until the club was taken over fully by Manchester City I was the chairman. We had quite a large committee at times running the club and that was important. I first got involved because my daughter was a keen footballer for Sale United when she was younger and then when she reached the age of ten she was told she couldn't play mixed football from then on. She was devastated. We managed to find a club in Stockport where Derek Heath was. He became a main driver of the junior sections at City. Derek did a lot with Stockport Ladies which was quite a big team in the area and he spotted my daughter at the Manchester Youth Games and suggested she play for Stockport. She played there for a while and then Derek announced he was going to leave Stockport and join Manchester City Ladies. His reason was that he had spoken to his committee and had said 'look if we're going to take ladies football forward we need to be connected to a major men's club because we can only take it so far.' I don't know the politics of Stockport Ladies at the time. I was just a dad. But I believe Derek spoke to City Ladies who had just one team back then and so they were keen to broaden the club out. So we moved with Derek and there was no bad feelings with Stockport Ladies. I suppose some may have thought we were deserting them but generally it was amicable.

"Derek did very well recruiting other young players and some senior players too to boost up the ladies team. The City ladies team was struggling for numbers at the time, so it was a good boost for them. My daughter eventually progressed through the football but she stopped playing. By that time I was entrenched as a volunteer. I had a bit of a determination to highlight ladies football by this time. I'd seen the attitudes of older men who used to say things like 'your daughter plays football? What's all that about?' They'd be laughing and I thought it was disgusting. It's difficult to imagine now but if you were involved in it at the time you knew. This was an everyday occurrence. It was totally unheard of in some areas of society. I got a bit of a bug for it and I wanted to drive it forward. "

Gary Moores became involved as a parent initially and about a year after arriving he: "became a committee member. I had helped collect subs and organise referees and stuff like that and started to get involved with a couple of the junior teams. It was probably 1999 when I became chairman. I think Rita Howard acted as the chair before me but I don't think she ever called herself chair or anything. She certainly seemed to have that role and led the committee meetings and so on. I was put forward for the role with no idea of what it would actually be. I'm not the most articulate or intelligent person but I'd got a passion for it and I wanted to help as much as I could… in any capacity. I think two or three names were put forward but it's all a bit of a blur. One part of the club wanted another guy and one part wanted me and there were a few false starts before it was all settled I think."

The 1997-98 season proved to be a successful one and began with a 10-0 win at home to Haslingden. Sadly, the game was expunged from the records later in the year as Haslingden withdrew from the league in November. The subsequent game then became the first official league match of the season and City managed a 9-6 victory over old rivals Wigan, placing them first in the North West Women's Regional Football League Second Division. League victories over Chester (twice), Liverpool District, Warrington and Trafford followed before the first set back - a 2-2 draw at Trafford. Derek's influence had been incredible. He had helped bring a plethora of talented youngsters to City, helped to establish a structure and the club seemed destined for success, however the Trafford game had come the day after some shocking news. Derek Heath had died after a short illness. Gary Moores: "I always remember Derek was brilliant at getting youngsters to play and it was hoped he'd do that at City but sadly he passed away quite soon after joining. He had cancer. It was only about twelve months after arriving and was so sad. It was also sad for the club because we'd have come on leaps and bounds with Derek. We did progress but he was a very good scout and he'd have helped develop so many other players. It was a massive loss losing Derek."

Derek's loss was felt throughout the club but some of the players he brought to the Blues continued to shine for many years, most notably Lindsay Savage. Gary Moores: "I remember him bringing Lindsay to play at Stockport and Dave Judge had left her on the sideline. Derek said 'are you not putting this girl on to play Dave?' And he said that

he hadn't seen her play but Derek persuaded him and he put her on. She was incredible and I think she scored at least two goals within no time. She was a great player and she lasted over ten years playing for the club. There was herself and Kelly McLellan and we celebrated them doing ten years at the club. I wouldn't like to name best players or anything but the one who did stand out was Lindsay Savage. She'd played with my daughter at Stockport. When she came to City she didn't play at under 16s, she went

LADIES MOURN LOSS OF DEREK

Tel: 0161 226 1782

We start this week's programme piece with some very sad news. After a relatively short illness, the membership secretary of Manchester City ladies team, Derek Heath, died in hospital from cancer on Saturday 8th November. Derek had recently moved from Stockport Ladies over to Manchester City and was instrumental in setting up a number of junior teams including the U-10s, U-12s, U-14s and U-16s girls' teams.

He arranged weekly coaching sessions for the girls at Wythenshawe Town FC, with around 100 budding young girl footballers attending. He was even known to go up to Blackley to collect youngsters who were unable to make their own way.

The funeral was held last Friday (14th) at Stockport Crematorium, attended by many of the girls from Stockport and City ladies and Alex Williams from the Community Office. Derek will be sadly missed by all the girls. Everyone at Manchester City FC would like to pass on their condolences to all Derek's friends and family and would like also to pass on our thanks

The sad news of Derek Heath's death, reported in the men's match programme November 1997.

for all the hard work he has put in to helping youngsters in Manchester.

We hope to invite his wife and family to one of our forthcoming games, possibly the Wolves match, to make a presentation on behalf of the football club.

City girls stay top

Manchester City Ladies are still riding high at the top of the table after beating Chorley Ladies 7-0, and recently enjoyed their exhibition match on the pitch against Crewe Alexandra, beating them 1-0 (ironically the same score as the men's team won by).

Pictured above is David Morley and the match sponsors Barrie Jones from Beejay & Co (Upholstery) with the best player from each side.

The ladies team have promised to continue the work Derek Heath began and so if any young lady is interested in playing for City ladies then please contact the Community

CABLE & WIRELESS

straight into the open age team and she was fabulous."

Lindsay, who came from a family of United supporters, was a member of Derek Heath's under 14s at Stockport. She remembers her debut at City: "I was 14. I was just a skinny kid playing in the first team and I was terrified. All the girls made me so welcome and really looked after me, and I think that was when I really thought-yes am ready and I can do this."

With Lindsay and the others City won the North West Second Division in style, winning 18 games and drawing two without any league defeats and won the division by 12 points. They had

N.W.W.R.F.L. DIVISION TWO
SEASON 1997/98

WELCOME
to the
GRANGE

v

MANCHESTER CITY LADIES F.C.

Sunday 29th March 1998
Kick-Off 2pm

Official Programme No. 52   50p

also netted 102 goals in their 20 league games with leading scorer Justine Mason, sharing the league's award for highest scorer with Bury's Diane McLean. Both had netted 25 league goals. This was a remarkable turnaround in only a year and meant that, for the first time ever, City had won a divisional title. They had also found success in a number of other tournaments including the Reebok Women's Soccer Festival and the Mansfield Smooth Bitter Cup. It was the most successful season the club had experienced to date and came only nine years after the Blues' formation in October 1988. A team photograph from this period includes Sally Rustige and Gail Redston, who had both been with the club since the inaugural season

■ Fury: Police escort City fans from the ground after fighting broke out within minutes of kick-off Picture: Alex Livesey

Going up!
Ladies ease
the Maine
Road blues

THEY ARE unbeaten this season, they're champions and they're Manchester City . . ladies.

While the men were tumbling into the Second Division, the gallant women of Maine Road were winning promotion to the First Division of the North West Women's Regional League after winning 17 games and drawing two.

On Sunday they beat Bury ladies to clinch promotion and true-Blue defender Gail Rothwell said: "Let's hope our lads can do the same as us next season."

■ Something to smile about: The triumphant Manchester City ladies

4 May 1998 - As City men are relegated, City Ladies celebrate promotion.

84

Jane Clark and Gail Redston holding the trophy, lead the Ladies' celebrations at Maine Road, 1998.

of 1988-89 and Tracey Blanchard who had joined for the second season. All three had played their part in the club's first promotion in 1991 and in the 1997-98 successes.

The team's return to the North West's top division began with a 6-0 victory at home to Bolton. In fact City won their opening seven games in all competitions, including a 6-2 headline grabbing win in the FA Cup over Brazil Girls, and led the table until late November. The number of postponed games affected the club's league position and after a game with Chester was postponed on 24 January 1999 City fell to sixth place due to falling behind in terms of games played. In the final weeks the postponements caused the club some real issues with the club having to play catch up throughout those final weeks. Ultimately, the club was unable to fulfil a fixture. Rita Howard, who was

by this point an active senior member of the committee, was not happy: "We were challenging for the league but was told that, due to all the postponements, we had to fulfil an evening fixture that we were unable to do because of work commitments. As a result we simply could not fulfil the fixture and we were fined and docked three points. Obviously, the points for the game were lost too. This meant it was almost impossible for us to get promotion. We appealed.

"Bev Harrop and I represented the club at a FA hearing, somewhere in Manchester. We won the appeal. The points were reallocated and the fine no longer stood. The league were furious but did not appeal the decision and we ended up finishing second thanks to those points – which we should never have been docked anyway!"

Sadly only one club was promoted at

MANCHESTER City Ladies l-r back: Reno Dionisiou secretary, Maria Fox, Louise Wakefield, Donna Davidson, Vicki Bloor, Maria Martin, Sally Rustige, Lindsay Savage, Kevin Scarborough manager. Front: Ellen Thornton, Tracey Blanchard, Kim Hines, Lyndsey Newman captain, Gail Rothwell, Bev Harrop, Charlie Johnson.

Brazil are Savaged by Girl Blues

BY RICHARD BURGESS

MANCHESTER City ladies have stormed back into action after their Championship-winning season.

The Blues have made the perfect start to their new campaign, with a 100 per cent record to date.

Hot-shot Lindsay Savage is firing on all cylinders, blasting five goals in three league games.

And in City's first round FA Cup tie, she claimed a fine hat-trick as they trounced Brazil Girls 6-2 at Wythenshawe Town FC.

Last season, the all-conquering City ladies clinched promotion to the Premier Division in emphatic style after topping the North West Second Division.

City beat Brazil in the FA Cup, 1998-99... and then Celtic!

that time from the North West Women's Regional Football League top tier to the Northern Combination. The players did receive runners up medals and so on but ultimately had City been able to play their fixture and won the game then the additional three points would have brought promotion. Blackpool Wren Rovers were the champions that season, winning the league by one point.

These were great days for the club with a mix of some of the originals from 1988-89, the new blood brought in via Derek Heath and other players added to the ranks through connections. With so many age related teams established, as well as a strong first team, the number of volunteers increased to support the club. Parents, like Gary Moores, would get involved and take on various duties such as fundraising, referee liaison and coaching. These were

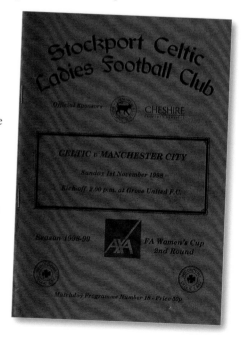

Stockport Celtic Ladies Football Club

Official Sponsors CHESHIRE

CELTIC v MANCHESTER CITY

Sunday 1st November 1998

Kick-off 2.00 p.m. at Grove United F.C.

Season 1998-99

AXA

FA Women's Cup 2nd Round

Matchday Programme Number 18 - Price 50p

Sally Rustige

Tracey Blanchard

vital cogs in an expanding Manchester City Ladies set up and this was already the club's most successful era until the WSL years. After finishing second in 1998-99 in the North West Women's Regional Football League Premier Division City had high hopes for the new season.

The 1999-2000 season met all expectations and proved to be a trophy winning campaign. As early as the third game City demonstrated their attacking flair with a 26-0 win in the FA Cup against Norton. At the time of going to press this remains the Blues' greatest win in the long-established national competition. Although no other result was quite so comprehensive that season there were still some exceptionally high scores in the league as City's quality shone, with several games seeing the Blues net seven goals. Inevitably City won the league title after a 3-2 victory over Trafford on 25 April 2000 but they also won the Premier Divisional Cup. Bev Harrop had some news: "I was captain at

the time and we had a Cup Final and I told my manager that I was pregnant. He was the only one I told. He said 'what do you want to do?' I said that I wanted to play and I said 'I'm not telling you for any other reason, other than if I come across any problems, that would be why.' So he said 'right, okay. Are you sure?' I said that I was and so he had no qualms about playing me. I was 13 weeks pregnant when we won the double."

As Bev mentioned City won that final 3-1 with a hat trick from Donna Davidson. All three City goals were netted in the final eight minutes of a great final. Bev: "We were a very good team. I was 32 I think in the final and I don't think being pregnant changed the way I played. I was relieved when the game was done and we'd finished and I knew that was it. It was summer and my child would be born in… well I thought it was going to be November, but she actually came in October. Football has given me the best friendships ever. The longest friendships. That is the one thing, other than the sheer enjoyment of playing, about being part of a team. Lesley Wright and Jane Morley have been friends right the way through… and in fact they're both God Mothers to my children."

Winning the league in 1999-2000 did not automatically bring promotion to the Northern Combination as that had to be achieved via a play-off process. There were three teams in the play-off – City, Barnsley and Darlington. Promotion was to be achieved by the two best teams with games played on a round robin basis. Darlington surprised everybody with a 2-0 win over Barnsley in the first match which meant that a City win would ensure they'd be promoted and the second match against Darlington would not be needed. City defeated Barnsley comfortably with the first goal coming after about twenty minutes. City Ladies website of the period carried this report of the goal: "Ellen Thornton picked up the ball just inside her own half and ran at the defence. Spotting the Keeper off her line, with the outside of her right foot, she curled the ball into the top corner from just outside the box. City continued to dominate and on the half hour the lead was doubled. Claire Jarratt swung in a left wing cross, and the Barnsley defender, under pressure from Kim Hines, only managed to steer a header into her own net."

Barnsley netted early into the second half but City soon regained control: "Attack after attack spelt further heartache for Barnsley as goals by Kim Hines, Donna Davidson (2), Lindsay Savage put the game out of reach. But City weren't finished as Louise Wakefield strode up from defence to notch her customary header. Gail Redston also got in on the act. The substitute picked up the ball on the edge of the box and drove a shot into the roof of the net which the Keeper could only watch fly by."

8-1 with goals from Donna Davidson (2), Ellen Thornton, Kim Hines, Lindsay Savage, Louise Wakefield, Gail Redston (one of the players from the 1988-89 season still playing) and an own goal. City were promoted to the Northern Combination, at the time the third tier of women's football.

Louise Wakefield felt the 1999-2000 was by far the best she experienced at the club: "We started winning everything. We used to play at Wythenshawe Town and somebody - I don't know who - put as you walked in to Wythenshawe Town 'the home of Manchester City Ladies' and as we walked in it was like one of the best moments seeing that. I remember thinking that I'd helped get us there and that song 'I'm Blue Dah Ba Dee' was out and we used to play that in the changing rooms. We had such a strong team spirit. If we'd get beat 'we'd be in the changing room: 'doesn't matter, doesn't matter, we go next week' and all that. They were definitely the best days. The best moments for me, being around that and being around those individuals there because everybody was your mate. At this time there was no bitching. There was no 'she's my mate, she's not your mate.' We were all together."

Right: Gail Redston celebrates the double success of 1999-2000.

Rita Howard leads out the team for a photoshoot at Maine Road in 1989-90.

Rita Howard – The First Female Manager

Although it is difficult to prove conclusively who managed the club for every moment of every season, it is clear that the majority of managers who have led Manchester City's women's team have been men. The club's first manager was Neil Mather and when he moved on at the end of the 1990-91 season a decision was made to appoint Rita Howard in his place. Rita, who had played for the historic Manchester Corinthians in the 1970s and 1980s became the first woman ever to manage a Manchester City team.

Rita Howard: "I don't remember being asked to become manager but I do remember when I said I'd do it. I remember vividly thinking 'we're not going to fold, so I'll do it.' At that time I really was coming towards the end of my playing days and we were at Platt Lane and one of the other players started to question me. She wanted to find out my integrity and wondered if I'd pick mates over best players and stuff like that. So I explained that 'I am a winner and I'll do it to the best of my ability and if that's not good enough or if you don't like it then I'll stop.' I carried on for a while but then we were a bit successful and I knew I couldn't spend a whole day at football when I've got three children and so on. At that time I was doing a roast dinner at 7am on a Sunday morning and plating it up so that we'd have our dinner when I got back. Then I'd be out the door to play football. I just wanted to make sure home kept running as it should."

Rita's husband and family supported her throughout her career which went on to see her contribute to the club into the 2000s. She was always perceived as a key voice at the club, representing it at disciplinary meetings and in other administrative areas. In the early 2000s with the promotions into wider geographically spread regions travelling to games and administrative duties were beginning to take an increasing amount of time. Rita: "When we became more successful I couldn't do much more. Kev Scarborough came in and helped out and we had parents on the committees and so on."

Bev Harrop, who arrived at City shortly before Rita became manager, always respected Rita's leadership attributes: "Rita is a character. And a fabulous Manager. She really was. She would make you believe that you'd won the game before you even went out. Yes. The things that she said in

Rita circa 1992-93.

the dressing room before we went out on to that pitch were motivational. We already knew we'd won before we stepped on to the pitch. She was an absolute character and also a really good player. When I first made my debut she was player-manager at the time."

Rita had breaks from City at times due to pregnancy – occasionally making the headlines too! – but she tried to keep involved for as long as possible. Rhoda Taylor, who had first played with Rita at Corinthians: "Rita is Rita. Always encouraging. Always pushing you on. Like Rita I took time out when I was pregnant and it got that way that when we had games whoever would be on the sidelines became

baby sitter. Quite a few children were born over the years."

Louise Wakefield, who joined City when the club was struggling for numbers, was unaware of Rita's history with City and football in general when she came back to help the club in the late 1990s: "She came in and I feel like she did an absolutely great job. I feel like she brought something different. She was one of the turning points as well when we started to grow. At first you'd think she wasn't a massive influential part of my time at City but she was. She came in and, in that couple of years, we won a couple of trophies. I was about 19/20, just coming back from my injury, and she just brought something so different. My best time at City, she was involved. She'd come in to the changing rooms and she was a big character. She'd have us laughing. She kind of brought us all together and we took that on to the pitch. You know when we were 2-0 down we'd all fight for each other. It wasn't an individual playing for an individual. Rita brought like a unity to us. Made us all like best mates on the pitch."

In a women's world

Rita, with Rhoda Taylor as Colin Hendry becomes President of the club.

Rita (back far left) celebrates promotion with the team 1998.

At one point in her City career Louise had missed most of the season due to injury as City pushed for a league title. She remembers Rita getting involved: "She really looked after me because we were winning the league that year and I'd come back from a really, really bad injury and I needed a few games so I could be part of that winning league. We were playing away and she took me to the side and she said 'I'm going to put you on today' and I was nearly crying because I'd not played, you know. I'd been in a wheelchair for four months. It was a big thing, so I played and every single player on that pitch was trying to get the ball to me to score. That was her that.. She brought that Rita. 'let's get her a goal' and all stuff like that. I'll never forget that and you could see her looking for me. You could see she wanted me to score because I'd just had this big massive injury. She brought that unity

and then it progressed from there for the club too.

"Rita was such a big character. When you did something wrong you'd know you'd done something wrong but she'd tell you in a constructive way. We'd not really had that."

Rita is proud of the fact that she managed City: "I didn't even think there was anything special about being the first female manager of the team until we met up for the 30th anniversary. It was mentioned to me and since then I've started to think about it and I'm quite pleased by it, although I don't know what it is that pleases me. I suppose it's about progress. So to be the first is really quite nice. I hope I did a good job. I was a player-manager too and so to pick the team when I'm in means that you have to be at least equally good as everybody else. You have to be up to the job and I was quick to recognise when it wasn't happening. There was a period of time when I was still trying to play when Reno Dionisiou made me sub. At the time I thought 'what is this?' Then when I got on I realised why. I struggled to put one foot in front of the other! Ah mobility, that's the reason."

The second female to manage City was Jane Morley and she was always aware of the value of experienced players and people who knew the club well. Jane had been a player at Manchester United and FC Redstar and was, like Rita, another experienced leader. She wanted consistency by ensuring Godfrey Williams, a longstanding City coach from the early years of the club, was her assistant: "There were a few people who stayed involved from the original team. Lesley (Wright) and Rita (Howard) were the two that captained the team for a long time. Rita became manager and for me her and Lesley are two of the pioneers. You had to have that connection and Godfrey was another. Wherever I've managed I've always wanted Godfrey to join me."

Both Jane and Rita's commitment to football has continued. In 2019 Jane is heavily involved with Stockport while Rita appeared in the Dick, Kerr's Ladies Walking Football Cup for a Manchester City community team. Looking back on her career Rita believes: "My best and my worst moment as manager go hand-in-hand. It was when we were going to be champions and we only needed a point from this game. I remember that we were winning something like 5-0 and it was quite obvious we were

Rita Howard at the Dick Kerr's Ladies Walking Football Cup 2019.

going to win. At the side I had a ghetto-blaster or whatever you call them these days… a machine that would play music loudly! Being champions was great and a real success for us and, while they were all playing and the other team was trying to beat us but failing badly, I played *We Are The Champions*. It appals me to this day that I did that, but I did. I can't turn the clock back. I'm disgusted with myself for doing that but I'm delighted that we achieved the success."

Joining City

The reasons players join a particular club can vary. Here's a small cross section of views from individuals connected with the club from its first season to the present day. We start with long serving player Gail Redston, who joined City prior to its first competitive season: "It was my older brother, Steve. He saw it in a newspaper and he said 'oh, Manchester City are starting a ladies team. Why don't you go down?' So I said 'where is it at?' He said 'Platt Lane.' Off I trotted to Platt Lane. But I was 30 and as I'm going there I'm thinking 'I won't get in, no way.' I went down and I could see, no disrespect to some of the players, but I could see they were a real mix of players. So I thought I might have a chance. Anyway, I kept going down and trained at Platt Lane and Neil was organising friendlies and things like that and then I just stayed and signed on.

"Being a Blue you want to wear that shirt. On the level of skill-wise I don't think it was tough but fitness… Fitness-wise you just work at that and it comes back. I just thought to myself this is what I wanted all them years ago when I was a girl. I think I pushed myself because I thought I'm one of the older ones and I'm thinking am I doing the right thing? I'd had my two kids by then and they were like 'oh Mum's going to football again.' I used to drag them everywhere but they were fine."

Gail had always wanted to play in a good, forward-looking team and about 1974, at the age of 14 or 15, she had a spell with Manchester Corinthians, but ultimately, the career was put on hold until she was about 30 in 1988. Fourteen years later she remained a City player and, in 2019 at the age of 61, she was still playing 11-a-side football for a team in Reddish.

Manchester Corinthians was a pioneering women's club for almost forty years and one of its captains was Rita Howard. She also joined City in the 1988-89 season: "Corinthians, later renamed Woodley, used to train at Platt Lane and it was brilliant. We used to use the little five-a-side pitch and it was great fun. Dave Ewing, a cup winner with City in 1956, was a coach there. I don't think he had community in his job title but he was in effect a football in the community coach. He was great and we had great fun there. Dave was brilliant. He was astounded that these girls were playing. It was all part of City's attempts to be inclusive I guess.

"Then after a few years new blood in Neil Mather and the others are there as part of the official Football in the Community programme. My teammate Lesley Wright and her mates were all Blues and they were

Dave Ewing (right with the Central League trophy and Ged Keegan, 1978) provided community coaching sessions at Platt Lane in the late 1970s and early 1980s.

all talking about City creating a women's team. Janice Smith, a great cultured footballer, was another Blue and they were all going to go and join City. So it became a no-brainer for me despite being a United fan. I wasn't going to leave this established group of players simply because it was City. So I went with them. You stay loyal to your mates and that was particularly true of Lesley Wright, Rhoda Taylor and Nicky Hunt. I'd had my first child by this time and so there had been some gaps in my career."

Helen Hempenstall

Rita's career continued into the 2000s with City. While Rita's move to City was to stay with her friends and footballing community, Helen Hempenstall's reason for moving had more to do with her interest in Manchester City: "I never really thought about playing for a women's team because I didn't think they existed. Then my dad read something in a local paper in Ashton about a team called Lady Blues and that they were looking for players. I had a trial and joined them.

"One day we were playing against City Ladies and I thought this is where I should be. I contacted City and they said 'come down'. I did and the next week I was in the team. It just went on from there. Lady Blues were a good team but once I'd seen City that was it. I needed to play in that kit. I've been a City fan all my life, watching games since I was 7 sitting in the Platt Lane. Lady Blues wasn't happy with it and when I played for City against them Neil Mather had to take me off the pitch because my legs were just black – they were at me from the minute go. It was Ashton United's ground where Lady Blues played."

The lure of City and other clubs eventually saw Lady Blues collapse and other players joined City as a result. A similar thing happened with FC Redstar, managed by Jane Morley: "After FC Redstar finished I spent time with Oldham but my knees were struggling. Then I met Lesley Wright socially and ended up coming down to City to watch a few games and then, as you do when you're on the sidelines, you start to get involved."

Jane's involvement was crucial at times. She managed the club but she also contributed significantly to the junior set up. In 2002 she was presented with a ball by the squad to mark her title triumph at a junior level that season. Jane, like many other women who contributed to City's development, was not a supporter of City's men's team. In fact she was a United fan but that did not stop her giving her all for the Blues while she was there. Another United fan was Louise Wakefield: "I joined in 1996. I was just turned 17 and I came from United. I started at United when I was 13. When I first joined City I was a striker like everybody does at that age and then, after about three or four seasons, I gradually moved to centre half. And then I always played across the back four. United wasn't as welcoming as City. From the first moment I arrived I felt at home. Everybody was so supportive and that's what I think I needed at that age."

Louise arrived at a the same time as Jane Clark, now Boardman. Jane had been to university in Manchester: "It would have been in the September/October 1996 when I started playing for City. I'd just graduated… just started my job with what was then A.A. and we took it in turns to wash the kit. We took it in turns to make the sandwiches for after the match… We took it in turns to sweep out the changing room after the match. The pitches were variable, shall we say, and you could generally tell the level of affiliation your opponents had with their sort of named counterpart men's club by the quality of the pitch. There were some clubs, like Middlesbrough, who were really getting behind their women's team who we used to go and play on their academy facilities and it was just like 'wow, you know?' 'Look the pitch is flat… look at the grass.' The simple things would really appeal to us. It was a great group of girls, but we did everything for ourselves."

When Jane arrived there wasn't a youth set up at City but within a couple of years that had all changed and players arrived at a young age to play within the various age related teams. One of these was Catherine Hyde: "I was doing a City in the Community activity – an out of school club - and I was scouted. I think it was something

Louise Wakefield   *Jane Clark*

like £5 for the time you trained with them or something like that. It was an extra to the school day. I was sent home with a letter from school suggesting I go for trials. We went up Altrincham way training. That's when I met Jane Morley and Lesley Wright. I would have been about 12.

"Laura Cheetham was scouted when I was at school as well. She carried on a lot longer than me and her family used to give us a lift because we obviously got scouted from the same school. Training was difficult because the pitch we trained on dog's used! You had to go around scooping dog poo up before you could train! I think at that time I would have joined any team. I just wanted to play football. When they sent me home with the letter they said 'don't open it until you get home'. My Mum was happy for me to do it. My Dad - he was over the moon and then, from that day, he used to take me on the fields every night after school playing football. Kicking a ball about and he'd say we'll get you there one day kid, but it wasn't to be my time. That time's now for young girls, not eighteen or so years ago."

Catherine's opportunities to play football professionally were limited, as they were for all women. A couple of clubs, most notably Fulham and Arsenal, had paid players at times but a professional structure was not in existence. This was still the case when Abbie McManus began playing. She became one of the first City players to cross into

Abbie McManus

Abbie wanted to play football for enjoyment and felt going to one of the FA approved training centres would make playing football more of a chore and not fun: "I could have gone to the likes of Blackburn or United because they had the Centre of Excellence, but it never interested me. It was more this is my hobby and I enjoy doing it. I always wanted to try and do it to the best of my ability though. Obviously now City provide stuff at that age and the younger girls have got more opportunity than I did. It means that the women's game will be increasing by investing in better value and better players."

Young players now have a variety of opportunities and young girls can genuinely dream of playing at Wembley and making a career out of the game. Supporters clubs have become established as well, meaning that professional female players are getting used to the interest that male professional players have had for some time. Dave Sheel is a member of City's women's supporters club. He's always been interested in anything Manchester City does, including the women's team. He believes that the female players are closer to supporters than in the male's game. This is part of the attraction for Dave. He has also tried to persuade male supporters of the men's game to watch City: "When City started signing what I would call marquee players I used to chat about it to the blokes that sit near me at the men's games. Some became interested but others remained blinkered. I said 'We've signed Toni Duggan – a player of real quality' and one of them said 'Who's he?' It gets to me. That's the ignorance. It has changed though and we now have a club that is known around the world. Players sign for City from all over because, for the first time since it was established in 1988, it is a leading player in a professional sport."

the professional era, but it was still amateur when she joined City: "I was 15 - so 10 years ago (2008) - and the reason why I joined was because I played for a local team that was struggling. At the time women's football wasn't grown and unfortunately the team that I was with just disbanded through funding. By chance Man City got a hold of me and I went down to a trial and ended up playing for the Under 16s team at the time. We used to train on a park in Wythenshawe… like a few horses could have probably tread over it you would never know! Ever since I've just been at City.

"City's women's team never had the FA Centre of Excellence so for most people your first thoughts are try and get yourself in the Centre of Excellence, but from a young age I wasn't thinking that. It was always my hobby, so I saw the Centre of Excellence as being 'too important' for me back then."

Referees and Discipline

For many years City had to find their own referee for games and this also meant that opposition teams would also provide referees for their home games. The quality would vary, as would the level of bias shown. Inevitably, away teams typically felt the referees favoured the home team. Neil Mather felt differently. He believed that City's own referees often over compensated and gave the opposition the advantage at times.

Rowena Foxwell who played in City's opening game at Oldham and remained involved with the club for about four years remembered that referees were often on the receiving end of considerable abuse during those seasons: "I remember playing Tranmere… there was one little girl. I say little girl, she was probably late teens or something, but she had a mouth on her, and the language! And I remember that was one difference I think for women's football at that time. By God, they argued with the referee! I'm not talking about fronting the ref like you do in the men's game now and respect for the ref… It was really a case of 'you're wrong ref and I ain't having it.' They used to have a proper barney at times with the ref, so I remember that Tranmere game and that one girl. It was a shock at the time."

The referee needs to give Gail Redston a word after the Dick Kerr's Ladies Walking Football Cup in 2019. Below: Advertising for referees in a City Ladies match programme, 1991.

Jane Clark, now Boardman, who arrived at City about eight years after formation, highlighted that referee inconsistency remained an issue for many years: "We used to have referees that were unreliable or ancient. There was one in particular who used to wear a black bin bag under his shirt because he must have been about 83 and he needed the extra insulation against the cold! He was deaf. He couldn't hear his own whistle. We used to have subs running the line, because we didn't have linesmen."

As City progressed up the pyramid system in the early 2000s leagues appointed their own referees for games but this was still not satisfactory: "They would provide referees but there was always a risk that your appointed ref didn't turn up."

Nowadays the players wear kits tailored for women, as seen in this shot of Esme Morgan in a photoshoot following the signing of a contract extension in 2019. All very different from 30 years earlier!

Kit

For most of its history the team has worn the kit and colours of Manchester City. Sometimes these were hand me down kits; sometimes these were provided new and free from the parent club, often via City in the Community; and sometimes these would be bought by the team or the players themselves. The kit hasn't always been blue and in the early days away colours were worn most often. Michelle Mather (now Middleton), who played in the first game in 1988, remembers: "The first kit was given to us by Tony Book and Glyn Pardoe and was the white Umbro kit with the black v neck and thin red stripe that belonged to the youth team. Short shorts and shirts that buried us!"

While Neil Mather was a member of City's community staff he was able to chat directly with those responsible for the kit and items no longer worn by the first or second team were often obtained. These were the days when the parent club was strict about the number of shirts available and first team male players were encouraged not to swap shirts or to hand items to fans. The kit provided at the start of the season had to last. The club was more strict when it came to reserve team and youth kit and those responsible had to account for every item. Kit would be expected to last two years and the white kit Michelle mentioned had gone from being the first team away kit to training wear and then City Ladies' first kit. What was most interesting about this kit though is that Manchester City's shirt sponsor changed by the time the Ladies had the kit, and some shirts had a patch sewn over the sponsor reading 'Umbro Training'. Donna Haynes and Heidi Ward wore these shirts initially and then for the third game, against Burnley, one – number 14 - was worn by Rhoda Taylor.

Neil did manage to get new items off the club from time to time and in 1989-90 the players and coaches were able to wear the same style tracksuits as the first team male squad. This allowed the Ladies to arrive at grounds looking official and was something Neil felt was important: "We had to look the part. We wanted to but I think our opponents expected it too."

Lesley Wright: "I can't remember having to buy my own kit at City but all the 'brother' (sponsor) kits we had were hand-me-downs from the first team or reserves. They were massive – far too big for us. We were given Umbro tracksuits." As well as getting tracksuits, Neil took steps to bring some income into the club. Gail

The original City Ladies kit from 1988-89.

Rhoda Taylor's original 'Intersleep Beds' kit.

Redston remembers: "We used to try and get sponsorship and I remember when we had the maroon and white striped kit - we managed to get that off City new - Neil managed to get us a sponsor and when we looked it said Intersleep Beds! I was like okay... that's good... Intersleep Beds on the women's shirts! Who thought of that?"

Ian Lees, another member of the community staff at City, had a connection to someone who owned the company 'Intersleep Beds', based in Ashton-under-Lyne. He asked whether they'd be interested in helping to fund the kit and the team and the sponsorship deal was made. This was the first shirt sponsor to actually provide any form of income to the Ladies team. Kate Themen recognised the significance of bringing money in but wanted consistency with the men's team: "I remember wondering 'why is ours different?' Surely there needs to be some sort of consistency there? But I remember the old Intersleep Beds... absolute consternation! You've kind of got a sponsor but it's not Saab, Phillips or Brother like the men."

Helen Hempenstall remembers the embarrassment she felt wearing the name: "We played in the Arsenal tournament and all the clubs affiliated in some way with a men's League team had their regular sponsors on their shirts but we had Intersleep Beds. When we were having a photo taken we all turned our backs at first to hide the sponsor! It was embarrassing. Intersleep Beds was a place in Ashton, near Penny Meadow, that sold beds. I also remember playing in a match once with that yellow kit that the men had worn once. They said they'd never wear it again because they got beat at Arsenal. Well, me being a full back I got Andy Hinchcliffe's shirt. Well you can imagine! I could've tucked the shorts in my socks. It meant something though wearing Hinchcliffe's shirt."

That yellow kit was worn once by the men in an embarrassing defeat at Arsenal in 1989. The club claimed it would be destroyed and that Manchester City would never wear yellow again. Of course, both the men's and women's teams have since worn yellow but the news that the 1989 kit was worn by the

The 1989 yellow shirt worn by the men v Arsenal and once by the women.

women that same season may surprise some. Photographs exist of Neil Mather wearing it and some shirts have survived and are held in supporter collections. Other than shirts worn in key successes, it is probably the most collectable City shirt.

Once Neil left, City Ladies constantly tried to get kits from the club. Gail Redston acted terrier-like, never giving up: "I'm like a dog with a bone, me. I used to just go round and mither Alex Williams to death for this, that and the other. We made sure that we stayed in contact with the club through the community programme.

Umbro Training covers the Saab sponsorship on the City Ladies first kit, 1988-89.

Sometimes we got kit and things like that, tracksuits. It was always down to the ladies and the coaches to try and push. We never actually got anything on a plate. We had to work hard at it. I was the Players Rep as well because I was the one that always went down and mithered Alex. If the players had an issue I'd try and sort it out. Whenever City were changing the kit I'd go and see Alex Williams. I remember going to Alex 'what are you doing with the old kit? We'll play in it!' He once said 'I don't think they'll allow you to, because you're still part of Man City' – meaning that we should wear same as the men not an old style. I replied 'right, who do I need to speak to then?' 'John Clay.' So I phoned John Clay up, and it was at the time they'd moved to Hart Road, in to the big house while the main stand was being renovated in the mid 90s. So I went to speak to John and he said 'well, there's a load of stuff in the basement, just go and help yourself.' So I did."

The MCFC badge on a City Ladies tracksuit, 1989-90.

Gail went in to the basement of the old house City were renting as office space and found boxes of unused, but no longer wanted due to brand/style changes by the parent club, kit: "Remember the quilted all-in-one subs' coats? I grabbed a box of them. I rooted through box after box, grabbing what I could and making journeys up the stairs and to my car… In the boot of my car…next box… Get that training kit… anything. It just gives you that edge to say 'look, we are Manchester City.' That kept us going for a bit."

Louise Wakefield was a young player who joined City in 1996. She always recognised the efforts Gail and the other experienced players made: "I was 13 years and was so impressed, especially people like Gail. What she did… the leg work she did. She was influential. She was massively influential. You're looking at her going 'look what she does.'"

Assistant manager Godfrey Williams was an important asset to the club during this time as he also worked for Umbro for a period. He used to raise money via selling football name cards and then use that to buy

The yellow and blue kit coach Godfrey Williams bought from Umbro used against Wigan in 1993.

action against Manchester City 26/9/93 WIGAN WIN 2 - 1

City kits on the Wakefield family's washing line on Trafford Road!

discounted kit from Umbro. He always tried to get the best possible: "I couldn't always get a full City kit because it was too expensive so once I got us this yellow and blue Umbro kit. It was good quality, proper Umbro and all that, but it wasn't City. It did the job though."

After this yellow kit Godfrey managed to persuade Umbro to provide a full City kit in 1995. City chairman Francis Lee posed with the team for a photograph and this seems to be the first occasion any Manchester City chairman appeared on a photo with the women's team. Rita Howard: "I can't remember when, after Neil left, we got a full strip…. I remember that when Francis Lee was chairman we managed to get a full kit off them. I do remember it as a sort of 'let's give them a kit and move on' but the kit never changed the perception of who we were. It never changed our perception. We were always Manchester City and recognised by all as such. Getting a kit or not getting one never changed that view."

Of course, getting a kit was only ever part of the story. It still had to be looked after and washed. Typically, in the late 1990s the players would take it in turns to wash the kit. Louise Wakefield: "It was my turn to take the kit home and wash it. I'll never forget it. I took the kit home, washed it and hung it out to dry. We lived at Trafford Road near Old Trafford. I went out and when I came back my Mum was sat on the couch like 'what are you trying to do to me?' and I went 'why?' She went 'all the United fans were walking past Trafford Road on their way to the United game and I had like 15 Manchester City kits hung on the line!' She said 'you're going to get our windows put in!' We took it in turns to take the kit home and wash them but the amount of times I turned them shorts pink was unbelievable!"

Louise had joined City at a time (1996) when the club was struggling for numbers and finance: "We didn't have training kit. We didn't have tracksuits. I used to turn up at Platt Lane in my United kit to train in. Obviously, so did Bev Harrop, you know. It didn't go down very well, but what else could we do? We started to get stuff slowly and it was only dribs and drabs… It was like very worn old stuff. The City laundry was at Platt Lane, in the back, so I think it was just the stuff we could manage to get out of there." Bev Harrop succinctly sums up this time: "We had to beg, borrow and steal kits, you know."

Jane Boardman remembers the relationship with City developing over time from her arrival in 1996: "In the initial stages we got nothing and then after a year or two, they started giving us the men's kit when they switched. So we'd play in last season's kit, but it was all massive or they'd give us an under-18s kit, but we were always sort of playing one season out of date. Then as time moved on they then gave us one first team kit. We were starting to build up the club and we went from having one first team to having first team and reserves and then slowly building up the junior sections all the way down to under-9s and the youngest girls that were playing were

The 1994-95 team pictured with City's then chairman Francis Lee.

sort of six and seven. So we were focusing on building up that side of things, but for many years we'd just get the left-over kit from the men, but everyone loved that, you know. People loved the fact that they were wearing a shirt that could have been worn by one of the male stars."

Catherine Hyde was one of the junior players who arrived as the various age related teams grew: "I have no idea where the kit came from but I know it was hard for us to get a kit at times. We'd have to wait and wait and wait. We were lucky if we got one. And then when we did get one it would smell of sweat and God knows what else. We always had to take it back. It would get

In touch with City…

CITY GIRLS KITTED OUT BY UMBRO

Lining up here for a team picture are the Manchester City Ladies Football Team who were recently presented with a set of spanking new kits at Maine Road courtesy of Umbro International.

Flanking the ladies on the right is team manager Godfrey Williams and Martin Prothero from Umbro, and on the left wing is City Chairman Francis Lee.

CENTENARY TIES

To commemorate the club's Centenary season, Manchester City have produced two exclusive Centenary ties (one in polyester, one in silk) which are available by mail order.

The polyester ties are priced at £7.95 (+50p p&p) and the fully lined, pure silk ties are available for £19.95 (+50p p&p).

Please complete the order form on the facing page (photocopies are acceptable), making cheques or postal orders payable to Manchester City Football Club. Cash will not be accepted. Stocks are limited, so we advise that you place your order as soon as possible.

Football in the Community

AN EQUAL

Numbers and Names and no hand-me-downs, City Women's first photoshoot after the relaunch.

washed at Platt Lane or whatever, and then we'd have to wait to get another kit the night before a game or one night at training. If it wasn't washed we'd just have to wear it."

In later years the volume of kits needed for the junior teams increased as the number of teams increased. Junior coach Tony Challoner recognises that considerable effort had to be made to fund and obtain shirts: "The First Advice kits and then the Thomas Cook kits were all arranged via Darren Brady in his tireless work for all the age groups as we had very little from Manchester City" Jane Morley (talking of late 90s/early 2000s) was always on the lookout to supplement whatever kit the club had: "I remember walking into a discount shop in Sale and buying Kappa tee-shirts for £1 each for all the girls. We all wanted to ensure we all looked like Manchester City." A young player during that era was Lindsay Savage: "Laura Gligan would always make

sure I would get the best and sort out some extras for me." John Stanhope, who followed Jane Morley as manager: "We got kit and that was huge because that's a huge help. It wasn't new kit. It's hand-me-down. I mean you don't want to sound as though you're being ungrateful for anything because you are grateful for everything you got."

One of John's big signings was goalkeeper Andie Worrall: "I think I wanted to applaud people that do all the background stuff in their own time because it's time-consuming. They were doing all the financial side of stuff, trying to find money from places and I think City would throw some money in, but it's nothing like now. Kits, they'd give you second-hand kits, or they'd give you men's kits. To people not involved this probably sounds really petty but you'd be given a man's kit. When you're 10 stone wet through and you've got a kit… it was Peter Schmeichel's goalie shirt! Have you seen the size of me and Schmeichel? It was an XXXXL and I think John Stanhope went 'I've got you a goalie top' and it was Schmeichel's. I'm like 'I could pitch it and go camping in it.' It was that big. You like to feel good don't you when you play? If you ask any of the current City team they'll tell you. You need to feel good when you play. I know City are big on the impression set now and on how people look. They like people to look like athletes. Back then you'd turn up in a mis-match. So we started getting tracksuits here and I'd buy all my own stuff. All my own gear. I always looked better than everyone else because I bought all my own stuff."

Jill Scott

From the late 2000s onwards the supply of kit by the male club was a normal practice. Ladies chair Gary Moores remembers: "Sometimes we did buy kit like jackets and so on from the souvenir shop. If it was anything more than the standard kit. Generally though we always received a full kit from City. It may not have arrived bang on time for the start of the season but the open age got a new kit every time the men's team changed their kit. Usually at the start of the season it would arrive. I think we had a fairy godmother somewhere who helped us out at the club. There may have been discussions that we were unaware of but someone always got us the kit."

Alison Smith, who was a coach and then secretary of the club (2008-14): "The one thing City did do for the grassroots club was provide genuine City kit - shirt, shorts, socks for all teams. The first team received a bit more training kit, jackets etc and this was expanded to junior teams in the later years."

Since the relaunch the club's professional approach has ensured that there is now no difference between how the men's and women's teams are treated kit wise. City's players are included in kit launches and their kits are designed, released and played in at the same time. Players no longer need to take it in turns to wash their kit, something England international Jill Scott still finds hard to believe: "[At other clubs] you'd have one set of kit. You'd wear it. You'd take it home. You'd wash it yourself and I remember the first year of being here, saying 'it's mad that we get our kit washed' and I can't remember if it was Nick Cushing, the Manager... He was like 'you need to stop saying all these things. You deserve these things. You deserve to be getting your food and getting your kit.' But we're all just so grateful and so appreciative of it. It was just such a change."

Role Models

It is important for any sport to provide role models. People children can look up to, idolise and so on, and so the question of who was your role model was an important one to ask the players interviewed for this project. Unsurprisingly, the majority of respondents talked of male footballers as, for most of the last sixty years, young girls growing up were unaware of leading female footballers. Many of the interviewees were unaware of women playing football at all. The following comments demonstrate how this has started to change since the development of the WSL and the growth of professional football as played by women.

Debbie Darbyshire: "I've been a Manchester City fan all my life so I was always a bit of a tomboy and played football in the park with the lads. My favourite player at the time was Peter Barnes - I had the Peter Barnes football trainer! So I always wanted to be a left footed footballer. I practiced and practiced and practiced for years with my left foot. I can't kick a ball with my right one now! That's how I got in to it."

Helen Hempenstall is another who loved City's 1976 League Cup final opening goal scorer: "In the 70s my hero was Peter Barnes. Always Peter Barnes. My husband wanted to call one of our children Tueart after Dennis Tueart and I said 'No! It sounds like a packet of Chewits! I can't have that.'"

Heidi Ward remembers growing up in the 1970s in a village on the outskirts of Manchester when Liverpool were the dominant team: "My role models were all from men's football teams. I liked some of the Liverpool players because Liverpool were doing really well at the time. My family always take the mickey out of me because they said I liked Ray Clemence, the Liverpool goalie, so I think that's when I started off playing in nets. My brother used to shove me in nets and I used to pretend I was Ray Clemence. I think that's what was happening! And then we started to come and watch City as a family. I was really young so players like Dave Watson, he was the captain of City in the 70s, and Peter Barnes and Dennis Tueart… and then all the way through the 80s like I remember

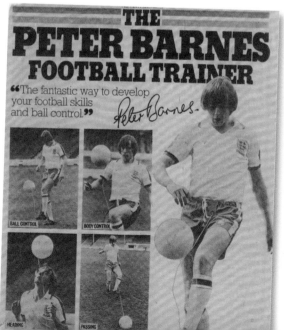

THE **PETER BARNES** FOOTBALL TRAINER

"The fantastic way to develop your football skills and ball control." *Peter Barnes.*

BALL CONTROL   BODY CONTROL

HEADING   PASSING

Dave Watson and Dennis Tueart, 1976.

For those that were children in the 1970s, 80s and 90s there's a common theme. Most role models were men. **Alison Smith**: "Colin Bell, Dennis Tueart and Rodney Marsh." **Michelle Middleton**: "Joe Corrigan, Trevor Francis." **Lindsay Savage**: "Steven Gerrard and Patrick Vieira"

Lesley Wright grew up in the sixties and early seventies: "When I was a ten year old I wanted to play football but society thought it was wrong for some reason. Now a ten year old girl can see that she has a chance. There are role models… clubs to play for… you can get paid to play and so it can be a career… You can dream of lifting the FA Cup at Wembley – it's possible now! You can go on the internet now and do a search 'women's football Stockport' and you'll find teams. For me it was different. If I hadn't spoken with Val Hall (a Manchester Corinthians player) in our school canteen and she said she had football training, I would never have known. It was chance. How did girls get to play football? Even if there was something in a newspaper the chances are it wouldn't be a local team and it was usually a story with a negative angle or a 'let's look at her, the girl who plays football'. You had to physically write to the Women's FA – but you may not have known that existed – and hope they send you details.

the City Youth Cup Winning Team of 1986. They were really good, like, David White, Paul Moulden and Andy Hinchcliffe. In terms of role model I don't know, I just like watching City play. Back then… it's really awful… I didn't have a girl/woman role model.

"I remember always wanting to play football and if anybody said 'what do you want to be when you grow up?' I'd say something like a PE Teacher, but I'd wanted to play football but I was aware that it sounded a bit stupid, playing football… and I did play football up to being 21… I think life takes over and you do different things, but if I was 18 again - actually if I was 12, because they've got lots of different age teams going on at City now haven't they? I think I'd have loved to have just been a part of it."

Lesley Wright, Dick Kerr's Ladies Cup 2019

"So I played for Corinthians which was run by George Aiken. He'd been involved for decades with the club and was certainly running it when I started playing when I was 14 or so. By that time he was running it with his partner Brenda. His funeral was just off Lloyd St in Hulme. He ran it with Marlene, Kim, Wendy… I don't know much about how he took it on. I do know he had a daughter who had played. I remember playing for them down

Briscoe Lane somewhere, near the Etihad, but we also played on Princess Parkway near the Parkway pub, not Hough End, further down. Corinthians moved to Woodley, now the Stockport Sports Village, and at the bottom was two pitches and a club house where we used to drink after the game. It was a lovely grass pitch at the time. Sadly, Woodley, the old Corinthians, finished when we moved to City. It couldn't survive."

Rowena Foxwell was a teenager when City Ladies began in 1988: "I think for me it's important that female sport is normalised, that a club the size of City has a women's team. My sons play football… one's still playing football and he has a really good female player in his team. And she's been down to the City Academy a few times and she can see a route for her if she wants to carry on, like he can. She can play with the best of them. We're finally moving forward. I think the fact that there is that pathway… I mean it's really difficult. I'm so glad I haven't got girls, because I would get so angry with sort of the female role in society, when you look at a lot of what the media still say and do. I think it's worse now than it probably was when we were sort of you know late teens maybe? You didn't have to fit a type. Now you look at the Kardashians or whatever. So for me to have professional athletes who are women recognised in football is incredibly important and you know I'm quite proud of the fact that City have put that investment in. If you think of the England team and they are winning games. They are in big tournaments. It's the same with the rugby and the cricket, the women are winning the cricket, winning the rugby.

"I mean, I've never had my nails done. Never had my eyebrows done. And I think you know if I was 30 years younger, I don't know where I'd start, that sort of

maintenance. You know it is that case of you don't need to be that hyper-feminine character to be a valued human being. How hard must it be to maintain some of that and play professional football?' That's the pressure of modern society. You have the right to look and play as you would like."

Louise Wakefield: "I didn't know any female football existed. I didn't so my role models were all males. It was like Mark Hughes, Lee Sharpe and Bryan Robson. Literally no females. Then once I started playing for City obviously Gail Redston, who was influential, and Bev Harrop - I always wanted to play football like Bev, you know, because she was very cool, calm and collected. She'd always have a go at me and I wanted to smack my nose in her face sometimes - just the way it is - but football-wise I always wanted to play like Bev. Spirit-wise I always wanted Gail's spirit, you know, and calmness-wise I'd always wanted to be like Rita Howard. There was a bit of them in all that. I used to play centre half with Lesley Wright and she was one of the people that like I ended up listening to a lot. I was captain for a while and that was probably down to listening and learning from her. She'd be like 'don't worry' and she'd talk a

Bev Harrop taking a penalty watched by Gail Redston, Dick Kerr's Ladies Cup 2019.

full back through the game. She was very, very encouraging. Lesley and the others used to give you a lot of advice on the game. They were a lot older. They were a lot more wiser. They knew football."

The support given to players like Louise by older female players is something that has come through loud and clear during the interviews. While female role models may not have been visible in the British media they were present at individual clubs. Older players had a duty to guide younger players, especially as schools neglected football as played by women for years. Louise found that as her career progressed she became the role model: "Before I knew it I started having girls under 10 asking me 'what position do you play?', 'how do you train?' and so on. I'm like 'I said stuff like that to Gail and now they're asking me. They want to play like me. They want to be like me.' I used to do that to Gail and Bev. They were my role models. Now I've got little kids saying it to me."

Even after decades of women playing football since the FA ban was lifted it is still often difficult for young female players to be accepted. **Jane Boardman**: "My son said this once. He was talking with his mates and he plays under 7s and every now and again they'll play against a team that has a girl in it. The first time this happened one of his mates went 'is that a girl?' and he went 'girls can't play football' and I looked at him and I went 'you of all people, saying girls can't play football.' He just sort of smiled and laughed and went 'yes, okay Mum' and then told all his mates 'my Mum used to play for Manchester City.' After the first time, they don't bat an eyelid now and a lot of these girls are holding their own in these lads under 7s teams because at that age they're physically very similar. You don't notice that they are girls a lot of the time. There's plenty of lads with long hair and you sort of think

well it could be a lad and that's just nice and that's how it should be, that you don't. But there should be more of them."

Catherine Hyde, a junior player in the early 2000s, is different from most contemporaries as she named a woman: "Kelly Smith she was my idol when I was growing up, that's why I wanted to be a striker, but ended up a centre half, don't know how that happened. If they were local then we'd go and watch England Women, but as far as other women's games, we didn't even know there was any going on."

Andie Worrall was a first team Manchester City player at this point. Like Catherine her role model was a female player: "If Karen Burke hears this, she'll probably cringe. Karen Burke was playing… it was Knowsley at the time, but they became Liverpool… Channel 4 used to air the women's cup final and it was Doncaster Belles v. Knowsley, but Knowsley had a Liverpool kit on if I remember right, and there was this winger… number 7 was Karen Burke, absolutely amazing but they got beat. Donny Belles had Karen Walker playing for them and Gillian Coulthard… all the England players, and I was like in awe watching this going 'I want to do that, that's what I want to do' and then obviously as I got older I got to play on the same team as Karen Burke."

Andie has witnessed a major improvement in the media presence of women footballers: "If you go on FIFA… a couple of the City girls got capped for England didn't they the other week like Abbie McManus and they're on FIFA. That's amazing! We're not there yet though. I mean Twitter is like negative opinions rule… 'the women's place in the kitchen.'

"I remember I'm on mancityfans.net and I arranged some 5-aside at Platt Lane.

One of the lads went 'oh we're going to come along and take the piss out of you because girls can't play football' and he said 'I walked in and I saw you smash a ball at about 70 mph and I about-turned and went' not going to say anything. So you always have to fight, I've always found that I've had to fight to change people's perceptions, and you do have to change people's perceptions because when they come with you, one to one, and they play football with you they go 'yes, she's quite good.' They need to realise that women's football is the standard it is because for years it's not been allowed to progress, but if 20 years ago they would have allowed us to progress it would be miles better than what it is now. But it's catching up rapidly. I look at when we were at City to the conditioning and the girls now. From when I was there the conditioning of Izzy Christiansen is 100 times different. And that's because they're in there every day. They are being fed properly. They are being trained properly. They have got proper recovery sessions and it's unbelievable to say that they are all under one roof, but people don't want to give City credit, because it's Manchester City and we don't get good press do we."

Stacey Copeland had a great footballing career with City and Doncaster Belles before becoming a major star at boxing. She was with City in the 2000s and has used her media presence to promote sporting activities for girls and women. On the *Greater Manchester* blog she discussed her career and commented: "I was made to feel like there was something 'wrong' with me as a youngster because I was a girl who loved football and boxing, so now I want to be the role model I did not have growing up." On the *Womanthology* website (31 May 2017) she added: "I think we must challenge myths around strength and femininity on many

different fronts. Firstly, in terms of physical strength, athletes like me must be visible role models to young girls, to show them that it is a great thing to be physically strong and to view our bodies as something that can help us to achieve amazing things, not just be looked at. As for emotional and mental strength, I think we should simply make it clear to youngsters that girls and women ARE strong in these ways, contrary to the ways we are often portrayed in movies, cartoons and other mediums."

Abbie McManus transitioned from City Ladies through the relaunch before joining Manchester United in 2019. Like most of the earlier players her role models were all men: "Always a male footballer back then because obviously there was no women out there

Abbie McManus with Patrick Vieira, November 2012.

that I could have looked up to. It just wasn't on TV, so I couldn't see it. My role models were the men that I used to watch as defenders, players like Rio Ferdinand, Vincent Kompany… just your typical centre half. I used to watch men's football with my dad and my brother. We used to always have debates about who was the best players and obviously back then City wasn't challenging for titles and so my heroes were at United really."

Goalkeeper **Karen Bardsley** inevitably sought out the best goalkeepers, including one who played for both Manchester

United and City: "I grew up absolutely obsessed with Peter Schmeichel. I just thought he was the best goalkeeper I'd ever seen and I tried to kind of emulate my game based on his and things like that. I was never really that bothered about female goalkeepers, I thought it was cool that Mia Hamm was you know as good as she was, but I never thought 'oh I want to be like Mia Hamm.' I wanted to be like Peter Schmeichel you know because my perception was that he was just at the top of everything, you know."

Karen's captain at City and England **Steph Houghton** grew up in the north-east: "As a big Sunderland fan I would have loved to be next to Kevin Phillips or you'd be dying to be the next [role model] to him. 10 years ago when people were doing the new England kit shoot I was always thinking 'one day I'd love to do that.' That was something I wanted to aim for but for years you don't really believe it could happen. Then it did and it's 'wow!'"

Today's Manchester City players are role models and for some the transition from fan to player is still something to get used to. **Jill Scott** remains modest about her achievements: "I still find that it a bit odd now after the game going to sign autographs. Obviously, it's a fantastic position to be in, but it does still feel weird now, because for me I'm just that young girl that played football – I just got older. That's the only way that I can put it. I think it's important now for the younger players to realise the way that that's going and, as I say, I was lucky enough to be around all the players that kept me grounded. I would never get carried away with things and I'm not really like out there on social media and stuff. I do post a lot but it's usually about football and family and I think I always say to the younger girls 'the best bit of advice I can give you with them social media things is would you shout that in the middle of a shopping mall in front of 1,500 people? Because that's how

Steph Houghton.

Jill Scott.

Karen Bardsley.

Gavin Makel with Esme Morgan.

many people are going to see what you're saying!' I think there are going to be different demands on the younger players now and if I look back and was to do it all again, I would rather keep my journey. We had that bit of normality, so it's important now that we kind of keep them grounded and keep them living in the real world, in case it is to take off too quick for them, if that makes sense."

All City's current squad seem to recognise the significance of acting responsibly as role models. **Karen Bardsley**: "I hope people feel like they can like look up to us. I still struggle to consider myself a role model because I'm just me and this is all I've ever known, you know? But I hope that we can inspire girls to want to play. To want to be professional athletes. To want to achieve and to do whatever they want to do, whether it is football or whether it's any other sport or dream. I want girls to go after their dreams relentlessly. I think that is what I want people to say 'you inspired me to do something that I didn't think I could do.' I think that would be pretty cool."

Abbie McManus: "Your social media goes crazy a lot when you make your international debut. I'm guessing a lot more people are looking at what you're doing as a player, so in a way, I would say that I know that a lot more people are looking at me…

but a role model? I'm not certain. Kids come up to us. They ask us for our autographs and ask questions. It's a great feeling, so I suppose I am."

The head of women's football at City is **Gavin Makel** and he is immensely proud of the way City's leading female players have adapted and become ambassadors for the sport and role models to the next generation: "If you are an eight year old boy living in Moss Side and you want to be Sergio Aguero or you want to be a Manchester City player, you have role models, you've always had role models to look up to. My hero was Gazza being from Newcastle. We all had role models but young girls have not had that. Now a young girl who is a Manchester City fan has the opportunity to look at Steph Houghton and the others and go 'okay, that's where I want to be.' It's no different and we are giving that opportunity and I think that gets missed. It's one of the things that I'm really proud of. Something we've achieved is that we can actually give opportunities and – I know this sounds a bit cliché, - we've given dreams really. We're creating dreams for girls. You can play football at the highest level."

Original boss of the women's team **Neil Mather** agrees: "And actually girls can become a top star and feature on the front cover of the *Shoot* Annual. It's always what I dreamt would happen and to see things like Steph being on the front cover of Shoot, and seeing that women are now treated the same is great. I love going to City's Academy and when I'm there I see the way the girls are treated exactly the same. To see that happen where they are treated exactly the same way… it's so different to how it was in the past. I'm delighted. I just wish I was 30 years younger and we'd all had the opportunities available now. I wish I was Nick Cushing!"

Under 14s 1996-97: Back (L to R) Carol Gregory (manager), Justine Taylor, Hayley Davidson, Rachel Smith, Kate Williamson, Kate Prince, Tracey Grainger, Stacey Skerritt, Amy Gregory, Gail Rothwell (coach);
Front (L to R) Kimberley Windran, Laura Griffiths, Lucy Webb, Sarah Darby, Amy Rothwell, Christy Rustage, Vicky Wray, Jenny Hunter, Nicola Goddard.

Hand me down kits, July 1997.

Junior Teams

Within a year of their first training session in October 1988 City established a reserve team to accommodate the large number of women and girls who wanted to play but this faded as time progressed. The number of players had reduced and City often struggled to find enough players for their first team, never mind a second. Then Derek Heath arrived from Stockport and brought with him several young players. Bev Harrop was a leading member of City's team at the time: "City built, with the help of Derek Heath, a whole junior section and Jane Morley pretty much ran that for several years. She contributed so much to that period and was a good influence on the young girls. We had children's teams for under 10s, under 12s, under 14s, under 16s... it was a proper structure."

By summer 1997 Derek announced via a City Ladies newsletter that the following would manage those age related teams:

Under 10s Bev Harrop, Assistant Manager Vicki Bloor; Under 12s Lesley Wright, Assistant Manager Joni Davies; Under 14s Carol Gregory, Assistant Manager Gail Rothwell (Redston); Under 16s Dave Judge.

Derek also applied for the under 12s and under 14s to play in a new Greater Manchester Girls Youth League set up by the Manchester County FA and the various age related teams entered, often winning, a number of tournaments. Lesley Wright: "We won the Moss Farm Tournament under 10s in our first year. That had never been done before. City had given us some of those Kappa tracksuits of the time but they were all men's and these were young girls! We played in the Lancashire League, which was the only girls league, so we had to travel to Morecambe, Preston and so on."

Jane Morley: "We actually beat Everton in the Moss Farm Tournament. That was some achievement then. Mo Marley came up to me and said that we'd got some cracking players. Lizzie Howells was one of our captains. Nat Taylor…Sarah Massey… Fran Kray… Nicola Twohig…Nicky Bell… I wish those girls we had in the 90s were at that age now because you'd be looking at England internationals. I'm being serious when I say that. They were that good. We had a good rapport with the parents. They were great. We did all our badges. The players were all looked after. The structure was there. In the years that have followed we've been to things like 30th birthday parties for some of the girls we coached. That's absolutely wonderful."

Lesley Wright: "Those girls were fantastic. You get spoiled and it's difficult to match that. It was a great group of girls and they could all play football well. Now you have to be sixteen to play open age football but there are youth leagues which there were very few of when I was playing for City in the early 1990s. There was a big gap and girls weren't able to play but we were one of the few clubs that looked forward and were progressive. Derek came from Stockport and he brought a lot of players across and asked me to run one of the teams. It was a good time for me to stop playing and to concentrate on developing the next generation. Some of the people who were in my under 12s are now in their 30s. I finished playing when I was about 36. I always thought I'd miss it but things weren't going right and I put my energy into the young players. It was a new challenge and I enjoyed it.

"Quite a few of us who'd been involved with City from the first season got involved as well as one or two others who we knew well from other clubs like Jane Morley. We had to do our coaching badges. Initially there was just a bunch of girls who wanted to play. We played at Brampton Road and the league became more structured and we started to play home and away games. Then watching the girls move up into open age was really good. Really satisfying. I left City after about five years of doing this. We were volunteers, bringing our own players in and so on."

Sadly, Derek died within a year of his arrival but the youth set up continued and developed. Louise Wakefield: "We put a shield up in his honour and every presentation night an individual - it didn't matter if you was under 10s or a Manager or a Coach or a Physio - you'd all be eligible to get that shield for that season for your contribution to the club.

"Jane Morley went on to do a lot for the youth section. She set the tone. She did the under 10s without her influence and her arranging stuff and all her efforts with the youth section… I don't think that City would have survived because it was her and certain individuals that were kind of building it all up. You don't realise that, even though you're part of it. I suppose we all helped in a way."

Laura Griffiths, June 1997

Manchester City B at Rhyl.
Back:LucyMoores.NickyBirtles.JacquiKeeler.DaveJudge(Mgr)
Front:RoxanneBrowe.KatePrince.AmyRothwell.LucyWebb.

Lucy on one of her many left-wing runs!

Coverage in the July 1997 newsletter.

Manchester City A at Rhyl.
Back:Carol(Mgr).HayleyDavidson.AliciaMassey.JustineTaylor.AmyGregory.Gail(Coa
Front:CeliaSimpkin.VickyWray.KateWilliamson.LauraGriffiths.

ABOVE.
Manchester City Under 10 girls who reached the Semi-Finals at Leeds Tournament.
Back:Vicky (Asst.Mgr).Carla Cleworth.Nicola Twohig. Leanne Rogers, Bev (Mgr).
Front:Bethan Worasko. Frances Crake, Frances Simpkin, Amy O'Shea, Michaela Goulding
Below.
Vicky Wray and Sarah Darby show off the City kit as worn by the Under14's
v. Cadishead.

118

Bev Harrop is proud of the work done by the players, former players and young footballers during this period: "That structure began working straight away and we had some of the kids that eventually came to play for the first team. We had some very talented kids then. Me and one of the others Vicki Bloor began running the under 12s. It would have been around 2000 and we played up at Haughton Green on a Saturday morning. I enjoyed it."

Emma McDougall playing for Blackburn Rovers.

Jane Morley: "It was great to see and manage the development of young players. It was tremendous. It was a very good club run by some great volunteers with some talented young players. Nat Taylor went to United's school of excellence. Emma McDougall was one of our girls at City when she started playing. She went on to play for Blackburn but died of cancer at 21. I started coaching her when she was 9. Seeing her photo up at Ewood Park was pretty special." Jane often asked Godfrey Williams to join her coaching set up and he remembers that Emma McDougall was a tremendous talent and views her as one of the best players he coached.

The age related teams varied from time to time with coaches sometimes staying with groups as they aged and teams being restructured based on competition requirements. By the end of the 2000-01 season the junior team had found the following successes:

Under 11: Tameside League champions & Tameside League Cup winners in 2001; Under 12 Lancashire League champions, Lancashire Cup finalists, Tameside League champions, Tameside Challenge Cup finalists & Tameside League Cup finalists in 2000; Under 13: Tameside League champions, Tameside Challenge Cup winners, Tameside League Cup winners in 2001.

The following 2001-02 season saw forty junior players as members of the club with three junior teams – under 11 (coached by Jane Morley), under 12 (Bev Harrop) and under 14 (Lesley Wright). There were problems from time to time with how football was structured for girls at a junior level. Lesley Wright: "One of the problems for junior football came when they developed the centres of excellence. You were only supposed to have one in each area, although somehow Liverpool and Everton both had one. In Manchester it was Manchester United that were given it – but they disbanded their women's team – and parents were told that 'if your daughter doesn't go to a centre of excellence then they'll never play for England.' That was said at a meeting I was at. Some of the girls wanted to stay at City but if they had ambition they were led to believe they had to be at a centre of excellence even though there was no progression into a United adult team. That was wrong."

Other issues came around 2002 when decisions at committee level alienated some coaches. There are many reasons and versions of what happened but in the end both Lesley Wright, an original member of the club, and Jane Morley, an experienced manager, felt they had no choice but to leave. The youth system struggled for a period as some players chose to follow their coaches. Lesley, looking for the positives, felt their departure allowed the parent club to become more involved: "Once Jane Morley and I left then City put more effort into the set up and so that worked out good for us all. They then became quite a successful youth set up – probably because we'd left, so that was good. I think City have always wanted a club and a good set up within women's football but, for whatever reason, City couldn't always fund or support it."

City's committee was now predominantly made up of parents of players rather than players or former-players. As with every era of the club up until the relaunch these were all volunteers. John Stanhope, who managed the club for a while in the early 2000s, felt parents contributed a great deal at that time. As well as acting as committee members and coaches they also contributed financially: "Well I know there were dads of kids in the youth - three of them – who chipped in five grand each. That was fifteen grand. It meant we could get to away games… could enter some tournaments and stay over and things like that. It was unbelievable but we were grateful."

Tony Chaloner was one of the parents who became more involved in the club. He became a youth coach between 2003-2007 and then acted as a manager/coach during 2007-2011 of some of City's age related teams. He got involved via interest from his daughter: "I took my daughter Olivia Chaloner who was having to leave Apollo Juniors boys team and Everton wanted her but she was a keen City fan. When I took my daughter I was coaching lads and I just thought the girls training was lacking a little. I was a little too vocal and I'm sure the coaches were not too happy but I was then welcomed on board and I set about working on new training regimes and more physically demanding drills which the girls benefited from immediately."

In 2009 the club won the under 14s Tesco Cup and then in 2011 they also won the under-16s Tesco Cup. Tony is rightly proud of these achievements: "the most exceptional successful group of players City Ladies had ever had, representing England twice in 3 years winning the Tesco cup playing in professional stadiums." Other achievements, according to Tony were: "Beating Manchester United was always special especially to lift the Lancashire League cup."

Between 2003 and 2011 Tony Challoner recorded that the junior teams won the following:

Under 10s
- Tameside league champions
- Tameside league cup champions
- Urmston tournament champions
- Poynton tournament champions
- Preston tournament champions

Under 11s
- Tameside league champions
- Tameside league cup champions
- Urmston tournament champions
- Poynton tournament champions
- Preston tournament champions

Under 12s
- Tameside league champions
- Tameside league cup champions
- Tameside challenge cup champions
- Urmston tournament champions
- Poynton tournament champions
- Preston tournament champions

Under 13s
- Lancashire league champions
- Lancashire league cup champions
- Urmston tournament champions
- Poynton tournament champions

Under 13 B Team 2003-04 seen here after 11-0 win over Denton Town.

- Preston tournament champions
- Thornton-Cleveleys champions

Under 15s (all girls under 14s but have to play up a year)
- Lancashire league champions
- Lancashire league cup champions
- Lancashire county cup champions
- Northern England Tesco Cup champions played at the Hawthorns
- English Tesco Cup champions at the Reebok stadium

According to Tony Challoner there were some problems: "There were many difficult times, from restrictions in the South Manchester League because the other clubs complained we were too good! And the Lancashire League didn't want us winning everything so we ended up playing 2 years above our age and still won everything! Darren Brady did everything for that club - we were two of the most successful coaches the club had ever known."

Another coach from the late 2000s was Alison Smith. She remembers the following achievements as being particularly significant at the time: "Winning the league and cup double with the U10s (2008); Cup finals in the West Lancashire Girls' Football League; and Darren Brady's U16 team going to the finals of a National competition about 2010." Alison believes the greatest players she worked with at the time were: "Amelia Kemp, Fiona Smith, Emily Taylor and Meg Stagg. I became an Assistant Coach… to help out… in 2008. Gained my FA Level 2 Coaching certificate and became a Coach. I became Club Secretary 2010. My family were supportive of my involvement as a coach and Secretary. Both my daughters played for many years in the junior teams. Training was well organised. We tried to get age groups to train together. Had a coach coordinator who developed a detailed player development plan. Collecting training subs, accounting and banking money was a lot of work."

At the relaunch the structure of the entire club changed and now there is a Girl's Academy at City. Gavin Makel, head of women's football said in 2018: "The Girl's Academy for me is a big piece of what we do. I'm very excited by that. Our under 14s in particular… we've got some unbelievably brilliant technical players within that age group, so in three or four years they could be knocking on the door. We might have another Jill Scott on our hands. Hopefully, because that's what the City Football Academy was built for. It's not just a team of all stars. It's building for the future, and the women's side of the club is no different to the men's. That's part of the sustainability of the football club. It is probably easier to do in the women's and girl's game than it is to do in the men's game… being able to bring players right the way through. We've got some exciting plans from a commercial and a marketing point of view. We want to be leading the way and I think we have been doing that over the last couple of years. So it's exciting."

Celebrating promotion to the Northern Combination in 1999-2000. 17 year old Lindsay Savage was top scorer with 26 goals. Below: the team are invited to Maine Road to show off their trophies: Olympic Trophies Challenge Shield, NW Women's Premier League, NW Women's Divisional Cup and the Darwen Ladies 5-aside Challenge Cup.

2000s Seasonal Summary

By 2010 Manchester City Ladies were established as a FA National North side after first achieving promotion in 2001. This was the second highest tier in women's football at the time, behind a national league. The winners of the FA National North would be promoted to the national league and, other than City's first two competitive seasons, this was the highest the club had ever reached, although back in 1989 to 1991 there was no national league (City played in the second tier of a regionalised structure, earning promotion at the end of their second competitive season). The decade had brought stability but there were some major issues too, most notably in 2001-03. Before that however, City began the first season of the new decade in the Northern Combination, after promotion at the end of 1999-2000.

The 2000-01 season began with an easy 6-1 victory over Doncaster Rovers with goals from Claire Jarratt, Ellen Thornton and four from Donna Davidson. Manager Greg Coniglio said in his programme notes for their first home game in the Northern Combination (V Middlesbrough, 10 September 2000): "I was more than delighted to come away from Doncaster Rovers with the three points in a 6-1 win. I have to be honest and admit that the result was not a true reflection of the game as Doncaster battled all the way and played some neat football at times. However, I do believe that we were far from our best and there is a lot of room for improvement."

A set-back followed that game with City losing 2-1 to Middlesbrough, but convincing victories followed in the next two matches – 6-0 at home to Newcastle and 4-0 away at Manchester United. These were exciting times as the team suddenly found itself challenging for promotion. Louise Wakefield felt the club was moving forward at a rapid pace: "You could see it. I mean I could see it anyway, from the progression, on a Friday night. Like you'd turn around at Platt Lane and there would just be a sea of girls and women playing football, training. Hoping to get into the first team. Chair Gary Moores agrees: "I remember beating Manchester United who, as far as I'm aware, never beat us in either the kids games or the open age games. We were always on top. There may have been the occasional draw but it was always us on top."

There was an interesting mix of player and committee members by this time with prominent parents taking on significant roles alongside players and some of the original players from the club's first competitive season. Early players still appearing for the first team of the club included Tracey Blanchard, Gail Redston, Sally Rustige, and Rhoda Taylor while Lesley Wright was a committee member and treasurer. Another original was Joni Davies who was the club's physio, while Godfrey Williams was a coach with the junior teams. Those links with the origins of the club were important to some. Louise Wakefield: "Gail was still there. She was getting involved with the reserves a lot more and it was kind of like that was her baby now… It was like watching Gail form a reserve team with my own eyes." The reserve team went on to win the North West

Women's Reserve League in 2000-01 – their first season in the competition - and they played at Brookway School, Wythenshawe. Dave Judge was the manager of the reserves but Gail Redston was certainly a major contributor at this time. As well as contributing to the reserves she was also the club's player representative.

As well as some of the long established names there were a number of new players brought in. "I realised that after promotion, the size of the squad had to be increased in order to compete with the established teams in the Combination. After months of scouting, the travelling paid off with the new signings of Louise Allwood and Sarah Morris from Stockport, Claire Timmis from Oldham and ex-Manchester United player Kate de-Mouilpied. I realised that there was also talent coming through the club and Roxanne Brown has earned a 1st team call up with some excellent performances for the under 16s," Greg wrote in the Middlesbrough match programme.

The club had moved grounds from Wythenshawe to Flixton FC and a new coach Terry John, formerly of Manchester United Ladies, had joined Greg's management team. It felt as if genuine progress was being made. However, as with the previous season, a number of postponements provided a false position for much of the season and, despite City performing well when they played, by the start of January they were sixth after seven league postponements. There were also postponements in the FA Cup which added to the pressure on the team. Despite this City had knocked out Manchester United (4-1), Stockport Hatters (3-1) and Walsall (2-1; goals from Rhoda Taylor and Lindsay Savage) to reach the fourth round where they were to face Fulham away. Rhoda Taylor: "That was a great experience. On our way down we were convinced we could beat them of course."

The Under 14s drew 1-1 with Everton in front of 20,000 crowd at Goodison Park for Joe Parkinson's Testimonial game v City in August 2000.

Louise Wakefield remembers the trip to Fulham: "Oh it was brilliant. We got an hotel. We played them and they were the first professional team. They paid their players and so everybody went there to play. It was just an amazing experience playing them though. It was the first time that I remember that we all came out suited and booted. We all had training kit. We all looked dead smart. We'd been in an hotel and stuff and it was like 'this is the start of things to come' and our manager said 'we're here as an experience. This is the start of things to come with women's football. You are part of this now. Look, there's money involved.' From there just being six of us at training to this... to go to Fulham away was just massive."

Fulham won the tie 8-0 to remind City of the gulf that still existed between the strongest and wealthiest women's clubs and the rest. Despite that setback the Blues progressed in the league but there were issues behind the scenes. Manager Greg Coniglio resigned. Gary Moores: "I don't know the ins and outs of it. When Greg left I suggested Dave Judge to manage. He'd been at Stockport Ladies and had come over with Derek Heath. He had run various age groups. Another part of the club wanted

Jane Morley and so what we decided to do was to create a joint management team. I think it was the first decision I had to make as chairman. I can't remember how many games were left but it was probably eight or more. They were in a good position but a long way off winning the League."

After a 3-2 defeat by Newcastle on 18 March 2001 City were fourth with eight league games remaining. Fixture congestion as a result of earlier postponed games meant that the team had to play occasional midweek games as well. The travelling was difficult for those with work and family commitments. Bev Harrop: "I stopped playing when we got in to the Northern Premier but I went back. Obviously I'd had a child and I was that bit older and the team had moved on. I wasn't enjoying it because of all the traveling… they were going up to the north east all the time. Four hours away from your baby, and that was just getting there." During the 2000-01 Northern Combination season City's furthest games were all in the north-east as Bev explained: Newcastle 141 miles, Chester-le-street 130, Darlington 108 and Middlesbrough 106.

Under Jane Morley and Dave Judge the team enjoyed a great run of results and rose to first place after defeating Darlington 5-3 on 29 April 2001. There were now two games left to play – Bradford City and

Blackpool Wren Rovers. Gary Moores: "I distinctly remember going to a night match at Bradford which was a really decisive match. They were quite good and we knew it was going to be a tough match. We went up midweek and it was a floodlit game. Just outside Bradford in a lovely valley. There was a bowling green and a cricket club and this little ground. It was a really exciting match because we were pushing for promotion and we won 6-1. We had a backlog of fixtures as there had been lots of postponements. There had also been a good WFA cup run, so all the league matches seemed to be shoved into the last few weeks, so it was quite exciting."

That day the goalscorers included Lindsay Savage, who netted a hat-trick, and Bev Harrop. Once Jane Morley was managing the team Bev had been encouraged to come back: "I came back towards the end of that season and played in a few games. I remember we were playing at Flixton at the time and we had to play against Blackpool Wren Rovers on the last day of the season and whoever won that game went in to the next league up. Jane put me in and I'd not been back playing very long. I was having a bit of a nightmare, but the game was very close, and she was joint managing with Dave Judge and I think he wanted to bring me off. Jane was like 'no, you're not bringing her off. Experience.' And we won that game and that took us where the team came from…the one that's professional now… that's where they came from. I think, given what they have today, I think that team could have gone on and done something very, very, special, I really do. We had some extremely talented players in that team."

As Bev suggested City had now arrived at a level – and at a time in both football and Manchester City history – which would allow a solid base for the future. The team never dropped below this level

Lyndsay Savage

Vicki Bloor

again and links with the male club became closer than they had been since the 1990s, helping to sustain the club. The credit for this achievement lay with a fantastic group of players and coaches and a committee that always managed to work together, thanks to the efforts of its chair Gary Moores. Gary was delighted with the success: "Between Jane and Dave they did an excellent job in getting us promoted that season. Promotion from the Combination into the Premier North in 2001. The Premier North was a tough league and we had about 12 years then before we got promoted again. That promotion in 2001 was a great achievement and it was a really good club spirit. We'd done it together and everyone around us, including the staff, the committee and so on felt we'd achieved something. We pulled it all together. I'd gone from being nominated as chairman to getting the role and helping out with the secretarial work for the first team. I was thrown into the deep end. I had to fill out team sheets and things like that. I felt all of a sudden that I was a part of it."

Jane Morley: "My greatest night in football as a manager ever was when we beat Blackpool Wren Rovers to win promotion as champions. It was at Flixton, our home ground then, and it went to extra time. There was a dog on the pitch at one point! It was 3-3 right to the last moments and then Donna scored and the scenes that night were just amazing. Blackpool were favourites. Half way through the season we were mid-table. We'd been shocking! Then we had a really good run of turning games around. That night just topped everything. I've managed another team to the Cheshire County Cup but that night was my best night as a manager. It was special. That promotion took the club higher than it had ever been and they've never dropped back. There had been a lot of hard work to get there by a lot of people. At that time we were like a family.

We would talk every day and we all seemed to have a shared vision. That soon changed but at the time it was a great atmosphere and a terrific feeling to be part of."

That Blackpool game ended 4-3 and the goalscorers were Donna Davidson (scored 2), who the following season described scoring the winning goal as the best moment of her career, Lindsay Savage and Tracey Blanchard. Tracey had first played for City when Neil Mather was managing the club. In nets was Vicki Bloor who was popular with the rest of the squad. Jane Morley: "Vicki Bloor was an excellent goalkeeper. Absolutely fantastic." Louise Wakefield remembers: "She was very, very, good. She was big and strong. She was agile, but not only that, she was dead encouraging to have behind you. She was intimidating to the opposition. No matter what you did, you felt better when she was in nets because she'd say 'oh, don't worry about that. Let's get on.' Not only that, she talked you through the game, she could obviously see what was happening and she'd talk. I feel that she could have definitely progressed. Definitely gone on and who knows? We had Lyndsey Newman in our team as well. She was very talented. She was very good with her feet but, just the same as all of us, she wasn't getting paid for it. Imagine what players like this could have been like if they'd been able to get paid to play and train? So considering that we didn't get paid… We had to pay and fork out a lot of money. I'd like to see if we did get paid what would have happened."

Winning promotion was perceived as the greatest moment for many members of the squad, including Gail Redston: "After winning promotion came my best ever day. We played United in a charity game and it was the day Keegan arrived at the men's team. There wasn't that many there but, because we'd won the Combination that year, Jane Morley said 'right, you all stay in the changing rooms before kick-off. Don't go out yet.' When we came out to the tunnel Manchester United, who we were playing, had done a guard of honour. They clapped us on and the League were there with the cup to present it to us. A Manchester United guard of honour! It was just a perfect day."

Gail enjoyed being a member of that squad and recognised the talented players the Blues had: "Lindsay Savage was youngest for a long time. Amy Gregory was another that was coming through from the Under 14s. I remember Roxanne Brown too. There was still players like Bev Harrop, Jane Boardman, Donna Davidson – a quality striker, Kim Hines, Vicki Bloor – a big strong keeper as well."

According to Gary Moores: "Lindsay Savage was one of the main reasons we got promoted in 2001 but I wouldn't want to pick any player out because it was the whole team that contributed. It was a collective success. Everybody contributed and Dave Judge and Jane Morley brought that success as managers." Lesley Wright agrees: "Lindsay Savage came from Stockport and was part of the youth set up who progressed all the way through. I never actually played with her but she was an excellent player."

"The club experienced the most successful season in its history, with four teams winning their respective leagues, one doing a league and cup double and the under 13s completing an unprecedented treble," the match programme for the game with Coventry on 2 September 2001 accurately reported but behind the scenes the politics of a growing football club were beginning to cause issues. Chair Gary Moores: "There was a lot more politics to the club than I'd expected when I took on the role of chairman. I felt, about 18 months into it, that I was trying to be a diplomat more than anything. I didn't like to see anybody ostracised or run out of town. Everybody

Lyndsey Newman   *Ellen Thornton*

that I spoke with seemed to understand that I was trying to find the best in everybody and smooth things over. I'm not sure I did it that well but I did try my best to bring everyone together."

One of the biggest issues concerned the role of manager. Jane Morley and Dave Judge had brought success together as a managerial duo but some within the club felt this was unsustainable. Jane: "Myself and Dave Judge were asked to manage the team. Collectively we brought back players who felt isolated and we changed the structure of how we played. Then there was that famous night against Blackpool Wren Rovers and we won promotion as champions. That summer I went to the FA meetings and was put down as the manager. I went to the AGM at the FA and then during that period something behind the scenes was happening. Parents started telling me of things that were happening."

Gary Moores: "The first year after we'd been promoted myself, Jane Clark and Jane Morley went down to be accepted into the league and we met at Soho Square, the FA Headquarters. It felt 'wow, this is big time.'

It wasn't a meeting at a working men's club in Lancashire somewhere, it was down in London at the FA!" Jane Clark: "I remember that first trip down to Soho Square and it felt weird, to be sitting alongside Doncaster Belles and Arsenal and all of these other clubs. Looking around and seeing all of these familiar faces and we felt a bit intimidated really!"

Gary recognised the contribution Jane Morley had made in getting the club to this point: "Dave Judge and Jane Morley worked well together and got us that promotion in 2001. They each came from different sides of the club really. Jane was friends with the older members of the club and Dave was part of the new regime coming through. We thought after a few committee meetings that it wasn't right and decided we'd go outside of the club for the next season's manager. We thought that the dual role wouldn't work moving forward and that if either one was given the job permanently on their own that it would upset one half of the club. We had several applicants for the job and all the committee decided to go for John Stanhope. It was still a voluntary role but we advertised it and did a proper recruitment process. We did have some who came for interviews who thought they were going to get paid. They soon had their bubble burst! John never came to the club saying he was an experienced manager as such but I think he did a pretty good job of it. I think it was tough because we were playing at a higher level than ever before."

As well as the changes at managerial level there were steps being taken by some members of the committee to get further support from the men's club. For most of the period up to the influx of players and committee members in 1996-97 the Ladies team had a good relationship with the male club via City in the Community. City Ladies had been established by Manchester City

staff and was perceived as a positive arm of the parent club, however support did vary. The men's team entered its worst ever period on the pitch around the same time as the women began to develop a new structure. The old contacts and relationships began to change and it seems, from interviews for this book, that a stronger City Ladies committee in the late 1990s meant there was less of a need to cultivate the relationship with the men's club. This is a shame but understandable. The late 1990s committee was more than able to manage and develop the women's club but some of the old relationships with the men's club seemed to be overlooked in favour of a vision solely for the women's club. By 2001 both the structure of the men's club and the women's club was somewhat different to what had existed in 1997. Club captain Jane Clark (now Boardman) believes the 2001 promotion allowed the women's and men's clubs the opportunity to talk about developing their relationship: "Before then it wasn't the right time because we weren't playing at the right level. We were working our way through the North West Leagues up to the Northern Premier League which ultimately we were in when I stopped playing for the first team, but we were happy with that. It was incremental and we could see that year on year [Manchester City] were showing more interest. They were giving us more and that was the right way to do it I think, building up that trust and making the relationship have longevity effectively."

Gary Moores: "There was a lot of confusion around this time because although we were openly recognised by Manchester City and the club helped us in certain areas, we weren't receiving money off the club. Any money we had had to be raised. City allowed us to do bucket collections and players paid subs. In some ways it was a big help having the Manchester City Ladies name in that it attracted players and coaches. There's no doubt about that. But the downside was that we didn't get any sponsorship hardly from anybody. That was a big downside plus we were always very conscious that we didn't upset the men's club by taking on opposing sponsors to the men's sponsors. We had our hands tied to some extent. We could get some sponsors for junior teams but we couldn't put anything on the kit because we always wanted them to wear the proper Manchester City kit."

Gary Moores and Jane Boardman decided it was time to strengthen the relationship and put it on a more formal basis. In essence to take it back to a relationship similar to that enjoyed in the early 1990s. Jane: "Me and Gary ultimately used my connections that I had through my work to finally getting in with the club, because one of my partners at work loved the fact I played for City, but he also knew that we didn't have any link with the club. He called me in one day and he said 'I've got you an hour with Chris Bird' (Manchester City's Managing Director). He said 'Go and tell him what you're doing.' I pulled together a PowerPoint slide deck setting out all the facts of what we were doing, what we wanted and what our ask was of the club. Very deliberately we decided we weren't going to ask for money - we wanted closer links, we wanted acknowledgement and we wanted opportunities to raise our profile that were going to cost the club nothing but could potentially be very lucrative relative to

Jane Clark.

how we were funding the club at that time. Things like doing bucket collections at the ground; things like having half a page in the programme, once every six months; having the opportunity to do announcements at half time when we'd won the League and that sort of thing... Walk around the pitch with our trophy, nothing huge. And so Gary and I did that meeting. I presented the whole thing and Chris loved it and said 'yes, we absolutely want to do this.' The fact that we'd gone straight to Chris at the start was great because his sponsorship was always there and he'd made it clear to Vicky Kloss (Head of Communications) that it was important to him and so she was able to sort of wave that mandate around."

During the late 1990s and early 2000s Chris was the key link between Manchester City and the fans. He had been raised in Hattersley and knew what life was like for the majority of supporters of the club. As a result he was keen to establish a number of fan related initiatives while also focusing on the resurrection of the club. He was keen to ensure that Manchester City represented all aspects of Mancunian life, including football as played by women: "I was involved and promoted the support of the team to board level and to potential sponsors. Supporting the team was something I felt was not only the right thing to do but also it was an opportunity to grow our community programme in schools and develop more girls playing in the future."

Jane Boardman: "Chris gave us an hour and a half of his time, which was very precious at that time, and he trusted us. I think he could see that what we were trying to do was, as professional as it could be, given the circumstances that we were in in terms of funding and everything else. All we wanted was to be recognised as being part of Manchester City and to be trusted to wear those shirts and represent the club. We didn't have a right to use the name but we wanted to affirm that right because we thought if we didn't affirm that right they could set up Manchester City Women and our club would just fall apart. But it was a gradual thing. For me and Gary that meeting with Chris Bird was a massive success. For some of the girls they were like 'what they giving us?' They expected that there would be some sort of helicopter coming past with a massive aid relief box that dropped on the pitch at Platt Lane and we'd suddenly be millionaires but it was very gradual. That was fine because we recognised we needed to build up the trust. We also wanted to keep the control, because everyone was emotionally invested in it."

As Jane explained the discussions between the women's team and the club continued for some time. It was a gradual process but according to some, discussions were going on without the full knowledge of the committee. It would all come to a head later in the 2001-02 season but before that occurred there was the small matter of playing in the FA National North for the first time. For this first season at that level the structure of the committee was recorded as Chairman: Gary Moores, Secretary: Pauline Fowler, Treasurer: Lesley Wright, Commercial Manager: John Pidgeon, First Team Manager: John Stanhope, Reserve Team Manager: Dave Judge, Under 14 Manager: Lesley Wright, Under 12 Manager: Bev Harrop, Under 11 Manager: Jane Morley, and Club Captain: Jane Clark.

John Stanhope began preparations for the 2001-02 season but he felt it was a difficult task at times. He knew that he was replacing the joint managership of Dave Judge and Jane Morley and understood why the committee decided to appoint a new face: "I think that was probably the right idea. You've got players who would play for one person more than they would another. They got on with them better or they knew that they were going to be guaranteed. A lot of the players thought Jane Morley was going to get the job. Then somebody else has come in and suddenly you're not now guaranteed the first team place because that person doesn't know you. That person doesn't know any of you, so somebody else who hasn't got in previously might suddenly get enthused. I noticed a lot of the younger ones were the ones that were getting enthused not necessarily the ones that had won things… they suddenly thought 'oh, I've got a chance here.'

"I remember playing Sheffield Wednesday. It was the first match and we got beat 3-0 and I knew Wednesday's manager, 'you've got a lot of women runners there.' I said 'I know. I'm pleased because the ones that are the willing workers are the young ones.' We then went and played Coventry twice, which was a blessing in disguise a little bit. We got two wins and they were bad. They'd come up and quite clearly you could see players hadn't realised but they had a manager who hadn't managed at this level. You could see him on the sideline and he was wide-eyed thinking what's going on here. I knew we were not the developed article, not by a long way, and yet we won 3-1 and 3-0. The flip side was that it back-fired a little bit on our girls because then they thought 'oh, we just walked two divisions and we can walk this.' That's why football so hard. I felt it was going to be a long winter and it was because games got

2001-02 at Maine Road.

cancelled. After the third game Gary Moores said 'you've got to be happy with that.' I said 'I am, but it's not going to work. It really isn't going to work.' I promised him I would give everyone a fair chance and wouldn't change anything until after Christmas. So there was nothing I could do. We just had to plod on and get through. Gary then got nervous because a team was going to fold and that would mean we'd be in the bottom two. I told Gary 'Don't worry about it. I've seen this before. We won't.' In November a team folded."

Records show that North Notts withdrew from the league after eleven games. John: "They went bump and I knew about the new league rules that meant only one team would go down if that situation occurred. I thought 'thank God for that. It's going to be Coventry, there's no doubt about it.' So I felt we were safe and that then gave me the green light to start doing the changes because I'd said to Gary Moores 'I promise you I will not do anything until Christmas, so that they all have their chance.' Now I could make my changes."

By the end of October 2001 City were tenth out of eleven surviving clubs. They'd suffered a 4-1 defeat to Aston Villa and a 4-0 loss at Sheffield Wednesday in consecutive weeks. In his programme notes for the Villa game John Stanhope gave his views on the Wednesday defeat: "Go to sleep, make mistakes and you get punished. I've no complaints, no excuses but we have got to learn very quickly."

Gary Moores: "Playing in the FA National Northern Division was a massive step up. I felt that as chairman but I know the players felt that as well. Some were disappointed because they felt they'd do one promotion and then another but it wasn't like that. It was just a little bit faster all over the pitch. I'm no football expert but in my amateur way of watching it was a little bit faster everywhere. Every team we faced had a little bit more in every area. Over all it was a massive leap because it all added up. In the combination you'd find teams with two or three outstanding players and the rest were making the numbers up but this was different. There was also the added complication that we were now dealing with the FA down in London and everything on my side had to be accurate and thorough. There was no room for mistakes because you could get serious fines or points deductions. All the leagues we had experienced were strict and their administration had to be right, but this was the FA and they were based in London, not around the corner. Tessa Haywood at the FA was helpful and she helped us settle."

John Stanhope felt the club needed to decide whether it wanted to push onwards and upwards or settle for life at the level they had reached: "They'd just had two back-to-back promotions and clearly morale was through the roof, as they had every right, you know and I thought this is good. I think the enthusiasm shone through rather more than the technical or the tactical cunning of what was going to be needed. You were going to need both. I remember one girl said 'I've not come here to do this, I want to play football' and I thought 'fair enough.' Maybe I could have learnt a little lesson there, because I wanted them to move on and have that drive that probably didn't really need to be there for them if you see what I mean. You win the title and then you get in to the Premier… the strain would have been unbelievable because then you'd have had to go to Arsenal and who is paying for all this? In a way you did well not to go up."

There's some logic in what John says. The 2001-02 season was perhaps the first when the long term direction of the club had to be discussed and assessed. By this time the structure of football for women was such that the FA wanted a strong national league supplemented by regional leagues of quality. To participate at the highest level needed a well-structured club. City had structure and depth but there were also issues. John Stanhope: "I noticed how a lot of it had become political and there were things

that were going on off the pitch… If you go back to the beginning, to 1988, none of that would have entered any of their heads. So you could see there, in an odd way, how far it had progressed. It's a strange way to look at it but it's valid."

Progression up the leagues at a time when the FA put more support and displayed more interest in women's football than at any time previous, brought issues of structure, finance, control and power within the club. John Stanhope: "That 2001-02 season I was doing the first team and then you had Jane Morley was looking after the youth section. Dave Judge was my Assistant and Eddie Gregory was the physio. I could have brought a couple of lads in but I thought these lads knew these players so I'll stick with them, you know what I mean? They were good lads and it was probably the best decision I made. They knew them, you know, and obviously Amy Gregory was Eddie's daughter. There is an argument to say we shouldn't have father and daughter, that could be bad, but it's two schools - it'll either work or it'll go wrong. Fortunately it worked but that was down to Eddie. He was a fair fellow. He would say if Amy hadn't done well or if she had done well. So we're all good and we used to have, every month, a Committee Meeting, and that would be Gary as Chairman, me and Dave representing the first team, Jane Morley and Lesley Wright representing the youth and then Reno Dionisiou, who was the secretary."

The rise up the divisions had happened so fast that the club had to move forward quickly. Ground requirements had to be met plus extra roles were needed. John: "We needed a first aid person for example." This rapid development was changing the feel of the club for some. Gary Moores: "So around 2001-02 the club was moving from a close knit group of friends to becoming part of the bigger club. That's what was developing and

City were getting more and more involved and we were asking to be more integrated. John and myself had been pushing really hard for a closer tie with the club. I'd always wanted the men's club to fully takeover the ladies team ever since I arrived. That was Derek Heath's dream and unfortunately we lost him, but he was right. John was getting some criticism and I think some thought I was being too pally with John but I wasn't. I just felt it was unfair to, again, get rid of another manager because some players didn't like him. We'd been through too many managers."

Gary Moores and Jane Clark were pursuing the discussions with City while John Stanhope was trying to build a team capable of challenging for promotion, but on the pitch the struggles of the new division continued. In January 2002 it was announced that John had signed Welsh international goalkeeper Andie Worrall. This was seen as a major acquisition and led to the player being introduced to Manchester City fans before a men's game at Maine Road. Within the next twelve months or so other significant names arrived including Mel Garside, Emma Davies, Nicky Davies and Stacey Copeland. John: "Nicky Davies was a great signing. She was a central midfield pocket dynamo that just broke everything down. I was determined to build our spine. That was important. Mel Garside came and she'd played for England. I think this is what Gary had seen in me that I could get these players in. Stacey Copeland was a good left winger. She'd whip balls in and she knew me from England youth tournaments so she was happy to come over. We got her from Doncaster Belles. So I was happy with that. Emma Davies we got from Everton and she was an international too. We were getting good players. We're getting proven quality and I was trying to keep the young kids happy too."

The 2001-02 season ended with City tenth out of eleven, avoiding relegation thanks to the resignation of the North Notts team. It was a relief in some ways when the season ended, however tensions over the final weeks were high off the pitch. According to John a number of established players began to make their feelings known: "We had two sort of divisions in the team and it came to a head at Aston Villa away. You pick the squad on the Friday night, 'see you on Sunday', and seven of them didn't turn up. We had 11! So anyway we went down there and we won 1-0 and people were really happy. You could see one or two in the dressing room that didn't feel comfortable having felt as though they'd let their mates down but played because they wanted to play. It was like there were three camps, you know, like a venn diagram."

For several long established players 2002 marked their departure from the club. Bev Harrop: "Worst moment was probably

Andie Worrall

towards the end in the way that we left. It had suddenly gone from this team, this really good team, that were all so close. It all then became really fragmented and there was a lot of stuff going on. I don't know if it was the fact that you know we'd built this team that had done so well. Maybe you know people couldn't see that that team could take it further. There were still some young players in that team that were very talented and that team broke up because of what happened. That involved people that weren't even playing."

Gail Redston: "I was playing for the reserves a little bit and now and again playing for the first but there was a little bit of controversy going on. I don't know what was going on. It was like we didn't exist. So four of us decided we're off, so there was the likes of myself, Rhoda Taylor, Bev Harrop and Clare Jarratt... we went to Oldham, playing in the same league. I played there for like two or three years."

John Stanhope: "I think one or two people weren't happy with the way the club was going. I wanted it much more professional. Looking back, I don't know, there's always give and take, but we had players who were approaching their 40s and in their 40s who wanted to play reserve team football. I said 'I want a definite link from the youth in to the first team.' I wanted it so that these kids can see a pathway."

For chair Gary Moores this was an upsetting time and one he had hoped he could have resolved by finding a way to keep the experienced players involved: "Hand on heart I would've loved to set up a veteran's team which may have kept some people part of the club." John agreed: "We looked to see if we could get an over 35s or a five aside team or anything, just to keep people playing, but there wasn't anything. It was hard enough getting fixtures at times you know what I mean. That side of the game

and that spread of it just wasn't there and it was hard. At times I felt we had to do things that you didn't really want to do to get the job done, but then again that is part and parcel of management anyway. What's the old saying? How do you keep your squad happy, or your first team happy? Keep the six that don't like you away from the five that haven't made their mind up."

The playing changes were not the only issues however as some committee members felt they were being excluded. The whole period is difficult to make judgements on as it seems every individual acted in what they thought was a reasonable manner. All of the people involved had been keen to see City develop and progress but, for whatever reason, that was not recognised or understood by all. Jane Morley: "My involvement ended in 2002. At that time there were meetings taking place with officials of Manchester City – the club – that only certain members of the committee were invited to. There was a meeting at Platt Lane when it all came out. Some of the parents were unhappy with the way it was all going as well. There were lots of unsavoury things at this time and I felt there was no option but to leave. I was then approached by Fletcher Moss who were setting up a girls section and I went there. People like Lesley Wright, Rita Howard, Rhoda Taylor, Gail Redston.... their dedication and years of service, keeping that club going and building the foundations seemed to be overlooked. I really felt for Lesley." Lesley Wright: "I love City and the way it has now gone but that period was awful. People don't see the whole thing. Jane Morley had achieved so much."

Once Lesley and Jane left many of the junior players who had been coached by them chose to join their new club Fletcher Moss, leaving many significant gaps in City's structure. John Stanhope: "What happened then was we ended up with one girl and I

Mel Garside

positions of Reserve Team Manager, Under 13s and Under 11s Manager were vacant. Within three weeks most of the positions had been filled with the match programme for the game with Ilkeston on 29 September 2002 recording that there was now a Junior Head Coach: Roger Bryan, a Player Rep: Sarah Jackson, an Equipment Director: Edmund Gregory and Becky Jones was under 13s manager.

The opening league game of the season saw City face Oldham Curzon which now contained four former City players – Bev Harrop, Clare Jarratt, Gail Redston and Rhoda Taylor. Both Taylor and Redston had appeared for City in the inaugural season of 1988-89 while Bev had joined shortly after. Their move to Oldham was a significant loss to City and they helped Oldham achieve a 3-1 victory over City. Gary Moores: It was a shame the way things happened because I think we could have found a way. It was a sad time. At this time Vicky Kloss (City's Head of Communications) was a massive help and she kept us sane – both myself and Jane Clark was heavily involved. Dave Judge, Eddie Gregory and John worked hard… Reno was back on board as well and they all worked hard because we'd lost quite a few players at all levels. We had a rebuilding exercise to do. There was a bit of a Dunkirk spirit."

Louise Wakefield and Lindsay Savage remained, and there were still several key players of quality alongside the experienced players John had brought in. Future boxer Stacey Copeland was one of City's stars. According to Louise Wakefield: "We'd signed quite a lot of big players by then and had signed like Stacey Copeland, who is a professional boxer now. She was up and down the wing. She was so strong. We signed her from Doncaster Belles and we'd signed Mel Garside from Donny Belles because John Stanhope was at City."

looked at Gary and Gary looked at me and he says 'what are we going to do about the youth section? We haven't got one.' A long summer followed. We went out. We went to schools. We asked City if they could help because in the summer they had the summer camps. We had a training open day at the end of July about 50 girls turned up. They all thought that they were going for trials, not knowing that the fact that they'd turned up got them in. By the time the season started we were absolutely made up because we had five teams and one of them, the under 11s, had two teams, we had to split them."

By September 2002 the structure of the club had changed and the match programme against Liverpool on 8 September that year listed Chairman: Gary Moores, Secretary Reno Dionisiou, Treasurer: Jane Clark, First Team Manager: John Stanhope & Dave Judge, Under 15s Manager Craig Richards & Steve Mills, Club Captain: Jane Clark, Trainer: Jimmy Shields, Club Doctor: Mei-Mei Ng, and Physio: Kate de Mouilpied. The

Amy Gregory

Lyndsay Savage

During 2002 John's mum was serious ill and the pressure of the rebuild and other changes were inevitably taking their toll. As with all City's officials the managerial role was unpaid at this time. John: "You're not just not being paid, you're losing money. I'm ringing Gary; Gary's ringing me. We had to do a programme - I was doing it on the Friday night when they come back from training. Getting that ready, then cobbling it all together on the Saturday morning. That's when I wasn't at youth matches, because I was helping Louise Wakefield - she was a first team player who wanted to do a bit of training and help the kids and all that. So I said to her 'if you'll do that, then I'll come down and help' and she said 'right, you're on'. It was good in a way, because then you could keep an eye on all the other teams that were playing at the same time and they could see that you were there as a first team manager. I was genuinely watching the kids thinking 'she's alright, she's not so bad', so you could see that link and Gary would come down

now and again when he could. He had his own business. He must have lost thousands over the years."

Jane Boardman: "You got a real sense that everyone was just playing their part and we had a really, really good team spirit. We'd meet either at Maine Road or at Tesco's in East Didsbury to get the bus on a Sunday morning and either Gary, as Chairman, or the Manager, would be driving the bus. City gave us a bus, you know, a pretty old bus, but it just meant we didn't have to hire a bus every week, or drive in cars, as we'd been doing before. It just created more team spirit because we were all in one place, all the way there and all the way back, and we'd have singing and stopping for a wee and all the other things that go with that."

Louise Wakefield: "Jane was very good for the club, you know. When she was captain and I was vice captain we'd go to functions. We used to go to City Supporters Club branches and they used to meet in these pubs and stuff. Me and Jane went and just sat there and there was all these men firing questions at us, like 'what's it like being a woman playing football' and stuff like that, I'd give them some sarcastic remark back whereas Jane would talk diplomatically and so she was really influential to the club."

The 2002-03 season was one of struggle and John Stanhope's mum's illness got worse: "She'd had cancer for a while, and I said to Gary I want to just step back a little bit, he said, that Dave Judge was there and he could do the job. I was asked if I'd want to do the reserves and I said 'you've still got the same problem, it's that time away. I'm not sure

how long she's going to live, so I'd rather spend that time on Sunday with my Mum than traipsing up and down the motorways' and I couldn't dedicate that time."

Gary Moores: "When John stopped managing we asked Dave Judge to become manager again. He was running the reserve team but came in for the back end of the season and kept us up. Losing John with 7 or 8 games left teetering at the bottom of the table. Dave Judge and Eddie Gregory kept us up. We had a couple of seasons of struggle."

Despite an influx of players City were still in survival mode in their second FA National Northern Division season. There had been some great moments, such as on 15 December when Mel Garside earned City a point with an equaliser in the 85th minute at Liverpool, but by the time of John stepping down the Blues had only managed two League victories – 4-0 against Middlesbrough in September (early goals from Laura Gligan and Louise Wakefield then two from Amy Gregory) and then a 3-0 win at Sheffield Wednesday in October. There had also been a disappointing third round defeat in the FA Cup. The game had gone to extra time and City had come close but opponents Leicester scored within the first additional five minutes and that was enough.

August 2003

Action from City v Liverpool in 2003/04.
Top Left: Mel Garside; Top Right: Louise Wakefield; Bottom: Chloe Llewellyn

On 23 February the home game with neighbours Oldham Curzon, with several former City players in their squad, ended 5-0 to the visitors and left the Blues tenth out of 12 clubs. Worse was to follow with a couple of postponements and then a 4-2 defeat at Wolves, leaving the club rock bottom of the Northern division for the first time ever. Gary Moores: "Every game felt like a cup final. I remember going to Ilkeston that was a six pointer and we had to win it (April 2003). Because the coaches were so busy I had had to go down to watch them play midweek. I'm no football expert but I said I'd go and watch them. I think it was luck rather than good judgement but I'd spotted that their 'keeper had a bad leg or something and she was getting one of the defenders to take the goal kicks. So I mentioned this to Dave Judge and so he put a forward on the edge of the box and we ended up scoring a couple of goals from the clearances because of course they wouldn't be offside."

Thanks to Gary's tactical suggestion, the coaching of Dave Judge and the dedication of the players the game with Ilkeston ended 5-0. It was their first victory in all competitions since 23 October 2002. Sadly, a 2-1 defeat to Middlesbrough followed but victories in City's next couple of games, followed by a goalless draw on the last day of the season at home to Sheffield Wednesday meant the team finished the season eighth out of twelve clubs.

A period that John Stanhope later called 'The tumultuous years' had seen the club survive at the highest level it had ever played at. The following season, 2003-04, City finished seventh out of eleven clubs, under Dave Judge. Survival in the division still remained the club's priority and, although ambition remained high, the next step simply didn't seem possible. On 27 March 2005 City were defeated 1-0 by Sunderland. Playing for Sunderland that day were Steph Houghton and Jill Scott. Lindsay Savage remembers playing against these future City stars that season: "Personally I hated playing against Jill Scott. She is never still and you feel like you had to run a marathon tracking her runs. Sunderland always had fantastic teams and wanted to get the ball down and play." That defeat had followed a 3-0 loss in August with Steph Houghton netting twice for Sunderland. Louise Wakefield, who was now one of the longest serving players and

Natalie Thomas and (right) Nicky Twohig in action v Sunderland, August 2004.

a major contributor to the direction of the club used to do her best to encourage some of the league's greatest players to join City. Louise Wakefield: "I tried my best to get Jill Scott and others to sign for us. I used to try and get them all the time. If ever I saw them 'I'd go oh please.' I remember going up to Jill, like on a drunken night out and I went 'oh, come on', and I'll never forget her going 'how am I supposed to get to training? I'm from Sunderland.' I tried whenever I saw someone from another team who I felt would add something. Then all of a sudden it got big and Jill and the others I'd tried were there."

The 2004-05 season ended with City tenth out of twelve clubs and it became the last one managed by longserving coach Dave Judge. According to reports at the time he stepped down due to health reasons. 29 year old Steve Walmsley, who had been a coach with the club for the previous year, became the new manager. Gary Moores: "We started to hit the bottom again. Dave Judge had done a good job but in his last season he had to go in for an operation on his leg and the committee thought at the time that we should ask Steve Walmsley to take over. Steve had been his assistant, along with Eddie Gregory. Steve had some good ideas and had got his coaching badges and so on. Dave left to concentrate on his leg operation but we left it open ended so that he could come back. As it turns out he never came back and Steve took over."

In 2005 Steve Walmsley told *femalesoccer.net*: "It's obviously fantastic for myself, but it has come as a bit of a shock. I would never have dreamed to have landed a position like this at my age. But at least it shows me I must be doing something right.

"You just want to get going as soon as possible. The season

Coverage of the opening of the 2004-05 season in the men's match programme.

ITY Ladies play host to top of the table Sunderland tomorrow looking for their first win of the season.

The Ladies, who play their matches at Abbey Hey F.C. in Gorton, kicked off their season with a 2-0 loss to Oldham on the opening day of the season and then went down 6-1 to local rivals Blackburn Rovers.

But Chairman Gary Moores is confident that the Ladies will be able to turn around their poor start to the season – starting with an upset tomorrow.

Gary said: "We have a couple of important players away at the moment which is making a difference - saying that we didn't deserve to win last week.

"I still think we will have a good season and hopefully we will cause an upset tomorrow.

"We have a good young squad, with some good individual players – we just need to start playing as a team."

Tomorrow's game in the FA Premier Northern Division kicks off at 2pm – entry costs £2 for adults, 50p for children and free for girls under 16.

For more information about Manchester City Ladies visit their website **www.mancityladies.com** or contact Chairman Gary Moores on 07802271 414.

LADIES GAMES...

15 Aug	H	Oldham Curzon	0-2
22 Aug	A	Blackburn Rovers	1-6
29 Aug	H	Sunderland	
5 Sep	A	Wolverhampton W.	
12 Sep	A	Middlesbrough (L/Cup)	
15 Sep	H	Tranmere Rovers*	
19 Sep	A	Stockport County	
26 Sep	H	Middlesbrough	
3 Oct	H	Wolverhampton W	
10 Oct		L/Cup	
13 Oct	A	Tranmere Rovers *	
17 Oct	A	Coventry City	
24 Oct	A	Aston Villa	
31 Oct	H	Sheffield Wed	
7 Nov		L/Cup	
14 Nov	A	Lincoln City	
21 Nov	H	Stockport County	
28 Nov	A	Middlesbrough	
5 Dec		FA Cup 3rd/Rd	
12 Dec	A	Coventry City	
19 Dec	H	Aston Villa	
9 Jan		FA Cup 4th/Rd	
16 Jan	A	Sheffield Wed	
23 Jan	H	Lincoln City	
30 Jan	A	Oldham Curzon	
6 Feb	H	Blackburn Rovers	
13 Feb	A	Sunderland	

Matches usually 2pm ko. (* = 7.30pm ko)
Home venue: Abbey Hey FC, Gorton.

FA Premier Northern Division

	P	Pts
Sunderland	2	6
Blackburn	2	4
Tranmere	2	4
Oldham	2	4
Sheffield W.	2	4
Lincoln	2	1
Wolves	2	1
M'brough	2	1
Stockport	2	1
Coventry	2	1
CITY	2	0

Midfielder Emma Sconce skips past an Oldham defender.

Winger Amy Gregory beats the full-back for pace in City's 2-0 defeat.

Reebok

CITY v CHARLTON

doesn't start until August, but I've got a whole summer of pre-season training. I have brought a few personal touches to the job already, like introducing fitness regimes and health meals. And I'd like to think I've changed things with Sport Science, but they are already at a high level. But I've got a good management team and a good structure behind me, and some good youth players coming through the system."

Steve had previously been manager of Darwen Ladies and Burnley Ladies in 2001 and was at Liverpool's Garswood for a time before joining City: "I know I have to keep my feet on the ground, and understand that chances like this don't come around all the time. Manchester City are one of the top 30 clubs in the country. They have been finishing in the top eight or nine consistently for the past few years, but my first aim is to get into the top six. After Christmas we will reassess things, but there are a lot of good teams and a lot of quality in this league."

The 2005-06 season brought some good victories, such as a 4-1 win at Tranmere in the third match of the season when Lindsay Savage, Natalie Thomas, Nicola Twohig and Levi Wensley all netted and a tense 6-5 win over Fulham in the League Cup, but the season was much the same as the previous ones and ended with the Blues eleventh out of twelve clubs, avoiding relegation by four points. Gary Moores: "We had another close scrape with the bottom of the table. We were still all volunteers and so the hours people put in were unbelievable. So many contributed. If I hadn't have been self-employed then there's no way I could have done what I did. I was spending time during the day 'phoning the FA or arranging referees or whatever. If I'd have been working for a company I couldn't have done that. I'd have been sacked. I wasn't the only one who did that of course."

To survive at this level of football was significant and a major achievement for all involved with the club. The playing squad included several players who had been there

Heidi Cullum

Jo Mitchell

for some time, most notably Lindsay Savage, and the involvement of people like Gary Moores, a prominent committee man since the 1990s, and Niki Taylor, who had become a key logistical figure, ensured the club was in good hands. It took an incredible amount of effort to sustain a club at this level and simply surviving in the Premier North was a major achievement. The relationship with City's men's club was still there of course and had got stronger through, specifically, the efforts of Jane Clark and Gary Moores, but Manchester City Ladies did manage its own affairs.

That season had seen City face old foes Arsenal, who had first met City back in 1990 at Arsenal's training ground, in the League Cup. Just as in 1990 one of the team's was surprised at the level of facilities the other possessed except, instead of

City being impressed it was Arsenal who were somewhat surprised. Gary Moores: "I remember us playing Arsenal Ladies in the cup at Flixton. Vic Akers wasn't too impressed. He wasn't happy at all and we put them in this tiny changing room which didn't go down too well. They appeared on the club coach and with bottles of Arsenal drinking water and when they opened the door of the changing room you could see their faces." Arsenal won 4-0 and the match was a culture shock to both clubs, though for different reasons.

In 2006-07 the Blues finished tenth again, three points above the relegation zone, and within weeks the team's website, *Mancityladies.com*, announced that Leigh Wood, who had been part of the coaching staff since 2005 and had guided the reserve team to promotion, would be the new first

NOVEMBER

CITY LADIES FIRST XI
2005-06

team manager. It was a positive step. Gary Moores: "Leigh had been about 12 or 18 months as reserve team manager before he became the manager. There had been some debate about whether Eddie Gregory should take on the role at the time but he didn't have the right badges, although he had a great football brain. I think it was a split decision with the committee. It was very tight but Leigh got it and did a wonderful job. It was a shame we didn't try Eddie for 12 months because of the amount of years he had been there but that would've let my heart rule my head. But we knew that Leigh wouldn't hang around, so if Eddie had been given the job we may have lost Leigh as well."

Louise Wakefield

In August 2007 the new coaching line up was announced with Chris Twohig as assistant manager; John Lucas as head physio and fitness instructor; Jenna Gilbert as physio; Martin Williamson and Tom O'Connell as sports masseurs; reserve team manager was to be Ryan Matthews (previously looked after the under 16s); assistant reserve team manager was former club captain Jane Clark who had joined the club shortly before the influx from Stockport in 1996. In her new role Jane came across a player who went on to become a star in the WSL for City: "There's one player now playing for City who I used to play with at City? Abbie McManus. She was playing for City reserves when I was captain in the reserves. I played alongside her at the back. You could see then she was a player. She was fantastic but you know she was 14 when I was 34 or whatever. Maybe until she stops playing I'll have that connection. It's nice to have been a big part of the history and it's nice for that history to be recognised, not

just to have been something that's taken off in the last few years."

One of the most positive aspects of the City women's team over the decades has been the longevity of players and committee personnel. Throughout the club's history there have been individuals who have helped guide the club through many, many years with several individuals such as Gail Redston, Lesley Wright, Louise Wakefield, Lindsay Savage, Jane Clark, Gary Moores, Eddie Gregory and Niki Taylor, overlapping and providing the continuity clubs need.

In August 2008, as he prepared for the new season Leigh Wood commented: "I have a great team of both players and support staff, all committed to improving City's fortunes this season through a mixture of teamwork, sports science, fun and of course fine good football thrown in for good measure. I am really looking forward to the challenges of first team football in what is always a highly competitive league. We have re-signed our experienced players like Lindsay Savage (captain), Nicola Twohig, Charlotte Farrell, Katie Brussell, Alex Merrill, Kelly McLellan, Laura Gligan and Levi Wensley. So we have a great spine to the team to build around."

Leigh's first season in charge was more successful than the previous couple with City ending the campaign seventh out of twelve teams, but it was the next season that demonstrated the quality of Leigh's management and the squad at his disposal. The season began with consecutive victories over Sheffield Wednesday (3-2 – with two goals from Sarah Penney and the other from Ellena Turner) and Curzon Ashton

(4-1 – Rebecca Lee, Levi Wensley and two goals from Katie Brussell). Long serving Lindsay Savage remembers this as a positive period with some talented players keen on contributing to the club as a whole. "It's not just the player but the person. Becky Lee she was the biggest nuisance on the pitch and would just let me just play. She loved doing the dirty side of the job, and now and again she would chip in with a wonder goal… total flukes of course!" Lindsay joked.

There were some setbacks along the way but this season proved to be the best experienced to date at this level and ended with four consecutive victories. This was the first time the feat had been achieved in the top flight by the team and the best winning run since Jane Morley and Dave Judge had guided City to eight consecutive league victories at the end of the 2000-01 season.

City ended 2008-09 in third place, ten points behind champions Sunderland. This season had seen the Abu Dhabi takeover of Manchester City and a perception existed that the women's team would now become a wealthy organisation, challenging for the game's top honours. Chair Gary Moores knew that this would not be likely for some time, if at all: "Always in my mind was the idea of being totally integrated with Manchester City men. A few others felt this too. We used to get parents thinking City would buy everything and we'd get into conversations 'what do you mean the club won't give her a training top? What kind of a club is this?' Especially after the takeover in 2008 everybody thought we had money. I remember we played in the north-east in the FA Cup… I think it was Bishop Auckland and the crowd were shouting 'look at you lot, moneybags.' We'd arrived in a 17 seater minibus that we'd borrowed off the club but we had nothing. I ended up saying to one of them 'these girls pay to play.' It was funny that we were suddenly seen as a team with money."

The 2009-10 season was another impressive one for Leigh Wood's team. League football was to be restructured with the establishment of the WSL and City hoped an improvement on the previous campaign would bring that reward as the top two clubs would be eligible for inclusion. The new WSL felt within their grasp. In the end City finished fourth and the top two teams, Liverpool and Lincoln were approved for the WSL. City had actually defeated Liverpool 2-1 in March and drawn with Lincoln in April but ended the season thirteen points behind qualification for the WSL. The quality of City's squad was there and the progression under Leigh Wood was clear.

Commonwealth Games Baton Relay

When Manchester was awarded the 2002 Commonwealth Games a decision was taken to stage a baton relay. The Queen's Jubilee Baton Relay took place before the Games with the baton visiting 23 nations and travelling more than 63,000 miles before it reached the UK. It was carried by 5,000 people. After an epic 137-day journey the Baton Relay reached its final destination, the City of Manchester Stadium (present day Etihad Stadium), where seriously ill young heroine Kirsty Howard handed the Baton to Her Majesty The Queen with the help of David Beckham. The Queen then took her message from within the Baton and declared the Manchester 2002 Commonwealth Games open.

The vast majority of the 5,000 baton runners were ordinary people and Manchester City put two players forward for the honour – first team male star Shaun Goater and City Ladies club captain Jane Clark. Jane saw this as official recognition of the role the ladies team played in the wider Manchester City Football Club: "Vicky Kloss needed to put forward two people to do two legs on behalf of City and she was the one in charge of that. She decided it was going to be the captain of the men's club, which was Shaun Goater, and the captain of the women's club, which was me. It was a big statement. We handed over the baton outside Maine Road and there was a picture of us together in the programme, with both our names at the bottom. I think that was a real turning point for what was then Manchester City Ladies and we were suddenly then part of the club and we got a slight subsidy on our use of Platt Lane."

shaun**goater**
jane**clark**
exchanging the
jubilee baton

City playing their first league game for two months
bounced back with vengence following their cup dissapiontment
And the resounding win was particularly sweet for
City manager Neil Mather for three reasons. Firstly it
came against fellow title chasers, Clitheroe going well
in the league will be devastated by this heavy defeat.
Secondly it's no secret that there's no love lost between
Mather and his Clitheroe counterpart Frank Cansell,
"It would be fair to say we're not the best of friends,
so I get an extra buzz about beating his side. grinned
Mather. Thirdly his gamble on playing a new 5-4-1
formation worked like a dream. He later explained the
new system. "I felt that we had two problems especially
in the Bronte and Hassocks Beacon cup defeats. One was
we were a little square at the back and susceptible
to the ball over the top the other was we were relying
on Rhoda and Donna too much up front. The midfield
wasn't getting forward in support and the front two were
running into a wall every time. By playing 5-4-1
when we defended we always had a player spare, Lesley
is quick and covers well who also possess a lot
of skill the ideal sweeper. And when we are on the
offensive at least one defender can commit themselves
to attack and all the midfield can push up and
join in too, it's simple and effective if played right."
City certainly played it right but Matthews charges
were significant. Newtons injury kept her out Blanchard
replacing her in a straight swop at right back but the
decision to drop Davies for Karlsson making her full
debut raised a few eyebrows "Joni wasn't playing well,
Malin deserved a chance and had a terrific game" Karlsson
often the provider of City's raids. As well as introducing
Wright as the sweeper he moved Haynes back into
midfield leaving Taylor alone up front. "As I said

... was curling and it was WARD who
...olled and spun in one movement sending a
...e half volley past Vickers. It was Ward's first
... in eleven games and the joy was evident.
... were now in a mean mood pining Clitheroe back
... driving towards goal and if Ward was happy with her
... the scorer of the second was ecstatic. Lesley
...'s role as sweeper had twice enabled her to

...re long ...
...right's blisteri...
...g high and t...
...ggling to e...
...fter a thor...
...g hounded e...
...enter Miche...
...about he...
...sing Haynes
...l and skil...
...38th minut...
...low Hayne...
...was perfec...
...ge Hayne...
...y pointed ...
...g Cansel...
...who ...
...l was ...
...his m...
...solutely
...side. T
..." of cha...
...ed to ...
...elt it, a...
...she sui...
...all feel she wa...
...hatrick" A lea...
...dodgy manner? S...
...by the incident t...
...left the field at...
...from Cansell.

Mather's Match Reports

Not that his ranting was to make any
second half, City were in no mood to
boosted ... he ... they continued with their policy of
... decisive goal

As early as the first game in November 1988 Neil Mather compiled match reports and sent them to various newspapers, predominantly those covering South Manchester. He would also often hand a copy to key players who featured in particular games. A copy was also stored in the office of City's community programme in their house on Maine Road. Sadly, as time progressed the majority of these have disappeared or been destroyed with only a small number surviving. This is a real shame as they do provide an interesting view of the state of football as played by women at the time and the views of club officials. This page provides sections from a detailed report Neil produced on City's 5-1 victory over Clitheroe on 20 January 1991. This was a 5-1 win, played at the University Grounds. Scorers: Donna Haynes (2), Rhoda Taylor, Heidi Ward and Lesley Wright.

rolling the
past her opponent leaving
then that Haynes should eventually score
worked the ball wide to Karlsson who in turn
... invited a volley but H
... ead. It was now beco

JANUARY 20TH 1991
... WEST REGIONAL LEAGUE DIVISION TWO
CHESTER CITY v CLITHEROE
... UNIVERSITY GROUND, MANCHESTER KICK OFF 2.00 pm

Clithroe up at wi
Karlsson slipped int
It seemed likely that
was quick off her line
who cleverly put the b
... ches wide. It hardly
he next time the ba
... r was five. Ta
and

Wing much to Mather's mirth
how come the sweeper scores
first shot at goal in years
runs down the wing?" Unfo
care approach cost City a
The defence undermaned, Woo
O'BRIEN beat Flynn, it was
but welcome relief for Clither
for her debut for Brady and h
shirt was to foul Parker on
The freekick went goalbound b
an air of contempt and there
action.

...E SHIRTS			
...E SHORTS & SOCKS			
M FLYNN	1	J. VICKERS	
T BLANCHARD	2	D. BARTON	
... HEMPENSTALL	3	V McCLOAD	
G DUNCAN	4	K ROOM	
C WOODALL	5	D O'CONNOR	
L WRIGHT	6	L COARD	
	7	P FEATHER	

147

Cushing's Interviews

While Neil Mather, the first City manager, wrote copious reports on every game, 2019 manager Nick Cushing became the first to have to face the media before and after games. This was a new experience for him. Here's what he said about his first experience of this new world (interviewed for the *Coachesvoice.com*):

"I tried to think logically. Calmly. But my mind wasn't co-operating. Because at that precise moment, nothing in my life was logical. I was standing in the dugout watching my team – Manchester City Women – take on Liverpool Ladies in the FA Women's Super League. It was the team's first game in the WSL. And the first time I had ever managed a side at that level of competition.

"I didn't feel prepared for it. And I wasn't prepared for what came with it, either. I'd coached a lot of 11-a-side academy games at City, so I was comfortable with the systems. I'd done my homework on Liverpool, too. But, as soon as I walked into Halton Stadium and saw the cameras, I realised that this was different. The game was being shown live on television. But before it even kicked off, I was looking straight down the lens of a camera for my first pre-match interview.

"Illogical. Uncomfortable.

"If I'm totally honest, the majority of the day was a pretty unpleasant experience.

"But without that day, I wouldn't be the coach I am now. I know that. Because it's those moments – those uncomfortable moments – that help to build you as a coach. It's the same as being a player. You need those experiences that push you outside of your comfort zone. The ones that force you to dig really deep to bring the absolute best out of yourself. They're the ones that put you on the path to success."

World in Action: Rowena Foxwell, Debbie Darbyshire and the rest of the team in the Maine Road Gym.

Kate Themen scores.

WAC90 and Other Media

Within the first two years of the club's formation, City's women's team was frequently featured on national television. This included two important programmes of the era – Granada TV's investigative programme World In Action and their Saturday morning children's show WAC90. WAC90 had started life as the Wide Awake Club and was a popular programme for school-aged children. Although it was light, in terms of presentation style, it often covered important topics. The key presenters were Timmy Mallett and Michaela Strachan.

Heidi Ward: "I remember the WAC90 programme because it was Michaela Strachan who was the main presenter. She was really big at the time, but when it actually came to the day, she didn't come. It was somebody else who was doing it, so a few people were disappointed."

Rowena Foxwell: "It was a Saturday morning and I remember them filming us in the changing room because we were singing after the game. We were singing Blue Moon and I know that made it on to the footage – all you could hear were our Mancunian accents – 'without a dream in my 'eart!' They filmed a game – we won easily. My other half Benny was on the sidelines. There was quite a bit of support there and they did some interviews. Benny was gutted because he ended up on the cutting room floor even though they had interviewed him and it'd been good. I think it was something to do with the tee shirt he was wearing though!"

Heidi: "I remember it was a reserve team game and at the time I was in the first team so we were all stood around and they said they were going to come and interview some of the first team whilst the game was going on. I just did not want to be interviewed at all, but they ended up interviewing Donna Haynes and Rhoda Taylor. Then they interviewed Benny, Rowena's boyfriend and they also interviewed Gary, my boyfriend, as well, but they asked him questions 'why do you prefer women's football to men's?' and he said 'well I don't. I come to watch my girlfriend play!' So obviously they didn't play that. I wouldn't be interviewed but it was good that it got the coverage and looking back it was quite sweet really what they did."

The feature was extremely positive about football as played by women and it was exactly the kind of positive coverage that, even today, the modern game is keen to foster but often struggles to get. Kate

Kate Themen with Mike Brosnan, WAC 90.

Rowena Foxwell (middle) singing Blue Moon.

Themen re-watched the coverage prior to being interviewed: "I'd not realised what a huge kind of deal it was, you know? It was quite a big deal. I remember that I was on it and that I'd scored a goal and I was expecting that when I watched it again the other day. I was like 'watch this, look, look, I score a goal here', and then I'd completely forgotten about the bit at the end where I'm there with the presenter! It was really funny to watch it but it was kind of nice seeing it again. It's like 'yes, that's actually presented in quite a positive light.' It's not that patronising, it was nice. I don't remember the details of the day but I do remember bits and pieces of it and then watching it again on video brings quite a few memories back. Singing songs in the dressing room and what have you - we were quite a boisterous lot!"

The WAC90 show may have played a part in encouraging some girls and young women to play football and Neil Mather does remember getting an increase in interest over the weeks that followed. The World In Action programme was expected to be another major positive for demonstrating the strengths of women's football. Debbie Darbyshire: "When we heard about World in Action and the fact that we could film it in City's gym – it wasn't very luxurious at the time – it sounded far

more glamourous than it was. It was quite exciting…. ITV coming to film you… in the proper ground."

Rowena Foxwell: "It was great knowing that World in Action were coming but then when the programme aired it was called Call for the Sisters or something and it was a group of men in a working men's club being interviewed about what effect women could have in football. It was the time of the national identity card stuff… the time of Margaret Thatcher… Of Luton being membership only. It was that time where football hooliganism was in the media an awful lot, so I think that's what the programme was trying to address, but obviously we hadn't had all this context.

"You had a lot of talking heads in the programme talking about 'oh there's no place for women in football… they should be in the kitchen…' The footage they had of us was really just the backdrop to the voices that were spoken over. It didn't make us look like good footballers either!"

Neil Mather: "Both World in Action and WAC90 had come through Linda Whitehead at the WFA I think. She said 'Get in touch with Neil.' You know so it was always the will for people to come to us. For the Women's FA to get maximum publicity for the women's game then using the biggest,

Alex Williams.

Linda Whitehead.

most recognisable club was good. So it was a good 'scratch your back' for everybody. We'd all benefit. I remember the World in Action one. I remember the producer ringing me up and I'm thinking is this someone having a laugh here or what, is this someone taking the mickey.

"The programme was a bit weird though because it was more about hooliganism and how to sort of stop hooliganism and stuff like that. They tried to say that if there's more women going to the game and more women playing football then hooliganism would be lessened and stuff like that. That was disappointing. We thought they were going to promote football as played by

women, not talk about men playing football. They came to film us training in the Maine Road gym and interviewed a few people and stuff like that. It was a bit of a weird one though. But again it was more publicity.

"There were other shows too. I was interviewed for one about a young girl who couldn't play. She wasn't allowed to play for a boys' team because she was a girl. I arranged for her to come training with us and I was interviewed for that at Platt Lane. At that time if there was anything ever that was on women's football on TV then they invariably came to us because we were Manchester City, and back then we were seen as the biggest club that had a women's team."

Debbie Darbyshire: "I think the biggest surprise for me was after the World In Action programme that was on the amount of people that recognised me after being on that. There was a kid and his dad on a bar at the Kippax… When it was all standing we used to stand behind a bar and a dad and his young lad used to sit on the bar. After the World in Action programme I remember him saying about it. Then when we went to the Gillingham play off (men's) at Wembley (in 1999 – approximately nine years later) they ended up near us. The lad was grown up by then. He was probably 16 or 17 and

Helen Hempenstall (left) Neil Mather drinking and the presenter Mike Brosnan.

Donna Haynes on WAC90.

the first thing he said was 'World in Action'. It obviously stuck in people's heads. What's really bizarre is that at Gillingham in the League (c.1998-99) somebody came up to me and asked for my autograph and I thought 'oh, yeah, right?' They said 'City Ladies.' Somehow they'd remembered. I went 'Really?' He went 'yes' – so I signed my actual signature. Afterwards I'm thinking 'oh, don't forge my signature on my cheque book now!' It was really bizarre."

Helen Hempenstall remembers World In Action for another reason: "It was down the tunnel at Maine Road in the old gym. I wasn't supposed to be there that night because I had a big abscess on my back but I went to Maine Road. Then when they're about to start filming someone booted the ball and it hit my back…. 'My abscess!' and I had to go off to get that seen to. I was there for the WAC90 game as well."

There were other TV shows involving some of City's early 1990s players. Rowena Foxwell: "There was another programme that got us playing football on concrete at the BBC on Oxford Road. You can't train on concrete, can you? It went out live, so I've never seen whatever they showed of us. I

can't remember much about it, but I know it happened. We were there for a couple of hours."

Gail Redston: "I remember we did odd little clips like on the news about this, that and the other, but there was one a series about a marriage bureau that organised your wedding and the storyline was a boy who was getting married to this girl. They both played football and she got contracted to go to Italy so the argument was that she wanted to go and he didn't. They said, 'right, what we'll do is we'll have a game of football. The team that wins…' Whichever team, hers or his, would decide what they're doing. I played in the game they filmed. I think it was myself, Donna Haynes and a few from other teams like Wigan. They filmed it over a three week course and most of it was done at Old Trafford football ground and I think it was at Dukinfield Registrar Office at Dukinfield Town Hall. I think that's where the wedding took place, but we were on set every day for three weeks. Most of the time we just sat there with big coats in the stand and took it in turns to play. A bit boring at times, but it was a great experience."

Over the decades newspapers often featured players. Inevitably the *Manchester Evening News*, regular or *Pink* edition, would focus on a player or an angle. Louise Wakefield joined Gail Redston for one article: "We didn't get much coverage but when we did everybody's like 'oh, bring it around', and everyone would have a copy and stuff like that."

City players have featured often in the media in recent years and now many City stars are regular faces. Back in 2007 though the TV drama series Waterloo Road used members of City's women's team as body doubles for the actress Shabana Bakhsh in football scenes for an episode.

Earliest Film

The earliest known surviving film of the team playing is of the game at Burnley in January 1989. This was City's third game and was filmed by Crosland Ward, Heidi Ward's father. Heidi: "I remember playing Burnley because my Dad came and he definitely videoed that, we've got video of it. There were no nets on the goalposts and we turned up at Burnley's ground and then had to walk to the pitch that we were playing on… on the top of a hill. If the ball went in the net it ran down the hill!"

Crosland captured about sixty minutes of the game but the tape is damaged. Attempts are being made by the North West Film Archive to preserve the footage. The film starts with the players leaving Turf Moor, Burnley FC's home, then shows them lining up in the goals prior to the game. Heidi: "If you notice I'm sort of like trying to hide my head a little bit because it's my Dad that's videoing and I'm just thinking this is so embarrassing. It was one of those big cameras that you put on your shoulder with a VHS video cassette in."

In addition to the Burnley game it is known that Heidi's father also filmed some of the inaugural game at Oldham in November. Sadly, film of this has not yet been rediscovered.

Images from the video: Burnley's Turf Moor stadium...
A bent cross bar and no nets ... Michelle Mather and
Neil Mather ... Lesley Wright (16) and Heidi Ward
prepare to start the game watched by Rhoda Taylor.

Lindsay Savage pictured in 2012/13 and profiled in the men's match programme in 2003.

Lyndsay Savage
Born: 25th February 1983
Position: Midfield
Occupation: Archiving Assistant
Previous clubs: Stockport Ladies
Honours: Champions of: Combination 2001, NW Premier Division 2000, 2nd Division 1998 Winner of: NW League Cup & NW Challenge Trophy 2000
Favourite players: Patrick Vieira and Sarah Morris

Longserving Players

One of the most positive findings during the oral history project and the research for this book is that there have been a significant number of players who have stayed with the club for more than a decade. It is impossible, due to the lack of material preserved, to create a comprehensive list of player appearances or even of longserving squad members. There are names that appear season after season of course but it is not always possible to identify specifically when someone arrived or left.

Several players from the opening season, such as Sally Rustige and Gail Redston, remained involved for about thirteen years. Gail: "I'm fortunate as well of the fact that I've not had any serious injuries. There were inevitably a few players like Bev Harrop, Rhoda Taylor and Rita Howard who had a break while they had children but they did come back too."

Another player who did around thirteen years is Louise Wakefield: "A lot of people flirted in and out, coming back after breaks, so it's difficult to know. I know I did 13 years. Jane Clark arrived at the same time as me but left before me, so I edged Jane. Some people flirted in and out and some came for a season or two." Players like Louise ensured the stability of the club over the decades. She has openly talked of the influence of people like Gail on her early career and, similarly, she became a major influence on those that arrived towards the end of her own career. This continuity is important.

While it seems impossible to prove conclusively who the longest serving player has been a number of players have suggested that the accolade belongs to Lindsay Savage. Lindsay was a junior player with the club and continued to play into the 2010s. At the time of the club's arrival in the WSL she was described on the *FAWSL.com* website as "the club's most influential figure on the pitch… leading them to Premier League Northern Division triumph in 2012 – a vital step in reaching the top flight of the Women's Super League."

Team mate Andie Worrall: "Lindsay Savage could have played at a very high level. She had the most appearances of a City player ever." Lindsay hasn't claimed the accolade herself but it does seem likely that her longevity has not been passed. When asked to pick a particular game as a highlight Lindsay Savage looked back on her long career and commented: "Every game teaches you and develops you as a player. Finals and high scoring games are great of course but I actually think that the hard battles and bizarrely the losses teach you a lot more and those are the games that stick in your mind." She was also proud of "captaining the side following Jane Clark's retirement for as many years as I did" and of "being one of the longest serving players for City."

Lindsay was at City for 17 years.

Nick Cushing

Managers

It has been somewhat challenging creating the following list of managers as there is confusion from time to time as to who played the lead role. Occasionally, the lead voice in team selection has been a committee member, and not the person listed as manager. At other times there have been interchangeable coaches and without newspapers, match programmes or other documentary evidence it is impossible to list specifically game by game who has managed the club. It is hoped the following provides an appropriate overview of the role. If anyone has any specific start and end dates then please let the author know.

October 1988 to May 1991 **Neil Mather**
May 1991 to 1996 **Rita Howard** with **Godfrey Williams** fulfilling the role between 1994-95. **Jane Morley** also filled the role at some point during this time for a brief period.
1996 to 1997 **Reno Dionisou**
1997 to 1999 **Kevin Scarborough**
1999 to 2001 **Greg Coniglio**
2001 **Jane Morley** and **Dave Judge**
2001 to 2003 **John Stanhope**
2003 to 2005 **Dave Judge**
2005 to 2007 **Steve Walmsley**
2007 to 2013 **Leigh Wood**
2013 **Nick Cushing**

A few comments on the managers from players and others:

Rita Howard: "Neil Mather was always full of enthusiasm. Some of us were longer in the tooth than he was and so that was a bit of a challenge for him and us. But for the

Neil Mather

love of the game you quickly get over those hurdles. We'd tell him what we thought and he listened. He was right for that time."

Neil Mather (dressing room etiquette) "The rule of thumb was I'd give them ten minutes to get changed and then I'm coming in. I'd knock on the door: 'everybody decent?' 'Yes.' I'd come in and the same afterwards 'you don't get changed until I've spoken to you, we'll sit and we'll chat about the match. We'll do the evaluation of the game and then you get changed'. There was never an issue with that whatsoever to me. The only issue I had was bloody pregnancy, Rita Howard getting pregnant. I'll never forget that one, that actually made *The Sun*. Your captain comes up to you and says 'oh by the way I'm going to be out for the next five or six months.'

Rita scores again!

MANCHESTER CITY LADIES soccer team boss Neil Mather has found himself with a problem which is unlikely to affect Howard Kendall or Alex Ferguson.

His captain Rita Howard is going to be out of action until well into next season . . . but it's for the best possible reason.

Rita has just found out that she is expecting her second child!

While it means that Neil has lost his centre half and influential skipper it does have a big plus in that Rita will now be giving him valuable help as his assistant manager.

Taking over Rita's role as captain will be Lesley Wright.

Reno Dionisiou   *Greg Coniglio (far left, back row)*

There was stuff like that I wasn't expecting. I learnt very quickly. It was great for me as a coach because psychologically you have to learn how to deal with different players."

Player and coach Bev Harrop: "Rita Howard was involved for a long time and she was the manager that gave me my first game. Then there was Reno. He worked with me in my job and he got involved and became manager. I don't know that he ever played himself. He was a football fan and he got his cousin, Greg Coniglio, involved as well. But between the two of them it was them that built that team, that double winning team."

Jane Morley: "Dave Judge came with Derek Heath from Stockport. Dave knew a lot about football. Gary Moores eventually became chairman. I had a spell as secretary as well. There was a committee. They worked well together. I had always run the clubs I was at and so knew what was needed but having a committee helped. Godfrey Williams came on board and worked with me as a coach. Wherever I've been I've always tended to work with Godfrey as a coach. His connections with City Ladies go back to the beginning of course. With Godfrey we managed to get on the big pitch at Platt Lane under the floodlights. It grew and grew. It grew quickly because there were some good people in every place. We all knew our roles and strengths. We met every month no matter what. We attended league meetings. We dealt with all our issues. That period of time was fantastic. The success of the teams at all levels was great. The six years or so that I was there were thoroughly enjoyable – apart from the last few months."

Goalkeeper Andie Worrall talking about John Stanhope: "I was really close with John, John was a friend from Wales, a really good guy. He knew all the coaches, knew all the girls. Leigh Wood did a great job. He'd got his licences and stuff, got some good coaches under him. I mean obviously without Leigh it wouldn't have been possible what's gone on since."

John Stanhope: "I was interviewed for the job by Gary Moores, Jane Morley and Dave Judge. They asked questions about my background. What could you bring? Do you know anything about women's football? Gary was very kind to say that my application stood out a mile. I'd been on tournaments with England. I'd helped the Swedish women's team and all sorts of stuff so I knew what was needed. They knew what was going on."

Chair Gary Moores: "John is an absolutely passionate football fan – and City fan! I think he'd done a lot of amateur men's football and he just loved City. "

John Stanhope

Dave Judge

Kevin Scarborough

Jane Morley

Player and coach Lesley Wright: "Is it good to have someone who doesn't know any of the players or someone who already knows them? I think it's best if it's someone you don't know because then there is never any accusation of favouritism or anything. Having said that there are positives for both. The way the women's game has changed adds to it of course. For me so long as those who get involved treat the women's game with respect and the focus it deserves then I don't think it matters whether the coaches are male, female, friends or not. I've been impressed with Phil Neville for England but he hasn't had a grounding in women's football and so he has a lot of work to do and I hope he succeeds. If he doesn't he'll be shot down for it. Nick Cushing has been brilliant for City. The perfect manager for this period of development. Gone are the days when we get someone coming to City saying 'I've got a mate who can manage the team.' That

doesn't work now. Maybe it didn't work then. People can talk a good game but they soon get found out."

Supporters Club member David Sheel: "When my step dad passed away Nick Cushing sent me a personal message on twitter. He's a very, very nice fella. He understands. When we went to Chelsea in the Continental Cup semi final in January. Nick Cushing came over to us, climbed into the stand and thanked us for the atmosphere. He said he had never heard anything like it and that he felt as if the club had been playing at home."

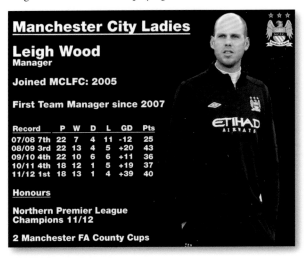

Leigh Wood infographic produced by City in 2012.

Manchester City Ladies

Leigh Wood
Manager

Joined MCLFC: 2005

First Team Manager since 2007

Record		P	W	D	L	GD	Pts
07/08	7th	22	7	4	11	-12	25
08/09	3rd	22	13	4	5	+20	43
09/10	4th	22	10	6	6	+11	36
10/11	4th	18	12	1	5	+19	37
11/12	1st	18	13	1	4	+39	40

Honours

Northern Premier League Champions 11/12

2 Manchester FA County Cups

City's number one training ground
Platt Lane in 1987.

Grounds

The club has played at many different grounds since formation. Occasionally they have used venues like Cheadle Town when their regular home was unavailable. As with identifying who played in every game, or what kit was worn it now seems unlikely we will ever be in a position to say conclusively which grounds were used for every single game. The following provides some thoughts on the club's main venues over the years.

1988-89 Platt Lane

■ Manchester City's first team training complex (at the time) staged home games for the inaugural season of friendlies and then staged other games at various times throughout the club's next decade or so.

1989 The University Grounds, Wythenshawe

■ Rita Howard: "We stayed a while down at the University Grounds. They were mint pitches. Then somehow we ended up at Wythenshawe Town."

Neil Mather: "The club sorted us out. I think they had a contact with the University Grounds in Wythenshawe from way back. Our pitch was the best pitch. It was quality. It was looked after."

Gail Redston: "When we played at the University Ground the pitches were immaculate and then, obviously, when we got bigger we had to move based on each league's rules but, going back to the University Grounds, there were decent changing rooms. You weren't getting changed in the back of the car or anything like that. We went to one ground on Merseyside and when we got there the goalposts were missing. The actual posts were in the pub. They said 'oh we've got to get them out the back of the pub.' They got them and walked across this road carrying the whole goal post, crossbar and everything. They said that if they didn't do this and just left them they'd get stolen! It was just unbelievable."

Lesley Wright: "When we had the University Grounds I remember that we'd arrive and be told 'you're on that pitch'. Often the one furthest away. You'd drag the nets across, put them up… If you wanted the toilet at half time forget it. You wouldn't have time to get back."

1998 Wythenshawe Town

■ Bev Harrop: "We played at Wythenshawe Town. It was the best. We had some very good games at Wythenshawe Town. The people that ran it were good towards us too. That was very helpful, but then we had to move. I think their ground was undergoing some kind of work and I think that was when we ended up at Flixton. We played at Wythenshawe for quite some time.

2000 and 2005 Flixton FC

■ Jane Boardman: "Through City we were given access to people who could find better places for us to play football, so we moved from playing at Wythenshawe Town to playing at Flixton. We were still paying but we were paying a subsidised rate in recognition of the fact that we were part of Manchester City."

Bev Harrop: "I mean towards the end,

when we got in to these other leagues, we had to change grounds, we ended up playing at Flixton because the regulations changed. You needed to be in an enclosed ground but the pitch at Flixton I think Jane Morley will tell you was costing us over £100 a game. We were just people that were working for a living that had to come up with this kind of money. It was very difficult. I don't recall really any sponsorship throughout the whole time. It was us that paid for it. And then we needed a referee and linesmen. That was another 50 quid a game."

Lesley Wright: "I remember us playing at Flixton but that cost us £100 a game. We played at Burnage Rugby Club when John Stanhope was manager. That was a good set up there. We played at Wythenshawe Town which is when we started the youth set up. There was a place opposite Wythenshawe that's now Manchester Health Academy... We've been all over. I can't even remember all the grounds from the early days. We raised money by selling name cards and stuff as well as paying our subs."

2001 Old Bedlians Sports Ground, Didsbury

■ According to match programmes, Old Bedlians became City's home from 2001, though a lot of games seemed to be played elsewhere. Gary Moores: "We played home games at Flixton, Mossley, Cheadle Town – where Stockport Ladies had played years ago. We went back to Flixton. I think we played Everton at Cheadle Town and that didn't go down well. We were supposed to play at the Regional Athletics Arena but it was a re-arranged fixture and we couldn't play it there. It was a FA Cup tie with Everton and they were massive then in ladies football. You felt you were playing royalty. I couldn't get a pitch... I'd tried everywhere and then we got Cheadle Town. Even the linesman wouldn't stay for a sandwich afterwards because he thought it was the

pits! Luckily the pitch wasn't too bad but the facilities weren't that good really. Everton won the game."

Andie Worrall remembers playing at Old Bedlians: "It's like a rugby place. We used to play over there. It wasn't brilliant. We played matches there but I don't know there was no structure to our training... like a couple of hours of week. At Everton it was a lot better and obviously they had goalie coaches, because that was always a big thing. I never had a goalie coach until I was about 21. I was never taught coaching. The first time I got coached was when I went to England at 21."

Regional Athletics Arena

■ Gary Moores: "We had spoken to the people at the Regional Athletics Arena a couple of seasons before we actually moved there. We asked City if they could help us and they put a good word in for us and we started playing there. We were quite nomadic for a number of years really before we moved to the Athletics Arena. Even that wasn't ideal because we were fighting against athletics events for the space at times. But it was the best we could get and it was the best we'd had.

"We got decent crowds at the Regional Athletics Arena. I know it doesn't sound massive but we got two maybe three hundred. They'd pay on the gate and buy programmes... We started running out of programmes every week. People would complain but they were being made by someone's dad on a Saturday night. He could only print so many off. We started being asked for reprints. It was all getting serious. I went through a period of doing them myself and it was a nightmare. I'd end up doing them on a Sunday morning sometimes because there had been some changes. John Stanhope made some when he was involved as well. There were other jobs like organising

The Regional Athletic Arena during City's game with Bristol Academy, 20 April 2014.

sandwiches for the visiting team. If you didn't do that you'd be in trouble."

David Sheel: "I'd been to watch the women, or Ladies as it was then, sporadically since it was formed but it was later on when I started to get more involved I suppose. I remember seeing them play at Abbey Hey a few times and then there were the games at the Regional Athletics Arena. It was always difficult to find out information as it wasn't covered much in the papers or anything. If a game was called off you wouldn't know for example. It was quite hard to follow so I didn't manage to get to many games. I do remember that sometimes it would be possible to see a game at the Regional Athletics Arena and then go to the stadium to watch the men on the same day. That helped. I dragged my partner along and she

got into it. Even then it was better than most people thought. There are some people even now who won't give women's football a try. They just won't even give it a chance. If you try it that's different, but to be blinkered is wrong."

Academy Stadium

■ The move to the Academy Stadium gave City their first purpose-built home. This was theirs and its proximity to the Etihad and the training complex was something former player Abbie McManus enjoyed: "It helps. For us, obviously, the more fans that are in the crowd the more we enjoy the game and we've said since the move that our fans have been amazing. They've come home and away so whether it is across the road, we've still got good enough fans that will travel away.

The Academy Stadium in October 2016
for the visit of Birmingham City.

They come to London. There was one of the fans that came to Russia. The fan base is improving and improving and we are now actually securing real fans that come back to every game to watch us play football at our own home."

Maine Road

■ No competitive game was played at Maine Road but there were mini-games played on men's match days and there was also a charity game for Football Aid against Manchester United. That was the most significant meeting for the women at the old stadium, but of course, the mini-games meant a large crowd would see them play.

Gail Redston: "We did about three mini-games at Maine Road. Barnsley and Sheffield Wednesday were two of them. It meant a lot to most of us, running out in front of 32,000 and them 32,000 now know we exist. I just wanted to take it all in. We got changed in the little gym, with the head tennis. We stood in the tunnel as the guys come out and then we ran out. My family knew that I was playing and they were there. They had come down to the wall (separating the pitch from the stands) and shouting us on and encouraging us. It was lovely."

Lesley Wright: "We played on Maine Road a couple of times and someone arranged for us to have a meal afterwards at Parrs Wood. I think the game was against Sheffield Wednesday. We had to sit in the stand in our kit. Freezing. Then when it was time we had to go down to the tunnel and we ran on at half time in the men's game. We played a short game and then we ran off again. Put on some Umbro tops that I think we'd bought ourselves and then we popped into the City Social Club after the game and people recognised us. It was great. It was the best thing to say we played for Manchester City. The level doesn't matter but to wear that shirt and to play on Maine Road felt like a major achievement. It was recognition too off the club. My best memory of it was running out of the tunnel at Maine Road. Benny (Rowena Foxwell's partner) said he'd give me a fiver if I ran out, knelt on my knees and kissed the pitch in front of the Kippax. And I did!"

Manchester United fan Louise Wakefield: "We played one of the last games at Maine Road as well. It was like the build-up to the closure of Maine Road and the City fans were brilliant. They were really good. We were just a bit of a park team back then, but when we won a trophy and we did the lap of honour, we all got a standing ovation. That little temporary stand (nicknamed the Gene Kelly – as fans were often 'singing in the rain') that was quite noisy. We got to that and it were just ecstatic in that corner there. It was absolutely brilliant. I loved it.

"The thing is my family call me 'Blue Lou' because I played so long and ended up going to a lot of City games because we got tickets and I used to go. I used to go to my brother 'it's brilliant, the atmosphere's brilliant.' They all called me Blue Lou."

Jane Boardman: "I can remember vividly we played Crewe Alexandra in the League and Crewe Ladies were in the same League we were in, so we saw that as an opportunity to try and set something up, at half time. At half time we went on to the pitch and we just played on a quarter of the pitch, small sided game and I remember we had a shot on goal and it went narrowly wide. You just heard this 'huuuhhh' from the crowd. It was

just a moment where you sort of stopped and thought 'oh my God, people are actually watching' and 'there's enough of them to make a noticeable noise.' I'd gone from feeling really quite relaxed about the whole thing to thinking 'oh my God.' My game just went to seed after that, but we won 1-0. We got a great round of applause.

Etihad Stadium

In 2014 City Women played Everton at the Etihad in a Continental Cup game. The Blues won 1-0 with an 89th minute winner from Natasha Flint. In July 2019 it was announced that the first WSL Manchester derby would be staged at the Etihad on the opening day of the season. New signing Aoife Mannion commented: "[The Manchester Derby] is going to be so exciting, it's going to be so immense…I'm so excited, especially with it being in the Etihad Stadium and I think we need to prepare really well in pre-season so that we can deliver the supporters the result that they want, which is a win to kick off the season."

City 1 Everton 0 at the Etihad in 2014.

The Re-Launch

Despite initially being formed as part of Manchester City's corporate structure in 1988 the women's team became its own entity affiliated to the parent club by the end of the 1990s. It had its own committees and structure but progression up the leagues had resulted in a need to re-establish closer ties. By the early 2010s it became clear a formal coming together was needed. This surprised some of the players and staff from the 1980s and 1990s, especially when articles appeared claiming the club had been established in 2002. Jane Morley: "It upset Lesley (Wright) that the full history had been ignored. There were stories that the club had been founded by a group of City fans and it came across that it was fairly insignificant. But that wasn't true. These were women who wanted to play football. Some were City fans but Rita Howard wasn't, Bev Harrop was a United season ticket holder – So was I. I went to United games with Bev."

Louise Wakefield: "I felt a bit like we'd been forgot and I thought 'is it just me?' but apparently a few of us were feeling left out. We'd done everything for the club. You know, turned up, swollen ankles, and had to play, you know? We felt a bit left out with it."

Michelle Middleton felt: "aggrieved that the media seemed to think that City had

The re-launch in January 2014 sees the team and coaches joined on the pitch at the Etihad Stadium by the men's team manager Manuel Pellegrini along with Claudio Reyna, Jason Kries and Patrick Vieira.

Debbie Darbyshire and Kate Themen, who were at the first training session in 1988, are pictured with Toni Duggan at the relaunch.

suddenly decided to have a women's team and didn't take the time to look into the history but I was happy that the club was still backing the women and were planning to make them as important a part of the club as the men."

Michelle had played at the formation of the club, with Lesley arriving that same season. Lesley stayed until 2002, with Louise joining the club in 1996, but it wasn't only players that had been involved before the 2002 date that felt aggrieved at times. Gary Moores: "The waters got muddied around this time and I think some people got a bit upset. I understood fully that what went on in the past is in the past and that it had nothing to do with the relaunched club. I know that upset a few people because some were still tying up the back end of

Gary Moores

Manchester City Ladies. Since the transfer of the club, I haven't been to games because it took so much time out of my life. I reached the point where I felt 'it's in safe hands now' and I felt that our part of the transition had been handled well and so I felt I could move away. Previously it had been like the guy spinning the plates… you couldn't stop because the plates would come crashing down but once City were handed control someone else was able to spin the plates and I could move on.

"I didn't pay much attention to those who suggested City were a new club because half of it was from people who had only just learned about women's football because of the birth of the Super League. They were speaking about something that they didn't actually know much about. They'd dipped into it occasionally. Also, there was the negativity because of the position of Doncaster Belles. That was a shame because we know what Doncaster Belles have done but then there's these people who see the money that Manchester City as an overall club was supposed to have and then it's suggested that City had used that money to buy their place but they hadn't. It was built on the back of years of commitment by players and volunteers. That first season after there were about half a dozen players who had been with us for years.

"I remember being on holiday about two years after the WSL place was given and there was a woman who was a big City Women fan there. We got chatting and I told her of my connection but she didn't believe me. She got her laptop out and started to quiz me. 'Okay, where did Krystle Johnston come from?' I said 'Manchester City Ladies' and she said that she'd played for one of the Sheffield clubs not City but that was the season when there was the transition from winter to summer football and the club had no games. The players went off to play for other clubs to keep fit but even on City's own website the previous club line gave the impression these had all arrived from other clubs. All of that added to this view that it was a new club. There were about six or seven players like this I think."

Inevitably there were going to be issues to resolve as the transition took place. As with the period in 2002 when some long established players and committee members felt the club was being taken from them, some of the

committee and players experienced similar feelings. Transformations are always difficult but with the media choosing to promote the view that 'new club' City were in the process of obtaining a WSL place at the expense of Doncaster Belles, it was always going to be tough to satisfy all former players and committee members. The noise, particularly in the media, did not overshadow what was actually happening however. Many current and former players were delighted with the potential for a stronger relationship. Rowena Foxwell: I think got a bit excited when City Ladies became more professional and then they changed the name to Women. I think because women's football was on the telly more, and it was great that our club was getting a professional team. We all thought 'if we were 20 years younger, we could have played in that'. So we got a bit giddy about it."

Rowena had seen some of the incorrect details of the club's birth and decided to be proactive: "I was clicking through and there was this piece on how City Ladies started in 2002 or whatever it was! So I emailed Vicky Kloss, the Head of Communication at City, and just said to her that I was part of the original team… still in touch with a lot of them… be great if we could get involved… do you know that some of the facts on there are wrong? I think the fact that we got angry

-----Original Message-----
From: Rowena
Sent: 18 December 2013 19:01
To: Vicky Kloss
Subject: City Ladies

Dear Ms Kloss,

Following all the recent media coverage on City Ladies signings and the start of the Women's Super League next year, I thought I'd contact you to highlight the fact that the original City Ladies team were founded 25 years ago.

I suspect next year will be the 25th anniversary of the team's first competitive game.

I attended the very first training session and am still in contact with several of those original players and can also track down the manager should you be interested in facilitating a reunion.

Whilst most of us are well past our playing days, some are still avid city fans and season card holders. There was even a few reds in that original line up!

I'm more than happy to provide further information if you are interested in following up.

Kind regards
Rowena Foxwell

Heidi Ward, who scored in the first City Ladies game, with present day goalkeeper Karen Bardsley at the relaunch.

about the fact that they'd got it wrong, just shows how passionate we were."

Debbie Darbyshire: "Vicky Kloss wanted it right. Vicky's good like that. She's always keen to make sure things are right. She called [Gary James] in and started the process of getting it all right."

Rowena's email was passed on to City's Damaris Treasure, then Head of Public Affairs. She was heavily involved with the relaunch and wanted to get the facts correct. She immediately contacted Rowena and pushed to ensure the history of the team was properly recorded and that those involved felt valued for what they had achieved. Rowena Foxwell: "Many of us were invited to the relaunch. We obviously rocked up to the Etihad. There were a few people that we hadn't seen probably since we played. So you know that was nice, and it was nice that City acknowledged us as the original team."

Damaris Treasure: "I started working with Don Dransfield on the then City Ladies when we announced the formalisation of the relationship with the Club in 2012. I was

then part of the core team who bid for the WSL license, and led the re-launch as City Women in 2014. The day of the re-launch as Manchester City Women will forever be a highlight for me. Thinking back on all that day and all the people in the room – the original City Ladies squad, the new City Women squad, more media than we thought possible, legends of the men's game (Patrick Vieira, Claudio Reyna), City leadership – it's actually quite incredible that all those people came together. But it's also indicative of just how right that moment was and how ready people were to invest in it."

Jane Boardman: "I think you know the club went some way to recognise that this was a relaunch and not a launch, which I think was very important. A number of us got invited to the relaunch event. I think it's important that the club continues to stay community-focused and I think that they do achieve that."

Heidi Ward: "I think I was really pleased that the relaunch got the press coverage that it did, because it lifted the women's game. I knew that City were going to put

Niki Taylor with Patrick Vieira.

Jane Boardman (bottom left) joins some of the originals at the relaunch. Back (L to R): Godfrey Williams, Rhoda Taylor. Middle: Heidi Ward, Rowena Foxwell, Neil Mather, Debbie Darbyshire. Front: Jane Boardman, Helen Hempenstall, Kate Themen, Donna Haynes, Lesley Wright.

money in to it and they were going to make the facilities and whatever. They are now absolutely brilliant. They wanted to give women the same opportunity as men and that's just absolutely amazing. To be fair, I didn't think it would get to the level where it is now, so that's incredible really. If you look at the players now, they all look like athletes. They are all similar shapes and sizes and they are all really fit and healthy. Look at Steph Houghton - her physique has changed and she's a complete athlete now. And the skills and the level of football has just raised in the last few years as well.

"I'm used to watching men's football and I've never wanted to compare it to men's football because it felt like a different game. I think there was a bit of a gap and now, at the highest level, I don't see that. There's

different skills and there's different strengths, but what City have done has changed things. I think it's amazing."

Kate Themen was delighted that City were investing but was unhappy with the media focus on the fate of Doncaster Belles: "I thought the FA could have handled it much better. I think that was a structural issue, because it was a shame that Doncaster had lost their place, but when the FA sets up a league structure, which is essentially a franchise structure then these things happen. It wasn't City's issue it was the FA's for having a structure whereby it allowed teams to do that."

Lesley Wright: "I remember Rowena Foxwell asking if we were going to the relaunch. It was very nice and it was great to be invited. I think most of us that went to the relaunch were City fans as well as players so it meant more in some ways. Manuel Pellegrini was there. I think it was good how it was done because it showed that City were taking it seriously. It was a major step forward. It wasn't just about using the money that Sheikh Mansour provided. It was the same as with the men. They invested in the club. They took the core of the England women's team and they've brought in others. The whole point of the WSL was to create a platform to develop English talent and so I'm pleased that City have focused on bringing in and developing English players. Along the way they've brought in people like Carli Lloyd to help of course, but they're developing talent the right way. It costs a lot of money and it can be difficult to sustain that but, like the men, they know what they want and they're developing the club to achieve that. Opening the Academy and creating that ground takes it to a different level again."

Damaris: "It was a really interesting time when we re-launched City Women, because there were teams that had been doing great things for a long time, Arsenal being the most notably successful, but we had a strong sense, which is generally how we do things anyway, of doing things well and doing things right by the highest possible standards. So, in some ways we treated this as a blank slate. Also, the way that we generally work at City is that we are all responsible for both the men's and the women's teams. Everyone working on City Women at that time was working in Premier League football as well as with the WSL, so there was a great range of experience being shared between the teams.

Neil Mather: "I was chuffed to bits as I still am and I still get a huge buzz going to watch them. It was always my dream that there would be a women's professional league and that they'd get the opportunities that the men got."

Louise Wakefield: "I'm really pleased because of where we've come from, you

Steph Houghton meets the media at the re-launch.

know? I hope people understand that rags to riches story. The Arsenals have always had that structure but I think the rags to riches story that City have had over all those years is remarkable. The media should push that. There could be documentaries on it. I was about two seasons away from the change. I wasn't far away at all. If it wasn't for an incident I had at a turning point where I was starting to progress, I'd have been in that era. I'd have been in every progression from 1996, apart from the current first team. If you've got that money behind you and you've got that training and you go training every day… and you're not playing on pitches that are up to here, you're going to progress. If I was 17 playing now I'd have been a lot better player."

Lindsay Savage was delighted when the relaunch occurred: "Brilliant, City is such a big club and it is great to see them challenging for everything. They are really inspiring young girls to follow their dream and are fantastic role models."

Rita Howard: "I was happy with the relaunch… No, I was jealous. Definitely jealous that this has happened and that I have missed out because of time. But very happy for women now and for girls coming through. They've now got something to aspire to. It absolutely heartens me when I see girls coming here to my school who are already in teams and it's a given that they are going to continue to play.

Welcome to the relaunched club, the Manchester City match programme

CONTENTS

Girls mud battle

WELCOME

To mark the re-launch of Manchester City Women's Football Club, we're dedicating this matchday supplement to our "sister" club, who celebrated their good news at a pre-season event at the Etihad Stadium last week.

It's an exciting time for City Women, as the Blues prepare to tackle England's top flight – the FA Women's Super League – for the first time. Over recent weeks, the club have made a host of marquee signings including Karen Bardsley, Steph Houghton, Toni Duggan, Jill Scott, Betsy Hassett and one more – but you'll have to turn to page 10 to find out who!

You can see photos from the launch on pages 4 and 5 and get to know all the players on pages 11 and 12…

On pages 6 and 7, we fill you in on the history of the club alongside an interview with the man who started it all, Neil Mather.

We also have discussions with the managerial team as well as club captain Houghton, who tells us all about her life as a footballer and away from the game she loves…

★★★

WOMEN

177

When I first started teaching here I was like a frontrunner of the girls football. We might have a good five-a-side team but struggle beyond that. Since then we have had a team that won a tournament."

The need for football lower down the pyramid to receive investment is there. Jane Morley, who is still involved in promoting the sport to young girls in the regions, hopes the wider public begin supporting community clubs financially: "It is important to remember that as great as it is what's happened to City and the other clubs in the WSL for most women's teams it is still as it has always been. You rent a grass pitch, a referee turns up, the opposition arrive and you play a game. The pitches vary, the conditions can be poor… it's not changed. You can still find games that have no dressing rooms…. Changing in cars and so on. I still think the women's game has to fit in with the men's game. Playing at 2pm on a Sunday to fit in with men's games in the morning."

It will take some time for benefits at the highest level to trickle down the leagues but football as played in female competition is in a much better place now than it was only a few years ago. City remain determined to see football as football, without a differentiation. Damaris Treasure: "Bringing City Women in to Manchester City formally was only the beginning of City's relationship with women's football. I now work for City Football Group based in Australia, and the blueprint created in Manchester was replicated with our team in Melbourne (who have since gone on to win pretty much everything going). In the same way as Manchester, the women's team are fully integrated with the men's team, train at the same facilities, and have been credited with raising the bar for women's football in Australia. We've got a girls academy at New York City FC, and long term we would love to see more women's teams as part of CFG.

Charter Standard

In 2001 the FA Charter Standard Programme was launched. It remains the FA's accreditation scheme for grassroots clubs and leagues and its aims are to raise standards, support the development of clubs and leagues and to recognise and reward them for their commitment and achievements. From its formation City's women's team was keen to be recognised via this award.

Jane Boardman: "We got charter standard after we'd invested a lot in areas such as paediatric first-aid, qualified coaches… all of the things that you need to do to become a charter standard club. Vicky Kloss (City's Head of Communications) was emotionally invested in what we were trying to do and that made all the difference."

Louise Wakefield: "Me and Jane did a lot of leg work for that. I think John Stanhope was around that and Gary Moores too. We did a lot of leg work. We received it at Maine Road at half time and I didn't really know the full extent of what it was all about until afterwards and then I saw that it meant we could progress. It opened so many doors and I was just thinking how every single season always relates back to that first season you started. How far you'd come but when we received that it was obviously a big turning point for the club. It was quite a proud moment.

Gary Moores: "We received a lot of help from the head of Girls Development at the Manchester FA. There was a lot of hard work to produce the mountains of documentation and setting out the schedules and procedures to apply for the Charter Standard. That was done by one of the volunteer dads, Craig Rickards. Without him I don't think we would have achieved it. He later emigrated to Canada with his family."

FA WOMEN'S PREMIER LEAGUE National Division

OFFICIAL MATCHDAY PROGRAM

Match Sponsor

Sue
Bluebird1
Clark

MANCHESTER CITY LADIES

Manchester City Women

Played

		Goals
1	Karen Bardsley	
2	Danielle Lea	
3	Steph Marsh	
4	Jess Holbrook	
6	Steph Houghton	
7	Krystle Johnston	
8	Jill Scott	
9	Toni Duggan	
10	Kimberley Turner	
11	Isobel Christiansen	
12	Betsy Hassett	
14	Nicola Harding	
15	Chelsea Nightingale	
16	Emma Lipman	
17	Lynda Shepherd	
18	Danielle Young	
19	Natasha Flint	
21	Andie Worrall	

Bristol Academy

Played

		Goals
1	Mary Earps	
2	Loren Dykes	
3	Corinne Yorston	
4	Jasmine Matthews	
5	Grace McCatty	
7	Natalia Pablos Sanchon	
8	Alexandra Windell	
9	Ann-Marie Heatherson	
10	Nicola Watts	
11	Ellen Curson	
13	Laura Del Rio Garcia	
14	Sophie Ingle	
16	Angharad James	
17	Lauren Haynes	
19	Jemma Rose	
20	Natasha Harding	
21	Vera Bernabe Payol	
23	Georgia Evans	
26	Ellie Leek	
27	Rhian Cleverly	

Match Officials

Referee:
Duncan Street

Assistants:
Aaron Bannister
Jonathan Carter

Fourth Official:
Anthony Ball

Mascots

Jorja Clarke
Amelia Wood

Ladies or Women

When Manchester City relaunched the name was changed from Ladies to Women. For some the importance of this move is clear. Others feel it is less important but Damaris Treasure, who worked on the change for the club, knew it was the right time to make this change: "The name change from Ladies to Women meant so much to me both personally and professionally. Ladies feels like an aged term and it felt particularly jarring when you're looking at these incredible athletes. It seemed like quite a simple thing but it said a lot about how we felt about those athletes, about the team and about the game. If that change hadn't happened, I think it could have undermined some of the other central messages about equity and inclusivity. Words are important."

Rowena Foxwell: "I absolutely see why they did it and I think it's the right thing because we were never ladies. Not in a month of Sundays. It does irritate me though that we don't say Manchester City Men but people say Manchester City Women though!"

Neil Mather: "I think it's a better idea to be called Women. Now I'm looking back I'm thinking, yes, it sounds right doesn't it? Women is better. Its sounds more strong, you know what I mean, but it was just that was what everybody else was called, so that's what we called ourselves."

Steph Houghton: "I just think it's really

empowering towards us as women and I think it gives off a really good impression. It's just very powerful to teams that come and play us for the perception of the whole Football Club is that we are taking it very seriously. We are professional athletes and we want to grow the game and we want to, more importantly, win things so for me I think it was the right idea to do that. It was the right time when we re-branded the whole club. The right decision and I think it just kind of exudes what this club's about."

Rita Howard: "I don't think the name really matters to me. Words can be made to mean a number of things but we are both women and ladies so it doesn't matter to me. It is a shame that there has to be a differentiation at all though. It should just be Manchester City."

Kate Themen: "Finally, that old archaic tag has gone. Things like that make a difference, because that's what frames people - the identity. The difference between the semantics of women and ladies. They signify different things, so for me, that was really important. I was really glad that they did it as well. A little change like that makes a big difference."

Lesley Wright: "I think changing the name was more about showing it's a fresh start. I'm not certain it mattered too much. The important thing was that City were taking it seriously. I've never understood

though why they need 'ladies' or 'women' if they're playing in the Women's Super League. The men are hardly likely to be in the women's league are they?"

Gary Moores: "I'd had meetings with the hierarchy at City. Several times it was said to us 'do you like the name Manchester City Ladies? Have you ever thought about changing it?' I could never understand why people had a bee in their bonnet about the 'ladies' bit. The name never bothered me and the name change didn't upset me either. The name was mentioned in passing several times over the years though."

Supporters club representative David Sheel: "To me the name change didn't, at the time, mean anything but I remember asking my partner and she was adamant that they are women and not ladies. To this day she hates any team called Ladies in the WSL. The club used it a lot in the club's branding but that's now gone to some extent and we see it as Manchester City."

The majority of women interviewed for this book supported the name change but

not all. Some felt it also signified a departure from the club's pre-2013 existence. Alison Smith, a committee member in the build-up to the relaunch saw the name change as "In some respect forward thinking" but she felt "It was also part of the 'separation' from the previous organisation."

The last word on this goes to Debbie Darbyshire. She was one of the first players to arrive at the initial training session in October 1988. She jokes: "We were never ladies!"

Dave Sheel with his partner Jayne.

Supporters

The club was always supported by a network of family, friends, partners and others with an interest in the sport. The first game to get a sizeable crowd was the first competitive derby in September 1990 when over 150 arrived at the University Grounds to watch the Blues beat the Reds 4-3. Around this time male first team players and former players occasionally came to games. Rowena Foxwell: "Colin Hendry was our president for a while and came to a few games. I remember Alex Williams used to come. He carried me off the pitch when I was injured so that man has a strong back!"

Over the years the significance of individual games and competitions, together with home ground facilities, have contributed to the development of supporters for the team. Once the club was relaunched the volume of fans increased significantly, especially once the club was playing in the WSL. To strengthen the link between the club and supporters City decided to establish a supporters club branch.

David Sheel: "I found this out later but Blandie was approached by the club to see if she would be interested in helping establish a branch of the Official Supporters Club of Manchester City for the women's team. Most branches are geographical but we also have the Canal Street Blues, the Disabled branch and others. So they invited Blandie to a meeting at Reddish where Steph Houghton and Izzy Christiansen were guest speakers. We went along – we've been before to

Supporters Club members on an Academy Stadium tour.

Reddish and know Howard Burr and the others who run it.

"We sat and chatted with Blandie and she told us that she'd been approached by the club to get together a group of regulars to come for a chat with Gavin Makel, the head of women's football, and Elliott Ward, from the publicity side of things. Just to have a chat about it. Blandie then set about finding a cross section of fans. She got a young lad called Craig, me and Jayne – as a couple of regulars, a lad called Mark who had run youth football teams…. There were a few of us. We went to the meeting and the club strongly felt that things were going so well that a supporters club should be established. This was in 2015. They liked the idea of it being official and they'd also help where they could. We formed a committee and of course that has evolved over time. Blandie became our first Chair, my partner Jayne is the secretary, Darren Page is on the committee. Jude Morris-King is the treasurer. It went

from there. The Supporters Club became established in 2015."

Former player Catherine Hyde is a member: "I've always followed the team and kept an eye on what they were doing. As soon as it got re-launched I started watching, because I knew that I'd never be here playing, because I was just too late. I just got in to it and started coming with my Dad. Then we joined the Supporters Club and joined the Committee there. It's stressful sometimes, but you're a bit part of it. You follow them everywhere. Go all the world with them. We constantly meet up and have different days out and they're a good bunch."

David Sheel "We instigated our first player of the year award for the 2016 season and Lucy Bronze won that. We had a great day and the Supporters Club was growing. We had a family funday and stuff like that. We did a few trips, like to the Football Museum. The success of the team brought more members too."

The Supporters Club has continued to grow and its bonds with the first team are strong. Some of the supporters of the women's team have no interest in the men's team at all and some support other men's clubs, demonstrating that City Women appeals to its own audience. There are people who support all aspects of Manchester City and there are some that support only one area. That perhaps confuses some, but it shows that the women's team are attracting support because of what they do and not simply because of interest in the full Manchester City club.

Awards night 2019. Below: Nick Cushing with the Supporters Club committee

Gavin Makel being interviewed at the 2014 re-launch.

Joining the WSL

Gavin Makel, City's Head of Women's Football, has been the driving figure behind the club ever since the decision was taken to develop a club capable of playing in the WSL. Here he explains his view of how City developed.

Gavin Makel: "In one of my previous roles at City in the Community - I think my title was Football Project Manager, or something of that ilk - I was kind of the contact point for Manchester City Ladies at that time. They were outside of the football club but we gave them kit. We gave them access to the meeting rooms… all of those kind of things. That was when I started to get involved, but there was no real commitment to it at all. We obviously had girls within our community setting playing football and things like that but there was nothing really specific to women and girls that I was necessarily involved in too much.

"I think one of the things that we recognised within City in the Community at the time was that we had someone who was focused on girls football part of the time, in terms of going out to schools. Participation increased amongst young girls, doing female sessions and that person reported in to me, so that was one of those reasons why I was kind of the contact point. We'd also applied for the Centre of Excellence as it was then, back in probably 2011. We were unsuccessful at that time for whatever reason. I wasn't a part of the application process, so I'm not entirely sure why we didn't get it. Probably we weren't ready for it at that time anyway and I think even if we had have got it it probably would have sat within

the community arm of the football club, in the same way that United's and a lot of the Centre of Excellences, or the Regional Talent Clubs as they are now do, They go in to the community Foundations. I was probably doing one day a month or something like that on it, or if it was when we got the new kit, for example, then it would be a little bit busier because we were liaising with the Committee from City Ladies as it was, to make sure that they had everything that they had. But I knew that there was an appetite from the club, at some point, for us to invest in women's and girls' football.

"Around the beginning of 2012 Brian Marwood was asked to go to a meeting with the FA to talk about entering a team in to the Women's Super League. Mike Green, who was my Line Manager at the time at CITC, said 'Brian wants you to go with them,' I didn't know much about the structure of the Women's Super League at the time. I'd seen how well Great Britain had done in the 2012 Olympics and I took interest in that, so I knew some of the players. I'm from the North East and obviously Steph Houghton is from the North East, so that kind of peaked my interest a little bit because she comes from down the road where I'm from. I knew that when we got the licence, that she would be my number one target to go and try and get.

"When Brian and I sat in that meeting with the FA and the FA asked who is going to pull the application together Brian went 'Gavin.' I was off to L.A. the next week and the application had to be in within two or three weeks and then I worked with Don

Dransfield, who oversees all the strategy element of the group, and we got it in by hook or crook and there was a lot of things that we had to consider about where they would be based, where would we play, the staff, umm, all of those kind of factors that I don't think we probably had thought about previously. Obviously our first year we played over at the athletics arena outside of the Etihad, but we knew that the CFA was coming up, and we knew that the Club had kind of already made that a commitment that we would play in here once it was ready."

The club had considered applying in 2011. Gavin: "The whole change at this football club was taking shape and to do it then would have been probably foolhardy in many ways. The focus was on getting the men's team up and running and changing the whole culture and everything about what had previously gone on within this football club. I think the opportunity two or three years later was a conscious decision by us, as a club, that if we're going to do it now is the time to do it.

"Brian Marwood was totally behind this. 100%, you know. After we got accepted in to the League there was a need for someone to head this department up, pulling together the whole application. There was never a point early on where I thought whether wanted the job or whether I was suitable. I'd never even given it a second thought. It wasn't until Don had a conversation about the structure of it with me. I was saying 'obviously there needs someone to come in.' He said 'Why don't you do it?' I'd never thought about it and he said 'What I would do is pull a couple of slides together on your thinking and take them in to Brian.' So I did that and I asked Brian for a meeting.

"I went in to the office with Brian all geared up to show him my slides and to say I want this job and he went 'Just before you do anything, I want to ask you a question:

how would you feel about taking it on?' Obviously, I had to go through an interview process and things like that, but that was it really. Brian has been very passionate about what we're doing. He's passionate about the club and he's passionate about the under 9 boys and girls. He knows every player and everything that's going on.

"I was probably working in the dark a little bit to begin with and that was where Brian was really supportive, you know. There was a lot of the on the job remit that I'd never experienced at that time in terms of dealing with player agents, putting on match day operations, match day experience… I'd project managed a lot of things here, previously, but not to the scale of what we needed to do, and I think the first thing that we did really well was develop a three year business plan. The biggest priority was players, so I started the job in the summer. I'd been on pre-season with the men to Hong Kong in the Barclays Asia Trophy back in 2013 and obviously with the WSL it was a summer season then and because of the way that the licence worked, we knew that all of the players in that League were running out of contract in November. Once it was announced that Manchester City were going to be part of the WSL a lot of the players probably were interested.

"We met with a lot of players but I'd submersed myself and when we were going through the application process I went to a load of games; looked at players; seen what facilities were out there; how match day is run; who the fan base were… So I had an idea of how we were going to approach it. We still had probably ten months before we would kick a ball in a game situation, so getting the team together was the main priority, given that players were going to come out of contract.

"Steph Houghton was my number one priority. She'd been made Arsenal Captain,

Toni Duggan was one of several key signings.

she was in the England team, she was on the verge of becoming the England Captain. I chased her, hounded her probably about three or four months, before she came and visited here. The CFA was a building site, we went around in the little truck with our high vis jackets and hats on and I said 'This is where the stadium is going to be. This is where you're going to train' and she took that leap of faith, as did Jill Scott, as did Toni Duggan, as did Izzy Christiansen and Karen Bardsley really. Those five."

Obtaining a WSL place wasn't without controversy and some in the media perceived City's arrival as being at the expense of Doncaster Belles. It wasn't like that as City applied and were accepted, following the rules of the governing body. City didn't make those rules and other clubs have also been parachuted into the top two tiers of the league pyramid. The idea of buying success is a lazy narrative by those who haven't looked deeper into what the club is doing. Gavin Makel: "We invest carefully in what we're doing in any part

of the business, and the women's team are no different. I have the pressures from the Chairman and the people above me that we need to be sustainable, as a women's team, we need to be sustainable. This football club are investing in the women's game and that's helped drive others on. Other clubs have followed suit so it needed that injection and to drive it forward because what the women's game has been crying out for years is for people to invest in it. I'm not just talking about the financial side of it, I'm talking about the investment in the people. Giving them the opportunity to be the best that they can be, whether you're a player, or whether you're a coach or a sport scientist or whether you're in my role. We're giving them the whole mechanism and support around that. We're very fortunate - we'll hold our hands up to that - that we've got an unbelievable facility to work in and we've got a host of expertise in different areas that we can use their knowledge and experience to help us kick on. That's what the game needs.

"Every Premier League team could do

Brian Marwood with the CFA under construction behind him.

what we're doing. Again, it's not about the cash that's going in, it's about everything we do like launching the new kit and having men and women players alongside each other. It's giving parity and being visible. People can see that we're really authentic in what we're doing, because this is what we believe in. Some women's clubs are still aligned with the foundation or the community department. It's starting to fade, which is good because when they're giving women and girls the opportunity to play football, they come and see it as an initiative. That baffles me. I've been in meetings around the country talking specifically about women in sport, and someone mentioned the Corporate Social Responsibility... Well if we keep thinking of it as a CSR initiative it will never ever evolve. It won't because we'll always just down play it. We have to think of it as it's football or it's tennis or it's rugby, whatever the sport might be, take it seriously, for what it is, and don't be almost condescending by saying 'Okay, let's put a

little bit of money to help young girls play football.' That really irks me!"

In 2013 when City's bid seemed likely to be accepted two important voices were quoted in the media – City Football Services Director Brian Marwood and existing City Ladies vice-chair Niki Taylor. Niki: "We are tremendously excited about the club's entry in to the Women's Super League. This is a huge milestone for Manchester City Ladies and I speak for the whole club when I say how honoured we are to be part of this. The support from Manchester City to make this possible is so valuable, and we look forward to what the future has to hold."

Brian Marwood: "The women's game is continuing to grow at a pace with 28 million girls and women playing football worldwide, making it the most popular female participating team sport. Manchester City is committed to the development of football in every community, and to sharing its football resources and coaching capabilities across a range of ages and abilities."

School & Family

Lesley Wright: "On a Sunday my mum and dad would take me to Sunday School and then the Conservative Club. That was our family day out – all I wanted to do was play football. I wanted to get a pair of boots and play. My mum and dad were supportive because it was sports. My brother was rugby and cricket and my auntie worked at Umbro in Wythenshawe and so we got discounted sportswear. She got me my first football boots. Puma…but not their best. It was the cheapest with no back on so you got blisters. My dad used to take me to play. When I started work I think people knew I played but your weekends are your own. For me it was watching City on the Saturday and playing football on the Sunday. I'd also go out after games on both Saturday and Sunday.

"My earliest memory of football was watching the 1969 FA Cup final on television. I always wanted to play football and I went to a grammar school where some girls did play and I remember meeting a girl at school, Val Hall, who said that she played for a team and I was like 'wow'. You had to be 14 then to play open age football and her mum and dad knew my mum and dad and so they took me to play for a team called Corinthians. This was about 1973. At the time they played in black and white stripes and they played somewhere near Briscoe Lane, not far from the Etihad. There was a pitch up there. We used to get beat by a lot of teams then because they were a lot older but for me just playing football was what I wanted. My school was an all-girls school and we played hockey, rounders, netball…

but no football. At primary school though I did play. On the 'boys' team I suppose you'd call it. At the time I thought I was the only girl who had ever wanted to play football because you didn't know of anyone else. Then when I went to Grammar School my friends were all sporty and could play any sport so then you realise.

"There were a lot of older women who played when I joined Corinthians. We used to play Macclesfield Town, Fodens… back then a lot of big companies had lovely sports facilities and tended to create women's sports teams, including football. There was a team called Ashton Brothers (based in Hyde)… there were a lot of works teams. When I was 16 I went to Spain with Corinthians. My mum had to write a note and I got my first passport. It was great to go abroad to play football and I think I went twice to Spain. Once we had to fly from Bradford because Manchester was iced-off. It was a great experience and football was everything to me. I couldn't wait to play and I got my season ticket to watch the men too. I used to go to Maine Road and stand on the Kippax or in the corner near the North Stand. My parents knew Rhoda Taylor's family and we got to know each other. We've now had season tickets together for…like forever!

"I used to play in the City Supporters Club five-a-side tournaments at Platt Lane. There was sports days at work where I'd play but some of the men didn't like it. Some would think you were trying to make them look foolish but it wasn't my fault that some of them were worse than me. I just wanted to play. If it was five blokes against five blokes and one scored that's all okay but if it's a woman who plays and scores that's different. Now attitudes have changed. Which is great. The blokes I sit with on the coach when going to watch the City men now talk about City Women and they've been to watch games. People are so much more aware of it now.

Rowena Foxwell: "I can't remember whether I was a City fan because I liked blue, or I liked blue because I was a City fan. I grew up in a single-parent family, no interest in football, Irish background… all I know is that myself and my best friend and one lad in the year above us, in the area we grew up in were City fans. Everybody else were Reds. We used to play football at break time at school and it was always, United versus Liverpool, so I used to play in nets for Liverpool, because it was the closest thing that you could be to playing for City. It was the lads and me, pretty much. No other girls."

Andie Worrall: "My Dad was a Sunday League footballer and it was a punishment to my Dad, because my Mum would blitz the house, cleaned it and he brought his whole football team back one weekend and I was about four, so my Mum said, from now on, the kids

Sexism in Schools

I am very concerned about sexism in schools particularly in the area of physical education. Female children are excluded from football and directed instead to netball. Male children are treated similarly. The children are being denied freedom of choice and girls and boys are being made to conform to society's stereotypes of male and female behaviour.

I am sick of it and so are my children. Is there a pressure group that is solely for children's liberation? Also I would welcome correspondence from like-minded parents on this and any other subject related to women's and children's liberation.

Your magazine is my only source of comfort these days.
Love, liberation
Elizabeth Panchaud
Reding House
Shalford
nr Braintree, Essex

Your best bet would be to write to the National Council for Civil Liberties, 186 Kings Cross Rd, London WC1. They are looking into the legality of different forms of sexism in schools in relation to the Equal Opportunities Act, and would be able to advise you.

football desperately needs them!

Little attention is paid to women's football and I think it could get a lot of support (and players) from the women's movement.

If anyone is interested in joining a team, here is the address to write to for further information:
Miss P. Gregory (Women's F.A.)
7 Mayfield Rd.
Hornsey N.8.
Tel: 01-340 6661
Yours in sisterhood,
Sharon Dunham.

*Dear Sharon
Coincidentally your letter arrived at the same time as this ad for Barclays Bank sent in by Fiona Aitken, Ashfield, Notts.

Women's Football

Until a few years ago the game of football was completely male dominated. Most men like to believe that women footballers are a bunch of man-hungry "dolly birds", who don't know the first thing about the game, will gladly be booked by the ref, and do everything on the field but have a game of football. This is of course totally untrue. If I don't come away from a game with at least a few bruises and a bit of mud on my legs, then I know I haven't made an effort and have had a bad game. I'm not saying that footballers are a load of masochists but when you go in for a tackle you go in hard and fight for the ball.

I play for a league side and I've met many women's teams, most of which have a high standard of play.

I haven't met any women managers or women referees yet though and I think that women's

Football is not one of her strong points.

But you wouldn't have her any other way. Because she's special. She's your future wife.

BARCLAYS

a good bank to get behind you.

Left and right: Spare Rib magazine regularly highlighted the issues facing women and girls wanting to play football in the 1970s. These articles are from February 1975, October 1976 and March 1978.

FOUL PLAY

NOTTINGHAM: Despite the hoo-ha in the national press, proclaiming 12-year old-Theresa Bennett's victory against the Football Association, the recent county court awards to Theresa on the basis of sex discrimination will have limited repercussions. The FA is appealing, and anyway Theresa won only because the judge ruled that at her age – before puberty – girls aren't at a physical disadvantage to boys.

After puberty the 'average' woman is physically weaker than the average man – and under the Sex Discrimination Act that means women can be kept out. It seems insane that if a woman is good enough, strong enough, fast enough to be selected for a team – and given male prejudices that means she'd have to be considerably better than any of the men applying– the notion that the *average* woman isn't, is considered relevant. It's not a question of considering the woman's safety, but of men fearing competition and worrying that their own sick sexuality would interfere with their concentration.

Theresa herself would like to play for an under-14 team next season – but she may not be able to as her victory applies only to under-12s.○

can go with you. I'd got a brother who was about eight, so there's four years difference between us. From being four to 18 I went with my Dad to Sunday League football, absolutely loved it. Where we lived it was all boys, so boys play football and there was hardly any girls so I never did any girly things, I just played football, and then obviously we'd go with my Dad on a Sunday. His nickname was Wellies because he always had wellies on, but we ended up with wellies on, me and my brother, so I learnt to play football in a pair of wellies so it was like he was Wellies, my Mum was Mrs Wellies and we were Little Wellies and I used to play football in wellies and could probably do it now. Me and my brother used to play football with all the other kids that had come with their dads.

"When I was about 10 my Mum read an article in the free *Advertiser*. An advertisement for a girls 5-a-side team for the Youth Games I went to the trial and there was myself, loads of girls turned up, and there was me and a girl called Maria Bertelli. She ended up playing volleyball for Great Britain, ended up at the Olympics.

She was one of the best footballers I've ever played with. So it was me and her that were the stand-out players, so that was Tameside and a guy called Mike McGlynn ran that. We ended up playing at the Youth Games and to me that was just the pinnacle at the time. I went in goal and I remember him saying 'you've got quite a talent' but I used to love playing out. Mike McGlynn used to get my Dad's ear going 'you need to keep her in goal.' So from that, Mike McGlynn is probably one of the biggest influences on me, he was like the Youth Development Officer in Tameside.

"I went to school in Dukinfield and some of the comments now they wouldn't get away with it now – 'girls can't play football.' That was a teacher, and he was a big Man United fan. 'You can't play football.' There was a tournament and I said to him 'well come and watch then.' He was our P.E. teacher and he ended up coming and was enthralled by it. He ended up getting so involved in it that he ended up coaching us. He got me up in assembly the next day and said 'I take it all back.' That was about 1993.

"When I was at school I spoke to the careers teacher. 'I want to be a footballer.' She's like 'you can't be a footballer, you can't do that.' She said 'what do you want to be?' 'I want to be a footballer' and she's basically like 'well, you'll work on a till or something you. You won't amount to anything.' So I was like 'I don't care, as long as my job can pay

Andie Worrall.

for me to play football, I really couldn't care less.' I was obsessed with football. You've got to understand this obsession. You'd come home, play football, play till it's dark, I'd play on concrete, I'd play anywhere.

"In the 80s they put a plastic pitch on Hyde United's ground and to me that was like someone going, well, there's Wembley on your doorstep, so I was really excited, Our school decided to have a game on there and then they went 'but you can't play in it because you're a girl' and then the teacher came up to me and he went 'I'm really sorry about that because you are the best player in the school, but girls are not allowed to play football.' I did get to play on it eventually because my Dad did a 5-aside with his work colleagues on a Monday so he'd always let me play five minutes at the end. My family always supported me but we never had a car 'till I was 16. We didn't have a lot, so I used to go everywhere on the bus… do all this travelling. Me and my Dad would go on our bikes everywhere to get to training."

Jane Boardman: "My Dad was a good

footballer, he used to play for Vauxhall Motors, and then ultimately became a P.E. Teacher so I spent most of my weekends on the touchline in the rain, in the mud, watching him. I've got a younger brother and my elder sister was a runner so she was never interested but my brother was interested at football. He used to play at sort of under 6s, under 7s and he wanted somebody to practice with and so he roped me in and we used to play in the street. Play between our gate posts, so he used to make me go in goal the whole time because he was a goal keeper for his team and he wanted to practice being outfield. In the evenings we used to go on to our local pitch, sneak in through a hole in the fence, and play in the goal. Sometimes in absolute pitch black and come back covered in mud. But really there were no women's teams in my vicinity then. I was living in Ellesmere Port.

"There was one girl I knew of who played football, as part of a boys' team, but she was the exception and so the only opportunities that we had really were informally, in the street, and as I got in to secondary school, I used to play informally again in the playground with the lads at school, but it was always difficult because (a) you'd have no coaching and (b) you were physically less strong than the boys, so there got to a point, when I was sort of 13, 14 where it was difficult to cope with the physical aspect against boys in the playground and so I didn't really play then until I got to university. I came to the University of Manchester. I knew there was a women's football team. I was quite a shy individual as a teenager, kind of growing up, but I'd made a decision that one of the things I wanted to do, when I got to Manchester University was to go and try out for the football team and I did and I got selected and that kind of is where it all started if you like."

"My Dad used to love coming down to watch me. At the time he was refereeing and he'd started to referee women's matches and so had seen the standard and been impressed with it. He used to come down and he was a centre half, just like me."

Abbie McManus: "I've got two older brothers you see, so from such a young age, it's how I got in to football. My parents taking my brothers to their football training and I was always the kid at the side wanting to join in and if they needed an odd goal keeper here or there or they were short of numbers I was always allowed to join in, so if it wasn't for the likes of my school teachers when I was younger, if it wasn't for the likes of Mum and Dad travelling me to here, there and everywhere for tournaments, games, fixtures…I thank them every day.

"It's funny because, as a girl growing up, your dream is to play football, because that's what you've always done. I've watched my

brother play for a professional club and my Dad's always going you'll get there, you'll get there, like obviously it's not just my dream, it's my Dad's dream. My brother's dream too. He loves it. My first England game, they all came and it was a special occasion, it's not just the fact that it's me, it's the fact this is now able to happen for young girls."

"Initially, it was a hobby. I did it after school. I did it during school. Football has always been a hobby to me, so at the age of 15 I don't think I ever thought it would turn in to my job. I knew there was a lot of people back then, when I was 15, 16, 17, in the backroom staff, trying to fight, trying to get the game recognised how it is now. I do think a lot of people have worked hard and unfortunately with the re-launch they are no longer here, but if it wasn't for them we wouldn't be where we are now."

"You got the typical nickname of being a tom-boy and obviously *She's The Man*, the film, when that came out, didn't help, because then it was *She's The Man*. But, apart from that, once they see you play they give you respect anyway. It was one of those like they point and laugh at the start and then when you used to take them on and stuff they'd be like 'oh, you can be on my team now.' You'd need to show them."

Bev Harrop: "My Mum said I could play football pretty much before I could walk. They never stopped me from playing. They bought footballs. Do you know what, when I was a child, even up to being in my mid 20s, I didn't tell anybody I played football that I didn't know. Because a lot of people, especially men, have this image of you know women not being able to play football and I just didn't want to go there. For a long time I didn't tell anyone that I was any good. It's only really quite recently with the game becoming high profile, like it is now, that you know that actually I'm proud of it.

"I played football all the time when I was

a child and then I wasn't allowed to play in school. The only time I could play at school was at break times at primary school. The boys were more than happy for me to play because I could play. I was just one of the lads, if you like. I played football in my spare time at home. In those days kids played out. We played football on the street, every single night. There was a field at the back of where we lived, we played on there. We had matches like our street versus other streets and it was really enjoyable. The police set up a five-a-side competition. I think I was aged 10 or 11, and we set up our own team from our street and went in to this competition. Back then I didn't even know that there were football clubs that you could join, but the teams we players were all football clubs and they were proper. We ended up getting in an older group than we were, but we did really well, and the police commended us on how well we played. I was the token girl really.

"When I started playing for teams my Mum and Dad came to watch. My Mum thought my playing football was 'oh it's just a phase!' My Dad took me to the Cliff on Friday nights, he enjoyed it. The older girls went to the pub afterwards and so we went. My dad enjoyed it and he went to the games. They didn't come to watch all the time. I remember getting the bus all around Manchester to play in the league."

Gail Redston: "I had four brothers, all older than myself, two years between all the boys and then I came along six years from the youngest boy and when they went out playing football I had no choice but to go and

A young Gail. Always with a ball.

kick a ball about. My Mum said to me that I was a really lazy walker and then I was sat on the beach one day and some kid had a beach ball. I just got up and ran after it and my Mum said ever since I've been chasing a ball.

"I was the only girl to play for my primary school. Some of the boys were supportive because I was a better player than them and when we went to secondary school a notice went up saying they were going to start a first year team. So a few of my friends said 'Gail, put your name down.' I put my name down and they just turned around said 'sorry, you can't play.' Because I'm a girl but all the guys said 'but Sir, she's better than me.' They tried but I wasn't allowed and I just lost a little bit of interest because I thought I'm being stopped from doing something that I love. When I was 14 though I played for the Corinthians. I only played about a season there and I think Les Wright was there at the same time."

Into her sixties Gail is still playing football: "My grandchildren love me playing. A lad said to my grandson 'Your Nana's sick at football.' When I was playing for Reddish, they'd sometimes go 'can we come train with you tonight Nana?' We'd be on the pitch and it would be like 'Yes Nana, down the line Nana.' I'd stop them and say 'It's Gail on the football pitch, not Nana!'"

Louise Wakefield: "I used to play in the street. I think I was the only girl who I knew played football so I used to play with all the lads anyway. The *Yellow Pages* came through the door, I wrote a letter to the FA in London. I was only

Steph Houghton

like 13. I said I play football; I've got my project coming up in school where you've got to go do work experience for a week. Is there anything I can do? They sent me the address of Manchester County FA and said get in contact with them. I wrote to them. They sent me the phone number of Manchester United's women's team manager. I phoned and then went to the Cliff every Friday night at 13, played for them, but they wouldn't play me. The manager was dead strict on his 11. So I did the same again. I wrote another letter to Manchester FA and they give me Gail Redston's number. She asked me to come down to Platt Lane, another Friday night. I went down and I think I signed the week after. That was 1996."

Steph Houghton: "My Dad was a big influence. I come from a really sporting family. In the North East they were football mad up there, so it was always kind of going to be football, but literally just kicking a ball about with my Dad in the yard and I think ever since I could run and was active it was always football, football, football, so as I say the rest is kind of history. They've been through every little step of my career as well. People see all these glory things that we speak about but they don't see like the hard times, like when I've been injured… I've missed major tournaments… I'm like a little bit stressed with football. The role that I play, there's a lot of pressure on you, you probably offload to them more. They travel all the way around the country, I don't get to see them much, so for them it's everything. You only know until maybe you miss a few games you realise that they don't know what to do with themselves because their whole lives revolve around driving down the M62 to come and watch me play so I think that's my motivation. To repay what they did when I was younger, taking us to all these holiday camps and taking us training when it's windy and cold and giving up their spare time together. I think that's a main motivator for me is to make them happy and to have them see you win things I think. That's what I play football for is to make them smile and see them in the crowd."

"I think primarily there was only a boys' football team at school but at break times we always used to play like 5-a-side competitions on the yard and there was girls playing then, me myself included. Then my first ever football team was actually the school team, so I was the only girl playing on that team, which was an 11-a-side team. Once they knew there was potential of more girls starting then they started to introduce a girls team.

"Opposition lads obviously wanted to make sure that they were better than us, but I was quite fortunate enough that I had a really good group of friends who always wanted me on their team. There was a few that would get a bit jealous and if you were playing ahead of them of course it's natural. It happens not just in schools, but in every day football. They kind of knew that I was pretty good at the sports, so they wanted us on their team as well. I loved it so much and I know for a fact I practised every single day. I knew that at some point I could kind of take it wherever I wanted to take it, but at the time, there wasn't that many girls' pathways to go on. For me it was something that I loved to do to keep active and be physical and fortunately the opportunities came around the corner.

"I used to go to like Sunderland Soccer Camps in the holidays. I went there and I got scouted by a coach from Sunderland. Sunderland were just starting their Centre of Excellence and asked us to go for trials. Ever since those trials you knew that there's potential to make it in to the first team. I think when I was 14 I made my Sunderland debut, my first team debut. I knew that football was definitely going to

be a part of my life and over the next few years the professionalism of the sport… the awareness… it started to grow and then England ask you to go for trials as well. You're like 'yes, I do want to be a footballer.' Whether it was working alongside education or something else. It was always going to be football. It was going to be always part of my life.

"I had a part-time job in a sports shop, which paid us about £20 a week, worked there four hours… eight hours a week depending on football. I went to university and got a degree. Always in the back of my mind I was like I just need to prepare myself to have something in line to be able to go down different routes. At one point I wanted to be a P.E. teacher. Another I wanted to be a sports scientist… I wanted to work within football… but also have playing football alongside it and fortunately enough, when I was in my university, I was studying, England brought in central contracts, which allowed us to train full time with England and do a training programme. You weren't relying on going out to go and work in schools or work in shops. You were allowed to dedicate so much of your time to your training rather than trying to go out and earn money.

"When I moved to Arsenal, I still wasn't on enough money to probably live off. It was all trying to get a part-time job at the university, working within primary schools, delivering sports. I think it was probably after the Olympics I thought 'right, okay, I could probably be involved in football for a very long time.' Whether that's playing as long as I can, or being involved within a team as a coach, or a back-room staff, whatever it is. I think that's when I probably thought 'well, okay, it's on television more, we're getting more people to games, there's more awareness, there's more profile of the players.' The Olympics was quite evident for me and I was like right, okay, there's a little bit more interest and people are taking them more seriously, so that's when it changed."

Catherine Hyde: "I played for Manchester City Ladies twice, once when I was 12, and I'm now 30, and again in 2005-2006. From the age of five I always had a ball at my feet. My Dad just used to take me on a field, asked me what I wanted to do and we just ran around with a ball and it was that ever since. I got bullied when I was in school for playing football, wanting to be like a tom boy, pretty much all the time. I'd always carry on. If I was doing something I was doing it. I used to hide my homework. Football was first. I wasn't bothered about the school to be honest. School didn't interest me. I just wanted to play football. If the lads can do it, I can do it. And that's all I wanted to do. I'm so competitive. When we was playing on our breaks at school I'd have to play against the boys and have to beat them and it felt good when lads said 'she is top, she can be on my team.' If I can kick a ball and I'm happy with the ball at my feet then you're not stopping me, it's simple as that.

"My sister Kerry Coclough took me everywhere I went to play. Week in week out. Snowy days, rained, horrible weathers, we used to have to travel. Well everywhere we played we had to travel because there was nothing really close by, three or four buses sometimes, maybe a train or a tram."

Rita Howard: "I've got three brothers all older than me. One of them was a really accomplished footballer who would have made it but for breaking his tib and fib which back then ended it all. He was in a cast from toe to thigh for months. Nevertheless when he was playing I went everywhere with him. Rain or shine. I followed him everywhere. I used to buy *Roy of the Rovers* magazine. Loved it. Read it from cover to cover several times and this one particular week it had an advertisement in it about women's football. Well, I was gobsmacked because I didn't know anything

with foreign coun-
England, though,
May, 1950 —
m in Brussels,
did the trick in

The following year, though, Spurs got some consolation in winning the Cup-Winners' Cup — the first British side to land a major European trophy.

have the nickname of "Magpies'
(PHILIP WESTMORLAND, Nott

● Don Revie scored four goals
full internationals for England
(JAMES DEVLIN, Co. Tyrone)

Female Soccer

I'd very much like to play for a ladies' team in my area when I leave school, but don't know how to set about finding the nearest. Can you help me, please?
ALISON KAILE,
BLANDFORD

● Well, Alison, new ladies' teams are being formed all over the place nowadays, and you shouldn't find difficulty in joining a suitable one not too far away.
For up-to-date information, your best bet would be to contact the Secretary of the Women's Football Association — Miss Pat Gregory, 7 Mayfield Road, Hornsey, London, N.8.
Good luck, Alison. I'm sure Miss Gregory will help fix you up.

● Four British players have "European Footballer of the Y Stan Matthews (1958). De (1964); Bobby Charlton (196 George Best (1968).
(BRIAN WOOD, Banffshire)

● Leeds' Scottish internation Joe Jordan was born on 15th D 1951.
(ERIK GONDER, Norway)

Our Expert would like to out that although all are read, he can only to published questions be of shortage of time.

orey
me how many
r, Peter Storey,

DREW LABAN,
DERBYSHIRE

defender has
drew. His first
reece at Wem-
his last in the
urin on 14th
d at Under-23

about women's football. So I saw this and thought this was absolutely marvellous. I wrote to the WFA at that time and I said I was interested but didn't know of any teams so they wrote back with details of two teams – One was Corinthian Ladies with George Aiken's name, God rest his soul. The other I think was Broadoak – or one out that way anyway. I rang George because his team was from Manchester and I was in Stockport and I thought it would work out. I was still at school then so it must be about 1976, after my dad had passed away. I didn't tell my mum that I'd written because she was dead against it but I did tell all my brothers who said 'Don't be stupid! They haven't got girls teams!' I'd always played with my brothers at football – I had to play in goal usually! Where I lived we'd often all go on the school playing fields City supporters against United supporters. You'd go to the men's match on the Saturday and then you'd relive it on the Sunday. I remember the first few weeks when I'd try to play with the lads and they'd all say 'no, no' then you'd manage to get in and then eventually it became 'Are you playing Rita?'

"So after writing the letter to George Aiken I got a call from him and he asked me to come to training. It was at Belle Vue behind the old Gorton Baths.... Gorton Park. I lived in Brinnington, Stockport. It was two bus rides away. I never thought for a minute my mum would let me go. The call was on a Sunday and I remember telling my brother Donal who was a footballer 'I'm going to this trial'. I was bigging it up in my head. I had no boots because I'd never actually owned any. He took me out in the yard and had a kickabout with me to show me a few things. But because I'd no boots I had to tell mum because I needed her help. She was dead against it. She did not want me to play football. I don't really know why other than the fact that she'd had three boys

then I came along. I suppose she was looking for leotards and frills. She didn't get that! She did later when she had another daughter though. She wanted me to be more of a lady and there was all that stuff about being a tomboy but it was never going to happen. Even going to watch football… I'm a United fan, always have been. Met my husband at Old Trafford… My mum didn't want me to go there but my brothers took me and then I started going on my own and she sort of went along with it.

"Getting the boots was an issue because we were young when my dad died and she was left with five of us. So there wasn't much money. But she let me choose a pair out of the catalogue. Pay weekly and I'll never forget it. They were called 'lightening' – nowadays kids would call these Adidas four stripe! You know what I mean? But I absolutely loved them and I looked after them with all my heart and soul.

"I remember one of the blokes at this 'trial' as I called it… he was one of the dads and you know how it is, if it wasn't for the dads and that you'd have no teams. His daughter Val played and he was called Ron. We were split into teams and I was playing on 'his' team and I remember we got a penalty and he's shouting 'let Ginger take it!', meaning me of course, and I scored.

"My brothers were definitely not against me playing and they saw the social benefit I got from playing. The playing was something I'd always wanted to do but when you're socialising with older girls in a team environment then it brings so many other social benefits. You learn so much. Life skills. My brothers never discouraged me. My mum never saw me play. A typical Sunday for me would see me get my boots, get on a couple of buses… I'm a Catholic so the only thing that wouldn't give was that I had to go to Mass and so that had to be fitted in. I couldn't give my mum any reason not to let me play. So I always did that. I'd get the bus in to Stockport and then one of the other girl's dads would pick me up. That in itself was a life skill. Travelling around.

"By the time I joined City I'd had a daughter and was married. My husband is the most fabulous man. I was playing football before we met and at no time since has he ever said 'I don't want you to play'. In 1993 I had my son James and I said 'I'm going to give up'. I was 31 and I felt like it was time to stop. My boots no longer fitted and I thought 'right, if I'm

giving it up, I'm giving it up' and I mooched about. Watched a few games taking the kids with me. I'm still feeding James anyway so wasn't able to play. Then Christmas day 1993 I get a pressie from my husband and I open it up and it's a pair of football boots and he said 'you're not ready to give up. Get on with it.' He was always supportive. Totally for me playing and that was a wonderful moment…. I have to tell you this though to change the mood. It's so funny. That pair of boots…. One was an Umbro and one was an Adidas! They'd packed them up wrong. I said 'you've robbed them!'

"My own children came to watch. In fact when I was still at Corinthians my daughter Leanne was six weeks old and I remember saying to my husband 'I'll just put her in the car. I'll take her and I'll watch the game.' I got there and they wanted me to play. Eventually I agreed to play in goal so my daughter was nearby! Lesley Wright

tells a story about the Umbro tournament at the University Grounds and James, my youngest, was born in the July. That tournament was usually in August and City got through to the semi-final or the final and I was sat on the touchline breast feeding. Lesley comes running down the touchline with the ball, sees me, stops and goes 'for god's sake, what are you doing?' So all my kids have been at my games over the years and it all was part of our normal life. James has since gone on to play football. I remember taking him to one of these soccer schools in the holidays at the local school. On the Friday afternoon they had a parent and child game so, of course, I go along with my kit. I'm the only mum playing and I'm holding back a bit and then I get the ball and do a decent pass. The lad who took the training said to me 'you can play, y'know' and I went 'yeah, I've played a couple of times.' At the end of the game I was given the player of the match. It was a bit embarrassing.

"In PE these days at my school where I teach girls play football as part of the curriculum. They join in and that's that. I am sometimes involved with school charity events and the like and I always say to the girls get a team in and they do. It's all an everyday part of life. Now when I was at school I remember saying to a teacher 'I want to do football.' 'You can't', 'but I want to'… it was an absolute no. Then a younger teacher came in and I said to him that I wanted to play. At the time there were two other girls – one was a brilliant sports person, she could do anything and she played football because I wanted to. Then there was an older girl who played as well. This new male member of staff then let us play football on a Friday after school. I never got to play in any competitive fixture or anything like that at school but he at least allowed us to play. That'd be about 1977 by then and I guess it was a move forward.

Helen Hempenstall: "Football was just natural in our house. My dad had played and I played with the boys at school. Growing up that's all I ever did on the estate. That's all any of us ever did. Play football all day every day. It was strange to some. Some boys didn't like it when I played because I'd get picked and they wouldn't some times. I never stopped playing though. I didn't really get much abuse from boys for actually playing but girls would often say 'why do you want to play football?' None of my 'girl' friends played football. I'd love to be that age now though, playing now. There's many more opportunities now. My youngest plays for Droylsden. She's only just ten but is too advanced for the tens and unders so she plays for the under-12s. She's got a really good football brain. We never needed to encourage her. It's funny really because the girls next door come home from school and are pushing prams

and stuff and all I can hear from ours is 'Agueroooooooooo!" and the bins getting leathered with the football! It reminds me so much of me at that age. At her age she's better than I was at that age and at Christmas everything is football or City. When I met my husband he knew I played for City and after he came to watch me he went back to his mum's and told her he was impressed 'I can't believe it, she's really good, mum.' He played as well on a Sunday morning."

Lindsay Savage was always aware of the efforts her family made to support her playing career: "Very much so, they travelled so many miles to support the team and me"

Heidi Ward: "Well I played football for as long as I can remember really. My brother used to play just in the street and then make me play alongside him. I just played and didn't think anything of it. I played at primary school but my head teacher wouldn't let me play on a team until the final year. I think my Mum got involved or we asked and my head said I could play

Spot Heidi Ward in the Broadbottom Primary School team 1981.

202

in the final year. I sometimes played half a game of netball for the girls and then half a game of football with the boys in my final year.

"There were no other girls that played football at all, so I was the only girl at primary school playing. We didn't even have a football pitch at school. We had a sloping tarmac pitch, so we just played on that and when we played against the neighbouring school we had to walk for about a mile and a half in our boots to get there. Then play a game of football and then walk back. Obviously I had to get dressed before we went because I wasn't allowed to get changed with the boys.

"I wasn't allowed to play at secondary school, so I just sort of like lost a little bit of interest. I still played in the streets… in the parks with my brother, and then my mum worked at City and she knew there was a tournament going on. I was about 13 or 14 and one of the sides was short of a player. I think it was a Supporters Club 5-a-side tournament and women were allowed to take part as well and one of these teams was short so my mum said 'oh my daughter plays a bit of football.' They said bring her along. So I went along and played with that team and some of them played for a team called Redstar and they asked me to come along and train with them. I was about 14 then.

"When I played for Redstar, I was obviously one of the younger ones so I was learning from the women there. I was fit because I was doing a PE Course, so I was doing PE sort of every day, but I'd liked to have been fitter and also a bit faster as well. I'd have liked to have trained in those areas. I didn't think about it at the time, I just wanted to play.

"It was really difficult when I first started playing for teams because I was only young. I wasn't aware of any teams around me. I lived near Glossop and it was about 15 miles

Jill Scott.

away from Manchester, so to get there, on my own, I'd have had to take like a train and a couple of buses to get to training for FC Redstar. My Mum wouldn't let me go on my own either, so sometimes my Mum would come with me to training and then other times I'd just completely miss training because I had no hope of getting there. They'd phone me up to say 'we've got a game, could you come and play' and then my Dad would take me. My Dad would come up to the away games as well, because Redstar didn't have any buses or anything. We all used to go like in a convoy in cars and then when I met Gary he came along with me as well."

Jill Scott: "I think it's weird when people ask us about starting to play football. I just feel like I just went in to football without it being a decision. I kind of went to school and just enjoyed it. I played football with the boys and I'm the type of person that I never really think ahead, probably just to the next day. I don't think I ever went in to it with the intention of it becoming a profession or whatever. I feel very lucky.

"There was only boys' teams and then I got in to junior school, which is like age seven to 11 and there was a teacher there at the time called Mr Burns and he let us play on the boys team. It was tough, obviously. You felt like you had to prove yourself and I remember being very young playing for like under 8s, under 7s and kind of just getting picked up by the coach which probably wouldn't happen now. Just going off playing football and my parents weren't there because I had other brothers and sisters and I used to get a lot of stick from the parents on the sides saying 'break that girl's legs' and stuff like that. I was only six or seven and I remember leaving the pitch in tears at times, but I always think back and think I must have loved it because I always got my boots ready and was waiting for my lift the week after. I was definitely the only girl playing on my team at that time.

"I think because they couldn't really take a girl doing better than them, the opposition boys used to try and go in a little bit harder. They used to call you names, but my team were quite supportive. When I think back, I had a lot of good friends in that team. I used to go to their house for tea after school and stuff like that. I can't really fault my team but I think the other team maybe were influenced by the parents. They probably didn't want to see their son getting beaten in a race by a girl.

"I got in to running, just from going to senior school, so from the age of 11, 12, I think as soon as you say you play one sport, you're suddenly at Badminton Club on a dinner time… you're at Netball on a night time. I don't think there was ever a day where I didn't pack a packed lunch to do something in lunchtime, but I just loved being active. I got in to running from there and went to a few school championships and did really well. I kind of had to make a decision. I went on to run for some of the Sunderland Harriers and was kind of breaking a few records there and I think I was the first girl to win the North East Championships, Northern Championships, and then it came up that I had to make a decision when I was about 14, because I had the opportunity to run in the English Schools and probably people argued that I could have gone on to maybe represent England. I remember when it came to making the decision, my Mum wanted us to do running, because I probably wasn't going to get kicked and it was a nice summer's day out, wasn't it? Running around the track… but my passion was always football. I hated running. I used to say to my coach 'well, what do I think about when I'm running?' and he's like 'well just concentrate on the race and what you're doing', but I was almost a bit bored. I think that feeling of winning on your own never really fulfilled us. I've always been a team person and I think when you win a game with a team it's nice to share them feelings, so the decision was always going to be football.

"I think at that time you had probably like Paula Radcliffe, Kelly Holmes and I'd seen them on the telly and they were winning things and obviously doing well but I think one thing my Mum had always supported us with was being happy. I think that's always something I thought. My decisions were always based on what made us happy. I'm probably a bit like that now. I tend to not do things that I don't like and people are like 'Jill, sometimes in your life you have to do things that you don't like.' I remember getting told that I couldn't play for the boys' team anymore and I thought that was going to be it and I was in tears because I thought football was going to be

Karen Bardsley at Bristol, 2018-19.

over when I was about nine or ten. Then I found a girls' team."

Karen Bardsley: "The difference lies in the culture and the perception of young girls and women playing sport in the States. It's widely accepted, you know, and it's almost encouraged that you know girls get active, girls go and do stuff, and once they find something that they really like, they are very encouraged to kind of carry on with it, especially football. It's almost perceived to be a women's sport in the States, which is kind of ironic really, especially when I have come over here and I've experienced it's not perceived that way (laughs). As a young girl in the States, I think you know there's all sorts of opportunities to play different sports and try different things and when you find something you like you just kind of carry on and see where it takes you. I discovered that I had the opportunity to get a scholarship to university. I ended up getting one and

then played semi-professional and then professionally. I ended up getting a trial and then getting drafted, so for me I always had this kind of dream that I wanted to be a professional athlete, but the fact that I didn't know any was never a deterrent. I thought if the men can do it, I can do it, and hopefully something will evolve along the way. Fortunately, it did, but we always had a very strong national team. Growing up there were you know the Mia Hamms… there's just too many to name them. They were always pivotal and influential and they kind of drove it from the top, which you know, obviously presented themselves with opportunities, but then also the future, so that really kind of drove me."

Izzy Christiansen: "Being a full time footballer was something which was beyond my wildest dreams. There was never that vision. There was never that clear pathway. In December 2013, just before I signed for

Izzy Christiansen.

City in February or January 2014, I was looking in to doing a PGCE, and just fitting football alongside because there was no pathway. It was only until the last three or four years that there's been a visible kind of distinct professionalism in the women's game and its meant that we were able to leave jobs, study, whatever it may be, to come full time."

Debbie Darbyshire: "When we started City Ladies Neil Mather's Mum and Dad looked after us. They fed us… they watered us… they washed our clothes… they let us stay overnight… they dried our tears. They were just there from the start to the finish and they were absolutely amazing. I'd like to mention those two because they were so good to us. We were like their extended family really."

Neil Mather: "The whole family were committed. My sister was in the first team as

well, she was a really enthusiastic player and was well in to it. My Mum loved it and loved the fact that it was women's football and my Dad was dead supportive. Everyone's family seemed to be there at times. Donna Haynes' family were always there. A lot of people gave up an awful lot of their time."

Rowena Foxwell: "We made lasting friendships through City Ladies. He'll probably hate me for saying it but it wasn't long after we started, probably early in 1989, when our coach Godfrey Williams had a very bad car crash. He was nearly killed and Debbie Darbyshire and I went to see him. He had broken his jaw. His mouth was wired up. He'd near enough lost the sight out of one of his eyes… And I can't say he was delighted because we turned up and he's sat there in the bed in his father's pyjamas! Godfrey married Rhoda Taylor. They got together at one of the parties. Godfrey was an Oldham player. They had two children and I'm godparent, so there's the overlap there."

Debbie Darbyshire: "Rowena met her partner Benny through City. Lots of friendships came through football."

Rowena Foxwell: "Benny was often around. We got together maybe a year or so after City Ladies had started. That's how we used to go out socially. We've been together now for over 28 years. We've got two kids… We're all season ticket holders at City. Debbie and I have been friends since that very first day of City Ladies."

Debbie Darbyshire: "On that first day I met Kate Themen too. Me and Kate are really good friends. I'd meet up with her after matches, home games now, umm, she comes to my Mum's for her dinner, randomly, too."

Neighbours

While the perception will always exist that Manchester United have always been City's rivals, for City Women the real rivals have varied over the years. Derby matches have been played against Manchester Belle Vue and other prominent local clubs. However, any game between City and United takes on extra significance. United fans established a Manchester United Ladies team in the 1970s with close ties to the men's club. This eventually was closed down by the men's club before re-emerging in 2018 as a WSL 2 club. In September 2019 the first WSL Manchester derby between City and United will occur. This will be staged at the Etihad. The first competitive derby was actually in September 1990 in the North West Women's Regional Football League Second Division when Neil Mather was manager.

Neil Mather: "I was nervous for weeks on end, and it was coming and coming and coming. I thought 'we've got to beat United in the first competitive Derby.' Being a big blue it was like 'whatever we do we've got to beat them.' We were 4-1 up with about five minutes to go and then had a five minute collapse where I thought we're going to blow this. At one point it had looked like we were going to get five or six and annihilate them and then we nearly lost it! Thank God we hung on for a 4-3 win, but I'll never forget that game. We had a girl called Jenny Newton who was a manic City fan and scored and I don't think I've ever seen anything like it. When she scored her eyes were bulging and it meant the world and a lot of our girls were City fans. It meant the world to beat them."

Heidi Ward: "It was exciting when we played United. There was a bit of interest there as well and we played at the University Grounds and we had quite a few people come to watch us just because it was City and United. That was quite nice actually. We were wearing City kits and they were wearing United kits. It felt quite special. I remember Rhoda Taylor was playing. She scored early on. When it was 4-1 I had a chance and instead of blasting it I tried to place it in the corner and the goalie saved it. I could feel the disappointment… Everybody was hoping to make it 5-1."

City Girls win cliff hanger

MANCHESTER City beat Manchester United 4-3 in the first derby game of the season, leaving the two sides separated only by goal difference at the top of Division Two.

No, this is not a flight of fancy but women's football. A crowd of more than 100 braved the weather and were rewarded with a thrilling seven goal game.

City started excellently with Rhoda Taylor opening the scoring in the eighth minute.

This was a testing time for United, but they showed the class that has won their opening three games with a 28th minute equaliser, a Williams header.

There was nothing between the teams until just before the interval when the in-form Rachel O'Shaughnessy scored, thanks to a wicked deflection.

The Blues carried on the good work after the break, Jenny Newton stealing in at the far post from a free kick on 50 minutes in a move that would have done Lineker proud.

City took command with Heidi Ward going close, and the by now, inevitable fourth goal being provided by Lesley Martin Peters, who beat three players to score.

With the crowd chanting "5-1" City began to show some of the qualities of their male profes-sional counterparts, conceding two quick goals from Holland and Bruce and leading to a worrying last five minutes for the City management.

"We must give credit to United. It was a night-mare last few minutes," City manager, Neil Mather, told Area News. "But the difference between the sides is that I think we wanted it more."

City's Tracey Blanchard was named as "man of the match."

The programmes from a charity 'derby' in 1992 and the 2000-01 FA Cup meeting.

Lesley Wright: "The first time we played United in a competitive game there was about 150 there. They were a really strong team. Better than us at the time and they'd been established a lot longer."

Rita Howard: "Despite being a United fan I loved playing as City Ladies against United. I absolutely loved it. Even though I'm a United fan I never contemplated joining them because the support from City, even when it waned a little, was far superior to anything United got. At best they'd get a kit and then it was 'on your way'. I know our closeness to City came from that beginning with Neil. His enthusiasm got us the kit, the tracksuits, the minibus…. All sorts of things. I know that wasn't happening at United and at that time I don't think any club connected in any way to a Football League side were as close as we were then. I think we got a lot

more recognition from the beginning and that has carried on to today. Look at what City have done and now it seems United are reluctantly coming on board."

Jane Morley: "I'm a season ticket holder at Manchester United but I was a manager at City Ladies. One day I'd been with City at a tournament and then went straight to Old Trafford for a men's game. I was sat there when the bloke next to me – who I didn't know – said 'what you doing with that on!' I realised I still had my City jacket on. I had to explain to him that I managed City Ladies."

Bev Harrop was a Manchester United fan playing for City: "I had a United shirt underneath my City shirt! (laughs) Most of the time. Not later on, I grew out of it eventually, but at first, I did."

Jane Boardman: "We attracted more players when United closed their open age

City to face United in the WFA Cup, 2000-01.

women's team we were the natural home. At that point it was sort of United, us and Stockport County, were the three main clubs locally. There were a lot of players that moved between the three and back again. I always stayed at City because I'd got my way in to the team and they knew my strengths and I didn't want to have to start again building up trust somewhere else.

Jane Morley: "It angers me when people say that Manchester United now have their first women's team. As with City when the relaunch happened that implies the stuff we did for the club years before doesn't count. I played for United in the 70s and 80s before a few of us broke away to set up FC Redstar. We left United because we wanted to test ourselves. We had some great players and

wanted to progress but those who ran United wanted to stay in a Manchester League and not join the North West League. So we broke away in 1985 and formed FC Redstar.

"Many of the teams we know today as WSL clubs are actually men's clubs that have taken over established women's clubs. Teams like Leasowe Pacific became Everton. I have to bite my lip sometimes when some clubs claim they created a women's team... no, you took and rebranded a team. There were quite a few big teams around the time City Ladies started such as Broadoak with Tracey Wheeldon."

Gavin Makel (talking in 2017): "I'm not bothered about any other club, what they're doing, we're focused on what we're doing, but I think in some ways, you know, let's get it right, Man United are a huge worldwide brand, one of the biggest football clubs in the world, there's no getting away from that. It would be fantastic to have a women's Manchester Derby here. We have that at youth level in the Girl's Academy, when they play each other. There are many big clubs who are starting to invest in to the game, which is great, and this is what it needs. From a playing perspective that's where it gets tricky, because the talent pool of players, at this moment in time, may not be big enough to go across everyone."

Right: The Football Aid Manchester derby played at Maine Road, May 2001.
Below: City v United, featured in the men's programme, August 2004.

■ Manchester City's Ladies winning squad: Vicki Bloor, Kim Hines, Jane Clark, Louise Wakefield, Tracey Blanchard, Sally Rustige, Lynsey Newman, Kate DeMouilpied, Ellen Thornton, Charlotte Johnson, Donna Davidson, Linsey Savage, Bev Harrop, Rhoda Taylor, Joanne Rutherford, Gail Hogarth, Wendy Tavendale and Christina Hogg

Ladies bring City cheers

By ROBERT HODGES

AT last, Manchester City have finally got something to cheer about. But I'm not talking about Mr you know who.

City's Ladies side have shown Keegan's boys how to do it by collecting the Northern Combination League championship with a win over United at Maine Road.

The match was the second of two days of football at Maine Road for Football Aid.

The charity, set up by Celtic fan, Craig Paterson, raises money for diabetes, as well as grassroots football.

It was set up a year ago and already 42 clubs have got involved with the cause.

Football Aid representative Scott Thornburn thinks that the charity is a great chance for football to use it's success to help others.

"Popstars have Live Aid so it makes sense for footballers to have Football Aid," said Scott. "It gives a chance for clubs around the country to raise some money and give their fans the chance to live out their dreams."

The charity organises matches involving amateur teams like Man-

chester City's ladies at the home of their idols. Then the proceeds from the matches are split between the governing bodies, the charity itself and a charity of the home club's choice.

"Clubs have been surprised by the response they get from the players, we give them all a book to write their comments in and the feedback has been tremendous," said Scott.

"We've already raised £300,000 for the cause and as more clubs get involved, it can only get bigger."

City's ladies side looked at home on the Maine Road pitch and showed the talent that has seen them take the Championship and promotion to the Premier League.

They were presented with their award by Radio Five Live's Susan Bookbinder who thinks the girls' achievements have shown the way for the men.

As for the match itself, City ran out 2-1 winners. The winning goal came from Tracey Blanchard in the dying moments.

■ IN CONTROL... City skipper Donna Davidson breaks up an attack

CITY GIRLS DEFEAT UNITED IN PRE-SEASON 'DERBY'...

Ladies Day

Manchester City Ladies got their preparation for the new season off to the perfect start by beating United Ladies 4-2 in July.

The match at Chorlton Sports and Social Club was staged to raise money for the Francis House Hospice and was a rare chance for City to face their rivals from Old Trafford who play in a lower division.

Wearing their new strip donated by Reebok, City raced to a 4-0 lead with goals from Lindsay Savage, Natalie Thomas (2) and Laura Oligan before United grabbed two consolation strikes late in the match.

The Ladies side play their home games at Abbey Hey Football Club, Gorton and last season finished seventh in the FA Premier Northern Division.

City Ladies Chairman Gary Moores said: "The result against United was fantastic and hopefully we can take our great form into the new season.

"We are very grateful for the support of Reebok and everyone at Manchester City for providing the first team with new kit for the season - hopefully the girls will now play as well as they look."

City Ladies run a number of teams from Under 10's to the first team, training on various nights of the week...

TUESDAY
7.30pm – 9pm, Under 10's, 11's & 13's, Chorlton Sport & Social Club, Hardy Lane, Chorlton.

THURSDAY
7.30pm – 9pm, Under 13's and 14's, Chorlton Sport & Social Club, Hardy Lane, Chorlton.

FRIDAY
7pm – 9pm, Open age training (15 upwards), Platt Lane Training Complex.

For more information about Manchester City Ladies please contact their Chairman Gary Moores on 07802 771 414 or visit the website www.mancityladies.com

LADIES GAMES...

First Team Fixtures 2004/05

15 Aug	H	Oldham Curzon
22 Aug	A	Blackburn Rovers
29 Aug	H	Sunderland
5 Sep	A	Wolverhampton W
12 Sep	A	Middlesbrough (L/Cup)
15 Sep	H	Tranmere Rovers*
19 Sep	A	Stockport County
26 Sep	H	Middlesbrough
3 Oct	H	Wolverhampton W
10 Oct		L/Cup
13 Oct	A	Tranmere Rovers *
17 Oct	H	Coventry City
24 Oct	A	Aston Villa
31 Oct	H	Sheffield Wed
7 Nov		L/Cup
14 Nov	A	Lincoln City
21 Nov	H	Stockport County
28 Nov	A	Middlesbrough
5 Dec		FA Cup 3rd/Rd
12 Dec	A	Coventry City
19 Dec	H	Aston Villa
3 Jan		FA Cup 4th/Rd
16 Jan	A	Sheffield Wed
23 Jan	H	Lincoln City
30 Jan	A	Oldham Curzon
6 Feb	H	Blackburn Rovers
13 Feb	A	Sunderland

Matches usually 2pm to. 0 – 7.30pm kick off. Some games played at Abbey Hey FC, Gorton.

CITY v LADIES

210

Tournaments

Before a national league the best way to compare women's teams from different regions was at annual tournaments. City participated in many of these over the years, such as the Mansfield Tournament. Occasionally, they won the tournaments and paraded the trophies at Maine Road or the Etihad before men's games or at half-time. These tournaments provided an opportunity for teams across the country to compare each other.

The first major tournament that City participated in outside of the north-west was organised by another new club, Arsenal, in 1990. Arsenal had been established shortly before City and both clubs were held up as positive examples of Football League clubs involvement in women's sport. City tended to get more media coverage back then, thanks to the support of Linda Whitehead at the WFA, but Arsenal seemed to invest more in their team. The Arsenal tournaments became memorable excursions for the original City Ladies players.

Debbie Darbyshire: "We went down to Arsenal for a tournament and we played at their main training complex. Arsenal had all the facilities. We were like 'wooh, look at this, we've got a posh changing room and showers.' At City we got the secondhand kit. The hand-me-downs."

Helen Hempenstall: "We stayed over at a university campus near Holloway Prison. We all did our own thing at night time and I remember Godfrey Williams saying 'None of you can drink a lot.' We ended up in this bar but a few of us didn't like it so me, Donna Haynes, Tracey Blanchard – we shared a room. Anyway, we left and ended up on the Underground then getting off and trying different pubs. Later we went back to where we were staying remembering that Godfrey had told us not to drink much. We pressed the lift button, the doors opened and there were Godfrey and Rhoda Taylor looking dazed in the lift after having too much to drink!

"I wasn't supposed to be playing in the

Joni Davies and Debbie Darbyshire, 1990.

Godfrey Williams

211

Rhoda Taylor passing to Gail Redston, Dick Kerr's Ladies Football Cup 2019.

tournament because I was injured and had had an operation. Things weren't going well in the tournament and Neil Mather asked if I could play if we strapped my leg up in some way. So we did and I played. It was a hot day and at the end of the tournament one of the Arsenal coaches came over and asked me

if I'd go and play for Arsenal. Arsenal were ambitious and were starting to pay players. That's how they developed so quickly and to me they were the first massive club to be involved in ladies football. I remember that as good as our club was there's seemed better then. They turned up in a full kit with tracksuits, matching bags and everything on the Arsenal coach… Some first team men's players came to watch too. It was a good setup. I didn't go because it was too far. I could've done it because my brother lived in Kent but I didn't want to leave home. Being a City fan too there's nothing more you want to do than play for City. It was a nice compliment at the time though. If I'd still been playing for Lady Blues and Arsenal had asked me then I would probably have done it but I was with City. I only told my mum. I was 21 and I knew my dad wouldn't have wanted me to go.

"That weekend we also watched City at

Rita Howard on the ball at the first Arsenal Tournament, August 1990.

Arsenal Tournament, August 1990.

Tottenham in the League and my husband – who I didn't know then – came up to us to talk to us. He knew some of the others and that's when we chatted."

Neil Mather: "[Arsenal] were clever to be fair, because they put players on Youth Training Scheme contracts. Any decent player that was a young girl was going to go there. It was about 28 quid a week wasn't it? But it was that or go and work in Tesco for

28 quid. It was a no-brainer, so that's how they were clever. That's how they became really strong, because all the young players went straight there. We couldn't do that. We didn't have the money at the time."

Gail Redston: "We hired a mini bus and argued over who was going to drive. I ended up driving there. Les Wright ended up driving back. I think Pam Rose got sent off in one of the games at Arsenal. She'd go through a brick wall, Pam, but it was interesting and it was nice the fact that we'd been recognised. We're Man City and Arsenal have invited us because they quickly became the top club. I used to say 'If all the guys would just donate sort of a £100 of their wages once a month in to the women's, they wouldn't miss it, and it would establish us to be a better team.' It would've made a huge difference. At the end of the day, we're all working. We're giving up time. Especially going to places like Arsenal. We're having to stay over for the weekend, so your weekend's gone. And you've got to pay for that."

Heidi Ward: "I remember the Arsenal tournament because me and my boyfriend were camping. We were going around Britain camping, so we didn't go down with the team but we met them there. I remember it being like loads and loads of pitches and loads of different games going on. The Arsenal girls… I think they'd just started or were just starting a Youth Training Scheme.

They were getting paid to play football and I remember thinking that would just be amazing, if you could be paid to play football. It was only something like £25 a week, but it was a job.

"I didn't even think that I could do anything like that, but looking back now, I would have loved the opportunity to have proper training… Told about what I should eat and thinking about all that type of thing. I'd have loved the opportunity just to give it a go. I thought it was amazing that Arsenal players were being paid. I don't know of any other places that did it. I think it was just Arsenal at the time and I don't know how long it lasted for either. But they were still playing in the same tournament as us… We were like eating a bag of chips and that. In no way, shape or form professional."

Kate Themen: "I remember the ball was put across to me and I was getting ready to head it… It hit the cross bar and came out and I just went running in to the net and grabbed the net. I couldn't believe it. I'd nearly scored against Arsenal. I was disappointed. I was later substituted and I remember getting told off by Godfrey Williams because I was annoyed that he'd substituted me at Arsenal. It was quite a prestigious tournament and they actually had girls on the books at Arsenal. Girl footballers on the books. That's kind of testament to them that they've done something revolutionary at the time, paying girls to play football."

Lesley Wright: "We went a couple of times to Arsenal and stayed in dorms. One time I went up for a header and cut my eyebrow quite bad but I wouldn't have stitches because I'm scared of needles! We did the Moss Farm Tournaments as well. This was always a good way to see clubs from outside the region and you'd be able to compare and see how far we had to go. There was no national tournament apart

from the FA Cup, so this is how we played Arsenal and others. Arsenal and Fulham became great teams because they were able to invest in their women's teams and start paying them, even if in Arsenal's case it was the old Youth Training Scheme. You can see the same now. The teams that attract players outside of the WSL are those that attract sponsors and can pay travel expenses. Which means that it doesn't cost you to play and so you attract the best players. Back when City started the great teams in the north were Leasowe and Doncaster Belles but down south they had more opportunities to develop because they had more clubs.

Lindsay Savage saw one of the regular tournaments that City played in as being her best memory of her time at the club: "The Mansfield Tournament when I was 14. I was just a skinny kid playing in the first team and I was terrified. All the girls made me so welcome and really looked after me, and I think that was when I really thought 'yes, I am ready and I can do this.'"

Bev Harrop: "There was a tournament in Mansfield every summer time, first weekend in September, and we played in that tournament for a few years. That was our chance to play against these better sides because there was Arsenal and Fulham and a couple of other big sides that were around. There was Doncaster Belles too. For us that was when we could see these teams and play against them. I mean they were better than we were but we gave them games, and some of them didn't like us giving them a bit of a challenge either. We've played against some of the players that everyone knows. I've played against Rachel Yankey. I tackled her once and she made it known that she didn't like it: 'What do you think you're doing?' I was like 'Get on with it.'

"There was the time we went down to Slough for the All England Five-A-Side Championships. Godfrey Williams must have been manager then and he took us. There were seven of us. At the time City wasn't winning anything but we went down there and we came runners up in the All England Five-A-Side Championships. I think Leasowe won. They beat is 1-0 in the final, but we played against some other big teams too. I don't know what happened to that competition, because we never played it again.

"The tournaments that we played at the start of the season every year were really good and that just bonded you because we went down to Mansfield and so on, stayed over and socialised. We went to Dublin once and played a couple of teams there. It was fun. We were a bunch of girls, women, that could play football that came together. Lifelong friendships were built from it. We went out as a team and then we played as a team."

Gail Redston: "When we went to Ireland we all got tracksuits and that. Godfrey was in charge then and we're walking around Dublin looking in the shops. We're in one and I'm looking at some stuff and there's two Irish kids. They were nudging each other 'it is', 'no, it's not.' Then I see they're looking at Godfrey and I hear 'It is. It's Andy Cole.' Godfrey's stood there with a City tracksuit on and this poor kid is wearing a United shirt and thinks Godfrey's Andy Cole. I went 'Yes, that's Andy Cole. Go and get his autograph. He won't mind.' They following him all around the shop. Godfrey's just looking at me, shaking his head."

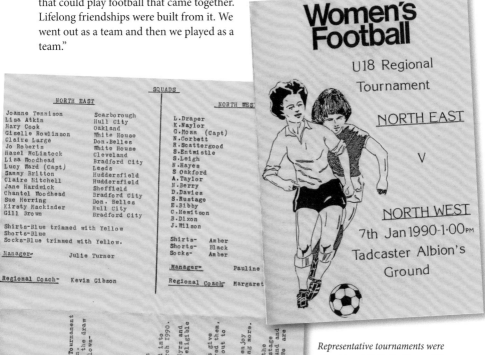

SQUADS

NORTH EAST

Joanne Tennison	Scarborough
Lisa Atkin	Hull City
Mary Cook	Oakland
Giselle Rowlinson	White House
Claire Large	Don.Belles
Jo Roberts	White House
Hazel McLintock	Cleveland
Lisa Woodhead	Bradford City
Lucy Ward (Capt)	Leeds
Sammy Britton	Huddersfield
Claire Mitchell	Huddersfield
Jane Hardwick	Sheffield
Chantel Woodhead	Bradford City
Sue Herring	Don. Belles
Kirsty Mackinder	Hull City
Gill Brown	Bradford City

Shirts-Blue trimmed with Yellow.
Shorts-Blue
Socks-Blue trimmed with Yellow.

Manager-   Julie Turner

Regional Coach-   Kevin Gibson

NORTH WEST

L.Draper
K.Naylor
G.Moss   (Capt)
N.Corbett
R.Scattergood
S.Entwistle
S.Leigh
N.Hayes
S Oakford
A.Taylor
N.Berry
D.Davies
S.Rustage
E.Bibby
C.Hewitson
B.Dixon
J.Wilson

Shirts-   Amber
Shorts-   Black
Socks-   Amber

Manager-   Pauline

Regional Coach-   Margaret

Women's Football
U18 Regional Tournament

NORTH EAST
v
NORTH WEST
7th Jan 1990 · 1·00 pm
Tadcaster Albion's Ground

Representative tournaments were often played. Sally Rustige and Donna Davies took part in this. Some of these players went on to win the WFA Cup and represent their country.

Jill Scott signing at the Etihad stadium with Nick Cushing.

Transfers

Interviewees were asked about their moves to City and how they came about.

Jane Boardman: "One of the last games I played for the university was a friendly against City Ladies and the university team won. At that time, the City Ladies were in a little bit of a difficult time. They didn't have that many players. I was finishing with the university soon after and at the end of that match they made an offer: 'If you are staying in Manchester, then come down and see us and have a trial and see how you get on.' I think she was captain in the team at the time and was sort of quite involved in all of the organisational stuff as well. At that point they were doing it all themselves, you know. She was probably captain, manager and treasurer and God knows what else… boot cleaner… kit cleaner. I went down and ended up signing for City, although you didn't really sign in those days. You signed a registration form with the League.

"I think there are a number of reasons, one was I was in Manchester and I was committed to staying in Manchester. I'd got a job in Manchester and the other thing was, because people have said that to me a lot over the years, people sometimes forget I'm not a City fan – I support Liverpool. I think the fact that we played them and we'd beaten them. So I got a sense that I'd have a chance to play. I knew I was never the best and so I wanted to find a team that I would get regular football with. Liverpool at that point were actually doing really well and had some good players and I knew that if I went there, the chances are I wouldn't get in. It felt more of a community and more something that

would be enjoyable whilst still competitive."

Andie Worrall: "I played for United in a game at Maine Road, the day Kevin Keegan come to City as a Manager. We got beat 2-1. It was conflicting having that shirt on.

I let the goal in at the end - I'm claiming credit for that because I ducked when I shouldn't have done, but whether people know if I did it on purpose or not I don't know! So we played there and then shortly after that John Stanhope was the City manager. He was a video analyst at Wales. He got me to come to City with all these promises of this, that and the other, but I didn't take it very seriously the first time around to be honest. Because I'd been at Everton, City were a step down then. Back then sometimes you'd get people's dads coaching. They'd sort of like develop and they'd get a coaching badge.

"City brought me out on the pitch at a men's game as a new signing. Victoria Derbyshire was there from BBC. My Dad and my brother came with me, and we had a few of us in a box. It was really good.

"The thing is in women's football you find people go in groups to other teams. I went back to Stockport when I left City the first time because Stockport was a better set up. It ended up Stockport was better run and the majority of us ended up at Stockport. Then something would happen at City and everyone would migrate back to City and that's how it happened."

Jill Scott: "I played for Sunderland till the age of 18… and then I joined Everton for seven years. The last couple of seasons we started to lose pace to different clubs. I think Liverpool had started off like a WSL Team and we lost a few players to there. I was going to make the decision to leave a year earlier, which I didn't make any secret of. I sat down with the manager and he offered us the captaincy of the team for the next year. I think I was about 25 at the time and I just thought it would be good for my development as a person as well as a player. I stayed another year, really enjoyed it, and then it's mad really to think that, if I had made that decision to go the year before, I probably wouldn't be sat here. Then Manchester City happened and it was just up the road and it kind of all fitted perfectly really.

"I'd heard a couple of rumours that Steph and Karen Bardsley were going to join and Toni Duggan at the time as well, because I knew them as players, I knew where the club was heading. I always think now, when I'm ever faced with a decision, I always think, if you're a positive person and you're willing to give it your all, then you can't really make a bad decision. I never look back and think 'oh I wish I'd never done that.' I think it's just part of your journey. I was excited, really excited. People always say was it about the money that you left but I was actually earning less money coming to

Izzy Christiansen.

Manchester City, at the time, because I had a couple of Ambassador roles with Everton. They looked after us really well, I loved my time there. For me it was just about the full time training really, and that's all I ever wanted to do, play football every day and this club was going to offer that.

"Whenever I think back to Sunderland I picture arriving 7 o'clock on a night, finishing half nine at night, getting in the house at 10 o'clock at night, going to bed. Preparing for school, college, work, whereas now your days are completely different. You wake up, you get your breakfast when you come in here, you get your kit and I remember saying this in interviews, when I first came, and can't remember if it was Nick, the Manager, he was like, you need to stop saying all these things, you deserve these things, he was like for your journey, you deserve to be getting your food and getting your kit, but we're all just so grateful and so appreciative of it because we'd never had it."

Karen Bardsley: "I have a great story about how I ended up signing for City. I was ready to leave Lincoln and literally go back home for Christmas. I'd just finished my contract and I was indecisive about whether or not to exercise my options and I spoke to my agent. I said 'Is City interested? What's going on over there?' He'd spoken to a few people and he said that they feel like they've got their spine already and they know who they want to go after. I was like 'Okay, it's not me. I haven't heard anything!' So I was on my way to the airport and I was staying at the Radisson at the airport. I got a phone call from my agent and he said 'Gavin wants to come and meet you' and I was like 'Well I'm at the airport tonight from this time until my flight tomorrow morning and so if we wants to come that's where I'll be.' I put the phone down, literally 30 minutes later, I got another call and was told 'He'll meet you there at eight.' So I ended up speaking to Gavin."

Gavin Makel with Karen Bardsley in 2017, three and a half years after rushing to Manchester Airport to persuade her to join the Blues.

Gavin Makel: "That spine that everyone talks about when you're putting a football team together, was really key. I remember I was moving house and I got a call telling me that Karen Bardsley's at Manchester Airport. She's flying back to California for the winter 'Are you interested in talking to her? Because she'd love to be a part of what you're doing.' I was literally moving house that day and was holding a box. I put the box down, drove to Manchester Airport, met her in the hotel, showed her a presentation."

Karen Bardsley: "Gavin got his laptop out and showed me this incredible presentation about what the idea of having a women's football team at Manchester City was and what it's going to look like and that just blew me away. I said to him 'When is this going to start?' 'This is three quarters of the way finished' and I was like 'what?' Obviously he was talking about this place, the CFA, and I was just blown away. I thought I've never had a Club actually do

what they said they were going to do, so that blew me right out of the water. There's been so many we'll do this and we'll do that and it just never really comes to fruition for the most part in the women's game. It might be the right way to do things and it's all well and good, you know, explaining to people how ambitious you are, but if there's nothing behind it, then it's just a lie in the end isn't it (laughs)?

"What attracted me to it was just the professionalism that the club has shown about really wanting to change the perception of women's football in this country and to be a part of a bigger something myself. To be a part of something bigger than just football and really starting to help the community and I think that really appealed to me. They wanted to be a pioneer of women's football. They want to build something and show people how it should be done, you know, and that really excited me. It was a gamble, I mean there

Aoife Mannion signs a two year contract after arriving from Birmingham in the summer of 2019.

were five of us I think that were full time at the time and that were of the required skill set, I would imagine."

Gavin Makel: "Karen went 'right, where do I sign' and that was it. Karen done. Signing Steph Houghton played out a little bit because she had offers elsewhere. Arsenal wanted to keep her as well. I look back at that and what an unbelievable leap of faith Steph made to leave a football club that had won trophies, year in, year out, and with no guarantee that that was going to happen here, but she took that leap of faith."

Gavin Makel about Jill Scott: "And that was solely because she wanted to play football and that's why you know you see those types of players and the kind of character that they have and they are reaping the rewards now I think for the sacrifices that they've made previously.

Izzy Christiansen: "If I'm really honest it took me a while for the penny to drop for me to think it's been the right thing for me to do. I struggled at first. I was still studying, finishing off my final year at university in Birmingham, so it was really difficult finishing that off whilst starting a new project with Manchester City as a player. We weren't full time but we were training a lot. So for me it was a really difficult time in juggling my degree, to complete it to the best of my ability, and to start at Manchester City because it wasn't easy at the start. Everyone was finding their feet, players and staff, and I was as well. I've spent a lot of my life on the M6 and it was really difficult because I wanted to fully invest myself in to Manchester City but I felt like I couldn't. Obviously since going full time, I've been able to do that, so things have changed for the better.

Blandie's Drum

David Sheel: "Blandie's drum gets the atmosphere going at games. Some people don't like the drum but the kids love it. There are a lot of kids at our games… a lot of families and the drum engages them. The drum gets the kids involved. Women's football is a lot more of a family experience and so it all helps contribute to the atmosphere."

"Blandie was going to games like we were and she was banging her drum. She started supporting the team because she liked women's football and it worked out right for her. She wasn't a supporter of the City men's team when she first came, so we do have a mix of reasons why people become supporters of the women's team."

"The people who wanted to make noise started to flock towards Blandie and her drum. She became the face of our support really. We laugh about it but I have said to her that people know you. She's a focal point."

Blandie with her original drum, presented to Izzy Christiansen, and the new bigger one signed by the squad

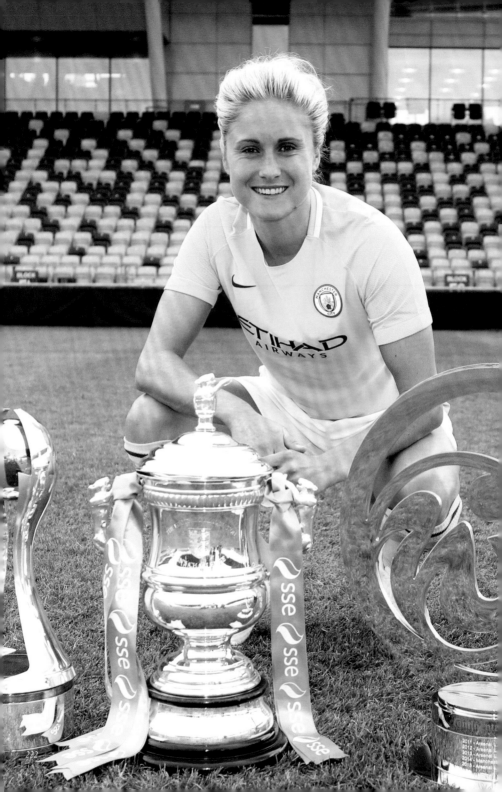

2010s Seasonal Summary

By summer 2010 City was a stable club with a strong and dedicated committee. Chair Gary Moores: "We had a core group of players that stayed for years but there were changes each year. Someone would move on for whatever reason and then somebody would know of someone who could fill that place. Plus we had a massive junior section by this time and some of those progressed all the way through. For example, Kelly McLellan was an under ten when my daughter was playing and she played all the way through the ages, playing quite a few years for the first team. She was only small but had the heart of a lion."

Leigh Wood was manager and he had contributed much to the direction of the club. Gary Moores: "When Leigh came on board I was able to take more of a backseat for the first team. He had a good assistant, Kevin Sims, and a good goalkeeping coach, Kurt de Klerk. He was self-sufficient if you like and he was an experienced sports teacher. He was an intelligent lad and I was able to offload much of the work that had come my way by this time back to them. I was still organising things like referees, the grounds and the travel but on match days I could leave them to it. The committee had the rest of the club to manage as well don't forget and a

Kelly McLellan.

massive part of this was the junior section. I didn't go regularly to the junior team games because we had others who were involved. Niki Taylor was massively involved in that. She was an important person in the ongoing development of this club. The money and the volunteers she brought in was incredible. She was like Derek Heath in what she gave this club. She was worth her weight in gold. We had little satellite committees around the main committee at this point and we had committees for raising money and so on. All answerable to the main committee.

"The club got bigger and bigger. Our junior section was the best in Manchester. We were knocking spots off everybody and anyone who didn't make the grade with us we were asking other clubs if they would take them on with the idea that they may come back in the year after. It was actually becoming a big juggernaut of a club. That's important – it wasn't just the first team."

The club relied on its volunteer committee. Alison Smith who was a coach and a committee member during the period 2008-14 believes that: "the friends made and the camaraderie of all the volunteers to get things done and done well" was the best aspect to the club during this period. She feels that "managing to keep a large, well respected grassroots club viable season after season and offering girls an excellent place to develop as young footballers" as the greatest achievement. There were issues however: "Too many to list! Financial difficulties constantly raising money through fund raising schemes; finding training and match day facilities around Manchester for

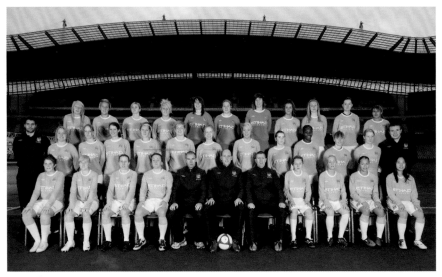

City Ladies 2010-11.

all teams that were affordable; finding quality and reliable coaches every season; dealing with parents; safeguarding and behaviour issues…." She felt that the person who did most during this period to ensure the club developed was "Gary Moores who guided the club through many difficulties."

Lindsay Savage agrees: "Gary Moores, as well as having the same birthday we moved from Stockport at the same time so experienced the journey together. Niki Taylor too. I think that the people behind the scenes sometimes don't get the recognition that they deserve and we had two of the very best with these two."

With Gary as chair and Leigh as manager City finished fourth in the division in 2010-11. They were five points behind champions Aston Villa. The next season, however, saw City achieve its highest position to date. Gary Moores: "Leigh Wood did a wonderful job for us and started getting us into good positions and he finally got us promoted in 2011-12. He developed a good team." Lindsay Savage,

who captained City to the Premier League Northern Division triumph in 2012: "I think the difficult times united the team and everybody involved with the club. The committee must have dealt with so much in the background which enabled us to go out week in and week out."

Abbie McManus was also a member of the squad. She remembers the community feel of the club: "It was just parents, family. It used to be like a day out for the family.

Lindsay Savage   *Abbie McManus*

Come and watch and we'll have a drink after, a cup of tea, or we'll go out for food after. Our parents used to go in, do the tea and coffee for the referees and like people used to bring oranges, Jaffa Cakes, jellies for half time. It's nothing like that anymore, but that's what it used to be like."

Gary Moores: "We got promotion in 2011-12 and I was still involved. Alex Williams, Vicky Kloss and others at City had been working closely with us from the early 2000s and that carried on right the way through. The big turn when we thought that the club would have to get more involved came with the FA introducing the Super League. We knew as a committee that there was no way we could take City Ladies into that Super League as a voluntary operation. We didn't have the time and we didn't have the money. You needed a substantial amount of money promised up front and we'd have had to get a loan. In my opinion we had two choices – we carry on as Manchester City Ladies in the north league because that's what was being suggested: A national

Sarah Buffel   Danielle Brown

Super League and a North and South next level. Or the club takes it on completely and takes it in to the Super League. The club was changing a lot at this time and we spoke to a lot of people but there was a lot of interest but someone at the club realised that it was the right time. Myself and everyone on the committee agreed it was time to move it over."

Before the club was 'moved over' the Blues had their 2012-13 campaign to

Celebrating winning the Premier League Northern Division in 2012.

Amanda Goodwin   *Becky Grocott*   *Krystle Johnston*   *Chelsea Nightingale*

consider. City's first season in a full national division was a success with the Blues finishing fourth on 25 points. Gary Moores: "There were eight teams in the Super League as it was so, in effect, we finished 12th in the whole of the country as far as I see it. This was a massive achievement for a voluntary committee. Everyone from the beginning through to that season had contributed to that development. The achievement of finishing twelfth in the country was down to all those people throughout that club's history. Competing with the strong sides like Everton and Liverpool…it was an incredible achievement."

Andie Worrall, who had left City for Liverpool and then stopped playing for a while, was aware of how things were beginning to change in Manchester. During the 2012-13 season she had returned to the club: "I came back just before they did the application for the WSL because City's 'keeper Dan Brown got injured. I remember I was sat in a pantomime and I was on Twitter and Dan Brown got a bad injury. I text Leigh and I went 'Do you want me to come back?' He went 'yes', so I was back within a week at Christmas. Dead unfit, got fit again, got my way back."

The formal transfer of the club to Manchester City occurred, along with the WSL application, and the decision was made that the club would join the Women's Super League for the 2014 season, played April to October. As the other women's leagues were in line with the men's season this meant that the club could not play in 2013-14. Many players went out to other clubs to ensure they played while the committee and the club worked out the logistical matters. Gary Moores: "When the transfer occurred those of us on the committee knew that would be it for us. My involvement fizzled out. We had a final 'hurrah' at the goalkeeping coach's house up in the Leyland area. We got all the players together and we had a bit of a party there in the afternoon. I think we knew that was the end. Leigh the manager and his assistant were going to be paid by the club and that was it really. We didn't get involved because it was between them and the club. There were some activities left for the committee though. We had to tie up the end of the season and satisfy the reporting commitments we had, including those with the Manchester FA. The final accounts had to be done and so on. This would have been 2013-14."

Abbie McManus: "Before the relaunch, we knew that it was going professional. I was actually on holiday with Man City Ladies in Madrid for one of the girl's birthdays at the time and we found out I won't lie, I did shed a tear, thinking 'Oh, my team's going to go.' They are going to bring loads of professionals in. 'We're not good enough.' Because this is our hobby and they are going to get people that actually go to the gym, where for us it was kind of a social event. We'd go, turn up, at the age of 19 or 20. After the game we'd go out, have a good time and we knew it was drastically going to change and that's what it did. Obviously, for the better for the club, for women in sport… I've had to adapt and change with that. It's no longer a social event. It's your job, so it's got miles better and it can only grow."

Andie Worrall: "I was one of the only ones that played at that level and I know what it's like and it's not like what it is with your mates. It's not like that. It becomes a job. It's got to be serious because City are in the business of winning. What this Club wants is to be at the pinnacle of everything and I just knew that, unfortunately, when you go on that journey, you leave people by the wayside. I got left on the wayside eventually."

City employee Damaris Treasure was a key figure for the club working on the relaunch: "In the very early days of formalising our relationship with then City Ladies there was some very understandable hesitation at what Manchester City's official involvement would mean and how it would impact both the players and the staff, many of whom had worked for years to build the club up. People like Niki Taylor were so important in ensuring that those voices were heard and that the relationship evolved in the right way."

In 2013 Niki Taylor, vice-chair and an influential member of the committee, looked back on her involvement with the club in an article which highlighted some of the key moments from her arrival in 2000: "We weren't too involved with City back then but we had the name. Since then it has just gone bonkers. We went out there and just pretty much grabbed any girl playing out in the park or playing at school. Going back to 1997, women's football was starting to grow but in the last few years it has just gone mad. We did the same thing with coaches

Action from the 2-0 Premier League Cup win over Preston at Wythenshawe in September 2012.

Lynda Shepherd tackled by Sunderland's Rachel Furness in the FA Cup, 17 March 2013.

as well, because they do it on a voluntary basis. We just worked really well and really hard at maintaining it. I am very proud of the club." She added: "The majority of the people that are involved started off with their daughters playing. I originally came down with my daughter, Katie. I started collecting the subs to help the coaches out. You just get embroiled and it becomes a real passion."

Carly Bayley

Sarah Danby

Talking of the links with the male club she commented on the support from City in the Community: "They are just fantastic, trying to involve us as much as they can with the club. Their coaches come along and spend some time with our coaches as well as the girls. They have lots of valuable information they can share with us. It is a great club to be involved with."

In 2013 Niki was full of praise for chair Gary Moores' efforts: "He has been pivotal – without him I don't think we could have carried on," she said. "He gets involved on a secretarial basis as well, organising the referees, the linesmen, the pitches – sorting out all this stuff behind the scenes."

Damaris Treasure: "Getting coverage in those very early days was definitely an uphill battle. I remember the first interview we did post the formalisation of the MCLFC relationship – Krystle Johnston came in to City@Home to speak to (I think) Tony Leighton on the phone. It felt like a real moment! And I think Krystle would probably agree that she was slightly terrified."

Damaris soon realised too that there is often a difference in approach when people discuss football as played by men and women: "Conversations about women's football are rarely just about the football - although this is changing, even in the seven years that I've been involved. You are also often talking about gender and opportunity in a way that you don't with the men's game. So that is a responsibility that you have when you're working with women's football."

Looking back Damaris highlighted a Manchester City employee who worked hard behind the scenes to ensure the club's approach was right at this time: "The work that Don Dransfield did behind the scenes in the early days of the formal relationship was incredibly significant – without the business plans that he created, and the internal championing, we may not be having this conversation! He recognised the opportunity and thought about it on a big scale, and I think starting the relationship with that scale of belief and vision was instrumental to its success."

Supporter Dave Sheel: "I spent a lot of 2012-13 ill so the rebranding came as I was starting to get better. It came end of 2013

City celebrate Krystle Johnston's 100th appearance v Coventry, 2013.

and beginning of 2014. I remember thinking that this was something I could get really enthusiastic about. There were stories of new players and investment and it seemed like a major change. Since the takeover of the men's club in 2008 it felt like everything they did they had got right – they did what they said they would do both on and off the pitch. The women's side needed investment and that's what they did. They wanted a top class women's side and I knew I wanted to be there watching it. It was exciting and the chance of seeing the women's team challenging for trophies was appealing of course.

"There was the controversy about us being fast tracked into the WSL, seemingly at the expense of Doncaster Belles. I can see that it is wrong. I understand what the FA were trying to do but it's wrong. It's not City's fault of course – you take whatever you are offered – but it shouldn't be like that. It's happened again of course with Manchester United going straight into WSL2. Football is about money these days and so I can see what the FA were doing. City didn't create that situation."

Gavin Makel: "When we decided that we were going to bring them in-house, we knew that Leigh Wood, who was the manager of City Ladies, had been successful in the

Rebecca Lee

Fliss Middleton

Women's National League and Northern Division and what have you. His back room staff - Kevin Sims, Kurt de Klerk (the goal keeping coach) – too. So we were going to give them a chance. We weren't going to go 'Okay, we're in the WSL, thank you very much, see you later.' We wanted to give them a chance. But it became very clear, quite early on, that maybe it wasn't the right thing. So there were some difficult decisions to be made, very early on. Nick was supporting Leigh because Nick knew the methodology. He'd been at the club a long time, and knew people around, and so it made sense to put someone from within the club alongside Leigh. But as I say we made that change very quickly. So there were some difficult decisions and conversations to have. Player-wise I think it was a natural process really." By the end of 2013 Nick Cushing became the

manager with Leigh Wood as head coach, before Leigh ultimately left the club.

One of the new players to arrive was goalkeeper Karen Bardsley: "It was a big gamble for us to go there the first season because it was an unknown entity so to speak in the women's game really. We discovered that the right people were in place, the right people were steering the ship, the resources and so on. Every single day as a player you want to improve and you want to develop, so knowing that those resources were there to go and train, to have the right coaching staff, to kind of get the information any time you needed it. Those were the things that kind of really set City apart at the time, I think.

"It was pretty crazy. I mean it started out being pretty weird because we started training at Wright Robinson College and we

Toni Duggan scored both City goals to kick-off the 2014 season with a WFA Cup win over Reading.

Izzy Christiansen on the ball in the opening WSL fixture away to Liverpool.

were kind of occasionally at Platt Lane, so it just kind of felt like we were all over the show for the first season. Once the Academy got hold of us and we needed some kind of stability that's when it felt like 'wow, this is the real deal, we're on even keel with the men. We're in the same building. Everything they get we get.'"

The 2014 season commenced on 13 April with a 2-1 FA Cup win at home to Reading. Supporter Dave Sheel: "The first game I went to after the rebranding was against Reading at the Regional Athletics Arena. They won 2-1 and Toni Duggan scored. There had been some media coverage going on about our signings and then we saw them. The new arrivals were all established players, most internationals. Names like Jill Scott, Steph Houghton, Karen Bardsley... these were brilliant international players. Jayne,

my partner, and I went to Liverpool next for the team's away game. It was at Widnes on an artificial pitch. It was an appalling pitch. Liverpool went on to be champions and were a very good side. Unfortunately, Karen Bardsley was injured and didn't play and we had Andie Worrall in nets. We lost 1-0 but it was good. This was history being made though and there were signs of promise.

"The first home WSL game was next against Bristol Academy. They were an established side and beat us quite easily. They were 2-0 up and I thought this is going to be tough. It takes time to establish a new team and there was only a few players left over from City Ladies at this point it seemed. There was Abbie McManus, Joey Johnson, Andie Worrall... maybe a couple of others. I thought it would take a long time to bed down. That first season we came to every

City players moments before the club's first WSL fixture away to Liverpool.

City's first home WSL fixture against Bristol Academy and Jess Holbrook is pictured in action.

home game and most of the away games. I saw that first season in the WSL as historic. I wanted to experience it all.

"There is a level of togetherness in the women's game between players and fans that you used to get in the men's game but it disappeared years ago. In the women's game it's still there now. At the Regional Athletics Arena I took a City ball and I managed to get all the players to sign the ball. There's a closeness between players and fans. Steph Houghton for example is such a big football star… a major international… but she remains approachable. She comes over at away games. They all do. They know our names. It has kept that closeness despite becoming a professional league. Women's football is about a community. I interact with more people at a women's game than I do at a men's. The crowds may be much smaller but I chat to more people. It's a togetherness that the men's game doesn't always have any more."

As Dave mentioned, Andie Worrall played in the opening games of the season. Andie: "I thought I would make this work. Obviously, I work a lot, well 40 hours a week, in my job, but I wanted to make this work, and that's what I think people didn't understand. I had a full-time job as well as my football and I was doing all that at City for free. And then eventually I think Nick Cushing got wind of that and then one day he went 'Sign this contract. We can't believe we've not paid you.'" Due to work Andie's training had to occur after her other commitments. This was the same for several players as the club was not full-time professional. There were tensions and the opportunity to train on an equal footing with the newer signings was not there: "I knew my time was at an end there because of my age and stuff. I wanted to stay and I didn't want it to be like that."

One person who seemed to thrive at the new 'City Women' was Steph

Right: City's first WSL match programme.

CITY

MCWFC OFFICIAL PROGRAMME
FREE

The FA
WSL
BT Sport

v Bristol Academy
Sunday 20 April 2014 2pm

ETIHAD   etisalat   AbuDhabi   aabar

Houghton: "I think first and foremost as a footballer I wanted to play full-time. I wanted to get up on a morning, come in to training, train, work hard, get better as a player, play in a fantastic stadium like this, amazing training facilities, so they were big factors. But I think for me I knew coming to this club it wasn't going to happen all in one year. It was going to take time and it has, but that was the risk that I took, but I really did put my trust in the people above, the likes of Gavin Makel, Brian Marwood, to really go, right okay, I want to be on this journey. I wanted to be on the journey from the beginning and since then the strides that we've made have been unbelievable.

"I think they want to be the best in England and they want to be the best in Europe. I think within women's football I've experienced places where you don't train at very good facilities, you don't play on the best pitches, you don't get looked after nutrition-wise, your physical performance then deteriorates because of that. So, for me, there were a lot of factors. My agent was big in making the decision as well. He had worked with the club quite a bit on previous players and he knew that, whenever Manchester City say they are going to do something, it normally generally happens. 99% of the time. 'Just put all your faith in that and just make sure you give it a good

go,' he said. It hasn't been all plain-sailing, it really hasn't. It's been ups and downs but it's been worth every minute."

Andie Worrall: "When we played that first WSL game against Liverpool we did alright. We held our own. I knew that I would only do that season, that would be it, because of my age. I played four games I think, because Karen Bardsley was injured. I played a couple of games in the FA Cup, played Liverpool and Bristol. It was nerve racking. All your mates watching, especially on telly. All my mates started coming. They'd got season tickets. I down play it but everyone in my family doesn't down play it. My sister-in-law came up to me 'I'm so proud of you. You're a pioneer and you need to know that.' I just went 'I like to play football.'

"The standard of training was brilliant then, like Karen Bardsley is an unbelievable athlete. She can jump like a man, she's an unbelievable athlete. She could play like a man could play in goal. I used to stand there and watch her in awe at how good she was. Really good, and Steph Houghton's driving for really high standards. Always driving."

Like Andie, Abbie McManus was a City Ladies player who remained post the relaunch: "It was hard. The job that I had wasn't one of the best jobs. It's funny because the company that I worked for was M2 at the time and they do all the printers and stuff

Nicki Harding   Betsy Hassett   Emma Lipman   Natasha Flint

around the CFA. It's actually quite funny to see the logo every now and then. It was an easy decision, as long as I could afford somewhere to live, food on the table, then I was going to dive straight in. Unfortunately, at first I wasn't given a professional contract but I said to the manager, Nick, when he took over, 'I don't need that at the moment, as long as you give me time off to go and work part-time somewhere and still earn money, I'll prove to you that next year I'll be able to get that professional contract.' Thankfully I did.

"At first, we continued to train at the night time, so there was some players on professional contracts who was training during the day with the Academy and then the others would join for a night time session. It was like two or three times a week, you'd be there for two or three hours. It was back at Platt Lane then. It was hard. You were tired to get up for work in the morning but, because of the love of the game, you don't really think about it. It's something that you just did and now you don't have to do it anymore.

"At first when they relaunched Manchester City Women they actually told me that they didn't want me to come back. That's when Leigh Wood was the manager. When I found out that Nick Cushing got

the job, I got his number off some of my friends and literally just rang him... must have been 96 times I rang him and he ended up answering. He did have a few of his defenders that had injuries and he just let me come down and he just said 'you can stay.'

"Steph and the others were already here with the relaunch because obviously they were already signed on and they were the professional players at the time. To play with the likes of Toni Duggan, Jill Scott, Steph Houghton... all these players that have been professionals before and they've got the England Internationals, it improves you massively as a player that's not been involved in them things. Nick Cushing gave me an opportunity and I hope I've repaid him. Nick's brought me on leaps and bounds and I can't thank him enough for that."

The opening weeks of the 2014 season were tough throughout the club. Steph Houghton: "We'd lost the first four. The training schedule wasn't as smooth as we probably wanted it to be. We had half a squad training full time. Half a squad still at work, which for a club of this stature was something that needed to change drastically. I can remember - and I always tell Nick Cushing this and Gavin Makel - ringing my agent saying 'I've made the wrong decision here.' We hadn't won in four or five games and we weren't playing too well and there's about three or four of us internationals that are thinking 'right okay, well we're trying our best but it's just not happening.' I think that was all part of the journey. You had to maybe suffer a little bit and when you've been used to winning, like at Arsenal, it's hard to come and lose the first four. That was a real learning curve."

For Steph the situation improved: "The whole structure of getting all the girls training during the day was massive and we had great facilities at Platt Lane as well. So to be able to do that and to get people in to the right shape and to know more about how the manager wanted us to play… It was really powerful and it really worked. I think obviously City at the time were spending a lot of cash in the men's game and obviously came here and pretty much built an amazing training facility. There was a lot of talk about

money etc. and I'd just moved from Arsenal who had just won two trophies. I was captain. I did get a lot of stick in terms of 'going for money' and being 'a traitor' and all this, but for the first time in my career, I had to be selfish and it wasn't about the money. It was about giving myself a platform to be the best and it was probably the best decision I've ever made."

Izzy Christiansen was another who found the opening of the 2014 season hard going: "I'd say definitely the worst part was in the first year. We had this vision. Sometimes things don't go to plan and we played Doncaster Rovers Belles away, I think it was on a cold Tuesday night, and we'd lost the previous two games and then we played Bristol and Liverpool and lost both those games. We then came up against Doncaster and there was a little bit of controversy around that because Doncaster got demoted

Steph Houghton leads City out at the Etihad Stadium with Everton the visitors, May 2014.

for Manchester City to be WSL1 candidate. For Doncaster Rovers Belles there was a huge incentive there to beat City and we weren't ready for that and we lost the game 2-1. I remember sitting on the pitch at full time… manager, players, sat there on the grass, cooling down, and we kind of looked at each other and we didn't know where to go. We didn't know what to do. We didn't know how we were going to move forward because we'd bought in to this project, this vision, but things were not going our way. Obviously, the lessons learned from that have been huge but that was definitely my worst moment."

Gavin Makel: "We played Doncaster Belles, which obviously had a little bit of intensity to it, given that we were perceived to have taken their place in the WSL1, and they beat us in the Continental Cup in the Group Stage. I remember it was kind of like 'Right, what do we do now?' We had

a young manager in Nick, who had never experienced it as well. I was obviously still new and learning. There were tears. There were people locking themselves in the toilets. I wouldn't blame them if the likes of Steph and Jill and those players brought in thought 'What have I done?' But it's about keeping faith in what you are doing. Not thinking short term, thinking long term. We all met on the Saturday morning, I think the next game was Everton at the Etihad - we actually played at the Etihad Stadium that day, again, in the Continental Cup. We won that game in the 90th minute, 1-0. Natasha Flint scored - a young player, 17 year old. Then we went on a four game winning streak.

"You learn from those failures and the heartbreak. I think those four games you look back now and it made us as a group stronger. It gave us the opportunity to remember when we were up against the wall… when our backs are up against

Toni Duggan celebrates after scoring City's first ever WSL goal, the winner away to Arsenal in May 2014.

the wall… what it felt like. How we coped with that situation and also remember that apart from five players, our squad was predominately made up of players who had never played in the WSL, that had been at Manchester City Ladies as it was. They were basically just training and on trial for about six months before we offered contracts to them. We were all learning on the job. The likes of Steph and Jill, who had that experience, helped us to drive along and that's why we made the conscious decision as well that we were going to go completely full time. We started to get there but it was a slow process and trying to put a methodology in to the team, in to the players, that they'd never been accustomed to previously as well."

Damaris Treasure recognised the efforts being made by everyone involved, with special praise for Gavin: "Gavin Makel has been the most incredible leader and ambassador for the team and for the women's game, right from day one. I think I remember him having to wash kits in the early days. He put his heart and soul in to City Women right from the start and has been both an internal and an external champion for the team and for the game."

For Gavin: "Our biggest challenge in our first year - and it's still my biggest challenge now - and it drives everything that we do, is changing and challenging perceptions. We focus on education in many areas. How you carry yourself. What you look like when you come to training. What you do around the lunch table. No phones. Wearing the right socks. Wearing the right trainers. What you do on social media. How you even live your life outside of here. There's been a whole education piece on that side, but I always say that one of the things early on was that we couldn't expect to just slap on the Manchester City crest."

The run of four victories that came in May included two Continental Cup games and WSL victories over Arsenal (1-0) and Everton (2-0). Players began to settle and enjoy their time at City. Jill Scott: "The best moment was probably that first year for me. I don't know if it's because it was just like arriving at a new club. It was like going to a new school. I remember the day before coming making sure I had like my new boots and everything and I loved that first year."

City continued to progress in the Continental Cup. Dave Sheel: "Unfortunately we were drawn against Chelsea in the semi. Now they'd given us a right hiding here in the FA Cup. It was 3-1 but could've been more. Now we played the Conti Cup game at Hyde I can't remember why. I remember sitting there thinking 'we're not going to do this. We're going to get hammered.' But City played out of their skin that day. They defended superbly and attacked well. Karen Bardsley was saving everything and I thought this might just be our day. One chance, that's all. Then after half-time we got half-a-chance and Toni Duggan stuck it in. The place erupted. We were all jumping on each other and started to think 'there's a cup final here if we win.' The watch seemed to be going slow. Time was standing still then the final whistle went. The celebrations that day were like we'd already won a cup. It was incredible. Through to a national final in the first season after the relaunch…. That's more than anybody could have expected. There's no way Gavin Makel would have said to Nick Cushing at the start of that season 'you must get us into a major final'. It just wouldn't have been on the radar. There had been some performances in the League but that semi was something else."

Jill Scott: "We had different arrays of talent at the time, but we had good people here and winning that Continental Cup in the first year… the odds were stacked against us to do it and I think sometimes when you

Celebrations after beating Chelsea at Hyde to reach a first Continental Cup final, September 2014.

win in that way, it makes it a little bit extra special. People will probably think that for my best moment I'd say winning the treble, but I think that first year was a really good feeling around the team."

City beat Arsenal 1-0 to win the Continental Cup at the end of the season. Karen Bardsley: "That was pretty amazing because obviously in the League we struggled in the first half of the season. I had a few injuries and I missed some games and that was difficult but we were new, so we weren't really expected to do a whole lot. I think with the name of Manchester City people thought we should be better, but you know the reality of the situation was that we were a new team with five players of the ability to be where we're at. Winning the Conti Cup was an incredible achievement for us in that first year, to come away with the trophy. We wanted it so bad and we were willing to kind of stick to the plan and do whatever it takes. I think we were a very good team for the most part in that year and that kind of carried over in to 2015, especially with the success of the national team in Canada and I think there was a lot of belief around. We were just like well-oiled machines, we just kind of got on with it."

The first WSL season ended with City 5th and Continental Cup winners. They were also FA Cup semi-finalists. Overall this was a more successful season than anybody could have anticipated, but it was the WSL where City needed to make the biggest impact the following season if the investment was to be considered a success to the wider football world. City were still building, however. Gavin Makel: "It takes you maybe two, three transfer windows, to change things how you'd like. In our first two, three transfer windows, we had like four, five, six players coming in, going out, and that was difficult. It wasn't really until the start of our second season in 2015 where we felt like we had a good squad. We probably didn't have a squad that was strong in depth, but we had a strong starting 11. Any of our players within that squad would get in a team anywhere, so that's the mark I think of a good team. But it took time.

"We ran Chelsea close in our second year to win the League. Really if you go back to the Notts County game (23 August 2015, tenth WSL game of the season) when we were 2-0 up with 10 minutes to go… We drew 2-2. We could have won the League in our second year, I mean that would have been amazing."

Supporter Dave Sheel was delighted with a season that saw City finish second in the WSL to Chelsea: "Some may see that as a dip because we didn't win a trophy but they'd over achieved the first year. There was

Krystle Johnston v Birmingham City, July 2015.

a whole debacle around the Conti Cup semi-final against Arsenal away. They were about to play on the Sunday but on the Friday afternoon the game was called off. They'd planned free coaches for fans and we were all geared up for it then it's off. Everyone asked why but it turned out that City had supposedly played an ineligible player at Sunderland in the FA Cup and they could be kicked out of the tournament. We'd been to Sunderland and I couldn't think who this ineligible player was. I remember getting the team sheet out to try and work it out. It turned out to be Keira Walsh I think but it

was a mistake by the FA. My theory is that her name had been misspelt and it said Keira Welsh not Walsh but that's my own idea. I'm not certain what the truth was. They re-arranged the game with only a couple of days' notice for a Thursday night. City had to come back and rush. City went to the game less prepared than they'd like and ended up losing 1-0 so that was the end of the trophy defence."

City's runners-up spot in the WSL was the highest finish any team from Greater Manchester had ever made in the highest national league but this was to be eclipsed in 2016 when the Blues won the WSL title for the first time.

Gavin Makel: "We went to Abu Dhabi for pre-season which was fantastic. We played a game against FC Rosengard, who are a great name within the women's game. We played them at the Academy Stadium and another Swedish team, Pitea IF, so we had a real strong pre-season and we won all of those games. That really I think catapulted us in to the season. I just got the feeling very early on that this was going to be our year in the league. You could see it amongst the team. The confidence, the way that we were playing. We'd finished the 2015 season after the World Cup really, really strong. So it almost seemed to be that our style had

Jennifer Beattie

Alex Brooks

Paula Radtke

Sarah Wiltshire

Kosovare Asllani

Daphne Corboz

Jane Ross

Tessel Middag

suddenly kicked in like that, overnight. It was very interesting to watch.

"We played Notts County in the first WSL game of the season, mid-week, and they frustrated the hell out of us and 'parked the bus' as the saying goes. It took the Steph Houghton free kick in the dying minutes of the game to win that game. That can really galvanise you winning a game in that style, even though we'd had about 30 chances, probably about 80% possession but we just couldn't score. Their keeper had a great game actually. We went on and then it was game after game, winning, winning, and then we went to Chelsea (19 May 2016)."

City had faced Chelsea in the FA Cup the previous month in a frustrating game. Dave Sheel: "We were drawn away to Chelsea and playing at Staines FC. The club put coaches on again and that's when everyone bonded. We scored late on – Jane Ross after about 72 minutes to put us 1-0 up. The City fans that day were all sat together and it was a proper away day. All singing, chanting together. It was a really great atmosphere. The team put everything they had into it and so did we as fans. But Chelsea equalised late on.

"It went into extra time and the difference between us was that we only had kids on the bench whereas they had experienced players. They snatched the winner in the last minute of extra time. Fran

Demi Stokes against Reading, August 2016.
Below: City v Sunderland, July 2016.

think Nick used the experience of that day to motivate and push the team. In the end the defeat may have been a good thing. It sounds odd saying that but it feels right.

"I was running the twitter feed for the Supporters Club by then and that's when I first got a Direct Message off Nick Cushing. He wanted to say how much the support that day had mattered to the players. It had changed everything. I think it was this day that the bond was created."

Jill Scott: "The worst part in those early days I would say was the semi-final, where we got beat off Chelsea. It was 2-1 and they scored in extra time and that really hurt at the time I think because there was expectation on us and suddenly we're out of the FA Cup, and I think again it was probably the way in which the game went. We gave everything. That was probably one of the hardest games."

Kirby scored. But the bonding that day… We got back on the coach and we were gutted. We were all there stunned by it all and I don't know what made me do it but I stood up and said 'I want every one of you to remember how this feels because it ain't going to happen again. When the good times come I want us all to remember this day.' I don't know why I did it but I felt it had to be said. It had been such an emotional day. The players were devastated to have lost and the bonding at the ground was really good. I

Gavin: "After that defeat, we knew that we wouldn't get beat off them twice. No way would we get beaten off them twice and we probably used that as even more of a motivation to go on and beat them in the League. I think it was always going to come down to the games between us, Arsenal and Chelsea. We did that and you know we just kept on going. We played some great

football. Probably should have scored more goals than what we have done, but it wasn't until we beat Chelsea to be honest, here (25 September 2016) to win the League, where I thought it was done. You just got a feeling that it was written in the stars for you that season but then to go and win the Continental Cup as well.

Dave Sheel: "2016 confidence was high in the League and that was the season when we were going for it. That was an incredible season and we went for it. They were outstanding. Best player of the year was Lucy Bronze. We were untouchable. The best team by a long way. They only let in one open play goal all season – we drew 1-1 with Liverpool (26 June 2016). Every other goal they conceded in the League was a penalty."

"I think the League was always the one the club wanted to win, although there is also an affinity with the Conti Cup. Nick Cushing is on record as calling it is his baby

Jenny Beattie's goal put Blues through to the Continental Cup final.

or something because they won it that first year and the second time his daughter was born the same day. The priority I think was always the League and when they won it they deserved it. They'd played well in virtually every game I can think of. They beat Chelsea away in the League quite easily. 2-0 and they were the nearest rivals too. Chelsea had

Celebrations after Demi Stokes' opening goal in the away league win over champions Chelsea, May 2016.

Memorabilia from a memorable season.

put Chelsea flags on all the chairs to stop us sitting where we had in that semi-final a few weeks earlier. So we moved and all sat together. Then we had to beat them at home to confirm the title. Which we did again. A massive crowd of over 4000 which was the record crowd. They didn't finish that far behind us but we were much better.

"We also won the Conti Cup final as well. That year they'd decided the final before a ball was kicked and they'd decided it would be at the Academy Stadium. Nick Cushing made a comment saying something like 'we're hosting it and we're not going to let anyone else lift the trophy here.' We got to the final against Birmingham. It

The moment City became WSL champions for the first time after beating Chelsea at home, September 2016.

WSL champions 2016.

was a tough final and it went to extra time but we snatched it 1-0. Great facilities here but I think the authorities would've saved themselves some earache if they'd announced the venue later on or staged it somewhere else when they knew the teams."

Winning the WSL and the Continental Cup was highly significant for Karen Bardsley. 2016 was an emotional year for City's players. Karen: "There were quite a lot of emotional stresses that we kind of had to endure. One being Zoe and her unfortunate passing."

18 year old Zoe Tynan had played for City in the FA Cup match with Sporting Club Albion in April and had been named as a substitute for the opening seven WSL games of the season. She had moved to Fylde Ladies for the 2016-17 FA Women's Premier League season but died in tragic circumstances in August 2016. The news of her death affected Karen: "It kind of made people realise that there's so much more than

football. There's so much more to what's going on outside in people's lives. I don't know how to explain it really, but it kind of rallied everyone together. It kind of brought everyone together. It was such an emotional time."

City players pay tribute to Zoe Tynan (pictured above), September 2016.

This had been a whirlwind period for all the players at City. Some had been desperately trying to make the transformation from amateur to professional, others had arrived with high expectations and significant media focus. For one young player the 2016 season was to see her gain individual national acclaim. Izzy Christiansen was voted the PFA Player of the Year: "It was my highest personal accolade. I couldn't have done it without the help from the club and the way in which they helped develop me as a player and as a person. How they've helped me unlock the potential that I've always known I've had. For me I've had to leave that to one side though. I got it, won it, enjoyed the moment, but then have left it on the table and moved on with my career. I look back on it most days and think that's mine and I've got that though. Those trophies… whether they be individual accolades or team achievements… they're just a bi-product of things that the media, the press, people in the outside world, don't see. It's the sacrifices, the work, the challenges, everything that goes on beneath the water, if you like.

"I think it's been incredible really, the way in which this club has encompassed the women's team, the programme, the scheduling, the channelling in terms of treating us not as females but as footballers. I think that's been a really important part of the transition and we've definitely reaped success from being part of the club's general programme as a footballer. We've had to obviously sacrifice a lot of our own natural instincts to change, to have that shift, whereas for a male counterpart, it's a bit more simple to run through an Academy as a younger player and then in to a first team, whatever it may be. It's more of a clear pathway but, for women, it's adaptable. It has changed and now it's good for the younger players coming through that they

Lucy Bronze   Nikita Parris

can look up to us and be like there's a sincere pathway that's going to allow them to maybe make a career out of football.

"I'm very proud of the fact that we went about 18 games unbeaten in that 2016 season. That's a huge achievement in any sport."

Due to the change in WSL calendar, the period 2016 to 2018 would see the 2016 season ending in November with a European tie; the 2017 season would be a shortened season called the Spring Series (each team played the other WSL clubs once) with the 2016-17 FA Cup and European competitions finishing during that Spring Series; followed by a traditionally timed 2017-18 full season. This meant that City's progression in both the 2016-17 FA Cup and European Cup spanned the 2016 season and the 2017 Spring Series. In Europe the Blues reached the semi-finals for the first time. Sadly, City were defeated 3-1 in the first leg to Lyon but won the second leg 1-0. Gavin Makel:" You watch our games against Lyon, the standard was of a very high quality. I mean we didn't do ourselves justice in the first leg, but it was a very high standard and that's the peak. That's the elite end of women's sport. So we've got to get that right."

Dave Sheel: "Europe is tough. There are some brilliant teams like Lyon and

Wolfsburg… Chelsea as well. Lyon buy every top star they can. For City to get to the semis the first time was an achievement because it is so tough. We beat Lyon in the second leg at their place which says something. They are the team to beat. It is a big step in Europe though.

"At the start of the 2017 Spring Series we got Carli Lloyd on loan. That was a big thing. She was the current World Footballer of the Year. She scored a hat trick in the World Cup final. We had the spring series where everyone played each other only once as it was that transitional season when the main WSL was moving to match the men's again. City's priority to me and most fans was clearly the FA Cup. That was what mattered that year. The signing of Carli Lloyd was another major turning point for me as it got headlines around the world. It was like when the men signed Robinho. It made another statement to the world. She was a superstar in the States. On the day she signed she

Carli Lloyd signed for City in February 2017.

OFFICIAL MATCHDAY PROGRAMME
MANCHESTER CITY WOMEN V LYON
22.04.2017

decided to follow our supporters club on twitter. The day she signed! I couldn't believe that and she started retweeting our stuff. That brought us new followers. It was incredible."

As Dave and everyone connected with the club hoped 2017 did see the Blues win the FA Cup at Wembley with a convincing victory over Birmingham City. The game ended 4-1 with goals from Bronze, Christiansen, Lloyd and Scott, meaning that City held all three major trophies at the same time. To achieve a domestic treble in either women's or men's football is incredible. A month after winning the FA Cup for the first time the Spring Series finished with City second.

Left: The match programme from City's first UEFA Women's Champions League semi-final in 2017.

City returned to Lyon for the Champions League semi-final in April 2018.
Back row (l to r): Abbie McManus, Steph Houghton, Karen Bardsley, Jill Scott, Jenny Beattie, Izzy Christiansen.
Front: Demi Stokes, Mel Lawley, Nikita Parris, Georgia Stanway, Keira Walsh.

There was a form of déjà vu about the 2017-18 season with City reaching the Champions League semi-final where they were defeated 1-0 on aggregate by Lyon; they finished second in the WSL and they reached the Continental Cup final. Sadly, they lost that 1-0 to Arsenal a mere seven days after the She Believes Cup Final between the USA and England featuring several City stars. Dave Sheel: "The girls were flying around America in economy jets for England. Phil Neville wasn't happy and we had nine players in that squad. They came back with only two days to go to play a cup final. Arsenal had pulled all theirs out. We got beat 1-0. Fair enough Arsenal were better but they were fresher. There was definitely an element to it."

It was a frustrating final but the Blues picked themselves up and ensured they challenged again in 2018-19. It was to be both a successful and a historic season in several ways. In December City celebrated the 30th anniversary of the club by inviting several members of the team from its inaugural season to be guests for the WSL game with Arsenal. It brought significant exposure to the club's history.

In the WSL they finished second again – considering the standard in the WSL this was no mean feat – but it was the cups that brought the Blues their next successes. In the Continental Cup a dramatic final ended goalless with Arsenal before a penalty shoot-out ended 4-2 in City's favour on 23 February 2019. Then on 4 May the club's second FA Cup final ended with a 3-0 (scorers Walsh, Stanway & Hemp) win over West Ham United before an impressive crowd of 43,264. This remarkable double coincided with the men's team achieving the domestic treble – a feat no male club had ever managed. When Pep Guardiola was asked about being the 'first' team to achieve a domestic treble he pointed out how the women had achieved that feat in 2016-17 and that he had guided the first men's team to it, but not the 'first' team.

When the season was finally over both the male and female teams enjoyed a historic homecoming parade through the streets of Manchester and Salford. As far as Manchester City was concerned these trophy successes were of equal significance and had to be celebrated together. It is this approach that impresses most, as Michelle Middleton, one of the players from the club's first game in 1988, comments: "I hope that they continue to lead the way in women's football, demonstrating the equal importance of the women's game to the men. When we started in 1988, had you said that I'd be watching women play professionally on a world stage with full media coverage I'd have laughed. The development and progression has been incredible, long may it continue."

The face of City Women since the relaunch has tended to be the club's – and England's – captain Steph Houghton: "I love the job. I think I'm really honoured to be the captain. It's something that I really take seriously. You've got to give a bit back and that's what I've always been taught when I've been younger that you can't just take all the time. The age that I'm at and with the experiences I've had, I like to think that I've got a chance to be influential to the younger generation coming through here at City but also for women's football in the whole of the country. It's something I really do enjoy and you see pleasure coming out of the girls with your name on their top, or when they come to the stadium to watch us play. I really think we can have a really positive influence on the sport as a whole.

"I didn't think it would happen to my generation. I thought it would still take a lot of time, but I feel as though this is the watershed moment for women's football in terms of the exposure. The fact that we're playing in bigger stadiums, we've got people coming to watch, which allow people to say actually well they're pretty good. In terms of effort, intensity, technical ability, I think we've really set a mark. We've kind of just grown and grown and grown, but potentially since the World Cup 2015, I think everybody just got this love of women's football,

Mie Leth Jans

Jess Park

Ellie Roebuck

Caroline Weir

2019 Victory parade for City's
men's and women's teams.

English football. You get a lot more people come to the games because of Manchester City, Arsenal, Chelsea… the majority of the England squad's made up of those players.

"To have your picture on the side of a stadium, I never ever envisaged that, but I knew that we'd be treated equally. I think they are very visual things to say the men's and the women's team are the same City. We have the same passion. We have an intention to make winning teams, to develop good people and this club's been fantastic for that. You can see the other clubs trying to copy, but they still haven't got the same power as what we had, because we started it off."

Today's successes are enjoyed by the fans of the club and by former players. Gail Redston, one of the 1988-89 side: "I love it. Love what we're doing. I tell you what, I'd be happy here being a kit woman for them.

Cat Hyde in 2019, playing for City's Walking Football team.

Honest to God. I'd be quite happy just doing that. It's difficult for me to get to see games because I'm still playing as well. I mean especially if my grandson's playing Saturday so I've got football Saturday, I've got football Sunday morning with him and then I've got football Sunday afternoon with me. When it's the European games… the night games, I drag my husband along. He loves it. I just wish I was born 30 years earlier. To have what the women have got now, I take my hat off to Manchester City for pushing it through and doing it and clap my hands to them all."

Catherine Hyde, another former player: "I think, since City's been re-branded, football has gone bigger because City have made the change. Everything has changed and I think it's City that's pushed it. Everybody's trying to keep up with City now."

Former committee member and coach Alison Smith hopes that in the future City: "continue to be a leading team in the women's game and recognise fully where the 'roots' of MCWFC came from." Looking to the future former player Lindsay Savage hopes City: "Continue to succeed at the highest level and to inspire the future generations." City Football Group employee Damaris Treasure feels the same: "I hope that we continue to raise the bar, to be challenged, and then to have to raise the bar again. We always want to be better – the more people in the game, the higher the standards we all have to live up to."

One of the areas that sets City apart from other clubs is the desire to plan for the long term. Gavin Makel: "I think where we're different is that we do think long term. We haven't even started the new season yet, but I'm thinking about the season after. I'm thinking about next summer. What we can do next summer and talking about what we can do further afield. What does our playing

The Supporters Club at the Continental Cup final Bramall Lane, 2019.

squad look like in three years' time? We're working on that now and I'm not sure that other clubs necessarily do that. I think they maybe look at seasons as silos and that's probably where we're slightly different and that's the way that we're going to be able to continue to kind of lead the way as much as possible really. I mean some of it obviously happens quite ad hoc. It's been a huge learning curve, how to deal with many different things, like how to deal with player agents for one! Which never gets easy. But it stands you in good stead and you know if we were to set up another club, elsewhere, we'd be in a better position to knowledge share."

The 2019-20 season was to begin with the first ever WSL Manchester derby, scheduled to be played at the Etihad Stadium.

Gemma Bonner

Pauline Bremer

Megan Campbell

Claire Emslie

All smiles in the Adams Park dressing room after City saw off Arsenal to win the Continental Cup for the first time in 2014.

The Continental Cup

The League Cup, sponsored by Continental and therefore known as the Continental Cup, was the first national competition won after the relaunch. As such it became highly significant.

David Sheel: "The club put on some coaches for us. It was night match – that doesn't help. It was played at Adams Park, Wycombe Wanderers' ground. There were two coaches. The first was full of parents and young academy girls and a few supporters with the second just supporters. All free. We went – sadly a lot couldn't go because it was a week night – and we played against Arsenal. A team full of established top players who had beat us 4-0 at City in the League. But, like semi final win over Chelsea at Hyde, there was just something about that night. Arsenal were all over us at times and did everything but score. Our defence was outstanding but we also had a few chances at the other end. Got to half-time nil-nil

Wild celebrations on the final whistle at Adams Park, 2014.

2014 – first trophy of the WSL era.

and you're thinking 'just one chance, please.' I can remember the goal… Joey Johnston went down the line, whipped the ball in and Izzy Christiansen, the smallest player on the pitch, headed it in. There were four of us sat together – the coaches had arrived just before kick off so we'd had to leg it in and grab the first spaces you could find. The four of us jumped up but we were surrounded by Arsenal fans. They started giving us some abuse. The goal was in the 73rd minute and we hung on.

"When the final whistle went I was as proud of that achievement as I was in 2011 when the men won the FA Cup. To me personally it was the same. I never ever felt I'd see the men win anything in my life and then the same was true with the women. I was so proud of the club. After that they did the trophy presentation and I picked up some of the tinsel that got fired out of the cannons when they did the presentation. All the players came over to the side afterwards.

Jill Scott was showing me her medal. They shared it with the fans. They even let me put my hands on the trophy. We were all there together. A bit like the men and their success in 2011 I think this told the outside world that City were here to do business. Inside the club the ambition was there but until you win a major trophy the other clubs may not take you seriously."

Abbie McManus: "That feeling of beating Arsenal, who have dominated women's football for years and years. At the time we were perceived to be a bunch of nobodies that have just thrown a team together and everyone was saying you're just throwing money at it. I didn't actually play that game. I got sent off the game before so I missed it! But watching the game and the feeling of that win. Being the underdog. I don't think that feeling will ever come back."

Izzy Christiansen scored in the final: "An amazing feeling to score in that game. There's no other words to describe it. It was

Above: 2016 – Final hosts and winners!
Below: 2019 – Shoot-out victory over the Gunners, and a new-look trophy.

just probably one of the best days of my life, the fact that the ball hit the back of the net. The fact that it meant that we, as a team, and a club, got our first trophy. That kind of set us off on our journey really. We had a taste of success at the start and that's where we've stayed, wanting success."

The Blues went on to win the Continental Cup in 2014, 2016 and 2019.

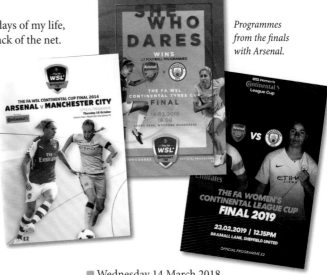

Programmes from the finals with Arsenal.

City's Finals:

■ Thursday 16 October 2014
Arsenal 0 Manchester City 1
City Scorer: Isobel Christiansen 73
Venue: Adams Park, High Wycombe
Attendance: 3,697
Team: Karen Bardsley, Nicola Harding, Steph Houghton, Emma Lipman (Paula Radtke 62), Georgia Brougham, Krystle Johnston, Keira Walsh, Isobel Christiansen, Natasha Flint, Jill Scott, Toni Duggan.
Subs not used: Alex Brooks, Chelsea Nightingale, Betsy Hassett, Emma Kete, Danielle Young.
Referee: Nigel Lugg (Surrey).

■ Sunday 2 October 2016
Manchester City 1 Birmingham City 0
After extra-time
City Scorer: Lucy Bronze 105
Venue: Academy Stadium, Manchester
Attendance: 4,214
Team: Marie Hourihan, Lucy Bronze, Jennifer Beattie, Steph Houghton, Demi Stokes, Jill Scott, Isobel Christiansen, Keira Walsh, Toni Duggan (Daphne Corboz 1060, Jane Ross (Tessel Middag 84), Nikita Parris (Kosovare Asllani 65).
Sub not used: Karen Bardsley.
Referee: Rebecca Welch (Durham).

■ Wednesday 14 March 2018
Arsenal 1 Manchester City 0
Venue: Adams Park, High Wycombe
Attendance: 2,136
Team: Ellie Roebuck, Demi Stokes, Jennifer Beattie, Steph Houghton, Abbie McManus, Keira Walsh, Jill Scott (Mel Lawley 82), Isobel Christiansen (Claire Emslie 56), Nikita Parris, Georgia Stanway, Nadia Nadim (Jane Ross 46).
Subs not used: Karen Bardsley, Mie Leth Jans, Ella Toone, Esme Morgan.
Referee: Amy Fearn (Derbyshire).

■ Saturday 23 February 2019
Arsenal 0 Manchester City 0
After extra-time. City won 4-2 on penalties.
Venue: Bramall Lane, Sheffield
Attendance: 2,424
Team: Karen Bardsley, Gemma Bonner, Steph Houghton, Jennifer Beattie, Demi Stokes, Tessa Wullaert (Janine Beckie 65), Caroline Weir (Claire Emslie 118), Jill Scott, Keira Walsh, Nikita Parris (Lauren Hemp 105), Georgia Stanway.
Subs not used: Ellie Roebuck, Pauline Bremer, Megan Campbell, Abbie McManus.
Referee: Lucy Oliver (Newcastle).

After City

Some players remained with City for over a decade, some moved on after a few games. The reasons for leaving varied. As did their post-City football careers. Interviewees were asked why they left and whether they played for other teams afterwards. Most did play elsewhere and several continue to contribute to football today.

Gail Redston: "I thought what would I do if I stopped playing? I mean I even took up golf and then I ended up with tennis elbow, so by the time I got to like the sixth my arm was killing. 'Hang on a minute, I'm going back to football.' When's the next game? (laughs) Hopefully, this Sunday against Curzon!"

Gail has continued to play 11-a-side football. She is now in her 60s and also participates in the City in the Community walking football activities each week.

Helen Hempenstall: "I stayed with City about three seasons. My daughter was born in 1993 and my football came to an end then. Life takes over and you can't get to training as easy. You're working and got a young family so it's difficult to get time for yourself. Now, I wish I'd carried on but then it seemed sensible to stop. You can't give 100% to football and you can't play if you only give 80%."

Bev Harrop: "I went back and played for a team quite recently, and one of the

Former City and FC Redstar team mates Heidi Ward and Bev Harrop at the Dick, Kerr's Ladies Football Cup, 2019.

girls that was involved was managing this team. I was 50 when I went back. You miss it all the time. I was still quite fit and I went and played and the manager says 'I'm going to start you off as sub.' I said 'what do you mean sub? I don't understand that word!' Eventually I got in that game and then played in every game after that as well."

Heidi Ward: "I got married in 92 and we moved over to West Yorkshire. I just thought it's too far to be travelling. If I was going to play football I wanted to get more involved and make sure that I was involved in things a bit more, so I decided to play for the nearest team. I played for Halifax Ladies for a while. They'd only just started a team. We played in the North East League I think. I stopped playing when I was pregnant.

"A few years back I started up a school team at the school I was working for. I'd wanted to do it for years and then an opportunity came up because the school I was working in the Head Teacher was very much in to his football. The first season we

Gail Redston about to score in the Dick, Kerr Ladies Football Cup 2019

did really well. We played some friendlies and then some tournaments. They were Year 4, 5, and 6 girls and that was great. The second year, because it was such a small school, we didn't have enough girls to make a team, and so we carried on doing training, but we didn't actually play as many games. I brought them to a women's game at City to encourage them and to let them see what you can actually do now. We also went to a football fun day in Keighley, set up to encourage girls to play football. Some of the older Doncaster Belles players came along and talked to the girls, so that was really good."

Louise Wakefield: "I was 29 when I stopped playing for City. It was heartbreaking, I just cried and everything when I left, I was really, really upset. It wasn't my choice! I went to Stockport and I fitted right in there. When I was 34 I was playing at Salford and I probably played the best football I've ever played, because the manager was the coach I'd always wanted. In training he'd say 'stop' and he'd walk me through my mistake. He'd walk me through my next move…my whole game changed and I wish I'd have had that earlier."

Kate Themen: "I started my degree in sociology and history when I was 23. I was a mature student. I finished my last exam, my finals, in 94. The women I played at City with still laugh 'you're a student.' I've been a bit studious and I did eventually get a doctorate. I only graduated the other year from Liverpool University. I was so pleased to get my doctorate. I mean, just absolutely made up, and I know my mum was really proud of me and really chuffed. I don't have to call myself Ms or Miss any more. I've got a nice androgynous title now. My PhD is on women's football. I did narrative interviews. Theoretically I'm a little more left field… I do post-colonial theoretic stuff and I'm just kind of more in to methodological things.

It's about bodies. Challenging and contesting bodies. There's kind of a direct line there from what I've experienced."

To commemorate thirty years of the club some of the players from the first season were guests at the City-Arsenal WSL game in December 2018. Kate was one of the original players there that day: "We'd done all the walk out and everything. That was amazing. When the team were coming out and we were just at the side and they all started clapping us, that was really lovely that. We got back to the stand and we were in padded seats and obviously Phil Neville, the England manager, is there. He was having a little bit of a laugh and a joke with us but we were a seat short for some reason and Donna Haynes needed everyone to move up. Phil was the last of our line and Donna shouted 'Gary, Gary, Gary, can you move up?' Someone went 'it's Phil!' Then it was 'Phil or whatever your name is, can you move up?" So funny but it was just kind of a typical Manchester City Ladies thing."

Lesley Wright: "The manager dropped a player. One of my mates. He didn't tell her particularly well and so we decided it was time to leave. So I actually left. A lot of things had changed and I'd been to a tournament where I actually played for the United team. That's how it was back then. In tournaments you'd guest for another team if they were short or if a friend needed help. City had players guesting and we guested for others. It wasn't an issue or anything. I'm a big City fan as you know but playing for United was just helping someone out. It was no big deal. City were at the tournament but I hadn't been picked as part of that squad. Afterwards the City manager came to me and said I'd not get back in the team. I packed in playing and concentrated on coaching the under 12s. I still went and watched the main team and they did quite well. It was good to see.

"I'm still involved as a committee member at Stockport County Ladies. I don't do too much but I help where I can. I'm also on the Cheshire Women's Youth committee, focusing on registrations and treasurer work. That's a county league. We're at the bottom of the women's pyramid – at least there's a pyramid now unlike the past when the best we had was a north west league and nothing higher. Some of the committee there now are people who were on the committee when I was playing. That's dedication. I used to think that when I stopped playing I'd be bored but you soon find stuff to fill your weekends. There was a time when I'd be coaching the City under 12s on a Saturday morning, watch the men in the afternoon and then play on a Sunday."

Jane Morley: "I'm the secretary of Stockport County Ladies and the secretary of Cheshire Womens Youth Football League. I'm also the secretary of the Cheshire Girls Football League Stockport Division. Lesley (Wright) is the registration secretary of the Cheshire Womens Youth Football League and treasurer of Cheshire Girls Football League Stockport Division and she's a committee member at Stockport County Ladies. I carry on because I want girls to be playing football in a safe, competitive environment and if I can still offer that via Stockport County Ladies then I will continue to do so. At the end of the day I love football. I just love football. I'm a big United fan but I will watch any football. There's nothing better than seeing a young girl make her first steps into the game. I've had an enquiry from the mum of a girl who is three asking if her daughter can come to our 'wildcat' centre. There's nothing better than helping a young girl enjoy the game and develop through fully qualified coaches in a safe environment. Grassroots football still needs volunteers."

Rita Howard: "I'm a maths teacher and

when I first started teaching at this school I took boys teams. We got through to a final and I really enjoyed that. Sometimes you have to fill up your timetable and so I take PE sometimes. When I first did that the PE teacher at the time said 'what do you want to take them for?' I said 'football' He said 'but it's raining.' I said that it wasn't a problem to me and we played football outside. The boys loved it and started asking me if I knew any drills. They loved the fact I could play. They said 'this is mint'. I get a lot satisfaction from doing this. It's great talking about football with the kids. It's a way to get on their level. They know I played for City but they assume that as it is now is how it was then. 'Miss, how much did you get paid?' "I paid them £2.50 a game to play! I had to wash my own kit."

Until recent years no female Manchester City player was paid and they tended to have separate careers or educational activities going on alongside their playing. Now with professionalism the need to consider a post-playing career exists. Jill Scott: "They've spoken to me about the transition since

coming here aged 26/27, and it really got my head around the question what happens when you've finished playing. You are going to have to think about what to do next. It's not that I take anything for granted, but I do feel like I have security here, where there will be a pathway hopefully for me to go in to coaching. The way that City have done it I think the world of. That's not to say that anything's handed to you on a plate. You've got to go out there. You've got to do coaching sessions off your own back and stuff like that. It's a fantastic club to be at

and you have to make sure that, if you're not playing for this football team and you want to work here, you've got to be willing to put the hours in to get the level that this club requires."

Below: Original members of City Ladies celebrate the 30th anniversary with the current team. City v Arsenal, December 2019. Fourteen of the people on this team photo have been interviewed for this book.

The FA Cup

City's first FA Cup tie was a 7-2 defeat at Robin Park, Wigan on 17 September 1989. This was only the second competitive game ever played by the club and came less than a year after formation. Since then, apart from a couple of seasons in the 1990s when the Blues decided not to enter, City have been regular competitors. In September 1999 City achieved their record score in the competition: 26-0 v Norton, WFA Cup Extra Preliminary Round. In 2017 they reached the FA Cup final for the first time.

Dave Sheel: "Everyone's aware that the FA Cup final will be played at Wembley in 2017 and because of the restructure of the season that became City's top target I believe. In the first round – I think it was officially round five – we played Reading at the Academy and it was absolutely throwing it down. This was Carli Lloyd's first big game and you could see she was having an effect. The younger players seemed to be learning from her already. She had her arm around Georgia Stanway at one point and it was like Obi Wan Kenobi and Luke Skywalker. That moment stuck in my head. Anyway, they won

City's first FA Cup tie v Wigan, 1989.

Goal spree Ladies in seventh heaven

Wigan Ladies 7, Man City Ladies 2

WIGAN Ladies played host to newly formed Manchester City Ladies in the first round of the W.F.A. Cup.

City, eager to do well in their first encounter in the cup, saw the home side slam seven goals past them.

Don't let the result fool you, this match was far from one sided with the visitors showing they will be a team in contention for honours at the end of the season.

From the kick off, City looked like they might score and went close in the opening minutes.

Wigan, however, withstood the pressure and went 2-0 up in the opening 20 minutes, goals coming from Lynn Arstall and Kerry Harding.

The visitors fought back and produced some good build-ups and, after 28 minutes, Lesley Peters fired in a shot well beyond Rimmer's reach.

For the next five minutes, Wigan were not in the game and City grabbed a well deserved equaliser when Donna Haynes hit a superb shot into the roof of the net.

Wigan, stunned by the fight back, had to go for goal and Vanessa McLeod put the girls back in front after 33 minutes. Wigan's Jo Wood hit number four just before half time.

City again came out in the second half looking to get the game back within their grasp, but Wigan held the pressure, and scored three more from Arstall (80 minutes), Entwistle (89 minutes) and Leach (89 minutes)

the game and faced Bristol City in the next round away. They weren't at their best and they struggled a bit. We took an early lead but they equalised and then we scored a last minute winner but it had been tough. Through to the semi-finals and we drew Liverpool at home. It was tense but a favourable draw. It was a tight game but we scored in the second half – Lawley who we'd got the year before. I start singing 'Wemberley, Wemberley' and my wife Jayne is saying 'Sush. Shut up. Don't tempt fate!' The final whistle goes and then we're at Wembley. I love the place. This is history though – it's the women's first Wembley final.

"We planned to do a massive group booking and then they announced the date of the final and it's the same day as the men's team are at home against Leicester. That game was 12.30 and the women's was about 5.30pm. Now there's some who managed to get to both by doing a mad dash. They left the men's game fifteen minutes early and rushed down to Wembley. We couldn't do that though as the Supporters Club were putting on subsidised coaches. Our

Celebrations after Lucy Bronze's opening goal of the FA Cup final against Birmingham City, 2017.

group booking meant we got the best seats behind the goal you can get. We had a whole section to ourselves. We ordered a full block of about 65 adults and 65 kids which were free. The clash with the men's was an issue though. I hate when the games clash. To me it's fairly easy to sort out. The FA could take the women's FA Cup final and move it to the Saturday before the last games in the Premier League as they're always on a Sunday. I know you could get a clash with Football League clubs, like Birmingham City, but in general it would work. They got a great crowd of 35,000 but it could have been 50,000. A lot of floating fans would come. Women's football can't take on Premier League football and you certainly shouldn't clash with your own men's team. It damages the product! I missed the Leicester men's game – it pained me to do so. We ended up

traveling down to Wembley early and then we watched the men's game on TV in the Green Man."

Gavin Makel: "We'd been so close to reaching the final with two previous seasons. We knew that was something that we wanted. We were desperate to win that competition and the carrot of being at Wembley, something that will always drive you on. It makes it even more special. For me personally, you know, and Nick Cushing, because of the spring series as well, we knew that that was our main target for that interim period of time. I went to wish the players good luck in the changing room just before the final at Wembley and I just said 'listen, not very many players, male or female, get the chance to play at Wembley and experience it. So love it, enjoy every minute of it' and I don't think there was ever

A dream come true as the Blues win the FA Cup for the first time, 2017.

any question that we would lose that game because I could see it. It was the same as the confidence that we had at the beginning of the League season the year before. Birmingham are a good team, but they've got young players and you wondered how they would cope under that kind of pressure."

Karen Bardsley: "I played at Wembley with England but there was something about just being there for the FA Cup. Playing at Wembley. I don't know what it was, it was just my family was there as well. They flew over for that, so it was pretty cool. It was just an amazing day."

Jill Scott: "That was a brilliant feeling, it really was, and I think to top it off on a personal level scoring at Wembley as well. My family were there. That was a really good feeling, but I would say the Birmingham game, without being disrespectful to them, we were always comfortable. We were 3-0 up at half time. So it was almost like you were winning the game as it went on."

Steph Houghton: "I think the fact that it was at Wembley. The crowd that we had and the way that we performed, like people

say it's about enjoying the day and it was great from the start to the finish. Being able to celebrate with your family and friends but also lifting that trophy, walking up the steps, it's giving us goose bumps now thinking about it. That's the moment you always dream of, when you know it's kind of possible. It's always a competition you want to win and historically people always talk about the FA Cup, whether it's male or female. To win in the way that we did in front of a record breaking crowd was unbelievable.

Heidi Ward: "I was there watching it at Wembley. When City came up for the cup I got quite emotional because I just thought when I was little I really wanted to play football. I didn't think about being in a girls' side, I just wanted to play football. So the thought of lifting the FA Cup up at Wembley was like a dream, a complete dream. There used to be films about it and TV programmes about people wanting to be a footballer, wanting to lift the FA Cup, and the fact that Steph Houghton, a City player, was lifting the FA Cup at Wembley was just

Wembley 2019...
Keira Walsh opens the scoring
against West Ham.

Lauren Hemp makes
it 3-0 in the closing
minutes.

City celebrate a second FA Cup win.

Steph Houghton lifted the cup for the second time with City.

amazing. I got really quite emotional about it. I don't think I would have ever got to that level, but just the thought that there's an opportunity now for girls to do that… they can dream… they can go and do that now."

Dave Sheel: "Winning the FA Cup was incredible. It was a lot easier than any of us expected. Birmingham were overawed and it was so different to the Conti Cup between us. Carli Lloyd was outstanding. I noticed as well that they kept trying to interview her but she kept pushing the younger players forward. She didn't want to take the spotlight off the others. That was nice to see."

"It meant as much to me as winning any of the men's trophies. More because I'd seen history. The first FA Cup win by the women. Historic. It's all so important. I even bought a half-half scarf… I don't buy half-half scarves but I did that day because it was the first FA Cup final by the women and it was at Wembley too. The longest running national women's competition."

Lesley Wright: "Who'd have ever thought when we started the club that we'd see City Women lift the FA Cup? It was something we all dreamed of but it never seemed likely."

City's Finals:

◼ Saturday 13 May 2017
Birmingham City 1 Manchester City 4
City Scorers: Lucy Bronze 18, Isobel Christiansen 25, Carli Lloyd 32, Jill Scott 80
Birmingham Scorer: Charlie Wellings 73
Venue: Wembley Stadium
Attendance: 35,271
Team: Karen Bardsley, Lucy Bronze, Steph Houghton, Megan Campbell (Abbie McManus 78), Demi Stokes, Keira Walsh, Jill Scott, Isobel Christiansen, Nikita Parris (Georgia Stanway 70), Carli Lloyd, Melissa Lawley (Toni Duggan 56).
Subs not used: Marie Hourihan, Jennifer Beattie.
Referee: Rebecca Welch (Durham).

◼ Saturday 4 May 2019
Manchester City 3 West Ham United 0
City Scorers: Keira Walsh 52, Georgia Stanway 81, Lauren Hemp 88
Venue: Wembley Stadium
Attendance: 43,264
Team: Karen Bardsley, Abbie McManus, Steph Houghton, Jennifer Beattie, Demi Stokes, Jill Scott, Keira Walsh, Caroline Weir (Claire Emslie 85), Tessa Wullaert, Nikita Parris (Lauren Hemp 82), Georgia Stanway.
Subs not used: Gemma Bonner, Pauline Bremer, Janine Beckie, Megan Campbell, Ellie Roebuck.
Referee: Abigail Byrne (Suffolk).

Funding

For most of its existence the women's team had to rely on the fundraising activities of its players, committee, supporters and family members. In the beginning Neil Mather had the support of City's community department as this was a Manchester City initiative but the players still needed to pay subs and training fees. At other times players had to buy kit and pay for their transport needs, while promotions occasionally resulted in the club having to find additional fees to be a part of a league or to fund an appropriately approved ground. Flixton FC's ground was utilised for a while and that is said to have cost £100 per game.

Jane Clark (now Boardman) fulfilled a number of roles following her arrival in 1996, including club captain and treasurer. She feels that a women's football club should be exactly that – a club: "I think it should be first and foremost a competitive football club with the same community side to it that the men's club has... grass roots football, girls, working in schools, coaching etc., but the problem is that the return on the investment

Above: Jane Clark.
Right: The opportunity to sponsor City Ladies, August 1999.

ADOPT A JUNIOR or the CITY LADIES

Do you want to get behind the future stars of Manchester City?

Well now you can because each Academy team and the MCFC Ladies are now available to adopt for £25. (Each team will have three sponsors).

The benefits are as follows:

- An invitation to an Academy Function (Academy sponsors ONLY)
- Framed photograph of your team
- Editorial mention in the matchday programme and the City Magazine
- On-pitch presentation during the course of a season with a representative from the Academy or Club.

The hard work of the MCFC Academy needs no real introduction to City supporters. the achievement of winning both the Foyle and Milk Cups at Under-14 level was a first in football, while many fans remember how close the Under-17's ran Blackburn Rovers in the final of the Academy Cup earlier this year.

MCFC Ladies are also looking for local supporters or companies with an interest in community activities. The ladies team do a great deal of work in promoting women's football in the local area and are always in need of support in these activities. They run a number of teams from Under-10's right through to open age.

If any companies or Supporters' Clubs are interested in getting behind the future of your club and/or supporting the MCFC Ladies then please contact Steve Sayer in City's Marketing Office on 0161 232 3064.

is never going to be a £50M player that you can sell to a lower league club. Or a £150M player who is going to get you 15 goals a season or whatever and that's the logical sort of financially-minded way that I've always looked at it. There were lots of players that I played with who were resentful of the financial discrepancy between women's football and men's football.

"I was Treasurer for a bit. It was awful, like wandering around the pitch with a sandwich bag trying to collect two quid off everybody, but my sort of comparison was girls pay to play netball, girls pay to go horse riding, boys pay to play basketball… whatever it might be. If there is no money coming in then somebody has got to fund it and at that point there was no commercial proposition for women's football. Some of that was because of the fact that the clubs weren't going out there and trying to promote it; some of it was because there wasn't the wider interest.

"I think generationally things have moved on because certainly my generation of male equivalents are far more family-oriented than even their 10 year older comparator group. You've now got a position where Dads as well as Mums want to get home to read bedtime stories and do bath time and everything else and they want their daughters to have the same opportunities as their sons. They are as likely to be going out watching their daughters play football on a weekend as they are watching their sons and so it's slowly changing but it's hard. There are plenty of men's sports that have failed to compete on financial terms with men's football as well. There are a lot of sports competing for what's essentially a defined income pool and if Sky are going to pay more over here they've got to pay less over there, so it's difficult.

"When I was actively involved [women's football] was 'very self-sufficient' (laughs) that's probably the political way of saying the girls did everything for themselves."

Season by Season Match Details

The following pages provide statistical material on the club's history for every season since formation in 1988. While it had never been an intention to include statistical material in this book it became apparent that what follows can be used to support the stories, memories and images that appear elsewhere through the book. Every effort has been made to identify games, scorers and lineups however, despite records being made at the time and submitted to various leagues and competitions, material has been difficult to locate. League archives have not been maintained and the club's own material, even from fairly recent years, is incomplete. The following is the most complete set of statistics ever compiled and published on the club (indeed it eclipses that published for most women's teams) and it is hoped that by publishing it now readers will be able to fill in some of the gaps.

It is known that from 2001 every league the club played in insisted that match programmes be published. As most of these carried past results it should be possible to fill in any gaps from 2001 onwards. If you have information and evidence which can help please email the author via **info@manchesterfootball.org** or contact him at **@garyjameswriter Facebook.com/garyjames4**

CITY'S FULL LEAGUE RECORD

Season	League	Position	P	W	D	L	F	A	Pts
1989-90	NWWRL Div 2	4th	14	5	3	6	42	52	13
1990-91	NWWRL Div 2	4th	18	11	2	5	65	37	24
1991-92	NWWRL Div 1	8th	18	4	2	12	30	52	10
1992-93	NWWRL Div 1	5th	12	4	1	7	26	49	9
1993-94	NWWRL Div 1	9th	18	5	3	10	47	56	18
1994-95	NWWRL Div 1	7th	18	6	3	9	20	51	21
1995-96	NWWRL Div 1	7th	16	4	3	9	37	44	15
1996-97	NWWRL Div 1	10th	18	0	2	16	19	99	2
1997-98	NWWRL Div 2	1st	20	18	2	0	102	26	56
1998-99	NWWRL Prem	2nd	18	14	2	2	68	31	44
1999-00	NWWRL Prem	1st	18	15	2	1	71	20	47
2000-01	Northern Comb	1st	22	16	2	4	80	36	50
2001-02	FA National Nth	10th	20	4	4	12	19	45	16
2002-03	FA National Nth	8th	22	5	6	11	31	37	21
2003-04	FA National Nth	7th	20	7	3	10	35	45	24
2004-05	FA National Nth	10th	22	7	3	12	29	45	24
2005-06	FA National Nth	11th	22	3	7	12	19	31	16
2006-07	FA National Nth	10th	22	6	6	10	27	35	24
2007-08	FA National Nth	7th	22	7	4	11	29	41	25
2008-09	FA National Nth	3rd	22	13	4	5	42	22	43
2009-10	FA National Nth	4th	22	10	6	6	36	25	36
2010-11	FA National Nth	4th	18	12	1	5	37	18	37
2011-12	FA National Nth	1st	18	13	1	4	58	19	40
2012-13	FA National	4th	18	7	4	7	32	25	25
Total (Pre WSL)			**458**	**196**	**76**	**186**	**1001**	**941**	**640**
2014	WSL	5th	14	6	1	7	13	16	19
2015	WSL	2nd	14	9	3	2	25	11	30
2016	WSL	1st	16	13	3	0	36	4	42
2017	Spring Series	2nd	8	6	1	1	17	6	19
2017-18	WSL	2nd	18	12	2	4	51	17	38
2018-19	WSL	2nd	20	14	5	1	53	17	47
Total (WSL)			**90**	**60**	**15**	**15**	**195**	**71**	**195**
TOTAL ALL LEAGUES			**548**	**256**	**91**	**201**	**1196**	**1012**	**835**

2pts for a win 1989-93, 3pts for a win from 1993-94 onwards

1988-89

	Date	Venue	Opposition	Result	City Scorers (where known)
1	Nov 27	Away	Oldham Athletic (Friendly)	W 4-1	Donna Haynes 2, Heidi Ward 2
2	**Dec 12**	**Home**	**Oldham Athletic** (Friendly)	**D 1-1**	Heidi Ward
3	Jan 22	Away	Burnley (Friendly)	W 5-3	
	Feb 4	Away	Crewe Alexandra (Friendly)	P-P	
4	Feb	Away	Oldham Athletic (Friendly)	W 6-0	Donna Haynes (4), Lisa Burnett, Julie Walsh
5	**Apr**	**Home**	**Burnley** (Friendly)	**W 4-1**	Nicky Hunt (3), Julie Walsh
6	**Apr 9**	**Home**	**Crewe Alexandra** (Friendly)	**W 4-3**	Heidi Ward, Rita Howard, Donna Haynes, Joni Davies
7	**May 3**	**Home**	**Chester City** (Friendly)	**W 12-0**	Kath Dickenson (4), Joni Davies (3), Lesley Wright (3), Helen Hempenstall, Nicky Hunt
8	**May 6**	**Home**	**Crewe Alexandra** (Friendly)	**W 3-0**	Donna Haynes (3)
9	May 13	Away	Bradford City (Friendly)	W 8-0	Kate Themen, ?
10		**Home**	**Bradford City** (Friendly)	**W 7-2**	
11		**Home**	**Manchester United** (Friendly)	**L 2-4**	

Home games (in bold type) played at Platt Lane

Notes

On 28th January 1989 City took a team to Brentford to compete in indoor friendlies. These were not classified as full games at the time.

Match 1 - City's first ever game was played at Boundary Park, Oldham.
Team: Michelle Flynn, Rowena Foxwell, Tonia Slack, Michelle Cox, Michelle Mather, Lisa Burnett, Kate Themen, Louisa Felton (capt), Heidi Ward, Donna Haynes, Alison Hewlett. Subs: C Morrison, M Braddock, Donna Davies, A Marland, Debbie Darbyshire, D Crystal, B Emerson.

Match 2 - Squad: Michelle Flynn, Donna Davies, Kate Themen, M Hewlett, M Braddock, Paula Hinchcliffe, T Slack, Michelle Mather, Louisa Felton, Donna Haynes, A Marsland, Debbie Darbyshire, Rowena Foxwell, Lisa Burnett, Heidi Ward, C Morgson, Helen Clark, J Walsh (Record of who started/subs not kept).

Match 3 - Team: Michelle Flynn, Rita Howard, Donna Davies, Louisa Felton, Carol Woodall, Nicky Hunt, Heidi Ward, Michelle Mather, Rhoda Taylor, Donna Haynes, Lesley Wright.

Match 7 - Team: Michelle Flynn, Louisa Felton, Helen Hempenstall, Rita Howard, Karen Martland, Joni Davies, Rachel O'Shaughnessy, Lesley Wright, Nicky Hunt, Donna Haynes, Kath Dickenson. Subs: Carol Woodall, Joanne Taylor, Estelle Scruton, Sharon Rowland, Sarah Jackson.

Match 8 - Team: Michelle Flynn, Carol Woodall, Donna Davies, Rita Howard, Lesley Wright, Joni Davies, Rachel O'Shaughnessy, Heidi Ward, Nicky Hunt, Donna Haynes, Helen Hempenstall Subs: Estelle Scruton, Bev Weir, Sharon Rowland, Rowena Foxwell, Karen Woods.

Match 9 - Team: Michelle Flynn, Carol Woodall, Donna Davies, Rita Howard, Lesley Wright, Joni Davies, Kate Themen, Gail Duncan, Rachel O'Shaughnessy, Donna Haynes, Helen Hempenstall. Subs: Carol Woodall, Joanne Taylor, Estelle Scruton, Sharon Rowland, Sarah Jackson.

City's record in the first season was Played 11, Won 9, Drew 1, Lost 1, Goals For 56, Against 15.
Top scorer Donna Haynes

Press cuttings from the 4-3 win over Crewe at Platt Lane in April 1989 and the friendly match with Australia Under 18s the following January.

Joni's gem is a winner

Man City Ladies 4   Crewe Alex 3

JONI Davies, making her City Ladies debut, scored a spectacular winner in this lively contest at Platt Lane

But it was Crewe who took an early lead totally against the run of play with a bizarre goal. City's keeper Flynn came off her line too late, collided with her own defender Howard and the ball trickled over the line.

Ward swiftly equalised after her first shot was parried.

In the second half City took control and it was only a matter of time before they took the lead through Howard.

City pressed on and Haynes kept up her superb scoring record with an overhead kick into the net.

City then lost concentration and let in Crewe to score twice in 10 minutes.

The game seemed destined for a draw . . . until Joni Davies drove home a fierce shot from outside the box.

Neil Mather

Girls mud battle

MANCHESTER City Ladies went down 3-1 to a team of girls from Down under at the weekend

The Manchester girls are only in their second season but their progress has been marked with an international prestige game.

The Australian under 18 team has been touring the USA and is now visiting Britain.

They are playing only two matches — one against Arsenal and in the other they took on City at the University Fields in Northenden.

The high wind and heavy conditions were not conducive to good soccer but both teams managed to put on a

By GEOFF GARNETT

fine display.

The Australians always had the advantage of the wind they went into a 3-1 first-half lead.

City's goal was scored by Welsh triallist Joni Davies who finished off a left-wing move by Lesley Peters and Rachel O'Shaughnessy.

The second half was goal-

less and City coach Neil Mather was very pleased with his team's battling and skilful performance and picked out centre-half Lesley Wright and striker Donna Haynes for special mention.

City Ladies are a flourishing club with their first team playing in the second division of the North West Regional League and their reserve team play friendly matches.

Their 34-strong squad originated from the Manchester City Community pro-

gramme and they are extremely grateful for the tremendous help they receive from the division one club.

Coach Neil Mather has world-wide experience of soccer at all levels but he is impressed by the flourishing ladies game.

He said: "They play a fast-flowing game with a high skill factor . . . and without any of the cynicism you often get in the men's game. The girls are very receptive to coaching."

	Date	Venue	Opposition	Result	Lge Pos	City Scorers (where known)
1	Sep 3	Away	Chorley	L 0-11	10th	
	Sep 10	Home	Broadoak	P-P	10th	
2	**Sep 10**	**Home**	**Burnley** (Friendly)	**W 4-2**		
3	Sep 17	Away	Wigan Athletic (WFAC 1)	L 2-7		Lesley Peters, Donna Haynes
4	Sep 24	Away	Rossendale	L 2-7	10th	Helen Hempenstall, Donna Haynes
5	**Oct 1**	**Home**	**FC Redstar**	**W 7-2**	8th	Nicky Hunt, Rhoda Taylor, Lesley Peters (3), Rachel O'Shaughnessy, Donna Haynes
	Oct 8	Away	Broadoak	P-P	8th	
	Oct 15	Home	Lady Blues	P-P	8th	
6	Oct 22	Away	Vernons (LC 1)	D 3-3		Lesley Peters, Donna Haynes, Own goal
7	Oct 29	Away	Petros	D 3-3	8th	Rachel O'Shaughnessy, Lesley Peters, Donna Haynes
8	**Nov 5**	**Home**	**North End**	**L 4-5**	8th	Howard, Donna Haynes, Rhoda Taylor, Nicky Hunt
9	**Nov 12**	**Home**	**Vernons** (LC 1 Replay)	**D 1-1**		(Lost 4-2 on penalties)
10	Nov 19	Away	Clitheroe	L 0-2	7th	
	Nov 26	Away	Wigan Athletic	P-P	8th	
11	Dec 3	Away	FC Redstar	L 1-2	8th	
12	**Dec 10**	**Home**	**Chorley**	**L 5-6**	8th	
13	**Dec 17**	**Home**	**Clitheroe**	**L 0-1**	9th	
	Jan 7	Home	Rossendale	P-P	9th	
14	**Jan 14**	**Home**	**Lady Blues**	**L 5-10**	9th	
15	**Jan 21**	**Home**	**Petros**	**W 9-0**	8th	
16	**Jan 28**	**Home**	**Australia U18** (Friendly)	**L 1-3**		Joni Davies
	Feb 4	Away	North End	P-P	8th	
17	**Feb 18**	**Home**	**Broadoak**	**W 7-3**	8th	Rhoda Taylor (3), Rachel O'Shaughnessy (2), Donna Haynes, Own goal
18	**Feb 25**	**Home**	**St Helens** (Div Cup 2)	**W 3-1**		Lesley Peters (2), Donna Haynes
19	**Mar 7**	**Home**	**Trafford**	**W 11-0**		Sally Rustige, ?
20	**Mar 11**	**Home**	**Broadoak**	**D 2-2**		
21	Mar 18	Away	Wigan Athletic	D 2-2	8th	Donna Haynes (2)
22	**Mar 25**	**Home**	**Crewe** (Div Cup QF)	**L 4-5**		Donna Haynes (2), Lesley Peters, Rhoda Taylor (pen)
23	**Apr 1**	**Home**	**Rossendale**	**W 2-1**	7th	Joni Davies (pen), Donna Haynes
24	**Apr 8**	**Home**	**Wigan Athletic**	**D 3-3**	6th	
25	Apr 22	Away	North End	W 4-0	5th	
26	Apr 27	Away	Lady Blues	W 4-1	4th	
27	Apr 28	Away	Preston North End (Friendly)	W 4-0		

WFAC = Women's FA Cup, LC = League Cup, Div Cup = 1st & 2nd Division Cup. Home games in bold type. League games on white background.
Home games played at the University Grounds.

Other games

City Ladies won the Trafford 5-a-side trophy. It was an all-City final as two teams were entered. The second team won the trophy. Michelle Brady scored the winning penalty in a penalty shootout.

Reserve Team:

Oct 20 -	Rochdale (a)	Drew 3-3	Sally Rustige (2), ?
Nov 10 -	Oldham (a)	Won 15-1	Kath Dickenson (9), Sally Rustige (2), Donna Davies, Pamela Rhodes, Jenny Newton, Helen Stapleton
			Team: Michelle Flynn, Susan Street, Donna Davies, Pamela Rhodes, Michelle Mather (capt), Joanne Taylor, Heidi Ward, Carole Hamilton, Kath Dickinson, Jenny Newton, Sally Rustige, Jean Dixon, Helen Stapleton, Debbie Darbyshire
Dec 2 -	Padgate (a)	Won 10-1	Sally Rustige (3), ?
Jan 21 -	Rochdale (a)	Won 4-3	Nicky Hunt (2), Taylor, Own goal
Feb 4 -	Port Vale (h)	Lost 2-4	Dickenson, Tarr
Feb 17 -	Bolton Bombers (h)	Won 10-0	Rustige (3), Hamilton (2), Duff, Foxwell, Tarr, Newton, J Taylor
Feb 24 -	Partington (h)	Won 18-1	Rustige (6), Dickenson (3), Hamilton (2), Hamnett (2), Hewlett, Mather, Yorke, Hudson & OG
Mar 12 -	Bury (h)	Won 2-1	Sally Rustige (2)
Apr 21 -	Tranmere Rovers (h)	Won 11-4	Sally Rustige, ?
May 6 -	Rochdale (a)	Lost 0-8	
May 20 -	Port Vale (a)	Lost 4-6	

Notes

Match 1 - This was City's first league game.

Match 3 - City's first FA Cup game was played at Robins Park, Wigan.
Team: Julie Yorke, Carol Woodall (Julie Taylor), Donna Davies, Karen Bretherton, Rita Howard, Joni Davies, Lesley Wright, Rachel O'Shaughnessy, Lesley Peters, Donna Haynes, Nicky Hunt. City were 2-0 down after 20 minutes but pulled it back to 2-2 on 33 minutes.

Match 21 - This was the first time a team had taken a point off Wigan since Wythenshawe on 20th December 1987 - a run of 21 matches. Wigan's last home defeat had been on 27th September 1987 when Clitheroe won 4-0.

10th May 1990 Annual Player of the year event at City's social club.

City Ladies was accepted into the NWWRFL at the NWWL AGM on Friday 7th June 1989. They were placed in Division Two (of Four) at a Special League Meeting on Friday 7th July 1989. Both meetings were held at Leyland. The League had been restructured that summer.

League Record **4th** (8* teams) Played **14** Won **5** Drawn **3** Lost **6** Goals For **42** Against **52** Points **13**

*Petros withdrew from the League on 18 February 1990 and FC Redstar withdrew on 4th March.

	Date	Venue	Opposition	Result	Lge Pos	City Scorers (where known)
1	Sep 9	Away	Rossendale	W 8-1	1st	Rhoda Taylor (3), Lesley Peters (4), Heidi Ward
2	Sep 16	Away	Daresbury	W 8-3	1st	Lesley Peters (6), Heidi Ward (2)
3	Sep 23	Away	Chorley	L 1-4	2nd	
4	**Sep 30**	**Home**	**Manchester United**	**W 4-3**	2nd	Rhoda Taylor, Rachel O'Shaughnessy, Jenny Newton, Lesley Peters
5	**Oct 7**	**Home**	**Blackpool** (WFAC1)	**W 6-0**	–	
	Oct 14	Away	Rivacre	P-P	2nd	
	Oct 28	Away	Clitheroe	P-P	4th	Waterlogged
6	**Nov 4**	**Home**	**Bury** (WFAC2)	**W 6-2**	5th	
7	**Nov 11**	**Home**	**Vernons**	**W 4-0**	4th	
8	**Nov 18**	**Home**	**Wythenshawe** (LC2)	**W 4-2**	–	
9	**Nov 25**	**Home**	**Broadoak**	**D 4-4**	4th	
10	**Dec 2**	**Home**	**Wythenshawe** (WFAC3)	**D 1-1**	–	
11	Dec 16	Away	Wythenshawe (WFAC3, replay)	W 3-2	–	
12	Dec 30	Away	Bronte (Div Cup 2)	L 1-2	–	
13	Jan 6	Away	Hassocks Beacon (WFAC4)	L 0-3	–	
	Jan 13	Home	Rivacre	P-P	5th	Frozen pitch
14	**Jan 20**	**Home**	**Clitheroe**	**W 5-1**	5th	Heidi Ward, Lesley Wright, Rhoda Taylor, Donna Haynes (2)
15	Jan 27	Away	Vernons	W 3-2	5th	
	Feb 3	Away	Broadoak	P-P	5th	
16	Feb 17	Away	St Helens (LC3)	L 2-4	5th	
17	**Feb 24**	**Home**	**Chorley**	**W 4-2**	4th	
18	Mar 3	Away	Rivacre	L 0-2	5th	
19	**Mar 17**	**Home**	**Nabwood**	**D 2-2**	4th	
20	Mar 24	Away	Clitheroe	L 1-2	5th	
	Apr 7	Home	Daresbury	P-P	5th	
21	**Apr 14**	**Home**	**Rossendale**	**W 7-1**	5th	
22	Apr 21	Away	Broadoak	W 3-1	4th	
	Apr 21	Home	Rivacre	P-P		
	Apr 28	Away	Manchester United (Friendly)	P-P		
23	Apr 28	Away	Nabwood	W 3-0	3rd	
24	May 5	Away	Manchester United	L 1-4	3rd	
25	**May 12**	**Home**	**Rivacre**	**L 2-4**	3rd	Donna Haynes, Rhoda Taylor
26	**May 14**	**Home**	**Daresbury**	**W 5-1**	3rd	Rhoda Taylor (2), Michelle Brady, Malin Karlsson (2)

WFAC = Women's FA Cup, LC = League Cup, Div Cup = 1st & 2nd Division Cup. Home games in bold type. League games on white background.
Home games played at the University Grounds.

League Record **4th** (10 teams) Played **18** Won **11** Drawn **2** Lost **5** Goals For **65** Against **37** Points **24**

Lesley Peters, Lesley Wright and Rachel O'Shaughnessy. Peters and O'Shaughnessy were on the scoresheet as City beat Manchester United 4-3 in the first League derby, September 1990.

Other games

July 22/23 1990 - Lancashire International Tournament. Lesley Peters, Donna Haynes and Jenny Newton participate as members of the Wigan team. Rhoda Taylor also invited but unable to compete.

August 26 - First Arsenal Tournament.

Oct 14 - This was postponed because of the Inter Regional Competition at Lilleshall involving Seniors and U21s for NW clubs.

Notes

The 1990-91 season was the second competitive season for Manchester City Ladies, playing in the North West Women's Regional Football League Second Division. Neil Mather remained the manager for this season.

Match 17 - City wore Sky Blue Shirts and Navy Blue Shorts and socks. Area News newspaper match report exists. Team: M Flynn, T Blanchard, H Hempenstall, G Duncan, C Woodall, L Wright, H Ward, M Brady, M Karlsson, R Taylor, D Haynes. Substitutes: M Nygren, S Kenyon, J Marcus, J Newton, F Billington.

Match 15 - Maroon & White Stripes, Maroon Shorts and Socks. Team: M Flynn, T Blanchard, H Hempenstall, G Duncan, C Woodall, L Wright, H Ward, M Brady, M Karlsson, R Taylor, D Haynes. Substitutes: J Newton, M Nygren.

Match 20 - Manager Neil Mather and two players sent off.

The Ladies Player of the Year event was staged on May 16th, 8pm at MCFC Social Club. Admission £2. Colin Hendry presenting the awards. Other City players in attendance.

	Date	Venue	Opposition	Result	Lge Pos	City Scorers (where known)
1	Sep 1	Away	Leasowe Pacific	L 1-4	10th	Rita Howard
	Sep 8		Manchester United	P-P	8th	
2	**Sep 15**	**Home**	**Huddersfield** (WFAC1 Group 5)	**L 1-4**	–	
	Sep 22	Away	Crewe Ladies	P-P	8th	
3	**Sep 29**	**Home**	**Vauxhall**	**D 2-2**	7th	
4	Oct 13	Away	Wigan	W 3-2	5th	
5	**Oct 20**	**Home**	**St Helens**	**L 2-3**	5th	
6	Oct 27	Away	Lady Blues	L 5-6	5th	
7	**Nov 3**	**Home**	**Wythenshawe**	**L 1-2**	5th	
8	Nov 10	Away	Vauxhall	L 0-1	6th	
9	Nov 17	Away	Sale (LC2)	W 11-0	–	Donna Haynes (5), Gail Duncan, Michelle Brady, Joni Davies, Sally Rustige, Jane Marcus, ?
10	Nov 24	Away	Preston Rangers	L 1-3	7th	
11	**Dec 1**	**Home**	**Lady Blues**	**W 3-2**	6th	
12	Dec 8	Away	Crewe Ladies	L 0-3	6th	
	Dec 22	Away	Manchester United	P-P	7th	Waterlogged pitch
13	**Jan 5**	**Home**	**Crewe Ladies**	**L 1-3**	8th	
14	**Jan 12**	**Home**	**Manchester United**	**D 2-2**	8th	
15	**Jan 19**	**Home**	**Wigan**	**W 4-1**	6th	
16	**Jan 26**	**Home**	**Manchester United**	**D 2-2**		
17	Feb 2	Away	Wythenshawe (Div Cup)	L 0-1	–	
18	Feb 9	Away	Tranmere Rovers (LC3)	D 2-2	–	
19	Feb 13	Away	Atherton (Charity Match)	W 13-0	–	
20	**Feb 16**	**Home**	**Tranmere Rovers** (LC3 Replay)	**W 6-2**	–	
21	Feb 23	Away	Liverpool University (Friendly)	W 14-0	–	
	Mar 1	Away	St Helens	P-P	6th	Waterlogged pitch
22	Mar 8	Away	Wythenshawe (LC QF)	L 3-4	–	
23	Mar 22	Away	Wythenshawe	W 1-0	6th	Bev Harrop
24	Mar 29	Away	Manchester United	L 0-1	6th	
25	Apr 19	Away	St Helens	L 1-5	8th	
26	**May 17**	**Home**	**Preston Rangers**	**L 2-3**	8th	
27	June 7	Neutral	Manchester United (Michael Wilson Memorial Cup)	L 3-4	–	

WFAC = Women's FA Cup, LC = League Cup, Div Cup = 1st & 2nd Division Cup. Home games in bold type. League games on white background.
Home games played at the University Grounds.

League Record **8th** (10 teams) Played **18** Won **4** Drawn **2** Lost **12** Goals For **30** Against **52** Points **10**

Rovers' girls score charity goal

ATHERTON Laburnum Ladies scored a charity goal recently to boost a Twins' Trust Fund.

The girls met Manchester City Ladies and the match raised £250 to help make life better for little David and Gillian Prescott, aged two, who both suffer from cerebral palsy.

Parents Rod and Josie Prescott and pictured with their lively twosome receiving the cheque with Rovers' lady captain Rhoda Taylor, City Ladies' captain Mary O'Grady and Rovers' press officer, John Bullen.(L0245).

Other games

July 21 1991 - Moss Farm Tournament This was the first Moss Farm Tournament. MCFC in a group with eventual winners Wigan.

July 27/28 1991 - Lancashire International Tournament. Guesting for Wigan from City were Rhoda Taylor (attack) and Gail Duncan (defence). Wigan won Group 2 but lost to Knowley 3-2 on penalties after a 1-1 draw (Knowsley won tournament).

August 18 1991 - Arsenal Tournament.

Notes

The 1991-92 season was the first season in the North West Women's Regional Football League First Division. Rita Howard replaced Neil Mather as manager for this season.

Sep 22 - Date of inter-regional competition held at Leicester involving North West Seniors and U21s.

Match 19 - Charity game kicked off by Garry Flitcroft for 2 year olds David and Gillian Prescott who had Cerebral Palsy.

Match 27 - Match programme produced, price 50p.

1992-93 North West Women's Regional Football League Division One

	Date	Venue	Opposition	Result	Lge Pos	City Scorers (where known)
	Sep 6	Home	Wigan	P-P		
	Sep 13	Away	Broadoak (WFAC1 Group 6)	P-P		
1	Sep 20	Away	Broadoak (WFAC1 Group 6)	L 1-3	–	Bev Harrop
2	Sep 27	Away	Chorley	W 2-1	5th	Tracey Blanchard, Gail Duncan
	Oct 4	Home	Chorley	P-P	5th	
3	Oct 11	Away	Crewe	W 4-3	3rd	Lesley Wright (2), Sally Rustige, Bev Harrop
4	Oct 18	Away	Preston Rangers	L 2-4	4th	
5	Oct 25	Away	Manchester Belle Vue	W 3-1	1st	Lesley Wright, Tracey Blanchard, Bev Weir
6	**Nov 8**	**Home**	**Broadoak**	**L 2-5**	3rd	
7	Nov 15	Away	Runcorn (LC2)	W 5-2	–	
8	Nov 29	Away	Manchester United	L 2-5	4th	
9	**Dec 6**	**Home**	**Chorley**	**L 2-4**	4th	
	Dec 20	Home	Preston Rangers	P-P	5th	
	Jan 3	Away	Wigan	P-P	5th	Frozen pitch
10	**Jan 10**	**Home**	**Preston Rangers**	**L 2-5**	5th	
11	**Jan 17**	**Home**	**Wigan**	**L 3-8**	5th	
12	**Jan 24**	**Home**	**Crewe**	**L 4-5**	5th	
13	**Jan 31**	**Home**	**Manchester United** (Div Cup)	**W 2-1**	–	
14	**Feb 7**	**Home**	**Manchester Belle Vue**	**D 1-1**	5th	Bev Harrop
15	**Feb 14**	**Home**	**Pilkington Ladies** (LC3)	**L 2-5**	–	
	Feb 28	Away	Broadoak	P-P	6th	
16	**Mar 7**	**Home**	**Manchester United**	**W 2-1**	6th	Sue Don-Bavond (2)
17	**Mar 7**	**Home**	**Pilkington Ladies** (Div Cup)	**L 2-5**	–	
18	Mar 14	Away	Broadoak	W 5-3	4th	Bev Harrop (2), Tracey Blanchard, Nora McGuire, Gail Duncan
19	Mar 28	Away	Wigan	L 0-11	4th	

WFAC = Women's FA Cup, LC = League Cup, Div Cup = 1st & 2nd Division Cup. Home games in bold type. League games on white background.
Home games played at the University Grounds.

Other games
Jan 23 1993 - All England 5-A-Side Tournament played at Salt Ayre, Lancaster. City in a group with Wigan (lost 1-2).

Notes
Sep 6 - Opening match postponed due to Wigan's commitment to play in the Invitational Hull Tournament.

Match 5 - This was Manchester Belle Vue's first League game.

Match 8 - City raced to a 2-0 lead in the first 30 minutes but United gained control and won it 5-2.

League Record **5th** (7 teams) Played **12** Won **4** Drawn **1** Lost **7** Goals For **26** Against **49** Points **9**

The division was reduced to 7 clubs: Lever Club folded on October 2nd 1992 and Crewe withdrew March 4th 1993. Manchester Belle Vue finished second to Wigan (a one goal difference!). City's Rhoda Taylor won the NWWRFL Player of the Year award at the Presentation Evening held at Leyland Motors on Friday June 25th 1993.

	Date	Venue	Opposition	Result	Lge Pos	City Scorers (where known)
1	Sep 5	Away	Preston Rangers	W 3-0	3rd	
2	**Sep 12**	**Home**	**Manchester United** (WFAC1)	**W 2-0**		
3	**Sep 26**	**Home**	**Wigan**	**L 1-2**	7th	
4	Oct 3	Away	Manchester Belle Vue	L 0-10	7th	
5	**Oct 10**	**Home**	**Manchester United**	**W 5-1**	5th	
6	Oct 17	Away	Bury (WFAC2)	L 1-4		
7	**Oct 24**	**Home**	**Bury**	**D 3-3**	6th	
8	**Oct 31**	**Home**	**Tranmere Rovers**	**L 0-5**	6th	
	Nov 7	Away	Broadoak	P-P	6th	
	Nov 14	Home	Chorley	P-P	8th	
9	Nov 21	Away	Stockport County (LC2)	W 1-0		
10	Nov 28	Away	Bury	L 0-5	8th	
11	**Dec 5**	**Home**	**Chorley**	**W 6-0**	7th	
	Dec 12	Away	Wigan	P-P	7th	
	Dec 19	Home	Rhyl	P-P	7th	
	Jan 2	Away	Wigan	P-P	7th	
12	**Jan 9**	**Home**	**Manchester Belle Vue**	**L 2-7**	7th	
13	Jan 16	Away	Manchester United	D 2-2	7th	
14	Jan 23	Away	Tranmere Rovers	L 0-2	8th	
	Jan 30	Away	Broadoak	P-P	8th	
15	**Feb 6**	**Home**	**Broadoak**	**W 2-1**	5th	
16	Feb 13	Away	Chorley	W 12-1	4th	
17	Feb 20	Away	Tranmere Rovers (LC3)	L 1-7		
18	**Feb 27**	**Home**	**Oldham Athletic** (Div Cup)	**L 0-1**		
19	**Mar 13**	**Home**	**Preston Rangers**	**L 0-2**	4th	
20	**Apr 10**	**Home**	**Rhyl**	**L 2-3**	5th	
21	May 8	Away	Wigan	L 3-5	8th	
22	May 13	Away	Broadoak	L 3-4	8th	

WFAC = Women's FA Cup, LC = League Cup, Div Cup = 1st & 2nd Division Cup. Home games in bold type. League games on white background.

Other games

July 4th 1993 - Premier UK Ladies Tournament. City finish third in Group A and do not qualify for knockout stage.
July 11th 1993 - Moss Farm Tournament
August 8th 1993 - Vernons Tournament. City reach quarter finals losing to eventual winners Wigan 0-1. City's Rhoda Taylor guests for the 'Friends of Gillian & David Representative Team', making 6 appearances (all games they played).

League Record **9th** (10 teams) Played **18** Won **5** Drawn **3** Lost **10** Goals For **47** Against **56** Points **18**

	Date	Venue	Opposition	Result	Lge Pos	City Scorers (where known)
1	Sep 4	Home	**Radcliffe Borough**	**L 0-2**	8th	
	Sep 7	Home	Preston Rangers	P-P	8th	
	Sep 14	Away	Manchester Belle Vue	P-P	9th	
2	Sep 18	Away	Manchester Belle Vue (WFAC1)	L 1-4		
	Sep 21	Away	Wigan	P-P	9th	
3	Sep 25	Away	Tranmere Rovers	L 1-5	9th	
4	Oct 2	Home	**Preston Rangers**	**D 0-0**	9th	
5	Oct 9	Home	**Blackpool** (LC2)	**W 3-2**		
6	Oct 16	Away	Rhyl	L 0-1	9th	
7	Oct 23	Home	**Leek**	**D 1-1**	9th	
	Oct 30	Away	Clitheroe (LC3)	P-P		
8	Nov 6	Home	**Bolton** (Div Cup)	**W 9-1**		
	Nov 13	Away	Clitheroe (LC3)	P-P		
9	Nov 20	Away	Leek	P-P	9th	
10	Nov 27	Away	Manchester United	W 1-0	7th	Sally Rustige
	Dec 4	Away	Preston Rangers	P-P	8th	
11	Dec 11	Away	Leek	W 3-2	7th	
12	Dec 18	Away	Tranmere Rovers	L 0-14	7th	
13	Jan 8	Home	**Manchester United**	**W 3-2**	6th	
14	Jan 15	Home	**Manchester Belle Vue**	**L 1-5**	6th	
	Jan 22	Away	Radcliffe Borough	P-P	6th	
15	Feb 5	Home	**Wigan**	**L 0-2**	7th	
	Feb 19	Away	Radcliffe Borough	P-P	5th	
	Mar 5	Away	Clitheroe (LC3)	P-P		
16	Mar 12	Away	Clitheroe (LC3)	L 1-6		
17	Mar 19	Home	**Oldham Athletic** (Div Cup)	**L 0-4**		
18	Mar 26	Away	Radcliffe Borough	W 2-1	6th	
19	Apr 2	Away	Manchester Belle Vue	L 2-7	6th	
20	Apr 6	Home	**Oldham Athletic**	**W 1-0**	5th	
21	Apr 9	Home	**Rhyl**	**W 1-0**	4th	
22	Apr 19	Away	Preston Rangers	L 2-4	4th	
23	Apr 25	Away	Wigan	L 0-3	6th	
24	Apr 27	Away	Oldham Athletic	D 2-2	5th	
25		Away	Shelbourne (Friendly)	L 0-2		

Other games
July 3rd 1994 - Premier UK Ladies Tournament at Padgate, Warrington
July 21st 1994 - Moss Farm Tournament
January 7th 1995 - NWWRFL Five A Side Tournament at Hyndburn, Blackburn.

WFAC = Women's FA Cup, LC = League Cup, Div Cup = 1st & 2nd Division Cup. Home games in bold type. League games on white background.

League Record **7th** (10 teams) Played **18** Won **6** Drawn **3** Lost **9** Goals For **20** Against **51** Points **21**

1995-96 North West Women's Regional Football League Division One

	Date	Venue	Opposition	Result	Lge Pos	City Scorers (where known)
1	Sep 3	Away	Blackburn Rovers	L 2-3	7th	
	Sep 6	Home	Manchester Belle Vue	P-P	7th	
2	**Sep 10**	**Home**	**Preston Rangers**	**D 3-3**	6th	
	Sep 14	Away	Manchester United	P-P	7th	
3	**Sep 17**	**Home**	**Oldham Athletic** (WFAC1)	**L 0-1**		
4	**Sep 24**	**Home**	**Manchester Belle Vue**	**L 1-2**	7th	
5	**Oct 1**	**Home**	**Liverpool Feds**	**D 2-2**	6th	
6	Oct 8	Away	Radcliffe Borough	L 4-8	7th	
7	Oct 15	Away	Wigan	W 5-1	5th	
8	Oct 22	Away	Manchester United	L 0-3	5th	.
9	Oct 29	Away	Manchester Belle Vue	L 4-5	6th	
10	Nov 5	Away	Vernons (LC2)	L 0-1		
	Nov 12	Home	Manchester United	P-P	8th	
11	**Nov 19**	**Home**	**Manchester United**	**L 1-2**	8th	
12	**Nov 26**	**Home**	**Blackburn Rovers**	**L 0-3**	8th	
	Dec 3	Away	Oldham Athletic	P-P	6th	
13	**Dec 10**	**Home**	**Oldham Athletic**	**L 2-6**	6th	
14	**Jan 7**	**Home**	**Radcliffe Borough**	**W 3-1**	6th	
15	Jan 14	Away	Preston Rangers	D 0-0	6th	
	Feb 4	Away	Oldham Athletic	P-P	7th	
16	**Feb 11**	**Home**	**Bangor City** (Div Cup)	**L 0-2**		
17	**Feb 25**	**Home**	**Wigan**	**W 5-1**	7th	
18	Mar 24	Away	Oldham Athletic	L 1-2	7th	
19	Apr 7	N	Manchester United (Charity Match)	L 2-3		
20	May 26	N	Bolton Girls (MCFA1)	W 5-0		
21	June 2	N	Manchester Belle Vue (MCFA SF)	L 2-6		

WFAC = Women's FA Cup, LC = League Cup, Div Cup = 1st & 2nd Division Cup, MCFA = Manchester County FA Trophy. Home games in bold type. League games on white background. N= Neutral Ground

Other games
MCFC prog October 29 1997 said there had been a game against Sheffield Wednesday at Maine Road this season.
July 2nd 1995 - Premier UK Ladies Tournament at Padgate, Warrington. City finish 4th from 7 teams in Group 2 and do not qualify for knock out stages
July 9th 1995 - Moss Farm Tournament

Notes
Match 19 - Played at Heaton Mersey Sports & Social Club.
Matches 20 & 21 - All games in this tournament played at Turn Moss Fields apart from the final (played at Cheadle Town) on 9/9/96.

League Record **7th** (9 teams) Played **16** Won **4** Drawn **3** Lost **9** Goals For **37** Against **44** Points **15**

Mold Ladies (formerly Rhyl) disbanded prior to the season's start.

1996-97 North West Women's Regional Football League Division One

	Date	Venue	Opposition	Result	Lge Pos	City Scorers (where known)
1	**Sep 1**	**Home**	**Radcliffe Borough**	**L 1-5**	9th	
	Sep 4	Away	Manchester United	P-P	10th	
2	**Sep 8**	**Home**	**Manchester Belle Vue**	**L 1-14**	10th	
	Sep 15	Away	Oldham Athletic	P-P	10th	
3	**Sep 22**	**Home**	**Newsham PH**	**D 1-1**	10th	
4	Sep 29	Away	Tranmere Rovers (Friendly)	L 0-9	–	
5	Oct 6	Away	Preston Rangers	L 0-4	10th	
6	Oct 13	Away	Bangor City	L 1-6	10th	
	Oct 20	Away	Oldham Athletic (LC1)	P-P	–	
7	Oct 27	Away	Oldham Athletic (LC1)	L 0-4	–	
8	Nov 3	Away	Manchester Belle Vue	L 1-9	10th	
	Nov 10	Home	Liverpool Feds	P-P	10th	
	Nov 17	Away	Radcliffe Borough	P-P	10th	
	Nov 24	Away	Newsham PH	P-P	10th	
9	**Dec 1**	**Home**	**Manchester United**	**L 3-5**	10th	
10	**Dec 15**	**Home**	**Preston Rangers**	**L 0-8**	10th	
	Dec 22	Home	Oldham Athletic	P-P	10th	
	Dec 29	Away	Newsham PH	P-P	10th	
	Jan 5	Away	Manchester United	P-P	10th	
	Jan 12	Away	Manchester United	P-P	10th	
11	Jan 19	Away	Radcliffe Borough	D 2-2	10th	
12	Jan 26	Away	Liverpool Feds	L 1-3	10th	
13	**Feb 2**	**Home**	**Blackburn Rovers**	**L 1-6**	10th	
14	Feb 9	Away	Newsham PH	L 3-5	10th	
15	Feb 16	Away	Blackburn Rovers	L 1-3	10th	
16	**Feb 23**	**Home**	**Oldham Athletic**	**L 1-4**	10th	
17	Mar 2	Away	Manchester United	L 1-4	10th	
18	Mar 16	Away	Chester (Div Cup 2)	W 3-2	–	
19	Mar 23	Away	Oldham Athletic	L 1-5	10th	
20	Mar 30	Away	Stockport (Div Cup QF)	L 0-6	–	
21	**Apr 13**	**Home**	**Liverpool Feds**	**L 0-8**	10th	
	May 9	Home	Bangor City	P-P	10th	
22	**May 11**	**Home**	**Bangor City**	**L 0-7**	10th	

LC = League Cup, Div Cup = 1st & 2nd Division Cup. Home games in bold type. League games on white background.

League Record **10th** (10 teams) Played **18** Won **0** Drawn **2** Lost **16** Goals For **19** Against **99** Points **2**
City relegated at the season's end.

The opening pages of the June 1997 newsletter.

THE COMMUNITY PROGRAMME IN PROFESSIONAL FOOTBALL

MANCHESTER CITY FOOTBALL CLUB PLC

Maine Road, Moss Side, Manchester M14 7WN Telephone: 0161 226 1702

MANCHESTER CITY LADIES F.C.

__INFORMATION SHEET__   14 JUNE 97

(1) TRAINING. Training seems to have settled down with Wednesdays being the regular evening for the Under 10's, Under 12's and Under 14's at 7.00 p.m. The Under 16's will be continuing on a Friday at least for the moment at 7.00 p.m. Numbers last Wednesday were 18 Under 10's, 17 Under 12's and 14's and this is quite enough to fill the Training Field at the moment.

Parents and Friends are invited to make use of the bar and facilities in the Clubhouse at Wythenshawe Town whilst the Training is taking place - our custom would be welcomed by the Wythenshawe Club. The players are interested in becoming Wythenshawe Club members simply in order to have access to the bar and Dressing Rooms etc., and parents are able to use the Club facilities if their daughters are Club members. So if your daughter is a Club member, invite you into the Club - at least, I think that's how it works!

With regard to Club Membership, we may have to ask the girls fairly soon to a Wythenshawe membership of £3 (Junior Rate) which I believe will last a year.

(2) TEAM MANAGERS. We now have Managers in place for all four junior teams and this is really encouraging, allowing for the fact that the first Training took place only a few weeks ago on May 7th. That first Wednesday, we had on a dreadful wet and cold night, then there were 41 the next week and after, (although that number included the Under 16's who are now ...

Inevitably, some of the girls who attended the first one or two sessions have not been recently and it may be that they realise that their team could be limited when the season starts - we have been surprised ... standards revealed at Training and it does seem that anyone hoping to be in one of the teams will have to be a reasonable standard to be ... school team standard at least. I am quite happy to say that the ... different views on this, especially the Under 10's where potential is important as already acquired skills - but it is true to say that the ... certainly in terms of space at the moment, are limited.

You may like to make a note of the four Team Managers and their names for future reference, and we would just say thankyou to all for ... ... but were often rewarding task of Team Managership! ... Vicky Bloor.

---

(4) MANCHESTER CITY CENTRE OF EXCELLENCE. More news on this - City are to set up around ten Centres of Excellence venues around Manchester with a main one at Platt Lane and girls will be able to attend as well as boys. Obviously, we hope that some of our players will be able to attend.

(5) MANCHESTER CITY LADIES F.C.   City Ladies are looking forward to next season and their Training evening is on a Friday at Wythenshawe Town F.C. (same evening as the Under 16's). Judging by the numbers already attending Friday Training (note 7.30 p.m. start), it will not be an easy task for Manager Reno Dionisiou to select his first squad when the season starts. City will play in Division Two of the North West Womens Regional Football League which includes teams from Bolton, Warrington, Chester, Leek, Haslingden, Wrexham, Wigan and Chorley, to name just some of the other Clubs involved.

(6) SUMMER TOURNAMENTS ETC.
June 22 (Sunday) 6-a-side tournament at Rhyl. We hope to take two Under 14 teams to this tournament (it is for Under 14's only!). You have to be Under 14 on the day of the tournament. Other teams entered include Tranmere Rovers, Liverpool, Brazil and Liverpool Feds.

July 5th (Saturday) 5 or 6-a-side tournament at Cadishead. Probably all ages will be able to play in this event, so we are hoping to have Under 10, Under 12, Under 14 and maybe Under 16 teams competing.

July 13 (Sunday)   7-a-side tournament at Northwich. Probably same teams as for Cadishead, with a Ladies Team competing also.

July 26 (Saturday) to August 2 (Saturday). Manchester Umbro International Tournament at Northenden. For Ladies teams and Under 14 teams with a possibility of a mini-soccer team at age Under 9 or Under 10.

(7) PLAYING RESULTS   Manchester City Girls had their first competitive games last weekend when the Under 10's played in a Tournament at Leeds and the Under 12's and Under 14's played 11-a-side Friendlies against teams from Cadishead Girls F.C.

The Under 10's did really well in reaching the Semi-Final at Leeds, going out to a very experienced Stockport side by only 1-0, and that was a penalty! Captain Nicola Twohig played brilliantly in goals - we didn't even know she could play goalkeeper until the second match of the tournament and the other squad members who all had great games were Frances Simpkin, Frances Crake, Amy O'Shea, Leanne Rogers, Carla Cleworth and Michaela Goulding.
Results:
Manchester City 1   Stockport   2
(Nicola Twohig)
Manchester City 5   Leeds City B 0
(Carla Cleworth 5)
Manchester City 8   Leeds City C 0
(Carla Cleworth 2, Nicola Twohig, Amy O'Shea 2, Frances Crake, Frances Simpkin, o.g.)
Manchester City 0   White Rose Ladies 1

Quarter Final
Manchester City 0   Leeds City A 0
(Manchester City win 5-4 on penalties)
Well done to all our 5 penalty-takers who all scored. Beth won it for us as well when she saved one of the Leeds penalty-kicks.
Semi-Final
Manchester City 0   Stockport 1

The Under 12's lost to Cadishead Under 12's on Sunday by 5 goals to 2 with Sarah Messham and Laura McGuigan scoring. Manager Lesley Wright gave the game to give trials to 20 players who all got a chance to show what they could do. Cadishead are a good little side who have played together for some time now so all things considered, the result wasn't unreasonable. Lesley and Joni (Asst.Manager) will have found this initial game very useful in assessing their squad.

PLAYING RESULTS (Continued)

The Under 14's had a great game against Cadishead Under 14's, winning 4-1 with striker Stacey Skerritt getting two goals and Amy Rothwell one own goal by Cadishead.

Carol Gregory and Gail Rothwell were delighted by the performance of players from Stockport Sarah Darby, Amy Gregory, Kate Williamson all added experience to an already talented squad.

Sarah Darby had a roving midfield role which she seemed to make her own on the right wing was a revelation with her pace and crossing and Kate and Vicky in defence (playing the 11-a-side game for the first time playing 7-a-side soccer) looked completely professional in the way they organised the defence over and over again.

Stacey Skerritt scored two good goals which don't try to score from ... the time - she will have a go at goal from way out which will get them in the future.

Left winger Claire Griffiths, who comes all the way from Sandbach for the game and combined well with Sarah in midfield. Amy Rothwell deserved a medal for having a crack from 20 yards and Kate Prince in goal dealt confidently with what little she had to do.

Sorry if I've missed anybody else out in this report but all played well on the day and staked their claims for future team places.

Certainly it was entertaining football with City playing with the right attitude and it worked ! - maybe City girls are setting the trend again in 7-a-side soccer.

Under 14 Team Photo below.

Back (L-R) Carol Gregory (Mgr). Justine Taylor, Hayley Davidson, Rachel Smith, Kate Williamson, Kate Prince, Tracey Grainger, Stacey Skerritt, Amy Gregory, Gail Rothwell (Coach)
Front (L-R): Kimberley Windran, Laura Griffiths, Lucy Webb, Sarah Darby, Amy Rothwell, Christy Rustage, Vicky Wray, Jenny Hunter, Nicola Goddard.

Other games 1996-97
MCFC prog October 29th 1997 said there had been a game against Barnsley at Maine Road during this season.
July 13th & 14th 1996 - Moss Farm Tournament
July 14th 1996 - Moss Farm Tournament

Notes
City did not enter the Women's FA Cup this season.

	Date	Venue	Opposition	Result	Lge Pos	City Scorers (where known)
1	Aug 24	Away	Chorley (Friendly)	W 6-3	–	
2	**Sep 7**	**Home**	**Haslingden**	**W 10-0**		*Result void*
3	Sep 14	Away	Wigan	W 9-6	1st	
4	Sep 21	Away	Chester	W 5-2	1st	
	Sep 28	Away	Chorley	P-P	1st	
5	**Oct 5**	**Home**	**Liverpool District**	**W 3-0**	1st	
6	Oct 12	Away	Chorley (LC1)	L 0-2	–	
7	**Oct 19**	**Home**	**Chester**	**W 3-2**	1st	
8	Oct 26	Maine Road	Crewe Alexandra (Exhibition Match)	W 1-0	–	
9	**Oct 26**	**Home**	**Warrington Grange**	**W 6-0**	1st	
10	**Nov 2**	**Home**	**Stockport County**	**W 2-0**	1st	
11	Nov 9	Away	Trafford	D 2-2	1st	
12	Nov 16	Away	Chorley	W 7-0	1st	
13	Nov 30	Away	Bolton (LC2)	W 2-0	–	
14	**Dec 7**	**Home**	**Wrexham**	**W 15-0**	1st	
15	Dec 14	Away	Stockport County	W 1-0	1st	
	Dec 21	Away	Haslingden	P-P	1st	
	Dec 28	Home	Wigan	P-P	1st	
	Jan 4	Home	Wigan	P-P	1st	
	Jan 11	Away	Liverpool District	P-P	1st	
	Jan 18	Home	Bury	P-P	1st	
	Jan 25	Away	Warrington Grange	P-P	1st	
16	Jan 3	Maine Road	Burnley (Exhibition Match)		–	
17	**Feb 1**	**Home**	**Bolton**	**W 6-3**	1st	
18	**Feb 8**	**Home**	**Chorley**	**W 5-1**	1st	
19	**Feb 15**	**Home**	**Wigan**	**W 4-1**	1st	
20	Feb 22	Away	Wrexham	W 12-0	1st	
21	Mar 1	Away	Manchester United (Div Cup 1)	D 3-3	–	
	Mar 8	Home	Manchester United (Div Cup 1 Replay)	P-P	–	
22	Mar 15	Away	Liverpool District	W 1-0	1st	
23	**Mar 22**	**Home**	**Trafford**	**D 2-2**	1st	
24	Mar 29	Away	Warrington Grange	W 6-1	1st	
25	**Apr 5**	**Home**	**Manchester United** (Div Cup 1 Replay)	Scratched		
26	**May 3**	**Home**	**Bury**	**W 7-4**	1st	
27	May 10	Away	Bury	W 4-2	1st	

LC = League Cup, Div Cup = 1st & 2nd Division Cup. Home games in bold type. League games on white background.
Home games played at Ericstone Park, Baguley, Manchester M23 9NT.

League Record **1st** (10 teams) Played **20** Won **18** Drawn **2** Lost **0** Goals For **102** Against **26** Points **56**

Other games

June 22nd 1997 - North West Soccer Sixes at Rhyl. Under 13s 'A' team reached the knock out final but lost to Brazil Girls 3-2 on penalties after a 1-1 draw.

July 6th 1997 - Cadishead Tournament. Under 17s. City's U17s finish 5th from 6 in Group A.

July 13th 1997 - Moss Farm Tournament. City finish 4th of 7 teams in Group 3 (ten groups).

July 30th 1997 - Umbro Tournament. Under 14s. City's U14s finish 6th out of 7 teams.

August 10th 1997 - Bamber Bridge 11 A Side Tournament at Bamber Bridge Leisure Centre. City finish 3rd out of 4 teams in Group B and did not qualify for later stages.

Notes

Match 2 - This match ended 10-0 to City but is recorded as void as Haslingden withdrew from the league on November 13th 1997.

Match 8 - MCFC match prog carried a photo and details of an annual game staged on the Maine Road pitch. Previous years had seen City play Sheffield Wednesday and Barnsley. The women's team were top of Bass North West League Division Two. Game was sponsored by Beejay & Co and they presented each player with a trophy and other awards.

Match 16 - Played at half time in men's game.

During the 1997-98 season City won the North West Women's Regional Football League Second Division title. It was the first league title the club had ever won.

Finished 12 points higher than second place. Out of 20 games they kept ten clean sheets.

Top Scorer: Justine Mason (29 goals)

Also Won: Reebok Women's Soccer Festival; Mansfield Smooth Bitter Cup Winners (according to August 25th 2001 MCFC men's match programme).

City withdrew from the 1st & 2nd Divisional Cup after drawn game with Manchester United.

City did not enter the Women's FA Cup.

NWWRFL Division Two Leading Scorer was Justine Mason (25 League goals), shared with Bury's Diane McLean.

On April 25th 1998 the Manchester City men's match programme carried an article under the title "Ladies mourn loss of Derek" - The City In The Community piece explains about Derek Heath's death after a short illness. He'd joined City from Stockport Ladies and was instrumental in setting up U10s, U12s, U14s and U16s girls teams. He had organised weekly coaching sessions at Wythenshawe Town FC with up to 100 girls attending.

1998-99 North West Women's Regional Football League Premier Division

	Date	Venue	Opposition	Result	Lge Pos	City Scorers (where known)
1	**Sep 6**	**Home**	**Bolton**	**W 6-0**	1st	
	Sep 9	Home	Trafford	P-P	1st	
2	**Sep 13**	**Home**	**Liverpool District**	**W 3-2**	1st	
3	**Sep 20**	**Home**	**Trafford**	**W 3-0**	1st	
4	**Sep 27**	**Home**	**Brazil Girls** (WFAC1)	**W 6-2**	–	
5	Oct 4	Away	Liverpool Feds	W 2-1	1st	
6	Oct 11	Away	Stockport County (LC1)	W 5-3	–	
	Oct 18	Home	Newsham PH	P-P	1st	
	Oct 25	Away	Blackpool Wren Rovers	P-P	1st	
7	Nov 1	Away	Stockport Celtic (WFAC2)	W 6-2	–	
8	Nov 8	Away	Chester City	D 3-3	1st	
9	Nov 15	Away	Blackpool Wren Rovers	D 1-1	1st	
10	Nov 22	Away	Newsham PH	W 5-3	1st	
	Nov 29	Away	Bolton	P-P	2nd	
	Dec 6	Away	Ilkeston (WFAC3)	P-P	–	
11	Dec 13	Away	Ilkeston (WFAC3)	L 1-2	–	
12	Dec 20	Away	Wigan	L 3-4	4th	
	Jan 3	Home	Liverpool Feds	P-P	4th	
	Jan 10	Away	Newsham PH	P-P	4th	
	Jan 17	Home	Blackpool Wren Rovers	P-P	4th	
	Jan 24	Away	Chester City	P-P	6th	
13	**Jan 31**	**Home**	**Bury**	**W 5-3**	3rd	
14	**Feb 7**	**Home**	**Bolton Wanderers Supporters Girls** (LC2)	**W 5-0**	–	
	Feb 14	Away	Trafford	P-P	3rd	
	Feb 21	Home	Liverpool Feds	P-P	3rd	
15	Feb 28	Away	Liverpool District	W 3-1	3rd	
16	Mar 7	Away	Bolton	W 4-3	2nd	
17	**Mar 14**	**Home**	**Chester City**	**W 2-0**	2nd	
18	**Mar 21**	**Home**	**Wigan**	**W 3-2**	2nd	
19	**Mar 28**	**Home**	**Newsham PH**	**W 4-0**	2nd	
	Apr 4	Away	Chester City (LC3)	P-P	–	
20	**Apr 11**	**Home**	**Blackpool Wren Rovers**	**L 2-3**	2nd	
21	Apr 25	Away	Bury	W 12-4	2nd	
22	Apr 28	Away	Trafford	W 3-1	2nd	
23	**May 2**	**Home**	**Liverpool Feds**	**W 4-0**	2nd	

WFAC = Women's FA Cup, LC = League Cup. Home games in bold type. League games on white background.
Home games played at Wythenshawe Town.

Pages from Stockport Celtic's programme for the FA Cup meeting in November 1998.

TODAY'S GAME

This afternoon we extend a warm welcome to the players, officials and supporters of neighbouring Manchester City for this 2nd Round AXA FA Women's Cup contest. For us, as a club that has existed for less than 18 months, it really is a special occasion. I doubt whether many people would have predicted that we would have progressed through the 1st Round of this major women's competition.

Having said that, we progressed on merit at Warrington and, along with Stockport County are the only NWWRFL clubs left who are not in the Premier Division. Once we had succeeded i progressing to the 2nd Round, it we inevitable that we would get an extreme difficult tie - and as the League Tabl show, there is a considerable g between the two clubs in this featur tie.

The appalling weather has not help our preparations for today's match ap

Women's Footba
» INFORMATION BULLET

Cups - AXA F.A. Wome Cup 2nd Round Draw

On Sunday 1st November 88 will compete. Notable ties Wimbledon (previous League Winners) v Premier League comp Berkhamsted and Leeds Uni Sheffield Wednesday. Our featu sees Manchester City plt the away to Stockport Celtic.

from the wasted progra over the past weeks. Whi stating the obvious to se we are the underdogs. confident that we demonstrate that we useful team. It wo wonderful if the game w (although my heart p couldn't stand it], but w the result, we know that c will go through to fly the the NWWRFL Good luc teams and let's all e game.

League Tables as at 26th October 1998

PREMIER DIVISION	P	W	D	L	F	A	Pts	Gl Diff
Manchester City	4	4	0	0	14	3	12	11
Chester City	6	3	1	2	16	11	10	5
Liverpool District	7	2	2	3	11	12	8	-1
Blackpool	3	2	1	0	9	3	7	6
Wigan	6	2	1	3	14	14	7	0
Trafford	5	2	1	2	9	10	7	-1
Bolton Ladies	5	2	1	2	8	13	5	-7
Bury	3	1	1	1	8	9	4	-1
Newsham	3	1	0	2	7	11	3	-4
Liverpool Feds	4	0	1	3	4	12	1	-8
DIVISION TWO	P	W	D	L	F	A	Pts	Gl Diff
Brazil	4	4	0	0	27	3	12	24
Ambassadors	5	4	0	1	27	6	12	21
Stockport Celtic	5	3	0	2	17	8	9	9
Manchester United Res	4	2	1	1	14	5	7	9
Moss Farm	7	2	1	4	16	14	7	2
Accrington Stanley	4	2	1	1	10	16	7	-6
Urmston	7	2	1	4	11	25	7	-14
Stockport County Res	7	2	1	4	15	41	7	-26
Liverpool Feds Res	7	1	3	3	9	24	6	-15
Rochdale	5	1	2	2	11	13	5	-2
Blackburn Rangers	3	1	0	2	4	6	3	-2

OUR VISITORS TODAY -

Manchester City Ladies Football Club

For this afternoon's Cup game, we welcome NWWRFL Premier Division leaders Manchester City. The last 18 months has seen a quite remarkable turn-round in fortunes for the 'sky blues'.

When we were accepted into the League in June 1997, City had just completed a quite miserable season in our old 1st Division. Not only were City in bottom place, they were 12 points behind the team immediately above them, having gone through the entire season without a League win. They had managed just two draws, had gone out of the League Cup in the 1st Round and enjoyed their one win of the season in the Divisional Cup at Chester before they were heavily beaten at Stockport in the next round.

As City started life in Division 2 in September 1997, they may well have believed that 'things could only get better' and better they have got - with a vengeance! Since the start of 1997-98, City have been unbeaten in the League, running away with the 2nd Division Championship, 11 points ahead of their nearest rivals, Trafford. Promoted to the new Premier Division, City have simply carried on where they left off, winning their first four League games of 1998-99 and standing proudly at the top, the only Premier team to have a 100% record.

In addition to their four League victories, City have maintained that 100% record in the Cup with a 6-2 home win against the strong Brazil Girls in the 1st Round of the AXA FA Women's Cup and a 5-3 League Cup win at 1st Division Stockport County who are strongly placed themselves.

City's record in the WFA Cup since 1989

Date	Rnd	Opponents	V	Res
17.09.89	1st	Wigan	A	2-7
07.10.90	1st	Blackpool	H	6-0
04.11.90	2nd	Bury	H	6-2
02.12.90	3rd	Wythenshawe	H	1-1
16.12.90	3rd	Wythenshawe	A	3-2
06.01.91	4th	Hassocks	H	0-3
15.09.91	1st	Huddersfield	H	1-4
20.09.92	1st	Broadoak	A	1-3
19.09.93	1st	Manchester Utd	H	2-0
17.10.93	2nd	Bury	A	1-4
18.09.94	1st	Manchester BV	A	1-4
29.09.95	1st	Oldham Athletic	H	0-1
29.09.96		Did not enter		
28.09.97		Did not enter		
27.09.98	1st	Brazil Girls	H	6-2

City's first Cup line-up in the 7-2 defeat at Wigan back in September 1989 was: J.Yorke, C.Woodall [J.Taylor], D.Davies, K.Bretherton, R.Howard, J.Davies, L.Wright, R.O'Shaunassy, L.Peters, D.Haynes, N.Hunt.

Although 2-0 down after 20 minutes, City fought back to level through L.Peters and Touchline Star Player Donna Haynes (who is still playing with Stockport County) before Wigan put the game out of reach.

Thanks to Rod and Josie Prescott for the details of City's Cup records and to Reno Dionisiou for the player profiles.

Other games

July 11th & 12th 1998 - Moss Farm Tournament

August 9th 1998 - Bamber Bridge 11 a side Tournament at Bamber Bridge Leisure Centre. City won Group C and lost to Oldham Athletic in the semi final 1-0.

June 13th 1999 - Farley's Fun Fives at Witton Park. City Under 12s reached 2nd round of knock out competition.

Notes

City were back in the North West Women's Regional Football League top division, now known as the Premier Division. April 4th - All NWWRFL Competition abandoned due to weather (except Div 3 knock out cup). City unable to progress.

League Record **2nd** (10 teams) Played **18** Won **14** Drawn **2** Lost **2** Goals For **68** Against **31** Points **44**

City were initially deducted 3 points for non-fulfillment of a fixture (v Trafford at home on Wednesday 9th Sept 1998) but had those points re-instated on FA appeal in February 1999. City received the Premier League runners-up medals from Harriet Miller (Chair); Rod, Josie, David & Gillian Prescott at the NWWRFL Presentation Evening held at Pavillions, Runcorn on July 30th 1999.

From season 1998-99, just one team from the NWWRFL was allowed promotion to the Northern Women's Combination. At the FA Women's Alliance Meeting held at Loughborough on November 21st 1998, it was agreed that one team would be promoted from the Northern Women's Combination League to the Premier League (North) and one team from each of the three Northern Regional Leagues would gain Automatic Promotion to the Combination. Thus there would be no Play Offs as originally proposed. The Lancashire FA had supported the NWWRFL in achieving this goal, which was very important at that time.

1999-00 North West Women's Regional Football League Premier Division

	Date	Venue	Opposition	Result	Lge Pos	City Scorers (where known)
1	**Sep 5**	**Home**	**Mond Rangers**	**W 6-0**	1st	
2	Sep 8	Away	Stockport County	D 1-1	3rd	
3	**Sep 12**	**Home**	**Norton** (WFAC Extra Preliminary Rnd)	**W 26-0**	–	
4	**Sep 19**	**Home**	**Chester City**	**D 1-1**	4th	
5	Sep 26	Away	Trafford (WFAC Preliminary Rnd)	L 1-2	–	
6	**Oct 3**	**Home**	**Stockport County**	**W 5-2**	3rd	
7	**Oct 10**	**Home**	**Wigan**	**W 4-0**	1st	
8	Oct 17	Away	Chester City	W 2-1	1st	
9	**Oct 24**	**Home**	**Liverpool Feds**	**W 3-1**	1st	
10	Oct 31	Away	Bury	W 7-2	1st	
11	**Nov 7**	**Home**	**Liverpool District**	**W 7-1**	1st	
12	Nov 14	Away	Mond Rangers	W 5-1	1st	
13	Nov 28	Away	Wigan	W 4-1	1st	
	Dec 5	Home	Wigan	P-P	1st	
	Dec 12	Away	Trafford	P-P	1st	
	Dec 19	Away	Bolton	P-P	1st	
14	Jan 16	Away	Liverpool Feds	L 3-4	1st	
15	**Jan 23**	**Home**	**Bury**	**W 5-0**	1st	
16	**Jan 30**	**Home**	**Crewe Alexandra** (LC2)	**W 7-0**	–	
17	Feb 6	Away	Liverpool District	W 3-1	1st	
18	**Feb 13**	**Home**	**Mond Rangers** (Div Cup)	**W 6-1**	–	
19	Mar 5	Away	Bolton	W 2-1	1st	
20	Mar 12	Away	Trafford	W 4-0	1st	
21	**Mar 26**	**Home**	**Stockport Celtic** (LC3)	**W 3-1**	–	
22	Apr 9	Away	Bolton (LC QF)	W 2-0	–	
23	**Apr 16**	**Home**	**Bolton** (Div Cup QF)	**W 4-3**	–	
24	**Apr 18**	**Home**	**Bolton**	**W 6-1**	1st	
25	Apr 23	Away	Bury (Div Cup SF)	W 6-4	–	After extra time
26	**Apr 25**	**Home**	**Trafford**	**W 3-2**	1st	
27	Apr 30	Away	Bury (LC SF)	L 1-3	–	After extra time
28	May 7	N	Newsham (Div Cup Final)	W 3-1	–	Donna Davidson (3)
29	May 14	Away	Barnsley (Northern Combination Play-Off SF)	W 8-1	–	Ellen Thornton, Own goal, Kim Hines, Donna Davidson (2), Lindsay Savage, Louise Wakefield, Gail Rothwell
30	May 21	N	Darlington (Northern Combination Play-Off Final)	Not Played	–	

WFAC = Women's FA Cup, LC = League Cup, Div Cup = Prem & 1st Division Cup. Home games in bold type. League games on white background.
Home games played at Wythenshawe Town.

294

■ Left to right (Back): Greg Coniglio (manager), Sally Rustige, Louise Wakefield, Jane Clark, Vicki Bloor, Lindsay Savage, Donna Davidson, Claire Jarratt, Tracey Blanchard; (front): Ellen Thornton, Charlie Johnson, Kim Hines, Lydney Newman, Bev Harrop (capt), Gail Redston, Jenny Higginson, Vicky Milner.

Other games

July 10th & 11th 1999 - Moss Farm Tournament. Comprising of U10s, U12s, U14s, U16s & Senior competitions. U10s player of the tournament was Carla Cleworth (Manchester City)

August 8th 1999 - Bamber Bridge 11 a side Tournament at Bamber Bridge Leisure Centre. City finished 3rd in Group B and did not qualify for knock out stages

Notes

Finished as Champions and NW Women's League Cup winners AND Challenge Trophy winners.

Top Scorer: Lindsay Savage, 26 goals

Lancashire County FA Girls League: U12s Group B - City finish 2nd from 8; U14s Group B - City finished 6th from 6; U16s - City finished 5th from 10.

MCFC v Nottm Forest men's programme (Aug 30th 1999) had an advert to 'adopt' MCFC Ladies. £25 would allow people to adopt the team, no limit on number of adopters. Ad claimed City had a number of teams from under 10s upwards and 'do a great deal of work in promoting women's football'.

Match 28 - Played at Ewood Bridge, Haslingden FC.

Team: Vicki Bloor, Kim Hines, Sally Rustige, Lyndsay Newman, Jane Clark, Tracey Blanchard, Ellen Thornton (Gail Rothwell 90), Bev Harrop (capt), Lindsay Savage, Donna Davidson (Louise Wakefield 90), Claire Jarratt (Rhoda Taylor 85). Subs not used: Roxanne Brown, Charlie Johnson. Ref: Ian Nolan, Assistants: John McCarrick & Tim Crompton. Trophy presented by David & Gillian Prescott. Player of the match awarded to Sally Rustige (selected by Rod & Josie Prescott). Donna Davidson's goals were scored in the 82nd, 86th and 89th minutes.

Match 30 - Game did not take place and both City and Darlington were promoted to the Northern Combination.

Girls face three-way play-off

GIRL power has propelled Man City ladies to the top of the league, but even an eight-point lead might not be enough to seal automatic promotion.

Last week's 6-1 thrashing of Wythenshawe Town sealed the North West Women's Regional Division title for the Blues.

However, the league have confirmed that City must enter a three-way play-off with Barnsley and Darlington, winners of the Yorkshire and Northern Conferences, to earn promotion to the Northern Combination.

"I was gutted when the league told us we would have to play-off," said the City manager Greg Coniglio. "But we will go up."

The players were not told of the league's stance ahead of their game with Wythenshawe.

"We didn't want to give them anything to worry about," said Coniglio. "They'll be all the more determined to go up now."

The possibility of losing out in a play-off would be a bitter blow for City, who missed out on going up by one point last term.

"After losing out to Blackpool on the last day of last season, the girls could have reacted badly," said the cl...

they've been ... in the divisi... Rino Dior ... Needing ... clinch the ... at Wythensh... nothing to ...

DOMINIC FIFIELD REPORTING

were 5-0 up after half an hour.

"We made a mess of it last season when we should have gone up," said Bev Harrop. City's two-goal captain. "We knew it was now or never this time around and got straight at them."

With the championship secured and the play-offs to come, City are on course for an unprecedented treble.

On Sunday they beat Bury 6-4 in the Divisional Cup semi-final and face the same opposition in the...

into the Northern Premier division, that could all change in the next few years.

"We've got the potential to get into the National Premier," added Harrop. "We have junior teams from under-10 level upwards and there are about 120 girls playing at the club now.

"It's about time the area made an impact on the women's game. The talent's there, but we've just got to bring it out."

LADIES NWWRFL PREMIER DIVISION , Season 1999/2000

WELCOME TO JACKSON'S BOAT HOME OF

TRAFFORD LADIES

V

MANCHESTER CITY

Sunday 12TH MARCH 00
Kick-off 2pm.

Issue No 28

Price 50p

League Record **1st** (10 teams) Played **18** Won **15** Drawn **2** Lost **1** Goals For **71** Against **20** Points **47**

City received the Premier Trophy and Premier Divisional Cup from Harriet Miller, Sylvia Gore and Rod, Josie, David & Gillian Prescott at the NWWRFL Presentation Evening held at the Pavillions, Runcorn on Friday 4th August 2000.

	Date	Venue	Opposition	Result	Lge Pos	City Scorers (where known)
1	Sep 3	Away	Doncaster Rovers	W 6-1	1st	Jarratt, Davidson (4), Thornton
2	Sep 10	Home	Middlesbrough	L 1-2	7th	Jarratt
	Sep 17	Away	Blackburn Rovers	P-P	7th	
3	Sep 24	Home	Newcastle	W 6-0	4th	Davidson (3), Hines (2), Wakefield
4	Oct 1	Away	Manchester United	W 4-0	4th	Davidson, Timmis, Savage, Wakefield
	Oct 8	Away	Stockport Hatters	P-P	4th	
5	Oct 15	Home	Stockport Hatters	W 1-0	3rd	Davidson
6	Oct 22	Away	Leeds City Vixens	D 5-5	2nd	Davidson (2), Jarratt (2), Savage
	Oct 29	Home	Manchester United (WFAC1)	P-P	–	
	Nov 5	Home	Chester-le-Street	P-P	2nd	
7	Nov 10	Home	Manchester United (WFAC1)	W 4-1	–	Jarratt (3), Savage
	Nov 12	Home	Darlington	P-P	2nd	
8	Nov 19	Away	Stockport Hatters (WFAC2)	W 3-1	–	Jarratt, Wakefield (2)
	Nov 26	Home	Doncaster Rovers	P-P	5th	
9	Dec 3	Away	Middlesbrough	L 1-2	6th	
	Dec 10	Home	Walsall (WFAC3)	P-P	–	
10	Dec 17	Home	Walsall (WFAC3)	W 2-1	–	(After extra time) Taylor, Savage
	Dec 24	Home	Manchester United	P-P	6th	
	Dec 31	Home	Stockport Hatters	P-P	6th	
	Jan 7	Away	Fulham (WFAC4)	P-P	–	
11	Jan 14	Away	Fulham (WFAC4)	L 0-8	–	
	Jan 21	Home	Bradford City	P-P	6th	
	Jan 28	Home	Bradford City	P-P	6th	
	Feb 4	Away	Darlington	P-P	7th	
12	Feb 11	Home	Doncaster Rovers	W 7-3	5th	Davidson (3), Savage, Thornton, Blanchard, ?
13	Feb 18	Away	Blackpool Wren Rovers	L 1-2	5th	Jarratt
14	Feb 25	Home	Bradford City	D 2-2	5th	Savage, Mason
15	Mar 4	Home	Leeds City Vixens	W 3-1	4th	Davidson, Savage, Morris
16	Mar 11	Away	Stockport Hatters	W 4-1	4th	Davidson (3), Own Goal
17	Mar 18	Away	Newcastle	L 2-3	4th	Jarratt (2)
18	Mar 25	Home	Chester-le-Street	W 6-2	4th	
	Apr 1	Away	Blackburn Rovers	P-P	4th	
19	Apr 8	Home	Blackburn Rovers	W 2-1	1st	Davidson, Savage
20	Apr 15	Away	Chester-le-Street	W 4-1	2nd	Davidson (3), Own Goal
21	Apr 22	Home	Darlington	W 4-2	2nd	Davidson (2), Savage (2)
22	Apr 25	Away	Blackburn Rovers	W 2-0	2nd	Davidson, Savage
23	Apr 29	Away	Darlington	W 5-3	1st	Davidson, Jarratt, Newman, ? ?
24	May 2	Away	Bradford City	W 6-1	1st	Savage (3), Gregory, Harrop, Newman
25	May 10	Home	Blackpool Wren Rovers	W 4-3	1st	Davidson (2), Savage, Blanchard
26		Home	Manchester United	W 4-1		*Specific date unknown*

NORTHERN WOMENS COMBINATION LEAGUE

Manchester City

vs

Middlesbrough

SUNDAY 10th SEPTEMBER 2000
Kick Off 2.00 pm

£1.00

FOOTBALL AID

FOOTBALL AID
MISSION FOR FOOTBALL,
COMPASSION FOR OTHER...

FOOTBALL AID CHARITY MATCH

Manchester City F.C.
vs
Manchester United F.C.

Ladies Teams

24 May, 2001

Kick-off: 3.00 pm

www.footballaid.com

WFAC = Women's FA Cup. Home games in bold type. League games on white background.
Home games at The Valley, Flixton FC

Other Games
July 8/9 2000 Moss Farm Tournament
Comprising of U10s, U12s, U14s, U16s and Senior competitions. U16s finished 3rd from 5 in Group 2.

Pre-Season Friendlies:
Aug 13 - Oldham (away)	Lost 2-3	Davidson (2)
Aug 20 - Derby County	Won 8-0	Allwood (3), Jarratt, Redston, Savage (2), Wakefield
Aug 28 - Chester City	Won 6-1	Allwood, Davidson (2), Savage (2), Wakefield

Notes
First names of listed goalscorers (left and above): Louise Allwood, Tracey Blanchard, Donna Davidson, Bev Harrop, Kim Hines, Claire Jarratt, Justine Mason, Sarah Morris, Lyndsay Newman, Gail Redston, Lindsay Savage, Rhoda Taylor, Ellen Thornton, Rhoda Timmis and Louise Wakefield.

League Record **1st** (12 teams) Played **22** Won **16** Drawn **2** Lost **4** Goals For **80** Against **36** Points **50**
The Northern Combination was the third tier within the women's league structure at this time.
City finished as champions and were promoted to FA National North Division.
Also won the Reebok Women's Soccer Festival Reebok Cup.
Reserves won the North West Women's Reserve League.

2001-02 FA National Northern League

	Date	Venue	Opposition	Result	Lge Pos	City Scorers (where known)
1	**Aug 19**	**Home**	**Sheffield Wednesday**	**L 0-3**	11th	
2	Aug 26	Away	Coventry City	W 3-0	6th	Gregory (2), de Mouilpied
3	**Sep 2**	**Home**	**Coventry City**	**W 3-1**	4th	Davidson (3)
4	Sep 9	Away	Birmingham City	L 0-2	6th	
5	Sep 16	Away	Ilkeston Town	L 1-4	7th	Gregory
6	**Sep 23**	**Home**	**Southampton Saints** (LC1)	**L 0-2**	–	
7	Oct 7	Away	Wolverhampton Wanderers	L 1-3	8th	Davidson
8	Oct 14	Away	Sheffield Wednesday	L 0-4	8th	
	Oct 21	Away	North Notts	P-P	9th	
9	**Oct 28**	**Home**	**Aston Villa**	**L 1-4**	10th	Savage
10	**Nov 4**	**Home**	**Bangor City**	**L 1-2**	10th	
	Nov 11	Away	Garswood Saints	P-P	10th	
11	**Nov 25**	**Home**	**Garswood Saints**	**D 1-1**	10th	
12	**Dec 9**	**Home**	**Bangor City** (WFAC3)	**L 2-3**	–	
	Dec 16	Home	Liverpool	P-P	10th	
13	Jan 13	Away	Liverpool	L 0-2	10th	
14	**Jan 27**	**Home**	**Ilkeston Town**	**L 0-5**	10th	
	Feb 3	Away	Aston Villa	P-P	10th	
	Feb 10	Home	Wolverhampton Wanderers	P-P	10th	
	Feb 24	Home	North Notts	P-P	10th	
15	Mar 10	Away	Aston Villa	W 1-0	10th	
16	**Mar 17**	**Home**	**Oldham Curzon**	**L 2-4**	10th	
	Mar 24	Home	Wolverhampton Wanderers	P-P	10th	
17	**Mar 31**	**Home**	**Liverpool**	**D 0-0**	10th	
18	**Apr 14**	**Home**	**Birmingham City**	**L 1-5**	10th	
19	Apr 21	Away	Bangor City	L 0-2	10th	
20	Apr 28	Away	Oldham Curzon	D 0-0	10th	
21	May 1	Away	Garswood Saints	D 2-2	10th	
22	**May 5**	**Home**	**Wolverhampton Wanderers**	**W 2-1**	10th	

WFAC = Women's FA Cup, LC = Axa League Cup. Home games in bold type. League games on white background. Home games at Old Bedlians.

Notes
2001-02 was the first season in the FA National Northern League.
All clubs are requested by the FA to issue programmes for their home League fixtures.
The 4th annual FA Women's Football Awards were held on Friday 24 May 2002 at the Grosvenor Hotel, London.

League Record **10th** (11 teams) Played **20** Won **4** Drawn **4** Lost **12** Goals For **19** Against **45** Points **16**

North Notts withdrew after 11 games. City had not played North Notts by the time of their withdrawal and North Notts record was annulled. City finished 14 points ahead of relegated Coventry City.

Known team line-ups 2001-02

Match 1 - White, Hines, Wakefield, Newman (Harvey 45), Brown, Timmis, de Mouilpied (Lodge 80), Thornton, Savage, Davidson, Jarratt. Unused subs: Howe, Cullum, Redston

Match 2 - White, Hines, Clark, Wakefield, Brown, Timmis, Savage, Thornton, Gregory, Davidson (de Mouilpied 82), Jarratt (Moores 86). Unused subs: Keeler, Johnson, Mason.

Match 3 - White, Hines, Clark, Wakefield, Brown, Timmis, Savage (Gligan 75), Thornton, Gregory, Davidson (Rustige 89), Jarratt.

Match 4 - White, Hines, Clark, Wakefield, Brown, Timmis (Morris 65), Savage, Thornton, Gregory, Davidson (Gligan 80), Blanchard (Rustige 80).

Match 5 - White, Hines, Morris, Wakefield (Newman 71), Clark, Savage (Shaw 80), Blanchard, Thornton, Gregory, Davidson, Gligan (Rustige 80).

Match 6 - White, Hines, Clark, Wakefield, Morris, Savage, Blanchard (Johnson 89), Jackson, Gregory (Gligan 73), Davidson, Thornton (Howe 73). Unused subs: Rustige, Moores.

Match 7 - White, Hines, Clark, Wakefield, Timmis, Savage, Thornton (Blanchard 61), Morris, Gregory (Brown 73), Davidson, Jarratt (Gligan 80). Unused: Jackson, Howe.

Match 8 - White, Hines, Wakefield, Morris, Clark (Brown 45), Gregory, Thornton (de Mouilpied 45), Timmis (Gligan 77), Savage, Davidson, Jarratt.

Match 9 - White, Hines, Clark, Wakefield (Rustige 85), Brown, Gregory, de Mouilpied (Jackson 67), Thornton, Savage, Davidson (Gligan 75), Jarratt.

Match 14 - Worrall, Wakefield, Timmis, Blanchard, Clark, Newman (Jackson 74) , Hines, Morris, Savage, Davidson (Gligan 61), Thornton (Howe 77). Unused: White, Harvey.

First names of players: Tracey Blanchard, Roxanne Brown, Jane Clark, Heidi Cullum, Kate de Mouilpied, Donna Davidson, Laura Gligan, Amy Gregory, Louise Harvey, Jenny Higginson, Kim Hines, Sammy Howe, Sarah Jackson, Claire Jarratt, Charlie Johnson, Jacquie Keeler, Debbie Lodge, Justine Mason, Lucy Moores, Sarah Morris, Lyndsay Newman, Christine Payne, Gail Redston, Sally Rustige, Lindsay Savage, Kirsten Shaw, Stacey Skerrett, Ellen Thornton, Rhoda Timmis, Louise Wakefield, Joanna White, Kate Williamson and Vicky Wray.

MANCHESTER CITY LADIES

COVENTRY CITY LADIES

AXA FA Premier - Northern Division
OLD BEDIANS SPORTS GROUND
SUNDAY 2ⁿᵈ SEPTEMBER 2001
KICK OFF: 2:00PM

2002-03 FA National Northern League

	Date	Venue	Opposition	Result	Lge Pos	City Scorers (where known)
1	Aug 18	Away	Oldham Curzon	L 1-3	9th	
2	**Aug 25**	**Home**	**Ilkeston Town**	**D 3-3**	9th	
3	Sep 1	Away	Middlesbrough	W 4-0	7th	
4	**Sep 8**	**Home**	**Liverpool**	**L 0-3**	7th	
5	Sep 15	Away	Aston Villa	L 1-4	8th	
6	**Sep 22**	**Home**	**Wolverhampton Wanderers**	**L 1-2**	9th	
	Sep 25	Home	Sheffield Wednesday	P-P	9th	
7	Sep 29	Home	Ilkeston Town (PLC1)	W	–	*City won but score missing*
8	**Oct 13**	**Home**	**Sunderland**	**L 2-3**	10th	
9	**Oct 20**	**Home**	**Lincoln City**	**L 0-1**	10th	
10	Oct 23	Away	Sheffield Wednesday	W 3-0	9th	
11	Oct 27	Away	Doncaster Belles (PLC2)	L 1-2	–	
	Nov 3	Home	Garswood Saints	P-P	9th	
	Nov 10	Home	Oldham Curzon	P-P	9th	
	Nov 17	Away	Ilkeston Town	P-P	9th	
12	Nov 24	Away	Bangor City	L 1-2	9th	
	Dec 1	Away		P-P	9th	
13	Dec 8	Away	Leicester City (WFAC3)	L 0-1	–	(After extra time)
14	Dec 15	Away	Liverpool	D 1-1	8th	
	Jan 12	Away	Ilkeston Town	P-P	8th	
	Jan 19	Away	Wolverhampton Wanderers	P-P	8th	
	Jan 26	Home	Bangor City	P-P	8th	
	Feb 2	Away	Sunderland	P-P	8th	
15	Feb 16	Away	Garswood Saints	D 1-1	9th	
16	**Feb 23**	**Home**	**Oldham Curzon**	**L 0-5**	10th	
	Mar 2	Away	Wolverhampton Wanderers	P-P	11th	
	Mar 9	Home	Garswood Saints	P-P	12th	
17	Mar 16	Away	Wolverhampton Wanderers	L 2-4	12th	
18	**Mar 23**	**Home**	**Aston Villa**	**L 0-1**	12th	
19	Mar 30	Away	Sunderland	D 0-0	12th	
20	**Apr 6**	**Home**	**Bangor City**	**D 1-1**	12th	
21	Apr 13	Away	Ilkeston Town	W 5-0	11th	
22	**Apr 20**	**Home**	**Middlesbrough**	**L 1-2**	11th	
23	Apr 27	Away	Lincoln City	W 2-1	8th	
24	**May 4**	**Home**	**Garswood Saints**	**W 2-0**	8th	
25	**May 8**	**Home**	**Sheffield Wednesday**	**D 0-0**	8th	

WFAC = Women's FA Cup, PLC = Premier League Cup. Home games in bold type. League games on white background.
Home games at Old Bedlians.

MCFC Ladies Official Match day Programme. Vol 2 Issue 02   Price £1.

MANCHESTER CITY LADIES

v

LIVERPOOL LADIES F.C.

AXA FA Premier League - Northern Division
OLD BEDIANS SPORTS GROUND
SUNDAY 8th SEPTEMBER 2002
KICK OFF: 2:00pm.

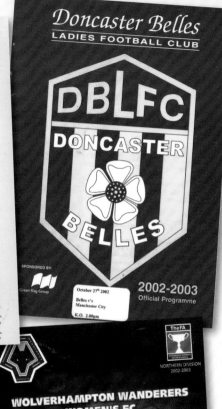

Notes

The 2002-03 season was the second season in the
FA National Northern League.

Match 24 - Result for game with Garswood Saints
unclear. Assumed to be a 2-0 victory based on end
of season stats.

Ilkeston Town and Garswood Saints were relegated
with Chesterfield and Stockport promoted in their
place.

5th annual FA Women's Awards took place on
Thursday 29th May 2003 at the Marriot Hotel,
Grosvenor Square, London.

League Record **8th** (12 teams) Played **22** Won **5** Drawn **6** Lost **11** Goals For **31** Against **37** Points **21**

2003-04 FA National Northern League

	Date	Venue	Opposition	Result	Lge Pos	City Scorers (where known)
1	Aug 17	Away	Bangor City	W 4-3		
2	Aug 31	Away	Oldham Curzon	W 3-2		
3	**Sep 7**	**Home**	**Stockport County**	**L 0-2**		
4	Sep 14	Away	Everton (PLC1)	W 3-0		
5	**Sep 17**	**Home**	**Curzon Ashton**	**W 2-1**		
6	Sep 21	Away	Wolverhampton Wanderers	L 1-6		
7	**Sep 28**	**Home**	**Chesterfield**	**D 4-4**		
8	Oct 5	Away	Chesterfield	W 4-1		
9	**Oct 12**	**Home**	**Liverpool**	**L 0-1**		
10	**Oct 19**	**Home**	**Lincoln LFC**	**L 0-2**		
11	Nov 2	Away	Middlesbrough	W 1-0		
12	**Nov 9**	**Home**	**Sheffield Wednesday**	**W 4-3**		
13	Nov 16	Away	Liverpool	L 0-1		
14	**Nov 30**	**Home**	**Middlesbrough**	**L 1-2**		
15	Dec 7	Away	Lincoln City (WFAC)	L 1-3		
16	Jan 25	Away	Sunderland	L 2-3		
17	Feb 8	Away	Lincoln LFC	L 0-4		
18	Feb 22	Away	Stockport County	L 2-3		
19	Mar 7	Away	Sheffield Wednesday	L 0-5		
20	**Mar 14**	**Home**	**Bangor City**	**W 5-0**		Mel Garside (4)
21	**Mar 28**	**Home**	**Sunderland**	**D 1-1**		
22	**Apr 14**	**Home**	**Bangor City**	**W 5-0**		
23	**Apr 25**	**Home**	**Wolverhampton Wanderers**	**D 1-1**		

WFAC = Women's FA Cup, PLC = Premier League Cup. Home games in bold type. League games on white background.
Home games at Abbey Hey.

Notes
Specific date unknown. Team played against CITC and amputee teams according to MCFC v Middlesbrough men's match programme (30/11/03) includes photos.

League Record **7th** (11 teams) Played **20** Won **7** Drawn **3** Lost **10** Goals For **35** Against **45** Points **24**
Liverpool promoted as champions. Chesterfield and Bangor City relegated.

City line-up before a pre-season derby against Manchester United in July 2004.

Back row (l to r): Lucy Martin, Gemma Horner, Natalie Thomas, Siân Payne, Ellen Thornton, Nicky Twohig, Jane Clark, Tania Watts.

Front: Laura Gligan, Nicky Aiyeqbusi, Lindsay Savage, Kelly McLellan, Amy Gregory, Emma Sconce, Louise Wakefield.

2004-05 FA National Northern League

	Date	Venue	Opposition	Result	City Scorers (where known)
1	July	N	Manchester United (Friendly)	W 4-2	Savage, Thomas (2), Gligan
2	**Aug 15**	**H**	**Oldham Curzon**	**L 0-2**	–
3	Aug 22	A	Blackburn Rovers	L 1-6	Dixon
4	**Aug 29**	**H**	**Sunderland**	**L 0-3**	–
5	Sep 5	A	Wolverhampton Wanderers	L 0-6	*Match void*
6	Sep 12	A	Middlesbrough (LC1)	W 3-1	Dixon (2), Thomas
7	**Sep 15**	**H**	**Tranmere Rovers**	**W 2-1**	Dixon, Gligan
8	Sep 19	A	Stockport County	L 0-3	–
9	Oct 10	A	Charlton Athletic (LC2)	L 0-6	–
10	Oct 14	A	Tranmere Rovers	L 1-2	Dixon
11	**Oct 31**	**H**	**Sheffield Wednesday**	**D 3-3**	Dixon, Sconce, Janes
12	Nov 14	A	Lincoln City	L 0-5	–
13	Nov 28	A	Middlesbrough	L 1-4	McClellan
14	**Dec 5**	**H**	**Sunderland** (WFAC3)	**L 1-2**	
15	Dec 12	A	Coventry City	W 3-2	Dixon, Wakefield, ?
16	Jan 16	A	Sheffield Wednesday	D 1-1	?
17	**Jan 23**	**H**	**Lincoln City**	**L 1-4**	Thomas
18	Jan 30	A	Curzon Ashton	D 0-0	–
19	**Feb 6**	**H**	**Blackburn Rovers**	**W 4-0**	Dixon, Gregory, Janes, Thomas
20	Feb 20	A	Wolverhampton Wanderers	L 2-4	Dixon (2)
21	**Mar 13**	**H**	**Stockport County**	**W 4-0**	Dixon (2), Savage, Sconce
22	**Mar 20**	**H**	**Aston Villa**	**W 2-0**	Dixon, Thomas
23	Mar 27	A	Sunderland	L 0-1	–
24	Apr 3	A	Aston Villa	L 0-3	–
25	**Apr 10**	**H**	**Coventry City**	**W 3-0**	Dixon (2), Savage
26	Apr 17	A	Middlesbrough	W 1-0	Thomas
27	Apr 24	A	Wolverhampton Wanderers	L 0-1	–

WFAC = Women's FA Cup, LC = League Cup. Home games in bold type. League games on white background.
● = Started, ◑ = Played as a substitute, U = Unused sub (League appearances in blue).
Home games at Mossley FC.

League Record **10th** (12 teams) Played **22** Won **7** Drawn **3** Lost **12** Goals For **29** Against **45** Points **24**

Sunderland promoted as champions. Sheffield Wednesday and Coventry City relegated. City one point above the relegation zone.

	Aiyeqbusi, Niccla	Brown, Danielle	Clark, Jane	Deyoung, Allison	Dixon, Caroline	Fizpatrick, Claire	Foley, Paula	Gligan, Laura	Gregory, Amy	Gulino, Rosemary	Horner, Gemma	Janes, Kimberley	Martin, Lucy	McCormack, Lauren	McClellan, Kelly	Merrill, Alex	Payne, Sian	Savage, Lindsay	Sconce, Emma	Shaw, Kirsten	Shelton, Katie-Louise	Shortiss, Siobhan	Thomas, Natalie	Thornton, Ellen	Twohig, Nicola	Wakefield, Louise	
			●		○			●	●		●	○		●	●				●	○			●	●	●		1
		◐	●		○			●	●	●	●	●		◐				●	●				●	●		●	2
		◐	●		○			●	●	●	●	●		●				●	●				●	●	●	●	3
				●	●			●	●	◐	●	●			●		●	●	●	●	◐		●		●	●	4
																											5
					●			●	●	◐	●	◐			●		●	●	●	●	◐		●		●	●	6
					●			●	●	◐	●	◐			●			●	●	◐			●		●	●	7
					●			●	●		●				●			●	●				●	◐	●		8
																											9
					●			●	●	●	◐	●	◐		●		●		●		◐	●				●	10
					●			●	●	●		◐			●		●	●	●					●	●	11
					●	◐		●	●		●	●			●		●	●	●	◐				●	●	12
					○			●	●	●	◐	●	●		●		●	●	●					●	●	13
																											14
					●			●	●	◐	●	◐			●		●	●	●				●	●	●	15
					●			●	●		●	◐			●		●	●	●				●	●	●	16
					●			●	●	◐	●	◐			●	◐	●	●	●	◐			●	●	●	17
◐					●			●	●		●	◐		●	●	●	●	●	●				●	●		18
◐					●				●		●	●		●	●	●	●	●	●				●	●		19
					●		●	●		●				●		●	●	●	●				●		◐	20
◐					●		●	◐	●	●				●	●	●	●	●				●		●		21
◐					●			●	●		●			●	●	●	●	●				●		●	◐	22
◐				●	◐			●	●		●			●	●	●	●	●				●			●	23
◐		●	●	●				●	●		●			●		●	●	●							●	24
◐		◐		●		○	●	●		●				●	●	●	●	●				●		●		25
◐		◐			●		●		●					●	●	●	●	●				●		●		26
																											27

Notes

Match 1 - Played at Chorlton Sports and Social Club sometime in July 2004 to raise money for Francis House. MUFC play in a lower division. Mention of City providing kit.

Match 5 - Result later expunged and game replayed on 24 April 2005.

	Date	Venue	Opposition	Result	City Scorers (where known)
1	Aug 14	A	Middlesbrough	D 1-1	Savage
2	**Aug 21**	**H**	**Aston Villa**	**L 1-2**	Dixon
3	Aug 28	A	Tranmere Rovers	W 4-1	Savage, Thomas, Twohig, Wensley
4	Sep 4	A	Nottingham Forest	L 1-3	Thomas
5	**Sep 7**	**H**	**Stockport County**	**W 2-1**	Dixon (2)
6	Sep 11	A	Fulham (LC)	W 6-5	Savage, ?
7	Sep 25	A	Wolverhampton Wanderers	D 0-0	–
8	**Oct 2**	**H**	**Nottingham Forest**	**D 0-0**	–
9	Oct 18	A	Stockport County	D 1-1	Sconce
10	**Oct 23**	**H**	**Arsenal** (LC)	**L 0-4**	–
11	**Oct 30**	**H**	**Liverpool**	**L 0-3**	–
12	Nov 13	A	Lincoln City	D 1-1	Sconce
13	**Nov 27**	**H**	**Wolverhampton Wanderers**	**W 1-0**	Farrell
14	Dec 4	A	Middlesbrough (WFAC3)	W 2-1	?
15	Dec 11	A	Newcastle United	D 2-2	Farrell, Forshaw
16	**Jan 8**	**H**	**Barnet** (WFAC4)	**L 0-2**	–
17	**Jan 22**	**H**	**Lincoln City**	**L 0-2**	–
18	**Jan 29**	**H**	**Middlesbrough**	**L 1-2**	Savage
19	Feb 26	A	Blackburn Rovers	L 0-2	–
20	**Mar 12**	**H**	**Curzon Ashton**	**L 0-1**	–
21	**Mar 19**	**H**	**Blackburn Rovers**	**L 0-1**	–
22	Mar 26	A	Liverpool	L 2-3	Savage, ?
23	Apr 2	A	Aston Villa	L 0-1	–
24	**Apr 9**	**H**	**Newcastle United**	**L 1-2**	
25	**Apr 16**	**H**	**Tranmere Rovers**	**L 0-1**	–
26	Apr 23	A	Curzon Ashton	D 1-1	?

WFAC = Women's FA Cup, LC = League Cup. Home games in bold type. League games on white background.
● = Started, ◑ = Played as a substitute, U = Unused sub (League appearances in blue).

League Record **11th** (12 teams) Played **22** Won **3** Drawn **7** Lost **12** Goals For **19** Against **31** Points **16**

	Baird, Elizabeth	Baker, Kerry	Brown, Danielle	Brown, Sharina	Butterworth, Amy	Clark, Jane	Clarke, Camille	Davies, Racheal	Dixon, Caroline	Duncan, Rachel	Farrell, Charlotte	Forshaw, Kathryn	Garvey, Colette	Gligan, Laura	Gulino, Rosemary	Hanlon, Elouise	Horner, Gemma	House, Elizabeth	Jackson, Kerry	Jackson, Sarah	Martin, Lucy	McLellan, Kelly	Merrill, Alex	Nkereuwem, Thessy	Payne, Sina	Phelps, Portia	Savage, Lindsay	Sconce, Emma	Shelton, Katie-Louise	Shortiss, Siobhan	Thomas, Natalie	Turner, Ellena	Twohig, Nicola	Vettor, Shannon	Watts, Tanya	Weaver, Amy	Wensley, Levi	
		◐			●				●		◐						●	●				●	●		●		●	●					●			U	◐	1
		◐			●			◐	●								●	●				●	●		●		●	●				●		●		U	U	2
					●				●								●	U				●	●		●		●	●	U		●		●	U		U	●	3
		◐			●				●		●						●	◐				●	●		●		●	●			●					◐	●	4
					●	U			●		●	U			U		●					●	●		●		●	●					U		U		●	5
	◐		●				●		●	U						●	●			●●◐◐	●		●●			●	●					U		U		●	6
	U		●				●		●	◐						●					●	●	U	●		●	●						U		U	◐	7
	U		●						●	◐						●					●	●		●		●	●						U		U	●	8
	◐		●						●	◐						●					●	●		●		●	●			●			U			●	9
	●		●				●		●	◐						●				●		●●		●		●●				●		◐			◐	10
	●		●			●	●	●	◐							●			●		●	●		●		●	●					◐			◐	11
	U		●				●	●	◐							●		●			●	●		●		●	●								●	12
	◐	●					●	●	◐							●	U				●	●		●		●	●								●	13
																																				14
	●	●					U	●	◐							●				●		●		●		●	●								●	15
																																				16
		◐ ●					●	●	U		●					●				●	●		●		●	●								U		17
		◐ ●					●	●	◐		◐					●				●	●		●		●	●									●	18
U	◐	◐ ●					●	U							●				●	●		●		●	●				U					●		19
◐	U	◐ ●					●	U							●				●	●		●		●	●					◐			●		20
U	◐	U ●					◐	●							●				●	●		●		●	●								●		21
	◐	◐ ●					◐ ●	●		●					●	U			●	●		●		●	●									U	22
																																				23
	● ●		● ●					U		● ●	●		●									●			●		● U				●					24
																																				25
																																				26

	Date	Venue	Opposition	Result	City Scorers (where known)
1	Aug 20	A	Wolverhampton Wanderers	L 1-2	L Savage
2	**Aug 27**	**H**	**Curzon Ashton**	**D 1-1**	Standring
3	Aug 30	A	Curzon Ashton (LC)	L 1-3	?
4	Sep 3	A	Lincoln City	D 1-1	S Arrowsmith
5	Sep 24	A	Nottingham Forest	W 3-2	Brusell, Berko, Jackson
6	**Oct 1**	**H**	**Aston Villa**	**W 3-2**	Brusell (2), Jackson
7	**Oct 8**	**H**	**Stockport County**	**L 0-1**	–
8	**Oct 22**	**H**	**Preston North End**	**D 1-1**	Gligan
9	Oct 29	A	Stockport County	W 1-0	K Savage
10	Nov 8	A	Tranmere Rovers	L 1-4	K Savage
11	Nov 12	A	Curzon Ashton	W 2-0	Berko, K Savage
12	Dec 2	A	Sheffield Wednesday (WFAC3)	W 5-3	? (after extra time)
13	**Dec 17**	**H**	**Tranmere Rovers**	**D 3-3**	Berko, L Savage (2)
14	Jan 13	A	Birmingham City (WFAC4)	L 1-3	?
15	Jan 28	A	Crewe Alexandra	L 0-3	–
16	**Feb 4**	**H**	**Lincoln City**	**D 1-1**	Gligan
17	Feb 25	A	Wolverhampton Wanderers	L 1-3	?
18	**Mar 11**	**H**	**Crewe Alexandra**	**W 2-1**	Berko, Twohig
19	Mar 18	A	Preston North End	L 1-2	Jackson
20	**Mar 25**	**H**	**Newcastle United**	**L 1-2**	L Savage
21	Apr 1	A	Liverpool	L 0-1	–
22	**Apr 8**	**H**	**Nottingham Forest**	**L 1-2**	K Savage
23	Apr 15	A	Aston Villa	L 0-1	–
24	**May 8**	**H**	**Liverpool**	**W 1-0**	L Savage
25	May 13	A	Newcastle United	D 2-2	K Savage, Twohig

WFAC = Women's FA Cup, LC = League Cup. Home games in bold type. League games on white background.

● = Started, ◑ = Played as a substitute, U = Unused sub (League appearances in blue).

League Record **10th** (12 teams) Played **22** Won **6** Drawn **6** Lost **10** Goals For **27** Against **35** Points **24**
City avoided relegation by 3 points. Curzon Ashton and Wolves were relegated. Liverpool promoted as champions.

	Arrowsmith, Donna	Arrowsmith, Stacey	Ashioti, Angela	Belcher, Louise	Berko, Nikki	Brown, Danielle	Brown, Rebecca-Jane	Brown, Sharina	Brusell, Katie	Crewe, Lisa-Emma	Dunford, Leanne	Farrell, Charlotte	Forshaw, Kathryn	Gligan, Laura	Horner, Gemma	Jackson, Kerry	Jones, Michelle	Lambert, Paula	Martin, Francesca	Martin, Lucy	McClellan, Kelly	Merrill, Alex	Pennington, Gail	Savage, Keeleigh	Savage, Lindsay	Sconce, Emma	Standring, Debbie-Claire	Turner, Ellena	Twohig, Nicola	Wensley, Levi	Young, Danielle
1			●	●	●		●			●			U	U	●	●					●			U	●			U		U	●
2			●	●	●		U						U	●	●	●	●				●	◑		◑	●		●	◑		●	
3																															
4	●	◑		●	●		U			U			U	●	●	●	●				●			◑			●	●		●	
5	◑	●		●	●		U		●				U		●	●					●	●		◑		●	●			●	U
6	◑	●		●	●		U		●					U	●	●					●	●		◑		●	●			●	U
7	◑	◑		●	●		U		●						●	●					●	●		U	◑	●	●			●	
8	●	U		●	●		U		●			●			●	●					●			◑	●		◐		●		U
9			●	●	●		U		●			●			●	●	●				●	◐		◑	●		U		●	●	U
10			U	●	●		●		●			●			●						●			◑	●		U		●	●	◑
11			●	●	◑		U								●	●					●		U	●	●		●	U	●	●	◑
12																															
13			●	●	●		◑		●		◑		●			●	●				●	U		◑	●				●	●	U
14																															
15			●	●	●		●		●			●	●		●						◑	U		U	●				●	●	◑
16			●	●	●		●		●				●	U							●	●	U	U	●				●	●	◑
17			●	●	●		●					●	U	◑		●		U		●	●	●		◑	●				●	●	◑
18			◑	●	●		●		U			●	●	●		◑		U	U	U	●				●				●	●	●
19			U	●	●		●		U	◑		●	●	●		◑	U		●						●				●	●	●
20			●	●	●		●			●		●	◑	●		◑		U				●	●				U		●	●	◑
21			●	●	●		●		U	●		●	●	●	U			◑	●	U	●	●	●				◑				
22			●	●	●		◑		◑	●		●	●	●				U	●	●	●	●			U					◑	
23			●	◑	◑		●	●		●		●	●	●		U	●	●			U	●	●			◐				●	
24			◑	●		●	●	●		●		●	U	●		U	●				U	●				◑	●		◑		
25			◑	●		●	●		●			●	U	●			●				●	●				◑	●	U	◑		

2007-08 FA National Northern Division

	Date	Venue	Opposition	Result	City Scorers (where known)
1	**Aug 19**	**H**	**Sunderland**	**D 2-2**	L Savage, Wensley
2	**Aug 26**	**H**	**Aston Villa**	**L 2-4**	L Savage, Turner
3	Sep 2	A	Tranmere Rovers	L 1-2	Turner
4	**Sep 9**	**H**	**Nottingham Forest**	**L 0-3**	–
5	Sep 12	A	Preston North End	W 2-1	Brussell (2)
6	**Sep 16**	**H**	**Sheffield Wednesday**	**L 1-3**	Young
7	Sep 23	A	Crewe Alexandra	W 5-2	Brussell, Davies, Gligan, L Savage, Turner
8	Sep 30	A	Watford (LC)	L 0-4	–
9	**Oct 7**	**H**	**Nottingham Forest**	**D 1-1**	Gligan
10	**Oct 10**	**H**	**Preston North End**	**L 0-4**	–
11	**Oct 14**	**H**	**Tranmere Rovers**	**W 3-0**	Farrell, Gligan, Davies
12	**Oct 21**	**H**	**Newcastle United**	**D 0-0**	–
13	Oct 28	A	Rotherham United	L 2-3	Brussell, Turner
14	**Nov 11**	**H**	**Stockport County**	**W 2-0**	Gligan, Young
15	Nov 25	A	Sheffield Wednesday	W 2-0	James, Young
16	Dec 2	A	West Auckland Town (WFAC 3)	W 4-1	?
17	**Jan 6**	**H**	**Watford** (WFAC 4)	**L 1-4**	? (after extra time)
18	**Jan 13**	**H**	**Rotherham United**	**L 1-5**	Brussell
19	Jan 20	A	Stockport County	W 3-0	Brussell, James, K Savage
20	Feb 10	A	Aston Villa	D 1-1	Farrell
21	Feb 24	A	Lincoln City	L 0-3	–
22	**Mar 2**	**H**	**Crewe Alexandra**	**W 1-0**	Brussell
23	Mar 9	A	Newcastle United	L 0-3	–
24	**Mar 23**	**H**	**Lincoln City**	**L 0-2**	–
25	Apr 13	A	Sunderland	L 0-2	–

WFAC = Women's FA Cup, LC = League Cup. Home games in bold type. League games on white background.

● = Started, ◑ = Played as a substitute, U = Unused sub (League appearances in blue).

League Record **7th** (12 teams) Played **22** Won **7** Drawn **4** Lost **11** Goals For **29** Against **41** Points **25**

Stockport County and Crewe Alexandra were relegated. City finished 6 points above the relegation zone. Nottingham Forest were promoted as champions

Brown, Rebecca-Jane	**Brown**, Sharina	**Brusell**, Katie	**Davies**, Rachael	**Farrell**, Charlotte	**Gilmore**, Laura	**Gligan**, Laura	**Hindley**, Lucy	**Howden**, Sarah	**James**, Shelley	**Janes**, Kimberley	**Kirby**, Naveen	**Lee**, Rebecca	**Martin**, Francesca	**McClellan**, Kelly	**Merrill**, Alex	**Morgan**, Nicola	**O'Boyle**, Shauna	**Pennington**, Gail	**Savage**, Keeleigh	**Savage**, Lindsay	**Sconce**, Emma	**Shirley**, Patrice	**Shortiss**, Siobhan	**Steadman**, Mary	**Stenson**, Michaela	**Thornton**, Ellen	**Turner**, Ellena	**Twohig**, Nicola	**Wensley**, Levi	**Young**, Danielle	
	●	●	●	●	●	●	U							●				U		●		◑				●	U	●	●	◑	1
	●	●		●		●	◑						●	●	●			◑		●		U			U	●	◑		●	●	2
	●	●		●		●	U				●			●	●					●		◑	U		U	●	●		●	◑	3
	●	●		●	●	●	●							●						●		◑	U		◑	●		●	●	◑	4
		●	●	●	●	●	●							●						●		U	U		U			●	●	●	5
		●	●	●	●	●	●							●				◑		●		U	U		U		◑	●	●	●	6
		●	●	●		●	●			U	●			●						●		U	◑		◑	U	●	●	●		7
		●	**●**	**●**		**●**	**●**				**●**	**◑**		**●**		**●**				**●**		**◑**	**◑**				**●**		**●**		8
		●	●	●		●	●				●	●		●		U	◑			●		U				●	U		●	◑	9
		●	●	●		●	●				●	●		●			◑					◑				●	◑		●	●	10
		●	◑	●		●	●				●	●		●		◑				●		●	U				●		●	U	11
		●	●	●	●	●	●				U	●		●		U				●		●				◑	◑		●	◑	12
		●	●	●	●	●	●					●		●		◑				●		●	U				◑		●	◑	13
		●	◑	●		●	●	●	●		●			●						●		U				U			●	●	14
		●	U	●		●	●		●		●	●		●						●		U					◑		●	●	15
																															16
																															17
		●	●	●			●		◑		●	●		●		U			◑	●		U					●		●	●	18
●		●		●		U	●		●			●		●		●			●	U		◑		◑			◑		●	●	19
●		●		●		●	●		●			●		●		●			◑		◑	U		U					●	●	20
	●	◑		●		●	●		◑			●		U		●			●		●	◑		●					●	●	21
●		●		●		◑	◑		●			●		●		●			●		●	U					◑		●	●	22
		●		●	●	●	U		●			●		●		U			●		●	U		●			U			●	23
●		●		●		U	●		◑			●				●			●	●	◑	◑		●			U		●	●	24
●				●			●					●				●			●	◑		●		●			●		●	●	25

2008-09 FA National Northern Division

	Date	Venue	Opposition	Result	City Scorers (where known)
1	**Aug 17**	**H**	**Sheffield Wednesday**	**W 3-2**	Penney (2), Turner
2	**Aug 24**	**H**	**Curzon Ashton**	**W 4-1**	Brussell (2), Lee, Wensley
3	Aug 31	A	Aston Villa	L 2-3	O'Connor (2)
4	**Sep 4**	**H**	**Preston North End**	**W 5-1**	Brussell, Gligan, Hindley, Johnston, Treanor
5	Sep 7	A	Rotherham United	W 2-0	Farrell (2)
6	Sep 14	A	Leeds (LC)	L 0-1	–
7	Sep 28	A	Lincoln City	L 0-3	–
8	**Oct 12**	**H**	**Rotherham United**	**W 3-0**	Brussell (2), Penney
9	Oct 26	A	Sunderland	L 0-1	–
10	**Nov 2**	**H**	**Tranmere Rovers**	**W 3-0**	O'Connor, Turner, Penney
11	Nov 9	A	Reading	W 2-1	Lee, Penney
12	**Nov 30**	**H**	**Lincoln City**	**L 1-2**	Penney
13	Dec 7	A	Leicester City	D 1-1	Penney
14	**Jan 4**	**H**	**Newcastle United** (WFAC 4)	**D 3-3**	? (After extra time, Won 8-7 on penalties)
15	**Jan 25**	**H**	**Everton** (WFAC 5)	**L 0-4**	–
16	Feb 1	A	Sheffield Wednesday	W 3-1	Brussell, Johnston (2)
17	Feb 22	A	Tranmere Rovers	W 3-1	?
18	**Mar 1**	**H**	**Newcastle United**	**D 0-0**	–
19	**Mar 8**	**H**	**Leicester City**	**L 0-3**	–
20	Mar 15	A	Newcastle United	D 1-1	Brussell
21	**Mar 22**	**H**	**Reading**	**D 1-1**	Penney
22	**Mar 29**	**H**	**Sunderland**	**W 1-0**	Turner
23	**Apr 5**	**H**	**Aston Villa**	**W 2-0**	?
24	Apr 12	A	Curzon Ashton	W 2-0	?
25	Apr 22	A	Preston North End	W 3-0	?

WFAC = Women's FA Cup, LC = League Cup. Home games in bold type. League games on white background.
● = Started, ◑ = Played as a substitute, U = Unused sub (League appearances in blue).
Home games at Flixton FC.

League Record **3rd** (12 teams) Played **22** Won **13** Drawn **4** Lost **5** Goals For **42** Against **22** Points **43**

City were ten points behind champions Sunderland (promoted). Tranmere Rovers and Rotherham United were relegated.

Match	Brusell, Katie	Champ, Francesca	Chapman, Natalie	Eadie, Jayne	Farrell, Charlotte	Gillespie, Laura	Gligan, Laura	Hindley, Lucy	Johnston, Krystle	Lee, Rebecca	McClellan, Kelly	Mussell, Sara	O'Boyle, Shauna	O'Connor, Jade	Pearse, Rachel	Penney, Sarah	Savage, Keeleigh	Savage, Lindsay	Steadman, Mary	Treanor, Jade	Turner, Ellena	Wensley, Levi	Worrall, Andrea	Worth, Bethany	Young, Danielle
1	●				●		U	●	◐	●	●	U	U			●	●	●		●	◐	●	●		●
2	●	●			●		◐	U	●	●	●			●			◐	●			◐	●	●	U	●
3	●	●			●		◐	U	●	●	●			●			◐	●		U	U	●	●		●
4	●	●			●		●	●	●	●	●				◐	U		●		◐	◐	●	●		U
5	●	●			●		●	●	●	●	●		◐		◐			●		U	◐	●	●		U
6	●	●			●		◐	◐	●	●	●			●		U		●		◐	●	●	●		●
7	●	●			●		●	●	◐		●			●		◐				U	◐	●	●	U	
8	●	●			●		●	●	U	◐	U			◐					●	●	◐	●	●	◐	
9	●	●			●		◐	●	●		●			◐	U	●		●		●	●	●	●		◐
10	●	●			●			●	●	◐	●			●		◐			U	◐	●	●	●		◐
11	●	●			●			●	●		●		●	●				◐		◐	●	●	●		
12	●	●		●	●	◐	●		U	●	U			●				●		●	●	●			
13	U	●		●	U	●	U	U	●	●				●				●		●	●	●		U	
14																									
15																									
16	●			●		U	◐	◐	●	●	●					●	●	●		◐	●	●		●	
17																									
18																									
19																									
20	◐	●		U	●		◐	●	●	●	●		◐					●		●	●	●	U	●	
21	●	●		◐	●			●	●	●	●			◐				●		●	●	●		◐	
22		●	U		●	●		●	●	●	◐		U			●		●		●	●	●	U	◐	
23																									
24																									
25																									

Note
Match 25 - Abbie McManus remembers making her debut as substitute in a game at Preston. Sadly, the full line up for this game isn't known but it seems logical this was her debut game.

2009-10 FA National Northern Division

	Date	Venue	Opposition	Result	City Scorers (where known)
1	**Aug 16**	**H**	**Sheffield Wednesday**	**W 4-0**	Farrell (2), E Turner, Wensley
2	Aug 23	A	Luton Town	W 1-0	Johnston
3	**Aug 30**	**H**	**Leeds City Vixens**	**L 2-3**	Farrell, Johnston
4	**Sep 3**	**H**	**Curzon Ashton**	**D 1-1**	Penney
5	Sep 6	A	Lincoln	L 0-1	–
6	Sep 13	A	Blackburn Rovers (LC 1)	L 2-4	Farrell, Worth
7	**Sep 20**	**H**	**Aston Villa**	**D 3-3**	Lee, E Turner, Young
8	Sep 27	A	Newcastle United	W 1-0	Grocott
9	Oct 4	A	Derby County	W 2-0	Grocott, Champ
10	Oct 7	A	Curzon Ashton	W 2-0	Grocott, Johnston
11	Oct 11	A	Leicester City	W 3-0	Beckford (2), Wensley
12	**Oct 18**	**H**	**Derby County**	**W 2-0**	Grocott, Young
13	Oct 25	A	Preston North End	L 1-3	Johnston
14	**Nov 1**	**H**	**Liverpool**	**L 1-2**	Farrell
15	Nov 8	A	Sheffield Wednesday	D 1-1	Grocott
16	Nov 22	A	Leeds City Vixens	D 1-1	?
17	Dec 13	A	Leeds City Vixens (WFAC 3)	L 0-1	–
18	**Feb 7**	**H**	**Newcastle United**	**L 1-2**	Grocott
19	**Mar 7**	**H**	**Leicester City**	**L 3-4**	Farrell (3)
20	Mar 14	A	Liverpool	W 2-1	Beckford, Farrell
21	**Apr 25**	**H**	**Lincoln City**	**D 1-1**	Grocott
22	**May 6**	**H**	**Preston North End**	**D 2-2**	Sconce, K Turner
23	May 9	A	Aston Villa	W 2-0	Grocott, Johnston
24	**May 16**	**H**	**Luton Town**	**H-W**	*(Home walkover, points awarded to City)*

WFAC = Women's FA Cup, LC = League Cup. Home games in bold type. League games on white background.
● = Started, ◑ = Played as a substitute, U = Unused sub (League appearances in blue).

League Record **4th** (12 teams) Played **22** Won **10** Drawn **6** Lost **6** Goals For **36** Against **25** Points **36**

City were thirteen points behind qualification for the WSL. Top two teams Liverpool and Lincoln were approved for the WSL. Sheffield Wednesday and Luton Town were relegated

Beckford, Lauren	Brusell, Katie	Champ, Francesca	Chapman, Natalie	Farrell, Charlotte	Gligan, Laura	Griffin, Emma	Grocott, Becky	Hindle, Rachel	Hindley, Lucy	Johnston, Krystle	Lee, Rebecca	McClellan, Kelly	McManus, Abbie	Pearse, Rachel	Penney, Sarah	Savage, Lindsay	Sconce, Emma	Turner, Ellena	Turner, Kimberley	Wensley, Levi	Worrall, Andrea	Worth, Bethany	Young, Danielle				

FA National Northern Division

	Date	Venue	Opposition	Result	City Scorers (where known)
1	**Aug 22**	**H**	**Coventry City**	**W 3-1**	Grocott, Johnston, McManus
2	**Oct 29**	**H**	**Leicester City** (LC Group 5)	**L 1-3**	Grocott
3	Sep 5	A	Leicester City	W 2-1	L Savage (2)
4	Sep 12	A	Derby County (LC Group 5)	W 3-2	Beckford, Johnston, L Savage
5	Sep 26	A	Preston North End	W 1-0	L Savage
6	**Oct 10**	**H**	**Nottingham Forest** (LC Group 5)	**L 0-1**	–
7	**Oct 24**	**H**	**Aston Villa**	**W 2-1**	Danby, McManus
8	Oct 31	A	Newcastle United	W 4-0	Danby, Grocott (2), Johnston
9	Nov 7	A	Leeds City Vixens	W 4-0	Grocott, Johnston (2), L Savage
10	**Nov 14**	**H**	**Rochdale**	**W 3-1**	Grocott, Johnston (2)
11	**Jan 9**	**H**	**Mossley Hill** (WFAC 2)	**L 2-3**	Wensley, Grocott (After extra time)
12	**Jan 16**	**H**	**Curzon Ashton**	**W 3-2**	Grocott, L Savage, ?
13	**Jan 23**	**H**	**Leeds City Vixens**	**W 0-3**	–
14	Feb 13	A	Aston Villa	L 1-2	Lea
15	Mar 6	A	Curzon Ashton	W 2-1	L Savage (2)
16	Mar 13	A	Derby County	L 0-1	–
17	**Mar 27**	**H**	**Preston North End**	**W 2-0**	Bayley, Johnston
18	**Apr 3**	**H**	**Derby County**	**D 1-1**	L Savage
19	Apr 7	A	Rochdale	W 3-0	Grocott (2), Johnston
20	**Apr 10**	**H**	**Newcastle United**	**W 4-0**	Bayley, Johnston, Jordan (2)
21	Apr 17	A	Coventry City	L 1-2	L Savage
22	**May 8**	**H**	**Leicester City**	**L 1-2**	Johnston

WFAC = Women's FA Cup, LC = League Cup. Home games in bold type. League games on white background.
● = Started, ◐ = Played as a substitute, U = Unused sub (League appearances in blue).

League Record **4th** (10 teams) **Played 18** **Won 12** **Drawn 1** **Lost 5** **Goals For 37** **Against 18** **Points 37**

City missed promotion to the National Division by 4 points. Aston Villa and Coventry promoted. Newcastle United and Curzon Ashton relegated

This season the Northern section became the 3rd tier as the Super League was established.

Bayley, Carly · Beckford, Lauren · Brown, Danielle · Champ, Francesca · Danby, Sarah · De Silva, Leanne · Grocott, Becky · Havelin, Roisin · Hindle, Rachel · Hindley, Lucy · Johnston, Krystle · Jordan, Saffron · Lea, Danielle · Lee, Rebecca · McClellan, Kelly · McManus, Abbie · Middleton, Felicity · O'Connor, Jade · Savage, Lindsay · Shepherd, Lynda · Simpson, Carrie · Turner, Ellena · Wensley, Levi · Worrall, Andrea · Worthington, Nicola · Young, Danielle

	Date	Venue	Opposition		Result	City Scorers (where known)
1	**Aug 21**	**H**	**Blackburn Rovers**		**L 1-3**	Savage
2	Aug 28	A	Rochdale		L 0-1	—
3	**Sep 4**	**H**	**Leicester City**		**L 1-2**	Goodwin
4	Sep 11	A	Derby County		W 3-1	Johnston, Lee, Buffel
5	**Sep 25**	**H**	**Sheffield FC**		**W 5-3**	Buffel, Jordan, Makin (3)
6	Oct 2	A	Rotherham United		W 4-0	Buffel (2), McManus, Savage
7	**Oct 9**	**H**	**Leeds City Vixens**		**W 11-0**	Buffel (3), Johnston (4), Young (2), Jordan, McLellan
8	Oct 16	A	Sporting Club Albion		D 1-1	Goodwin
9	**Oct 30**	**H**	**Rochdale**		**W 2-0**	Johnston, Savage
10	Nov 6	A	Leicester City		W 3-0	Savage, Young, Grocott
11	**Nov 13**	**H**	**Derby County**		**W 7-1**	Buffel (3), Farrell, Johnston (2), Young
12	Nov 27	A	Sheffield United		W 2-1	Goodwin, McLellan
13	**Dec 4**	**H**	**Rotherham United**		**W 4-0**	Buffel, Grocott (2), Lee
14	**Jan 8**	**H**	**Leeds City Vixens** (WFAC 2)		**W 9-1**	?
15	Jan 29	A	Preston North End (LC Group 1)		W 4-2	Johnston (2), McManus, Bayley
16	**Feb 12**	**H**	**Oxford United** (WFAC 3)		**W 4-1**	?
17	Feb 26	A	Enfield Town (WFAC 4)		W 2-0	?
18	**Mar 4**	**H**	**Preston North End**		**W 3-2**	Johnston, Young, Carroll own goal
19	**Mar 11**	**H**	**Everton** (WFAC 5)		**L 1-5**	?
20	**Mar 13**	**H**	**Blackburn Rovers** (LC Group 1)		**W 7-0**	Goodwin, Johnston, Lee, Savage, Young (2), Jordan
21	Mar 18	A	Leeds City Vixens		W 5-1	Bayley, Goodwin, McLellan, Young (2)
22	**Mar 20**	**H**	**Rochdale** (LC Group 1)		**H-W**	*Match awarded to City*
23	Apr 1	A	Sunderland (LC 1)		L 0-4	—
24	Apr 15	A	Preston North End		W 4-0	Bayley, Buffel, Johnston (2)
25	**Apr 22**	**H**	**Sporting Club Albion**		**W 1-0**	Buffel
26	May 8	A	Blackburn Rovers		L 1-3	Buffel

WFAC = Women's FA Cup, LC = League Cup. Home games in bold type. League games on white background.
● = Started, ◑ = Played as a substitute, U = Unused sub (League appearances in blue).
Home games at Manchester Regional Arena.

League Record **1st** (10 teams) Played **18** Won **13** Drawn **1** Lost **4** Goals For **58** Against **19** Points **40**
Finished as champions, five points clear of runners-up Sheffield FC.

| Bayley, Carly | Brooks, Alex | Brown, Danielle | Buffel, Sarah | Champ, Francesca | Farrell, Charlotte | Flanagan, Chelsea | Fryer, Hannah | Goodwin, Amanda | Green, Josephine | Grocott, Becky | Harding, Nicola | Havelin, Roisin | Hey, Alice | Johnston, Krystle | Jordan, Saffron | Lea, Danielle | Lee, Rebecca | Makin, Lagan | McClellan, Kelly | McManus, Abbie | Middleton, Felicity | Nightingale, Chelsea | Savage, Lindsay | Simpson, Carrie | Turner, Elena | Worthington, Nicola | Young, Danielle |

2012-13 FA National League

	Date		Venue	Opposition		Result		City Scorers (where known)
1	Aug	19	A	Barnet		W	3-0	Lee, ?, ?
2	Aug	26	A	Charlton Athletic		D	4-4	Buffel, Danby, Nightingale, Shepherd
3	**Sep**	**2**	**H**	**Preston North End** (LC Group 4)		**W**	**2-0**	Young, Savage
4	**Sep**	**9**	**H**	**Portsmouth**		**L**	**2-3**	Danby, Goodwin
5	Sep	23	A	Wolverhampton W (LC Group 4)		D	4-4	Buffel, Farrell, Goodwin, Johnston
6	**Sep**	**30**	**H**	**Sunderland**		**L**	**2-3**	Lee, Savage
7	**Oct**	**7**	**H**	**Coventry City**		**W**	**2-1**	Buffel, Goodwin
8	Oct	14	A	Blackburn Rovers (LC Group 4)		D	1-1	Young
9	Oct	21	A	Watford		D	1-1	Danby
10	Oct	28	A	Aston Villa		L	0-1	—
11	**Nov**	**11**	**H**	**Leeds**		**W**	**3-0**	Danby, Goodwin, Young
12	**Nov**	**18**	**H**	**Barnet**		**W**	**1-0**	Johnston
13	**Dec**	**2**	**H**	**Charlton Athletic**		**L**	**1-2**	Johnston
14	**Feb**	**3**	**H**	**Sheffield FC** (WFAC 3)		**W**	**3-2**	?
15	**Feb**	**10**	**H**	**Watford**		**D**	**1-1**	Danby
16	Feb	24	A	Coventry City (WFAC 4)		W	1-0	?
17	Mar	3	A	Portsmouth (LC 1)		L	1-2	Bayley
18	Mar	17	A	Sunderland (WFAC 5)		L	0-4	—
19	Mar	24	A	Cardiff City		L	2-3	Bayley, Johnston
20	Mar	31	A	Coventry City		W	3-0	Buffel, Johnston, ?
21	**Apr**	**7**	**H**	**Cardiff City**		**W**	**3-1**	Johnston (2), McManus
22	Apr	21	A	Sunderland		L	0-1	—
23	May	2	A	Leeds		L	1-2	Buffel
24	May	12	A	Portsmouth		W	2-1	McManus, Savage
25	**May**	**19**	**H**	**Aston Villa**		**D**	**1-1**	Shepherd

WFAC = Women's FA Cup, LC = League Cup. Home games in bold type. League games on white background.
● = Started, ◑ = Played as a substitute, U = Unused sub (League appearances in blue).
Home games at Manchester Regional Arena.

League Record **4th** (10 teams) Played **18** Won **7** Drawn **4** Lost **7** Goals For **32** Against **25** Points **25**

Bayley, Carly · Brown, Danielle · Buffel, Sarah · Danby, Sarah · Farrell, Charlotte · Flanagan, Chelsea · Goodwin, Amanda · Harding, Nicola · Johnston, Krystle · Jordan, Saffron · Lee, Rebecca · McClellan, Kelly · McManus, Abbie · Middleton, Felicity · Nightingale, Chelsea · Savage, Lindsay · Seasman, Elizabeth · Shepherd, Lynda · Turner, Kimberley · Worrall, Andrea · Worthington, Nicola · Young, Danielle

Manchester County FA Women's Cup

Date		Opponent	Result	Scorers
Jan 20	H	Middleton Athletic (QF)	W 17-0	Grocott (3), Jordan (4), Nightingale (2), Bayley (2), O'Keefe, Brougham, Foster, Ward, Harbinson, own goal
Feb 17	H	Curzon Ashton (SF)	W 7-0	?
Mar 21	H	City of Manchester Ladies (Final)	W 2-1	?

Following the relaunch City Women warmed up for a first campaign in the Women's Super League with a training camp in La Manga, Spain (left), and travelled to Scotland to play Glasgow City in a friendly (above and right)... before lining up against Reading in the FA Cup at the Regional Arena (below).

FA Women's Super League

	Date		Venue	Opposition	Result	Attendance	City Scorers and Goal times
1	**Apr**	**13**	**H**	**Reading** (WFAC)	**W 2-1**	**253**	Duggan 7, 79
2	Apr	17	A	Liverpool	L 0-1	1,572	–
3	**Apr**	**20**	**H**	**Bristol Academy**	**L 0-2**	**1,253**	–
4	**Apr**	**27**	**H**	**Chelsea** (WFAC)	**L 1-3**	**597**	Duggan pen 13
5	May	1	A	Doncaster Rovers Belles (CC)	L 1-2	308	Duggan 90
6	**May**	**4**	**H**	**Everton** (CC)	**W 1-0**	**1,462**	Flint 89
7	**May**	**14**	**H**	**Liverpool** (CC)	**W 2-1**	**746**	McManus 4, Christiansen 52
8	May	18	A	Arsenal	W 1-0	829	Duggan 11
9	**May**	**21**	**H**	**Everton**	**W 2-0**	**947**	og 25, Scott 46
10	June	29	A	Birmingham City	L 0-2	759	–
11	**July**	**6**	**H**	**Sunderland** (CC)	**W 2-0**	**670**	Houghton 74, Duggan 78
12	July	13	A	Durham (CC)	W 3-0	379	Johnston 27, Duggan 38, Scott 83
13	**July**	**17**	**H**	**Notts County**	**W 1-0**	**820**	Flint 17
14	July	20	A	Chelsea	L 1-2	476	Flint 27
15	**July**	**27**	**H**	**Liverpool**	**W 1-0**	**920**	Johnston 17
16	Aug	24	**H**	**Arsenal**	**L 0-4**	**891**	–
17	Sep	3	A	Notts County	D 1-1	498	Duggan 61
18	**Sep**	**7**	**H**	**Chelsea** (CC SF)	**W 1-0**	**752**	Duggan 51
19	Sep	21	A	Everton	W 3-0	512	Scott 6, Johnson og 56, Duggan 90
20	Sep	28	A	Bristol Academy	L 0-1	374	–
21	**Oct**	**5**	**H**	**Birmingham City**	**L 1-2**	**520**	Scott 63
22	**Oct**	**12**	**H**	**Chelsea**	**W 2-1**	**1,292**	Scott 23, Duggan 34
23	Oct	16	N	Arsenal (CC Final)	W 1-0	3,697	Christiansen 73

WFAC = Women's FA Cup, CC = Continental Cup. Home games in bold type. League games on white background.
● = Started, ◐ = Played as a substitute, U = Unused sub (League appearances in blue).
Homes games at Manchester Regional Arena (except Match 6 at Etihad Stadium and Match 18 at Hyde FC). N = Neutral venue (Match 23 at Adams Park, Wycombe).

League Record **5th** (8 teams) Played **14** Won **6** Drawn **1** Lost **7** Goals For **13** Against **16** Points **19**

| Bardsley, Karen | Brooks, Alex | Brougham, Georgia | Christiansen, Isobel | Duggan, Toni | Flint, Natasha | Harding, Nicola | Hassett, Betsy | Holbrook, Jess | Houghton, Steph | Johnston, Krystle | Kete, Emma | Lipman, Emma | Marsh, Steph | McManus, Abbie | Nightingale, Chelsea | Radtke, Kathleen | Scott, Jill | Shepherd, Lynda | Turner, Kimberley | Walsh, Keira | Worrall, Andrea | Young, Danielle | | | |

Other Games

Feb 9	H	**Celtic** (Friendly)	**W**	**3-0**	Christiansen (2), Marsh
		(Played as 2 x 60 min games which finished 3-0 and 0-0)			
Feb 23	A	**Glasgow City** (Friendly)	**D**	**0-0**	–
Mar 23	A	**Durham** (Friendly)	**W**	**7-0**	Duggan 26, 46, 90, Hassett 28, Scott 45, Houghton 75, Young 90
Mar 30	H	**Aston Villa** (Friendly)	**H**	**2-0**	Johnston 3, Duggan 44

	Date		Venue	Opposition	Result	Attendance	City Scorers and Goal times
1	**Mar**	**22**	**H**	**Doncaster Rovers** (WFAC5)	**W 3-1**	**514**	Parris 35, 80, Duggan 90
2	Mar	29	A	Birmingham City	D 0-0	757	–
3	Apr	1	A	Sunderland	W 1-0	1,433	Parris 21
4	**Apr**	**12**	**H**	**Birmingham City** (WFAC6)	**W 3-1**	**450**	Duggan 16, Parris 67, Scott 87
5	**Apr**	**19**	**H**	**Arsenal**	**L 0-1**	**1,167**	–
6	Apr	26	A	Liverpool	L 1-2	1,022	Parris 53
7	May	4	N	Chelsea (WFAC SF)	L 0-1	867	–
8	**May**	**10**	**H**	**Chelsea**	**D 1-1**	**750**	Duggan 37
9	**July**	**12**	**H**	**Birmingham City**	**W 1-0**	**2,102**	Duggan 55
10	July	18	A	Bristol Academy	W 3-0	946	Duggan 29, 69, Corboz 82
11	July	23	A	Doncaster Rovers (CC)	W 3-0	1,274	Christiansen 48, Parris 68, Duggan 83
12	July	26	A	Chelsea	W 2-1	1,857	Duggan 12, Rafferty og 86
13	**July**	**29**	**H**	**Durham** (CC)	**W 5-0**	**1,185**	Johnston 12, 87, Parris 24, 41, Christiansen 30
14	Aug	9	A	Arsenal	W 3-2	1,142	Bronze 23, Christiansen 60, Duggan 68
15	Aug	15	A	Sunderland (CC)	W 3-1	1,514	Parris 11, Houghton 15, Duggan 90
16	Aug	23	A	Notts County	D 2-2	1,683	Houghton 44, 54
17	Aug	27	A	Everton (CC)	W 2-0	526	Duggan 19, Stanway 88
18	**Aug**	**30**	**H**	**Liverpool** (CC)	**W 2-0**	**1,890**	Duggan 15, Christiansen 71
19	**Sep**	**6**	**H**	**Sunderland**	**W 1-0**	**992**	Christiansen 32
20	**Sep**	**10**	**H**	**Liverpool**	**W 2-0**	**1,009**	Christiansen 45, Harding 75
21	**Sep**	**27**	**H**	**Bristol Academy**	**W 6-1**	**1,300**	Scott 9, Christiansen 34, pen 75, Bronze 38, Parris 48, Stanway 78
22	Oct	1	A	Arsenal (CC QF)	L 0-1	720	–
23	**Oct**	**4**	**H**	**Notts County**	**W 2-1**	**3,180**	Parris 13, Christiansen 45

WFAC = Women's FA Cup, CC = Continental Cup. Home games in bold type. League games on white background.

● = Started, ◑ = Played as a substitute, U = Unused sub (League appearances in blue).

All homes games at Academy Stadium. N = Neutral venue (Match 7 at Adams Park, Wycombe).

League Record **2nd** (8 teams) Played **14** Won **9** Drawn **3** Lost **2** Goals For **25** Against **11** Points **30**

Bardsley, Karen	Beattie, Jennifer	Bronze, Lucy	Brooks, Alex	Brougham, Georgia	Christiansen, Isobel	Corboz, Daphne	Duggan, Toni	Flint, Natasha	Harding, Natasha	Houghton, Steph	Johnston, Krystle	Lipman, Emma	MacIver, Alex	McManus, Abbie	Nightingale, Chelsea	Parris, Nikita	Radtke, Kathleen	Seasman, Elizabeth	Scott, Jill	Stanway, Georgia	Stokes, Demi	Tynan, Zoe	Walsh, Keira	Wiltshire, Sarah		
●	●	U	U	●		◐	◐			●	●			U	●	●			●		●		●	●		1
○	○	U		●		○	●	◐	U	U	●			○	●	◐		○		●		○	U			2
	○		●		●		◐		◐	○			●	●	●	●	U	○		●			●			3
	●	◐	●		●		●	U	●		U	U		●	●	●	●	U	●		●					4
	○	●	●	U	○		●	◐	●		U	◐		●	U	●		U	○		●		U			5
U	○	●		U	○		●	◐	●	◐	○	U		●	U	●					●		U			6
U	●	●	●		●		●	◐	◐	●	◐	U		U	●	●	●				●					7
○	○	○	U	U	●		●	○	●	●	U	U		◐	●	●					●		U			8
○	○	○	U	U	○	◐	●		●	●	◐	U		U	●	●		●		◐						9
○	○	○	U	U	○	◐	●		●	●	U	U		○	●	●		●		◐						10
●	●	●	U	U	●	●	●		●	U	◐		◐		●	●	●		●		●					11
○	○	○	U	U	○	●			●	◐	U	U		○	●	●		●		○						12
●			U	◐	●	●	●	◐		●	●	●		●		●			◐	●	U					13
○	○	○	U	U	○	●	U		●	◐	U		◐		●	●		●		○						14
●	●	●	U	U	●	●	●	U		●	◐	U		U	●	●		●		●		◐				15
○	○	○	U	U	○	●	U		●	◐	U		U		●	◐		○		●		●				16
●	●	U	U	◐	●		●	◐		●	●	●		●		●		●	◐	U		●				17
●	●	●	U	U	●		●	◐		●	●	U		◐		●	U		●		●		●			18
○	○	U	U	○			◐	●	●	●	U		◐			U			●	●	●		○			19
○	○	○	U	U	●			U	●	●	U		U		●	U		●	◐	●		○				20
○	○		U	●	◐			●	●		U	U	◐		●	U		●	◐	●		○				21
●		●	U	●	●		◐	◐	●	●	●	U	U	◐		●	●		●		●		●			22
○	○	●	U	●	●		◐	●	●	●	◐	U	U	U	U	●	◐		●		●		○			23

Other Game

Feb 21   H   **Aston Villa** (Friendly)   W 5-0   Parris 15, 79, Christiansen 39, Flint 43, Beattie 87

	Date		Venue	Opposition	Result	Attendance	City Scorers and Goal times
1	Mar	19	A	Liverpool (WFAC 5)	W 2-0	743	Stanway 30, Parris 64
2	**Mar**	**23**	**H**	**Notts County**	**W 1-0**	**1,173**	Houghton 90+1
3	**Mar**	**28**	**H**	**Arsenal**	**W 2-0**	**1,914**	Ross 65, Duggan pen 78
4	**Apr**	**3**	**H**	**Sporting Club Albion** (WFAC 6)	**W 2-0**	**1,270**	Parris 7, Ross 22
5	Apr	17	A	Chelsea (WFAC SF)	L 1-2	2,278	Ross 72 *(after extra time)*
6	Apr	24	A	Birmingham City	W 2-0	956	Corboz 35, Ross 90+5
7	Apr	29	A	Sunderland	W 2-0	1,411	Parris 40, Duggan 75
8	**May**	**2**	**H**	**Doncaster Rovers**	**W 6-0**	**2,227**	Bronze 7, Scott 10, Ross 40, Beattie 44, Asllani 45, Duggan 74
9	May	19	A	Chelsea	W 2-0	1,518	Stokes 44, Beattie 48
10	May	25	A	Liverpool	D 0-0	936	–
11	**June**	**26**	**H**	**Liverpool**	**D 1-1**	**2,172**	Ross 66
12	July	2	A	Aston Villa (CC 1)	W 8-0	492	Ross 16, 90+1, Parris 3, 17, 59, Middag 32, Corboz 79, Scott 90
13	July	24	A	Notts County	W 5-1	1,627	Ross 5, 41, Scott 25, Stanway 45+1, Christiansen 73
14	**July**	**31**	**H**	**Sunderland**	**W 3-0**	**2,026**	Stanway 17, 55, 82
15	Aug	3	A	Reading	W 2-1	592	Christiansen 38, Duggan 81
16	**Aug**	**7**	**H**	**Doncaster Rovers** (CC QF)	**W 4-1**	**1,153**	Christiansen 38, Stanway 76, Duggan 82, Ross 88
17	Aug	11	A	Doncaster Rovers	W 4-0	740	Ross 1, Christiansen 15, Bronze 62, Corboz 90
18	**Aug**	**28**	**H**	**Reading**	**W 2-0**	**1,950**	Beattie 48, Houghton 87
19	**Sep**	**4**	**H**	**Arsenal** (CC SF)	**W 1-0**	**1,643**	Beattie 79
20	Sep	11	A	Arsenal	W 1-0	1,686	Ross 50
21	**Sep**	**25**	**H**	**Chelsea**	**W 2-0**	**4,096**	Scott 34, Duggan pen 50
22	**Oct**	**2**	**N**	**Birmingham City** (CC Final)	**W 1-0**	**4,214**	Bronze 105 *(after extra time)*
23	**Oct**	**6**	**H**	**Zvezda-2005** (UWCL R32-1)	**W 2-0**	**1,149**	Scott 34, Bronze 90+3
24	Oct	12	A	Zvezda-2005 (UWCL R32-2)	W 4-0	3,500	Beattie 22, 53, Bronze 32, Christiansen 74
25	**Oct**	**30**	**H**	**Birmingham City**	**D 1-1**	**2,440**	Stokes 54
26	**Nov**	**9**	**H**	**Brondby IF** (UWCL R16-1)	**W 1-0**	**1,296**	Walsh 74
27	Nov	16	A	Brondby IF (UWCL R16-2)	D 1-1	2,513	Duggan 65

UWCL = UEFA Women's Champions League (2016-17 season), WFAC = Women's FA Cup, CC = Continental Cup. Home games in bold type. League games on white background.
● = Started, ◑ = Played as a substitute, U = Unused sub (League appearances in blue).
Home games at Academy Stadium. N = Neutral venue (Match 22 at Academy Stadium but officially a neutral venue).

League Record **1st** (9 teams) Played **16** Won **13** Drawn **3** Lost **0** Goals For **36** Against **4** Points **42**

Asllani, Kosovare	Bardsley, Karen	Beattie, Jennifer	Bronze, Lucy	Campbell, Megan	Christiansen, Isobel	Corboz, Daphne	Duggan, Toni	Holland, Ceri	Houghton, Steph	Hourihan, Marie	Kemp, Amelia	McManus, Abbie	Middag, Tessel	Parris, Nikita	Paul, Alethea	Roebuck, Ellie	Ross, Jane	Scott, Jill	Stanway, Georgia	Stokes, Demi	Toone, Ella	Tynan, Zoe	Walsh, Keira	
●	●	U	●		●	●	●		●	U		●		◐			●	●	◐	●		U		1
●	●	U	●			●	●		●	U	U	●		●	U		●	●		●		U		2
●	●		●			●	●	U	●	U	U	●		●	U		●	●		●		U		3
●			●		●	U	U		●	●	◐	●			●	●	U	●		◐	●		●	4
●	●	◐	●			●	●		●	U		●		●	U		●	●		◐	●	U		5
●	●					●	●		●	U	U	●		●	U		●	●		◐	●	U		6
●	●					●	◐	U	●	U		●		●	U		●	●		●		U		7
●	●					◐	●	U	●	U	U	●		●			●	●		●		U		8
●	●			U	◐	◐	●		●	U		●		●			●	●		●		U		9
●	●		●	U	◐	◐	●		●	U		●		●			●	●		●		U		10
●	●		●	◐		●	●		●	U		●	◐	◐			●	●	U	●	U			11
●	U	◐	●	●		◐	U		●	●		U	●	●			●	●	U	●	◐		●	12
	●	●		●	●	U	◐		●	U		●	◐	●			●	●	●	◐	U	U	●	13
	●	U	●	●	●	◐	◐		●	U		◐	●	●			●	●	●	U		●		14
	●		●	●	●	◐	◐		●	U		●	●				●	●	●	U		◐		15
	●	●		●	●	●		●	●			●	●		U	◐	U	◐	●	U		●		16
	●	●		◐	●	◐		●	U			●	◐				●	●	●	U		●		17
U				●		◐	●		●	U			◐				●	●	◐	U				18
◐	U	◐	●		●	U		●	●			U	●				●	●	◐	●		●		19
◐	●	●	●			●	U		●	U			◐	●			●	●	U	●		●		20
◐	●	●	●			◐	◐		●	U			◐	●			●	●		●		●		21
◐	U	●	●		●	◐	◐		●	●			◐	●			●	●		●		●		22
●	●	●	●		●	U	◐		●	U			◐	◐			●	●		●		●		23
●	●	●	●		◐	◐	●		●	U			◐	◐			●	●		●		●		24
●	●	●	●		U	U	◐		●	U			●	◐		◐	●	●	◐	●		●		25
●	●	●	●		●	U	●		●	U			◐	◐		U	●	●	◐	●		●		26
◐	●	●	●		●	U	●		●	U			◐	●		U	◐	●	U	●		●		27

Other Games

Feb 7	H	**Rosengard** (Friendly)	**W**	**3-1**	Christiansen 22, Duggan 47, Houghton 70
Feb 17	N	**Melbourne City**	**W**	**3-0**	Houghton 34, 75, Christiansen 50
		(Fatima Bint Mubarak Ladies Sports Academy Challenge in Abu Dhabi)			
Feb 25	H	**Pitea IF** (Friendly)	**W**	**2-1**	Duggan 23, Asllani 42

FA Women's Super League - Spring Series

	Date		Venue	Opposition	Result	Attendance	City Scorers and Goal times
1	**Mar**	**18**	**H**	**Reading** (WFAC 5)	**W 1-0**	**891**	Bronze 84
2	Mar	23	A	Fortuna Hjørring (UWCL QF-1)	W 1-0	2,036	Lloyd 36
3	Mar	26	A	Bristol City (WFAC QF)	W 2-1	594	Houghton 7, Parris 88
4	**Mar**	**30**	**H**	**Fortuna Hjørring** (UWCL QF-2)	**W 1-0**	**2,152**	Bronze 41
5	**Apr**	**17**	**H**	**Liverpool** (WFAC SF)	**W 1-0**	**3,059**	Lawley 58
6	**Apr**	**22**	**H**	**Lyon** (UWCL SF-1)	**L 1-3**	**3,548**	Kosovare 9
7	Apr	29	A	Lyon (UWCL SF-2)	W 1-0	19,214	Lloyd 57
8	**May**	**3**	**H**	**Birmingham City**	**D 1-1**	**1,003**	Bronze 58
9	May	7	A	Reading	W 3-2	579	Parris 6, 76, Scott 78
10	May	9	A	Bristol City	W 3-0	875	Duggan 43, pen 51, 57
11	May	13	N	Birmingham City (WFAC Final)	W 4-1	35,271	Bronze 18, Christiansen 25, Lloyd 32, Scott 80
12	**May**	**21**	**H**	**Yeovil Town**	**W 5-1**	**1,153**	Heatherson og 11, Scott 13, Ross 38, 62, Asllani 68
13	**May**	**25**	**H**	**Chelsea**	**W 1-0**	**1,069**	Duggan 28
14	**May**	**28**	**H**	**Arsenal**	**L 0-1**	**1,808**	–
15	May	31	A	Sunderland	W 1-0	1,054	Stanway 90+1
16	June	3	A	Liverpool	W 3-1	1,508	Scott 30, Lawley 45+3, Campbell 63

UWCL = UEFA Women's Champions League (2016-17 season), WFAC = Women's FA Cup. Home games in bold type. League games on white background.
● = Started, ◑ = Played as a substitute, U = Unused sub (League appearances in blue).
Home games at Academy Stadium. N = Neutral venue (Match 11 at Wembley Stadium).

League Record **2nd** (9 teams) Played **8** Won **6** Drawn **1** Lost **1** Goals For **17** Against **6** Points **19**

Players (column headers, left to right):

Asllani, Kosovare · Bardsley, Karen · Beattie, Jennifer · Bronze, Lucy · Campbell, Megan · Christiansen, Isobel · Duggan, Toni · Houghton, Steph · Hourihan, Marie · Lawley, Melissa · Lloyd, Carli · McManus, Abbie · Middag, Tessel · Parris, Nikita · Roebuck, Ellie · Ross, Jane · Scott, Jill · Stanway, Georgia · Stokes, Demi · Toone, Ella · Walsh, Keira

Other Games 2017

Feb 5	A	**Turbine Potsdam** (Friendly)	L	**1-4**	Duggan 85
Feb 10	H	**Frankfurt** (Friendly)	L	**1-2**	Parris 75
Aug 20	A	**Frankfurt** (Friendly)	L	**0-3**	–
Aug 25	N	**Montpellier** (Toulouse International Ladies Cup)	L	**2-4**	Ross 61, 80 (in Toulouse, France)
Aug 27	N	**Lyon** (Toulouse International Ladies Cup)	W	**3-2**	Christiansen 6, 37, Bremer 86 (in Toulouse, France)

Other Games 2018

July 24	N	**Paris Saint-Germain** (Friendly)	W	**1-0**	Nadim 49 (in Portland, USA)
July 26	N	**Lyon** (Women's International Champions Cup SF)	L	**0-3**	– (in Miami, USA)
July 29	N	**Paris Saint-Germain** (Women's International Champions Cup 3rd Place Play-off)	W	**2-1**	Scott 41, Jans 45 (in Miami, USA)
Aug 12	H	**Barcelona** (Friendly)	W	**2-0**	Lawley 75, Parris 89 pen

	Date		Venue	Opposition		Result	Attendance	City Scorers and Goal Times
1	Sep	24	A	Yeovil Town		W 4-0	1,302	Christiansen pen 7, Ross 38, Scott 58, Stanway 83
2	**Sep**	**30**	**H**	**Arsenal**		**W 5-2**	**1,646**	Ross 40, Houghton 45+3, Stanway 70, Christiansen 75, Scott 79
3	Oct	4	A	St Pölten	(UWCL R32-1)	W 3-0	2,337	Stokes 23, Houghton 31, Parris 35
4	Oct	7	A	Everton		W 3-2	735	Houghton 12, Parris 13, Bremer 19
5	**Oct**	**12**	**H**	**St Pölten**	(UWCL R32-2)	**W 3-0**	**1,041**	Parris 35, Scott 44, Lawley 85
6	**Oct**	**29**	**H**	**Birmingham City**		**W 3-1**	**1,465**	Christiansen pen 76, pen 90+8, Beattie 90+1
7	Nov	2	A	Oxford United	(CC)	W 6-0	777	Christiansen pen 44, Stanway 45, 53, Emslie 57, Beattie 79, og 86
8	**Nov**	**5**	**H**	**Everton**	(CC)	**W 2-1**	**873**	Christiansen 25, Parris 80
9	Nov	9	A	LSK	(UWCL R16-1)	W 5-0	1,226	Stokes 26, Christiansen pen 40, Emslie 69, Ross 74, 78
10	**Nov**	**12**	**H**	**Bristol City**		**W 4-0**	**1,256**	Christiansen pen 8, Emslie 38, McManus 59, Beattie 87
11	**Nov**	**16**	**H**	**LSK**	(UWCL R16-2)	**W 2-1**	**716**	Christiansen 46, Parris 72
12	**Dec**	**3**	**H**	**Birmingham City**	(CC)	**W 2-0**	**1,077**	Parris 18, Emslie 36
13	Dec	6	A	Doncaster Rovers	(CC)	W 3-2	924	Emslie 4, Ross 55, Stanway 59
14	Dec	17	A	Bristol City	(CC QF)	W 2-0	352	Parris 60, Beattie 87
15	Jan	7	A	Reading		W 5-2	951	Nadim 6, Emslie 32, Christiansen 43, Scott 56, 58
16	Jan	14	A	Chelsea	(CC SF)	W 1-0	2,595	Nadim 18
17	Jan	28	A	Sunderland		W 3-0	978	Parris 36, 72, Christiansen 56
18	Feb	1	A	Chelsea		D 0-0	2,648	–
19	Feb	4	A	Brighton & HA	(WFAC4)	W 2-0	1,372	Christiansen 45, Emslie 66
20	**Feb**	**11**	**H**	**Liverpool**		**W 4-0**	**2,356**	Parris 1, 60, Christiansen pen 56, McManus 73
21	Feb	18	A	Birmingham City	(WFAC5)	W 3-1	641	Nadim 13, Stanway 97, Emslie 119
22	Feb	21	A	Birmingham City		L 0-2	803	–
23	**Feb**	**24**	**H**	**Chelsea**		**D 2-2**	**1,417**	Parris 49, Stanway 86
24	Mar	14	N	Arsenal	(CC Final)	L 0-1	2,136	–
25	**Mar**	**21**	**H**	**Linköping**	(UWCL QF-1)	**W 2-0**	**1,259**	Parris pen 38, Ross 55
26	Mar	25	A	Sunderland	(WFAC6)	W 4-2	522	Stokes 72, Ross 90, 96, Toone 114
27	Mar	28	A	Linköping	(UWCL QF-2)	W 5-3	1,903	Ross 13, Stanway 23, 32, Beattie 41, Christiansen 64
28	**Apr**	**1**	**H**	**Reading**		**L 0-2**	**1,274**	–
29	Apr	15	A	Chelsea	(WFAC SF)	L 0-2	3,048	–
30	**Apr**	**18**	**H**	**Sunderland**		**W 3-0**	**943**	Stanway 15, 87, Nadim 90+4
31	**Apr**	**22**	**H**	**Lyon**	(UWCL SF1)	**D 0-0**	**2,876**	–
32	Apr	29	A	Lyon	(UWCL SF2)	L 0-1	20,837	–
33	May	3	A	Bristol City		W 6-1	568	Scott 41, Emslie 51, Ross 57, Parris 58, Nadim 80, Lawley 90+3
34	May	8	A	Liverpool		L 0-1	653	–
35	May	11	A	Arsenal		L 1-2	1,514	Nadim 10
36	**May**	**16**	**H**	**Yeovil Town**		**W 5-0**	**715**	Emslie 45, Parris 48, 74, 76, Christiansen pen 81
37	**May**	**20**	**H**	**Everton**		**W 3-0**	**1,605**	Scott 21, 60, Parris 57

UWCL = UEFA Women's Champions League, WFAC = Women's FA Cup, CC = Continental Cup. Home games in bold type. League games on white background.
● = Started, ◑ = Played as a substitute, U = Unused sub (League appearances in blue). Home games at Academy Stadium. N = Neutral venue (Match 24 at Adams Park, Wycombe).

Bardsley, Karen	**Beattie**, Jennifer	**Bentley**, Fran	**Bremer**, Pauline	**Campbell**, Megan	**Christiansen**, Isobel	**Emslie**, Claire	**Fletcher**, Serena	**Houghton**, Steph	**Hourihan**, Marie	**Lawley**, Melissa	**Leth Jans**, Mie	**McManus**, Abbie	**McPartlan**, Brenna	**Middag**, Tessel	**Morgan**, Esme	**Nadim**, Nadia	**Park**, Jess	**Parris**, Nikita	**Pattinson**, Poppy	**Roebuck**, Ellie	**Ross**, Jane	**Scott**, Jill	**Spetsmark**, Julia	**Stanway**, Georgia	**Stokes**, Demi	**Toone**, Ella	**Walsh**, Keira	
	●			◑	●	●		●	U			●			◑			●		●	●	●		◑	●		●	1
	●		◑	U	●	●		●	U			●			U			●		●	●	●		◑	●	U	●	2
	●		◑	●	●	◑		●	U	U		●			U			●		●	U	●		●	●		●	3
	◑		●	●	●	●		●	●	◑		●			U			●		U	●			◑	●	U	●	4
	●			◑	●	◑		●	U	◑		●			U			●		●	●	●		●	●		●	5
U	●			◑	●	◑		●		●		●						●		●	●	●		◑	●	U	●	6
U	●			●	●	●		●	●	U	U	●			◑			●			◑	●		●	U	◑	●	7
●	●			◑	●	●		●	U	◑	U	●			U			●			U	●		●	●	U	●	8
●	●			●	●	◑		●	U	◑	U	●						●			●	●		◑	●	U	●	9
U	●			◑	●	●		●	U	●		●			U			◑		●	●	●		U	●	◑	●	10
	●			●	●	●		●	U	◑	◑	●						●		●	◑	●		U	●	U	●	11
●	●				●	●		●	U			●			●			●		U	●	●		◑		◑	●	12
U	●				◑	●	U	●	●	◑	●	●	U		●		◑		U		●			●		●	●	13
●	●		U		●	●		●	U	◑		●			U			●			●	●		U	●		●	14
	●				●	●		●	U	◑	U	●			U	●		●		●	U	●	U	U	●		●	15
●	●				●	●		●	U	◑	U	●				●		●			U	●	◑	U	●	U	●	16
●	●				●	●		●		◑	U	●				●		●		U	◑	●	◑	U	●	U	●	17
●	●				●	◑		●		●	◑	●			U	●		●		◑	U	●		U	●	U	●	18
	●	U			●	●				●	●	●			U	◑		◑		●	●	●		U	●		●	19
	●	U			●	●				◑	●	●			U	●		●		●	U		U	●	●	◑	●	20
	●	U			●	◑				●	●	●			U	●		●		●	U	●		◑	●		●	21
	●	U			●	●				U		●			●	◑	U	●		●	◑	●	◑	●	●	U	●	22
U	●				●	◑				U	U	●			●	●		●		●	◑	●	●	◑	●	U	●	23
U	●				●	◑		●		◑	U	●			U	●		●		●	◑	●		●	●	U	●	24
U	●					◑		●		●	U	●		◑	U	◑		●		●	●	●		●	●	U	●	25
U	●				●	●				●	●	●		●	U	◑		◑		●	●			●	●	◑		26
U	●				◑	◑		●		●	◑	●		U		U		●		●	●	●		●	●	U	●	27
U	●				◑	◑		●		●	U	●		U		◑		●		●	●	●		●	●		●	28
U	●				●	◑		●			U	●		U		●		●		●	U	●		●	●		●	29
U	●				◑	◑		●		●	U			U	●	◑		●		●	●	●		●	●	U	●	30
●	●				●	◑		●		●	U	●		U		U		●		U	U	●	U	●	●		●	31
●	●				●	◑		●		●	U	●		U		◑		●		U	U	●		●	●	U	●	32
●	●				U	●		●		◑	U	●		U	●	◑		●		U	●	●		●		U	●	33
●	●				●	◑		●			U			U	●	●		●		U	◑	●	U	●	●	U	●	34
●	●				◑	U		●		◑	◑	●		U	U	●		●		U	●	●		●	●		●	35
●	●				◑	●		●		●	U	●		◑	●	U		●		U	U	●		●		◑	●	36
●	●				◑	●		●		●	●	●		U	U	◑		●		U	U	●		●		U	●	37

League Record **2nd** (10 teams) Played **18** Won **12** Drawn **2** Lost **4** Goals For **51** Against **17** Points **38**

For other games in 2017 see page 331.

2018-19 FA Women's Super League

	Date	Venue	Opposition	Result	Attendance	City Scorers and Goal Times
1	Aug 19	A	Birmingham City (CC)	D 0-0	572	(City won 5-4 on pens)
2	**Aug 26**	**H**	**Leicester City** (CC)	**W 4-0**	**1,609**	Wullaert 54, 80, McCue og 71, Nadim 83
3	Sep 9	A	Chelsea	D 0-0	2,501	–
4	Sep 13	A	Atletico Madrid (UWCL R32-1)	D 1-1	1,671	Bonner 15
5	Sep 16	A	Bristol City (CC)	W 3-0	451	Emslie 52, Nadim pen 65, Weir 72
6	Sep 20	A	Everton	W 4-0	296	Stanway 14, Parris 63, 67, Emslie 90
7	**Sep 23**	**H**	**Bristol City**	**D 2-2**	**1,338**	Parris pen 83, Houghton 90
8	**Sep 26**	**H**	**Atletico Madrid** (UWCL R32-2)	**L 0-2**	**1,178**	–
9	Sep 30	A	Birmingham City	W 3-2	824	Weir 54, Parris 64, Wullaert 72
10	**Oct 14**	**H**	**West Ham United**	**W 7-1**	**1,245**	Weir 2, Parris 7,17, Stanway 72, 80, Houghton 76, Wullaert 86
11	Oct 21	A	Brighton & Hove Albion	W 6-0	815	Stanway 20, 63, 68, Weir 43, Parris 87, Emslie 90
12	**Oct 26**	**H**	**Reading**	**D 1-1**	**1,015**	Stanway 33
13	Nov 4	A	Liverpool	W 3-0	661	Fahey og 50, Parris 59, pen 85
14	Nov 25	A	Yeovil Town	W 4-0	1,153	Parris 17, Weir 40, Houghton 83, Emslie 88
15	**Dec 2**	**H**	**Arsenal**	**W 2-0**	**2,149**	Stanway 18, 64
16	**Dec 5**	**H**	**Sheffield United** (CC)	**W 6-0**	**1,079**	Beckie 7, 24, 48, 78, Park 14, Stanway pen 52
17	**Dec 9**	**H**	**Birmingham City**	**W 1-0**	**1,157**	Stanway 12
18	Dec 13	A	Aston Villa (CC)	W 4-0	458	Bonner 21, Beckie 27, Park 77, Hemp 82
19	Jan 6	A	Bristol City	D 1-1	812	Parris 35
20	**Jan 10**	**H**	**Brighton & Hove A** (CC QF)	**W 7-1**	**786**	Parris 4, Hemp 23, 86, Weir 59, Emslie 88, Stanway 90, Beckie 90+2
21	Jan 13	A	West Ham United	W 3-1	640	Weir 15, Hemp 38, Parris 85
22	**Jan 27**	**H**	**Brighton & Hove Albion**	**W 3-0**	**1,279**	Parris pen 3, 41, Bonner 31
23	**Feb 2**	**H**	**Watford** (WFAC4)	**W 3-0**	**883**	Parris 62, 69, Bremer 86
24	Feb 6	A	Chelsea (CC SF)	W 2-0	1,358	Parris pen 49, 81
25	**Feb 10**	**H**	**Chelsea**	**D 2-2**	**3,078**	Wullaert 12, Stanway 24
26	Feb 17	A	Tottenham Hotspur (WFAC5)	W 3-0	1,153	Houghton 37, Hemp 39, Bonner 51
27	**Feb 20**	**H**	**Everton**	**W 3-1**	**864**	Walsh 47, Beckie 55, Parris 90
28	Feb 23	N	Arsenal (CC Final)	D 0-0	2,424	(City won 4-2 on pens)
29	Mar 13	A	Reading	W 4-3	449	Parris pen 13, 36, 39, Stokes 54
30	**Mar 17**	**H**	**Liverpool** (WFAC QF)	**W 3-0**	**1,366**	Beckie 25, Stanway 69, 88
31	**Mar 31**	**H**	**Liverpool**	**W 2-1**	**1,568**	Emslie 28, Beattie 90+5
32	**Apr 14**	**H**	**Chelsea** (WFAC SF)	**W 1-0**	**1,726**	Eriksson og 90+2
33	**Apr 28**	**H**	**Yeovil Town**	**W 2-1**	**1,369**	Parris pen 30, Hemp 65
34	May 4	N	West Ham United (WFAC Final)	W 3-0	43,264	Walsh 52, Stanway 81, Hemp 88
35	May 11	A	Arsenal	L 0-1	2,200	–

UWCL = UEFA Women's Champions League, WFAC = Women's FA Cup, CC = Continental Cup. Home games in bold type. League games on white background.

● = Started, ◖ = Played as a substitute, U = Unused sub (League appearances in blue).

Home games at Academy Stadium. N = Neutral venues (Match 28 at Bramall Lane, Sheffield; Match 34 at Wembley Stadium).

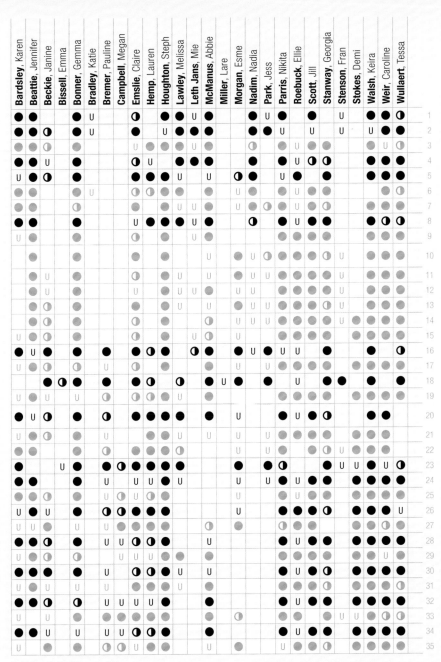

For other games in 2018 see page 331.

League Record **2nd** (11 teams) Played **20** Won **14** Drawn **5** Lost **1** Goals For **53** Against **17** Points **47**

City in the WSL era 2014 to 2018/19

Player		WSL Apps (sub)	Goals	CUPS Apps (sub)	Goals	TOTAL Apps (sub)	Goals	International
Kosovare	**Asllani**	12 (3)	2	11 (4)	1	**23 (7)**	**3**	Sweden
Karen	**Bardsley**	52	-	46	-	**98**	**-**	England
Jennifer	**Beattie**	66 (2)	6	44 (2)	6	**110 (4)**	**12**	Scotland
Janine	**Beckie**	2 (8)	1	3 (5)	7	**5 (13)**	**8**	Canada
Emma	**Bissell**	-	-	1	-	**1**	**-**	-
Gemma	**Bonner**	14 (3)	1	13 (1)	3	**27 (4)**	**4**	England
Pauline	**Bremer**	2 (4)	1	3 (3)	1	**5 (7)**	**2**	Germany
Lucy	**Bronze**	33 (1)	5	24 (1)	6	**57 (2)**	**11**	England
Alex	**Brooks**	4	-	2 (1)	-	**6 (1)**	**-**	England Under 19
Georgia	**Brougham**	4	-	1 (3)	-	**5 (3)**	**-**	England Under 19
Megan	**Campbell**	8 (10)	1	6 (4)	-	**14 (14)**	**1**	Republic of Ireland
Isobel	**Christiansen**	51 (10)	18	46 (3)	14	**97 (13)**	**32**	England
Daphne	**Corboz**	10 (10)	3	8 (3)	1	**18 (13)**	**4**	USA U23 / France
Toni	**Duggan**	39 (5)	19	26 (5)	15	**65 (10)**	**34**	England
Claire	**Emslie**	18 (13)	8	16 (15)	8	**34 (28)**	**16**	Scotland
Natasha	**Flint**	9 (10)	2	8 (7)	1	**17 (17)**	**3**	England Under 19
Natasha	**Harding**	8 (2)	1	2 (1)	-	**10 (3)**	**1**	Wales
Nicola	**Harding**	3 (2)	-	5	-	**8 (2)**	**-**	England Under 19
Betsy	**Hassett**	11 (2)	-	8	-	**19 (2)**	**-**	New Zealand
Lauren	**Hemp**	7 (3)	2	5 (5)	5	**12 (8)**	**7**	England Under 20
Jess	**Holbrook**	5	-	2 (1)	-	**7 (1)**	**-**	England Under 20
Steph	**Houghton**	81 (2)	9	63	5	**144 (2)**	**14**	England
Marie	**Hourihan**	4	-	8	-	**12**	**-**	England U23 / Rep of Ireland
Krystle	**Johnston**	18 (7)	1	11 (4)	3	**29 (11)**	**4**	-
Amelia	**Kemp**	-	-	0 (1)	-	**0 (1)**	**-**	-
Emma	**Kete**	2 (2)	-	0 (1)	-	**2 (3)**	**-**	New Zealand
Melissa	**Lawley**	14 (8)	2	19 (10)	2	**33 (18)**	**4**	England
Mie	**Leth Jans**	2 (2)	-	6 (3)	-	**8 (5)**	**-**	Denmark
Emma	**Lipman**	12 (3)	-	11 (2)	-	**23 (5)**	**-**	-
Carli	**Lloyd**	3 (1)	-	8	3	**11 (1)**	**3**	USA
Steph	**Marsh**	2	-	3	-	**5**	**-**	England Under 19
Abbie	**McManus**	54 (6)	2	46 (5)	1	**100 (11)**	**3**	England
Tessel	**Middag**	5 (6)	-	4 (8)	1	**9 (14)**	**1**	Netherlands

Player		WSL Apps (sub)	Goals	CUPS Apps (sub)	Goals	TOTAL Apps (sub)	Goals	International
Esme	**Morgan**	11 (2)	-	5 (2)	-	**16 (4)**	**-**	England Under 19
Nadia	**Nadim**	9 (6)	4	8 (5)	4	**17 (11)**	**8**	Denmark
Chelsea	**Nightingale**	10 (3)	-	5 (1)	-	**15 (4)**	**-**	-
Jess	**Park**	0 (2)	-	4 (1)	2	**4 (3)**	**2**	England Under 19
Nikita	**Parris**	65 (7)	37	44 (11)	25	**109 (18)**	**62**	England
Alethea	**Paul**	-	-	1	-	**1**	**-**	-
Kathleen	**Radtke**	13 (3)	-	10 (1)	-	**23 (4)**	**-**	-
Ellie	**Roebuck**	28 (2)	-	12	-	**40 (2)**	**-**	England
Jane	**Ross**	28 (5)	13	22 (6)	12	**50 (11)**	**25**	Scotland
Jill	**Scott**	81 (3)	17	58 (1)	6	**139 (4)**	**23**	England
Lynda	**Shepherd**	0 (2)	-	3	-	**3 (2)**	**-**	England U23 / N. Ireland
Julia	**Spetsmark**	1 (2)	-	0 (1)	-	**1 (3)**	**-**	Sweden
Georgia	**Stanway**	32 (20)	22	23 (18)	14	**55 (38)**	**36**	England
Fran	**Stenson**	-	-	1	-	**1**	**-**	England Under 19
Demi	**Stokes**	62 (1)	3	49	3	**111 (1)**	**6**	England
Ella	**Toone**	0 (5)	-	1 (4)	1	**1 (9)**	**1**	England Under 21
Zoe	**Tynan**	-	-	1	-	**1**	**-**	England Under 19
Keira	**Walsh**	62 (4)	1	52 (2)	2	**114 (6)**	**3**	England
Caroline	**Weir**	16 (2)	5	11 (1)	2	**27 (3)**	**7**	Scotland
Sarah	**Wiltshire**	1	-	1	-	**2**	**-**	England U17 / Wales
Andrea	**Worrall**	2	-	2	-	**4**	**-**	Wales
Tessa	**Wullaert**	14 (4)	3	9 (4)	2	**23 (8)**	**5**	Belgium
Danielle	**Young**	0 (6)	-	1 (2)	-	**1 (8)**	**-**	-

Figures in brackets are additional appearances made as a substitute.

WSL figures include the 2016 Spring Series.

Cups include UEFA Women's Champions League, Women's FA Cup and Continental Cup.

Kathleen Radtke was also known as Paula Radtke whilst with City.

Alex Brooks, **Nicola Harding**, **Krystle Johnston**, **Abbie McManus**, **Chelsea Nightingale**, **Lynda Shepherd**, **Andrea Worrall** and **Danielle Young** also made appearances for City prior to 2014.

The Derbies

Manchester City v Manchester United Competitive Record

HOME RECORD	Played	City Wins	Draws	United Wins	City Goals	United Goals	Goal Difference
NWWRFL Division 2	1	1	0	0	4	3	1
NWWRFL Division 1	6	3	1	2	16	13	3
Northern Combination	1	1	0	0	4	1	3
NWWRFL Divisional Cup	1	1	0	0	2	1	1
Women's FA Cup	2	2	0	0	6	1	5
HOME TOTALS	**11**	**8**	**1**	**2**	**32**	**19**	**13**

AWAY RECORD	Played	City Wins	Draws	United Wins	City Goals	United Goals	Goal Difference
NWWRFL Division 2	1	0	0	1	1	4	-3
NWWRFL Division 1	6	1	1	4	6	15	-9
Northern Combination	1	1	0	0	4	0	4
NWWRFL Divisional Cup	1	0	1	0	3	3	0
Women's FA Cup	0	0	0	0	0	0	0
AWAY TOTALS	**9**	**2**	**2**	**5**	**14**	**22**	**-8**

FULL RECORD	Played	City Wins	Draws	United Wins	City Goals	United Goals	Goal Difference
NWWRFL Division 2	2	1	0	1	5	7	-2
NWWRFL Division 1	12	4	2	6	22	28	-6
Northern Combination	2	2	0	0	8	1	7
NWWRFL Divisional Cup	2	1	1	0	5	4	1
Women's FA Cup	2	2	0	0	6	1	5
OVERALL TOTALS	**20**	**10**	**3**	**7**	**46**	**41**	**5**

Note:

In 1997-98 City and United drew in the NWWRFL Divisional Cup however postponements and related issues meant City decided to scratch from the tournament and the game was never replayed.

The above statistics include every first team competitive fixture, i.e. League, respective league cups and the Women's FA Cup. It excludes friendlies, charity matches, representative charity matches, and minor cups such as the Michael Wilson Cup (they met in 1991-92).

Walking Football

The story of City's women's team has come full circle in some ways with City in the Community playing a key part in providing opportunities to participate in sport to women often excluded from physical activities. City's community arm now has Walking Football sessions every Friday for both men, and most importantly, women. These have been set up to enable footballers – and those who have never played in a team – the opportunity to keep active and participate in a friendly, supportive environment. Some of City's original players, most notably Gail Redston, participate as do women with a variety of experience, including relative novices.

There's even a competitive angle for those who want to pursue that side of sport still. In July 2019 City in the Community entered two teams into the Dick, Kerr's Ladies Football Cup (a walking football competition) with the Over 50s team being made up of former City Ladies players. Both teams performed well in the tournament with the Over 40s team reaching the semi-finals (and came close to progressing further!) and the Over 50s were finalists.

If this book has inspired any reader to return to football or to make their first moves into the game then please look at what City in the Community offers and get involved. Whatever your age there are now pathways available.

Below: The CITC Walking Football teams at the Dick Kerr Ladies Football Cup, 2019. Above: Rita Howard congratulates goalkeeper Anita Clarke after she saved and then scored in the penalty shoot-out.

City's Full History

Although there isn't the space to go into detail about the research methodologies attached to this oral history project, it is important to provide a brief overview of theories being utilised and findings being reached. This book has been produced with the aim of publishing for the first time the stories and voices of the people involved with the club since its formation in 1988 but it is only a small part of a much bigger project I have been undertaking for several years. For approximately six years I have been capturing and researching the history of women and football using Manchester as the case study. A detailed history of the subject will be published at a future date when it will all be contextualised and interpreted using an all-encompassing framework based on the work of French historian Fernand Braudel. [1]

Braudel argued that historians should consider three categories of social time. I have documented how this can be applied to football research in a number of publications, and so I will keep the methodological explanations brief here. The three Braudel time periods can be understood as the long-term, cyclical history and the history of events. [2] It should be stressed however that cyclical history does not mean that this is a repetitive process, rather that this definition refers to the fact that activities at that level are cycles within a larger timeframe. This is an embracing concept, providing the unifying element of human history. [3] Braudel aimed to show that the historian's focus solely on event led history was flawed and that only by considering the long-term, and indeed the cyclical, or middle level, can we establish a true understanding of the manner in which a society was established. Braudel's longue durée, as he termed it, encompasses the full history of a subject and it is worth considering how the framework is relevant to football and to this publication. [4] My research into Manchester City's women's team uses a version of Braudel's framework based on three levels of time:

Full-time

Based on Braudel's highest level of time, the longue durée, this project uses the term 'full-time' for the full duration of the club from 1988 to the present. Full-time allows us to contextualise events and their significance over the life of the sport.

Transformational Level

This level is characterised by periods where Manchester City's women's team has developed or been transformed in some way. Dramatic fluctuations or attention grabbing events can be better interpreted within cycles, with the trend becoming apparent the more we understand the individual events and the circumstances that surround them.[5] The way these middle level time periods are organised provides the structure and the 'coherent and fairly fixed series of relationships between realities'.[6] These cycles, with their influences, outputs and inputs, demonstrate the general tendencies over time without being obscured by the attention-grabbing individual events. An individual game may be significant, but in terms of history it is the general pattern demonstrated within cycles that proves whether the individual game is part of a wider development or simply a one-off with little wider significance. The aim of this level is to determine links and comparisons with individual episodes acting as rungs in a ladder moving the development of the club onwards. Transformational cycles vary in length as there are some periods where rapid development of the club occurs, such as the relaunch as Manchester City Women and entry into the Women's Super League.

Episodal Level

Event led history is perceived as important to football fans where we often fixate on specific games, goals, trophy successes and so on. Unfortunately, events are often selected either retrospectively, once a pattern is known, or by those who have something to gain from highlighting an event at the expense of another.[7] It is important to remember that events

on their own are not the 'story'. We may remember the league title winning games but, in truth, they are part of a longer series of matches that bring trophy success. The role of the historian as a challenging, interpretive analyst is important and historians must look at every angle to search for an event's true significance. Similarly, an interviewee may be keen to promote a particular moment as the 'turning point' in the club's history but the interviewer must investigate further. We must not abuse or misuse the records of the past. [8] Analysis is vital and we must consider if events are relevant to a wider theme; Eureka moments; or inconsequential occurrences.

It is the investigation of events that adds to transformational cycles which progress football clubs, and during the research for this book it has become apparent that Manchester City's birth owes a great deal to a number of events that occurred prior to November 1988. These events include activities specifically at Manchester City of course but, and this may surprise some, it also includes discussions and actions at other organisations, while the success of the organisation owes a great deal to other football clubs, one of which dates back to the 1940s. The interactions of individuals tell us a great deal about how Manchester City's women's team developed and it is that level of detail, analysis and interpretation which is required at all clubs. Webs of social activity can be identified and their influence on the wider history of football can be determined. Social interactions lead to invention and innovation and help progress the longue durée of any topic, including the history of Manchester City. [9]

This framework has been used to assess every event/episode identified to date connected with City to consider how those activities form part of transformational cycles connected with the establishment and ongoing development of the club. It was essential a critical reading of the data available was reached, and by researching at three levels of time it became clear how the club developed. I can't go into detail here but to summarise, I believe there are six key transformational cycles in the club's history:

The Full Time History of Manchester City's Women's Team

Cycle	Origins	Birth	Growth	Stability	Relaunch	Business as Usual
Dates	1988 and before	1988 to 1996	1996 to 2002	2002 to 2012	2012 to 2016	2016 to present
Sample Events	Establishment of Football in the Community	Birth of the club	Decision of eight players to continue the club	Establishment of structure	Decision to bring club back inhouse	Ongoing successes
	WFA becoming established in Manchester	First training session	Arrival of Derek Heath	Managerial appointments	Signing of key players	World Cup impact
	Establishment of community initiatives at MCFC	Opening game	Addition of junior section	National League restructures	Joining WSL	
	Club investment in facilities at Platt Lane	Arrival of former Corinthians players and others	Promotions	Promotion	First trophies	
		Joining a league			CFA build	

Each cycle has a number of linked events that have moved the club forward in some way. Events are important and are remembered but they are only significant as part of the wider cycle.

[1] J. Clark, J. Harrison and E. Miguelez, 'Connecting cities, revitalizing regions: The centrality of cities to regional development', Regional Studies, 52:8 (2018), 1025–1028; F. Braudel, 'Histoire et science sociale: La longue durée', Annales 13:4 (1958), 725–753.

[2] I. Wallerstein, Unthinking social science (Philadelphia: Temple University Press, 2001), 136.

[3] D. Tomich, 'The order of historical time: The longue durée and micro-history', The longue durée and world-systems analysis, (Binghamton: Binghamton University, 2008), 2.

[4] F. Braudel, 'History and the social sciences: the Longue durée', in R. E. Lee (ed) The Longue durée and world systems analysis (Albany: State University of New York, 2012), 241-276.

[5] P. Stanfield, '"Pix biz spurts with war fever": Film and the public sphere – Cycles and topicality', Film History: An International Journal, 25:1-2 (2013): 222.

[6] F. Braudel, On history (Chicago: The University of Chicago Press, 1980), 30–31.

[7] M. Ermarth, 'On history. By Fernand Braudel', The Business History Review, 56:1 (1982): 90; Wallerstein, Unthinking, 137.

[8] R. Aldrich, 'The three duties of the historian of education', History of education: Journal of the History of Education Society, 32:2 (2010), 136.

[9] A. P. Molella, 'The longue durée of Abbott Payson Usher: A. P. Usher, A history of mechanical inventions', Technology and Culture, 46:4 (2005), 796.

I have avoided dividing this book into these cycles but feel it is important, as a summary piece, to record them here. Each cycle was important in the club's history and allowed the club to progress. Sometimes there were blips, setbacks and issues but these cycles catch in general terms the progression of the club and the key moments of transformation. The development of the club through these cycles owes a great deal to a large number of individuals who have played, worked, guided and supported the club over the years. In a book of this size it is impossible to list all who have helped along the way but it is important to say thanks to the following:

Firstly, the players, managers, coaches and committee members of the club who have given up their time to be interviewed or have provided material in other ways. Interviews took place between September 2017 and July 2019 with many individuals dedication several hours of time. Most interviews were performed by myself but Steph Alder has also performed some. If there is anyone who feels they would like to contribute their stories or material then please contact Steph at Manchester City. If a full interview was not possible then questionnaires were occasionally used. The following individuals need to be thanked for their support and time:

Karen Bardsley, Chris Bird, Vicki Bloor, Jane Boardman (played under the surname Clark), Tony Chaloner, Izzy Christiansen, Kerry Coclough, Stacey Copeland, Debbie Darbyshire, Joni Davies, Rowena Foxwell, Bev Harrop, Helen Hempenstall (now Pounder), Steph Houghton, Rita Howard, Catherine Hyde, Ian Lees, Gavin Makel, Jane Marcus, Neil Mather, Michelle Mather (now Middleton), Abbie McManus, Gary Moores, Jane Morley, Roger Reade, Gail Redston (also played under the surnames Duncan & Rothwell), Sally Rustige, Lindsay Savage, Jill Scott, David Sheel, Alison Smith, John Stanhope, Niki Taylor, Rhoda Taylor, Kate Themen, Ellen Thornton, Damaris Treasure, Louise Wakefield, Heidi Ward (now James), Alex Williams, Godfrey Williams, Andie Worrall and Lesley Wright.

Phil Neville considers his next England squad. Back (L to R) Lesley Wright, Neil Mather, Heidi Ward, Phil Neville, Anita Clarke, Karen Bretherton. Front (L to R) Rita Howard, Debbie Darbyshire, Gail Redston and Donna Haynes. The 30th anniversary game, December 2018.

Special thanks also to Rowena Foxwell's family, in particular her partner Benny. I appreciate how difficult 2019 has been and would like to thank you for your understanding as this project has taken shape.

In addition to the above I would like to thank the following for their support, time, interest and material: Mercedes Antrobus, Noel Bayley, Vicky Kloss, Brian Marwood, Dave Masey, Will McTaggart, David Mooney, Caroline Oatway, Steve Rigby, David Scally,

Ric Turner, Rebecca Walkden, Dave & Sue Wallace, and the Manchester City Women's Official Supporters' Club, especially Dave Sheel, Jayne Comer, Blandie and Dave Coop (who has also provided some significant images for this book). Thanks also to the British Library, National Football Museum, Manchester Central Library, the Football Association, Manchester City Football Club, Oldham Library Services, the North West Film Archive at Manchester Metropolitan University, Manchester Evening News, delegates at the International Football History conference, the British Society of Sports History, and the North American Society for Sport History.

Special thanks to Trevor Hartley for his design work on the layout and cover of this book. It really is appreciated. Also, thanks to my family for their continuing support. Thanks are also due to the journalists, photographers, fans and officials who have helped chronicle the club over the years, especially those photographers who have captured the club over the last few years, including Victoria Haydn, Tom Flathers, Matt McNulty, Sharon Latham and Dave Coop. Also, thanks, of course, to Manchester City's staff and officials for their support throughout the process.

For the first time this book includes a statistical record of the club ever since formation. It had never been my intention to do this but a couple of factors helped me make the decision to include the material. Firstly, I was gathering match reports and programmes throughout the project and whenever I found a line-up I entered it on to a spreadsheet for my own research purposes. Then Sally Rustige allowed me to borrow her scrapbooks which contained further squad related material. My designer Trevor Hartley had the line-ups from all WSL seasons and additional material was located from other players. Soon I had details for every season then I met with Rod Prescott who had compiled detailed records of results for the North West Women's Regional Football League. Through Rod I was able to fill in the gaps in fixture lists. Rod and the rest of the Prescott family were good friends to Manchester City during the club's first decade or so and he sent me this message to include: "Rod, Josie and

David Prescott considered it an honour to provide our statistical record of Manchester City Ladies (1989-2003), as a thank you to all the players and officials of their club, who so kindly played a Charity Match for our family in February 1992 at Atherton LR Ladies. This is our way of saying thank you for your kindness."

There remain a number of blank line-ups and there are some missing competitive games but the statistical material provided here is the most comprehensive detail I have at this moment. If you have material to add (for example, from about 2001 match programmes always carried line up details – if you have programmes from end of season games then we can use those to fill in the gaps) then please let me know via facebook.com/garyjames4 or twitter: @garyjameswriter of via Steph Alder at Manchester City.

I am certain there are many other people who have helped along the way. If I have overlooked your contribution please don't feel slighted in any way. This has been a long process and it has been difficult keeping track of everyone who has contributed to this process. Obviously, I'd like to thank everyone named or quoted in the text too. Special thanks have to go to the people listed in the Subscriber list too. These people backed this book before publication and, in effect, made it happen. I am grateful for that support.

Finally, I hope you've enjoyed reading this book and that it has given you a greater understanding of the team's entire history. This was never meant to be the definitive story but I do hope that, through the voices of the people there at the time, an appropriate oral history of the club has been produced. I hope future generations take this book not as the final word on the club's first 31 years but as the starting point for further analysis and research. Let's fill in the gaps and ensure every moment of the club's history is there forever. Thanks again.

Dr Gary James
Twitter: @garyjameswriter
Facebook.com/garyjames4

The Honours

Founded
■ The women's team was established as an initiative via City in the Community.
1988 Manchester City Ladies FC
2014 Relaunched as Manchester City Women FC

League Successes:
■ **Women's Super League** Winners 2016, Runners Up 2015 & 2018
■ **FA Women's Premier League** Northern Division Winners 2012
■ **Northern Combination** Winners 2001
■ **North West Women's Regional Football League Premier Division**
Winners 2000, Runners Up 1999
■ **North West Women's Regional Football League Second Division**
Winners 1998, Promoted 1991

Major Cup Successes:
■ **FA Women's Cup** Winners 2017, 2019
■ **FA WSL Continental Cup** Winners 2014, 2016 & 2019, Runners Up 2018
■ **North West Challenge Trophy** Winners 2000
■ **North West League Cup** Winners 2000

Rowena Foxwell

One of the first people interviewed for this project was Rowena Foxwell, who was one of the first to arrive at the initial training session in October 1988 and played in the opening game v Oldham at Boundary Park the following month. She was a keen supporter of the project and attended the 30th anniversary game in December 2018 as one of the guests of the club. Sadly, Rowena died the following month. As a tribute, I'd like to end this book with an image of Rowena and a few simple words taken from her interview concerning the establishment of a women's team at City. These words are brief but they capture perfectly the significance of Manchester City's women's team in 1988 and today.

This was something different. This was something special.
I think for me it's important that it normalises female sport that a club the size of City has a women's team.

Above: Rowena Foxwell (middle) with Rita Howard and Kate Themen at the
30th anniversary game, December 2018.

Presentation Copies

Subscribers

61	Larry Patrick
62	Guest 1717253341
63	Paul Risby (Prestige Car Repairs)
64	Nick Smith
65	Katie Davidson
66	Chris Bolsmann
67	Brian D Bunk
68	Neal Dickson
69	Sam Gowers
70	Joseph Hyde, True Mancunian Blue
71	Andy Jones
72	Julian Shawcross
73	Sandra Hampson Lifelong Blue and Manc through and through!
74	Stuart Banner
75	Stanley Millership
76	Jonathan Hunt
77	Sienna Arakawa
78	Peter Coppock
79	John Dickinson
80	David Skade
81	Peter Thornton
82	Paul McGarraghy
83	Corisse Ledward
84	Colin Henrys
85	Amelia-May Smith
86	Conor Heffernan
87	Karen Grunwell
88	Mark Simmonds
89	Topias Kauhala
90	George Bryson Allison

91	Craig McIntosh
92	Julie Phillips
93	Tucker Smith
94	Richard Donlan
95	Neil Van Swol
96	Aoife Grace McBride
97	Lucy Brindle
98	Louise Morgan
99	Andrew Winterbotham
100	Nigel Laverick
101	Matthew J. Reeves
102	Neil Errington
103	Eleanor Kelly
104	Colin Hinchley
105	Adam Pomfret
106	Stuart Parker
107	Paul and Sarah May
108	Jessica Gabrielle Harris
109	Amy Higginbottom
110	Andrew Scott
111	Katherine Hainey
112	Allan Fairweather
113	Amy Rudd
114	Jessica Visco
115	Katy Mitchell
116	In memory of Rowena Foxwell (from Andrew Wilson)
117	Mike and Tricia Tierney
118	Brian Houghton
119	Martin Hunt
120	Pete Lyons

121	Pete Lyons		151	Grace smith
122	Simon Pott		152	Aeryn Kelly
123	Craig Atkinson		153	Amy Tapper
124	Jane Patel		154	Richard Boddie
125	Paul McConnell		155	Stephen Atkinson
126	Crystal Short		156	Rita Howard
127	Simon Mills		157	Anna James
128	Jennifer Knott		158	Michael James
129	Ella Paige Patterson		159	Julie Whitfield
130	Nigel Rothband		160	Andy G. Robinson
131	Damaris Treasure		161	Mike Smith and
132	Simon Dean			Philippa Dudek-Mason
133	Joe Troop & Maried Lopez		162	Dr Marion Stell
134	Mark Francis		163	Alyson & Neil Buckley
135	Dr J Simon Rofe		164	James Thornton
136	Andrew Waldon		165	Sam Thornton
137	Paul Fallows		166	Lindsay Thornton
138	Maurizio Valenti		167	Paul & Marjorie James
139	Aberystwyth Town Ladies FC		168	Barbara & Alan Clarke
140	Carol Osborne			
141	Sue Walton			
142	Dil Porter			
143	Sue Turner			
144	Tom Casey			
145	MCFC Boston			
146	Louise Orain			
147	Bartley Ramsay			
148	John Hutchinson			
149	Louise Morgan			
150	Michael Horrocks